Decentering the Center

A
Hypatia
BOOK

DECENTERING THE CENTER

Philosophy for a
Multicultural, Postcolonial, and
Feminist World

EDITED BY

UMA NARAYAN & SANDRA HARDING

Indiana University Press

BLOOMINGTON AND INDIANAPOLIS

This book is a publication of

Indiana University Press
601 North Morton Street
Bloomington, IN 47404-3797 USA

http://www.indiana.edu/~iupress

Telephone orders 800-842-6796
Fax orders 812-855-7931
Orders by e-mail iuporder@indiana.edu

Library of Congress Cataloging-in-Publication Data

Decentering the center : philosophy for a multicultural, postcolonial, and feminist
world / edited by Uma Narayan and Sandra Harding.
    p.   cm. — (A hypatia book)
Includes index.
ISBN 0-253-33737-2 (cloth : alk. paper) — ISBN 0-253-21384-3 (pbk. : alk.
paper)
    1. Feminist theory. 2. Feminism. 3. Multiculturalism. 4. Pluralism (Social
sciences). 5. Women—Developing countries. I. Narayan, Uma. II. Harding,
Sandra. III. Series.

HQ1190 .D43 2000
305.42—dc21

99-053662

1 2 3 4 5 05 04 03 02 01 00

Contents

Contents

Introduction

UMA NARAYAN AND SANDRA HARDING

A considerable amount of feminist thinking today works across borders in ways that unsettle familiar philosophical and political frameworks. It cuts across the borders of traditional disciplinary configurations, borrowing, incorporating, and transforming the methodological approaches as well as the concrete concerns of the disciplines. Moreover, feminist work is increasingly attentive to factors such as class, race, ethnicity, sexual orientation, and religion that configure the lives of different groups of women and men in multiple ways within contemporary cultures and nation-states. This work also crosses regional, national, and continental boundaries, as feminists find they must "think globally, act locally," as the popular slogan has it. What happens "here" affects what can be thought and done "there," and vice versa. This kind of feminist work is committed to articulating a political vision that is responsive to the difference such interconnections make, both in the perspectives of feminist theorists and in the interests of women. The shape of the conceptual frameworks that guide public policy can be a matter of life and death for both men and women, not only locally but also in other nation-states.

Most significantly, these essays bring to their focuses on philosophical issues the new angles of vision created by the multicultural, global, and postcolonial feminisms that have been developing around us. Their concerns cannot simply be added to those of the mainstream feminist philosophies of the last few decades without disturbing the latter, any more than the mainstream feminist concerns could be added to conventional philosophical categories and assumptions and leave the latter untroubled. Indeed, these multicultural, global, and postcolonial feminist concerns transform mainstream notions of experience, human rights, the origins of philosophic issues, philosophic uses of metaphors of the family, white antiracism, human progress, scientific progress, modernity, the unity of scientific method, the desirability of universal knowledge claims, and other ideas central to philosophy.

It is worth recollecting that the deepest forms of sexism and andro-centrism—the ones most difficult even to identify, let alone to eradicate, have not been those visible in the intentional actions of individuals (which is not to excuse such overt or covert sexism and androcentrism). It has not been sexist or androcentric motivations or prejudices of individuals—their false beliefs and bad attitudes—that has given women the most trouble. Rather, it has been the institutional, societal, and civilizational or philosophic forms of sexism and androcentrism that have exerted the most powerful effects on women's and men's lives—the forms least visible to us in our daily lives. The discouraging news for Enlightenment enthusiasts is that being very smart and well intentioned has not been sufficient to prevent us from enacting and supporting the most egregious of sexist and androcentric practices. Similarly, these multicultural and postcolonial works draw our attention to the institutional, societal, and philosophic forms of racism, ethnocentrism, and Eurocentrism. They take a perspective (a standpoint, as some would put it) "from elsewhere" to reveal the frameworks that structure our thought and actions "here."

"Multicultural," "global," and "postcolonial" have many different meanings and referents in contemporary life. While these terms themselves continue to be contested and debated, they have, in a number of different ways, become central to the concerns of feminist theorizing. The growth of feminist political movements in a large number of nation-states has given feminist concerns an increasingly global presence. Issues such as women's human rights or economic development not only cut across national borders, but also raise important questions about how feminists should understand and engage with the continuing effects of colonial history and with the persistence of neocolonial economic and political relationships. Feminist movements in a variety of national contexts also continue to struggle to make feminist agendas responsive to the concerns of heterogeneous national populations, making debates on multiculturalism crucial to their political success.

This collection originally appeared as two special issues of *Hypatia*. It was envisioned as a forum that would encourage such border-crossing reflections on philosophic concerns in particular. We also wanted to bring together writings representing a diversity of approaches to such concerns. We sought essays that would explore, for both philosophers and thinkers in other disciplines, the extent to which feminist philosophy must and does draw on the texts, data, and concerns of work in other disciplines, responding to the challenges these pose and the illuminations they provide. The situation is similar in the history of mainstream Western philosophy, in which influential new directions have developed through borrowings and interchanges with the natural and social sciences; to take recent examples, with projects in medical sciences, psychology, linguistics, and artificial intelligence. At the same time, we wanted to show how feminist work in other disciplines both draws on and produces philosophy: feminist philosophy is done in many disciplines these days. The authors of these essays are located in political science, social geography, economics, and psychology, as well as in philosophy departments.

Those in philosophy departments bring to their analyses the strengths of diverse traditions in the discipline.

We hope that the issues raised in these papers will provide resources for more complex and fruitful thinking within feminist philosophy at all the sites and in all the forms in which it is engaged. We hope, too, that these issues will challenge readers to reflect on how changes in social relations always generate the need for revision in philosophic frameworks. As the "Others" of modernity's ideal humans—such as women, and peoples of non-European races and cultures—increasingly are recognized as fully human, we should expect transformations in the fundamental landscapes of Western metaphysics, epistemology, ethics, political philosophy, and even philosophies of science. These essays collectively emphasize the degree to which the landscape of contemporary philosophy is being enriched and transformed by postcolonial and multicultural feminist engagements with issues that are both intellectually and practically urgent.

The authors of the essays in this volume are all interested in exploring how multicultural, global, and postcolonial institutions, cultures, and practices create opportunities for raising new questions, engaging in new kinds of dialogues and discussions on new topics with new conversational partners, and organizing different kinds of social relations than might be likely or, perhaps, even possible otherwise. The contributions can be understood as attempts to envision and to participate in democratic, nondogmatic, and open-ended dialogues of the sort that are crucial to feminist attempts to imagine and facilitate more inclusive and egalitarian institutions and practices. The arguments of these papers often conflict with each other in ways that we hope will encourage further reflection. Such tensions are usually a sign of the difficulty or impossibility of arriving at uniquely "right answers" to the complex questions that arise in the contemporary world.

The first five essays here by Alison Jaggar, Susan Okin, Ofelia Schutte, Lorraine Code, and Uma Narayan are later versions of papers initially presented at an invited symposium on "Cultural Relativism and Global Feminism" at the American Philosophical Association's Pacific Division meeting at Berkeley in March 1997. The session was organized and chaired by Professor Deen Chaterjee and cosponsored by the APA Committee on the Status of Women and the APA Committee on International Cooperation. In "Globalizing Feminist Ethics," Alison Jaggar draws on both the dialogical tradition in Western moral philosophy and the discursive practices of feminist activist communities to develop an account of practical moral reason that is respectful of cultural difference. Jaggar explores the possibility that a feminist conception of moral discourse might at times justify the exclusion of some people from particular dialogues without running counter to the ideal of free and open discussion. She provides a detailed account of the ways "closed communities" have been, and continue to be, epistemologically and politically indispensable even while they have their moral and epistemological dangers.

Jaggar examines the possibility of global feminist dialogue, especially between Western feminist communities and communities in the Third World that are struggling to advance women's interests, and engages the difficult question of who may participate in such discourse. She cautions against assuming that there is a single or monolithic global feminist community, and urges that we recognize such a community to consist of multiple and overlapping discursive networks, a community-in-the-making that is constantly being reimagined. Jaggar points to a number of ways in which exchanges between such feminist discourse communities across the world can be the sites of important critical perspectives on ongoing economic, political, social, and environmental issues that are crucial to feminist agendas both within and across national contexts.

Susan Okin's essay, "Feminism, Women's Human Rights, and Cultural Differences," focuses on the real world successes of one transnational feminist discourse community—that of activists and thinkers engaged in making international and national human rights agendas responsive to the predicaments and interests of women. Okin points to some interesting tensions between the universalizing rhetoric that has been part of the successful development of feminist human rights activism and certain Western feminist critiques of essentialist overgeneralizations that have been hesitant or ambivalent about the deployment of universalizing notions. Okin argues that such feminist agendas have challenged the conventional notion of human rights formulated by Locke and, more recently, by the 1948 Universal Declaration of Human Rights. These agendas also challenge the presumed immunity of family and religious practices from human rights considerations. Okin's analysis in many ways bears out Jaggar's thesis about the importance of multiple and overlapping feminist discourse communities as sites of critical political challenges to the national and international status quo.

Ofelia Schutte's essay, "Cultural Alterity: Cross-Cultural Communication and Feminist Theory in North-South Contexts," explores another set of issues that pertain to conversations between differently located feminists, using phenomenological-existential and poststructural concepts of alterity and difference to think about issues of cross-cultural communication. Underscoring the need to develop a model to understand subaltern cultural differences, Schutte analyzes the locations of those who are constructed as the "culturally different Other." Schutte cautions that the possibility of perfect translations should not be assumed in communications between culturally differentiated subjects, suggesting that there will always be an important residue of meaning that does not get across and that constitutes an element of cultural incommensurability. Drawing on Anzaldúa's figure of the multi-hyphenated *mestiza* self and Kristeva's figure of the stranger within, Schutte argues for a feminist notion of difference that facilitates the recognition of alterity both within and outside the self. She enlists personal experience to delineate the construction and implications of a culturally different Latina identity in Anglo-American contexts. Schutte uses her exploration of cultural alterity to caution Western feminism against making an "Other" of women whose path to emancipation it fails to understand or recognize, and argues for a postcolonial feminism that pays serious attention to the experience of Western colonialism and its ongoing contemporary effects.

In "How to Think Globally: Stretching the Limits of Imagination," Lorraine Code engages concerns about how transnational feminist agendas are to deal with issues of difference, including cultural difference. Code articulates her own temptation to relativism, provoked by Western assumptions about "having the one true story." At the same time, she acknowledges that situations such as the treatment of women by the fundamentalist Taliban in Afghanistan pose severe test cases for such relativist temptations. Code analyzes a variety of strategies employed by Chandra Mohanty's account of women in various sites in the global economy in order to explore avenues of analysis that might enable feminists to negotiate the conundrums that seem to result from difficult choices between universalism and relativism. She also reflects on how her location as a Canadian might filter her feminist perspectives on issues of cultural difference and on transnational feminist cooperation.

The issues of cultural difference that are the core concerns of the essays by Schutte and Code resurface in Uma Narayan's essay, "Essence of Culture and a Sense of History: A Feminist Critique of Cultural Essentialism." Narayan points to the ways in which attempts to avoid gender essentialism by taking into account cultural differences among women sometimes lead to culturally essentialist pictures of particular Third World cultures and of their contrasts to Western culture. Narayan analyzes the common characteristics of essentialist pictures of culture and proposes a number of strategies that Third World feminists may find useful in challenging the culturally essentialist agendas of Third World fundamentalists. While acknowledging the salience of Schutte's point that feminists need to deal with cultural alterity, Narayan insists that this be done in a manner that does not replicate imaginary colonialist-essentialist understandings of the differences between Western and Third World cultures. Narayan cautions that forms of cultural relativism buy into essentialist notions of cultural differences and pose dangers to feminist agendas as significant as those posed by universalism.

Multicultural and postcolonial feminist writings often do not look much like contemporary philosophic work in either their styles or their concerns. Nevertheless, many of these writings have contributed important insights and analyses to feminist philosophy. We asked several authors briefly to review for the diverse Hypatia readership what is especially relevant for philosophy in several such recent bodies of work. In "It's Not Philosophy," Andrea Nye takes a fresh look at some influential writings from the 1980s by Trinh Minh-ha, Patricia Hill Collins, Gloria Anzaldúa, Maria Lugones and Elizabeth Spelman, and Regina Harrison. While many feminist philosophers have already been using the insights of such writings to transform the categories and assumptions that shape their ethics, epistemology, or concept of the self, the easier and more prevalent practice is simply to mention such works in a footnote without taking the important step of using them to rethink the kinds of projects we learned and are still encouraged to think of as uniquely philosophic. Nye's reflection on these works illustrates how, in periods of intellectual change, it is on "the cusp of a redefinition of 'love of knowledge' " that new forms of thought are positioned.

The notion of experience has played a central role in numerous philosophic texts and has been evoked by feminists engaged in struggles over self-representation. Shari Stone-Mediatore uses the work of Chandra Mohanty, as well as of Gloria Anzaldúa and Samuel Delany, in her essay "Chandra Mohanty and the Revaluing of 'Experience' " to explore possibilities for a robust and philosophically useful notion of experience that can avoid the troubles encountered by both empiricist and certain features of poststructuralist approaches. Along the way, she identifies why it is that narratives are so crucial for revealing the tensions between language and experience that often can lead to valuable conceptual innovations.

In "*Sitios y Lenguas:* Chicanas Theorize Feminisms," Aída Hurtado provides a needed historical overview and synthesis of the various contributions of Chicana feminism, ranging from Chicana activism in the 1960s to contemporary writings by influential Chicana feminists. She challenges non-Chicana scholars to engage not just with the few exemplary Chicana texts, but also with the diverse concerns visible in a far broader range of these writings. She ends with reflections on challenges to Chicana feminism in the future. Along the way, Hurtado documents Chicana feminism's use of different methods of producing knowledge, and draws attention to the internal variety within the Chicana communities of the United States, even as she points to some overarching similarities in how sexism is experienced and reproduced in these communities.

In "It's All in the Family: Intersections of Gender, Race, and Nation," Patricia Hill Collins examines how metaphors of the family have provided ways of thinking about various aspects of social organization in the United States—both structures of domination and discourses of resistance. She examines six dimensions of the traditional family ideal that have been metaphorically extended to other relationships, starting with the use of "blood ties" to construct not only notions of nuclear families and kinship networks, but also of "racial families" and "ethnic nationalism" that are used to define membership in the United States political nation. Unpacking other familial metaphors, Collins examines the roles played by space and territory, ideas of naturalized hierarchy, normative justifications for distributions of social wealth that reproduce class hierarchies, and idealized representations of rights and responsibilities that define family membership. Collins concludes with a discussion of metaphors of "family planning" that have permeated public policies, ranging from historical eugenic racial hygiene doctrines to contemporary linkages of family values to questions related to welfare, poverty, and reproduction. She is concerned here also with how the metaphor of the family itself illuminates the intersections of race, gender, nation, and other such structural and symbolic social relations.

Issues of Third World so-called development have been glimpsed in some of the earlier papers. But the next group of essays takes a direct and more extensive look at philosophical implications of the reevaluations of Third World development projects that have been appearing in the last few years. They draw on different literatures and have divergent specific concerns. Both Southern and Northern feminists have contributed to these assessments. The accounts by Barker, Ferguson, Wright, Lange, and Harding provide new angles of vision on familiar categories and assumptions in ethics, metaphysics, epistemology, and philosophies of science.

We asked development economist Drucilla K. Barker briefly to identify, for *Hypatia* readers who might not be familiar with this literature, some central philosophical themes in the most recent writings on gender, environment, and development. Focusing on epistemology, she points to the romantic narrative of "the Enlightenment dream" in which development economics conducts its business, and to the importance of so-called nonmodern knowledge systems as a resource for constructing epistemologies for "collective emancipatory projects without reproducing patterns of hierarchy and domination." The task, then, is to identify the resources of both kinds of knowledge systems without romanticizing either.

Ann Ferguson's essay, "Resisting the Veil of Privilege: Building Bridge Identities as an Ethico-Politics of Global Feminisms," explores a set of issues that have interesting parallels with Alcoff's and Bailey's explorations (see below) of whites' resistance to racial privilege. She focuses, however, on the problems raised by the privileged identities of Northerners who work in various contexts of the global South. Ferguson argues that Northern feminist researchers and scholars, as well as Northerners working on development projects in the South, might need to think about and work against their own privileged locations. She points out that an Enlightenment ethics of modernity is assumed to be desirable and unproblematic not only by institutions such as the International Monetary Fund, the World Bank, and Northern-based nongovernmental organizations, but also by most feminist researchers. Northerners, she argues, are socialized into a "universalized code ethics that then becomes part of the horizon of ignorance" of researchers and scholars. Feminist researchers must develop a more situated ethics so as to avoid becoming part of the problems that plague the objects of Northern development strategies. Ferguson shows how a "negative identity politics process" can be a resource for a "bridge identity politics" that is useful in such a project.

"*Maquiladora Mestizas* and a Feminist Border Politics: Revisiting Anzaldúa," by Melissa Wright, examines how political and institutional forces work in constructing the identities of various women in the U.S.-Mexico borderlands. Wright provides an ethnographic account of two professional women, one Mexican and one Mexican American, who work in the administrative sector of a U.S. *maquiladora* firm and whose race-culture and gender affect their negotiations of professional status. The Mexican woman's story reveals how her attempts to Americanize her dress, language, and professional demeanor win her credibility and consolidate her professional status. The Mexican American woman, conversely, jeopardizes her professional standing, competence rating, and eventually her job by insisting on a self-presentation that signifies "Mexican" rather than "American." Wright points to the ways that scripts of race-culture and gender define the working spaces of the border *maquiladoras*, and the ways that women rewrite, change, and sometimes subvert them. Wright uses such constructions of *mestiza* identity to interrogate and rethink Gloria Anzaldúa's use of the borderlands figure and the political implications of that identity for feminist politics.

Lynda Lange's contribution, "Burnt Offerings to Rationality: A Feminist Reading of the Construction of Indigenous Peoples in Enrique Dussel's Theory of Modernity," like Uma Narayan's essay, thinks through the implications of colonial history for postcolonial feminist perspectives. Lange approaches the issues via a reading of Enrique Dussel's *Invention of the Americas*. Dussel contends that European modernity is constituted by a relationship with non-Europe, and that a constitutive part of such modernity is a Eurocentric, irrational, "cultural myth" that prompted Europeans to see non-Europeans exclusively in terms of European categories. South and Central America were "invented" as undeveloped as a consequence of this myth, regardless of their various peoples' actual levels of development. Lange draws on this analysis to raise critical questions about what Dussel calls the "developmental fallacy" and to explore its connections to current policies that induct areas of the Third World into European forms of subordination and "development" under the rubric of "forcing them to be free." However, postmodernist rejections of such modernist projects share more with them than their adherents imagine. She raises questions about how philosophical projects have been constituted through colonial interests rather than emerging from politically unmotivated searches for eternally true principles, as main tendencies in philosophy have held.

In "Gender, Development, and Post-Enlightenment Philosophies of Science," Sandra Harding is concerned with identifying ways that some of the most recent writings on gender, environment, and sustainable development illuminate problems with the still-prevalent Enlightenment philosophies of science. Harding's paper focuses on the roots of these accounts in other recent critiques of development, and on how these analyses reinforce and expand arguments made by other recently influential schools of science studies. She argues that philosophies of science adequate to these new understandings of nature, science, and philosophy can abandon the ideal of universally valid scientific claims, develop more realistic representations of knowers and of knowledge systems, successfully resist relativism and idealism, understand nature-as-an-object-of-knowledge as socially mediated and as always emerging, and internalize democratic ethics and politics in both sciences and philosophies of science—in themselves.

Linda Alcoff's essay, "What Should White People Do?," assesses the strengths and limitations of various proposed approaches to whites' resistance to white supremacy. While Alcoff is aware of how white antiracist efforts are often flawed, she also wishes to affirm and explore the possibility of sincere and genuine antiracist efforts against white supremacy that would go beyond self-criticism to a pro-active position. Alcoff explores a variety of strategies that have been suggested for "becoming disloyal to whiteness." She critically analyzes the feminist debate, the liberal approach of Judith Katz, the more radical approach of Ignatiev and Garvey, and the antiracist strategies proposed by Michael Harrington. She goes on to suggest that whites need to generate their own versions of the "double consciousness" that W. E. B. Du Bois identified in African Americans. This double vision would continually have to mark white identity constructions in contemporary patterns of inequality and exploitation, but it would also reawaken the memory of the many "white traitors to white privilege" who have, since the days of John Brown and earlier, struggled to help create an inclusive human community.

Alison Bailey's essay explores how the social location of white traitorous identities might be understood. In "Locating Traitorous Identities: Toward a View of Privilege-Cognizant White Character," Bailey examines some problematic implications of Sandra Harding's standpoint framework description of white traitors as "becoming marginal." Bailey argues that the location of white traitors might better be understood in terms of their "decentering the center." She distinguishes between "privilege-cognizant" and "privilege-evasive" white scripts. Drawing on the work of Marilyn Frye and Anne Braden, Bailey gives an account of the contrasting perceptions and behaviors of whites who animate one type of script and those who struggle to forge the other type. Bailey uses María Lugones's account of identity and notions of "world traveling" and "loving perception" to explicate the ways whites, and white feminists in particular, might cultivate a traitorous character conducive to an antiracist politics.

In "Multiculturalism as a Cognitive Virtue of Scientific Practice," Ann Cudd argues that multiculturalism can be understood as a cognitive virtue without abandoning the conventional analytic framework that still appeals to so much of contemporary Anglo-American philosophy. She shows how multiculturalism improves the content of science as well as its claims to objectivity. Her examples are from economics: Amartya Sen's analysis of the causes of famine and the political economy of families.

We hope you enjoy reading these essays as much as we have enjoyed bringing them together in *Hypatia* and now in this volume.

Decentering the Center

1

Globalizing Feminist Ethics

ALISON M. JAGGAR

The feminist conception of discourse offered below differs from classical discourse ethics. Arguing that inequalities of power are even more conspicuous in global than in local contexts, I note that a global discourse community seems to be emerging among feminists, and I explore the role played by small communities in feminism's attempts to reconcile a commitment to open discussion, on the one hand, with a recognition of the realities of power inequalities, on the other.

Global trade and interaction are not new but their current intensification is unprecedented.[1] Local communities have never been completely closed but now their boundaries have become so porous that people speak of community disintegration. Economies have never been entirely self-sufficient but never before has international trade been so crucial to the prosperity and even the survival of local economies. These developments have raised new problems for moral and political philosophy and so for feminist ethics.

Women are located at the center of these contemporary developments. They constitute a large and increasing portion of the labor force in many newly industrializing as well as industrialized countries; they (with their children) constitute 80 percent of the world's refugees; they are trafficked in a world wide prostitution trade; and their bodies are the site of technological interventions designed both to promote and to control fertility. At the same time, women are frequently taken as emblems of cultural integrity, so that defending beleaguered cultures becomes equated with preserving traditional forms of femininity, especially as these are manifest in traditional female dress and practices of marriage and sexuality. Thus, women are situated in the vortex of contending social forces: on the one hand, centripetal tendencies toward increasing globalization and integration and, on the other hand, centrifugal tendencies toward nationalism and fragmentation.

Contemporary moral theory reproduces these tensions, counterposing a universalistic discourse of human rights against approaches such as communitarianism and postmodernism which emphasize the local and so are often construed as relativist. In this context, philosophers' increasing rejection of moral foundationalism makes it difficult to see how conventional and local norms may be subjected to systematic moral critique. My larger project, from which this paper emerges, is to develop an account of practical moral reason that shows how respect for cultural difference may be combined with claims to postconventional moral objectivity. In developing this account, I draw on the dialogical tradition in Western moral theory that stretches from Plato, through Locke and Kant, to Rawls and Habermas, and I take seriously the values that lie at the heart of this tradition, including the values of discursive equality, openness and inclusiveness. In addition to being inspired by this philosophical tradition, my own understanding of practical discourse is also shaped by reflection on the discursive practices of recent feminist grassroots activism in North America.[2]

As developed by Karl-Otto Apel and Juergen Habermas, classical discourse ethics defines moral justification in terms of universal consensus in conditions of domination-free communication. This definition is often derided as utopian—and so ultimately skeptical—for reasons that include not only practical difficulties of establishing universal discourse but also what appear to be insurmountable difficulties of principle, notably the impossibility of implementing like domination-free communication. Yet even though such problems are even more conspicuous in global than in local contexts, the beginnings of a global discourse community nevertheless seem to be emerging among feminists. These beginnings are most visible in official and semiofficial venues, such as the several UN Conferences on women since 1975 and their accompanying nongovernmental organization (NGO) fora, but they are also evident in a multitude of ongoing interactions among grassroots groups, such as the Network of East/West women and the Women's Global Network for Reproductive Rights.

One respect in which a feminist conception of practical moral discourse differs from that of classical discourse ethics is that it addresses directly issues of discursive equality and openness in situations inevitably structured by power. This paper begins to explore the role played by small communities in feminism's attempts to reconcile a commitment to open discussion, on the one hand, with a recognition of the realities of power inequalities, on the other.

ILLUSTRATING THE PROBLEM

My own conception of practical moral discourse seeks to reconstruct the norms guiding the discursive practices of many late twentieth-century groups of North American feminist activists. These groups have often limited discursive openness in two related ways. One way is by limiting their agendas:

activist groups typically come together around certain moral convictions, such as opposing militarism or violence against women; rather than debating these basic moral commitments, they devote themselves instead to exploring their implications. Unquestioned within the group, such commitments become foundational for groups' moral perspectives. The second way in which groups have often limited discursive openness is by restricting participation in their discussions, excluding individuals who do not share the basic commitments of the group or who do not have "standing" because they are outsiders.

The exclusion of outsiders or the closure of moral agendas are sometimes de facto but sometimes are matters of explicit and fierce insistence. For example, some prostitutes' groups have emphatically rejected middle-class feminist analyses of them as victims of sexual exploitation; African American women have sometimes asserted that domestic violence and rape by African American men are topics off-limits to European Americans; some lesbian women have sought to exclude heterosexual women from discussing certain lesbian practices; and, outside the West, some North African women have objected to Western feminist criticisms of the practices of clitoridectomy and infibulation. One especially bitter controversy arose around an article co-authored by two Australian women, an anthropologist of European descent and a "traditional" Aboriginal woman. This article exposed astronomical rates of violence and rape, including frequent gang-rape, committed by Aboriginal men against Aboriginal women. The truth of the allegations was undisputed, but some Aboriginal women objected that it was inappropriate for this topic to be broached by a white woman, even in collaboration with an Aborigine (Bell and Nelson 1989; Larbalestier 1990; Bell 1990, 1991a, 1991b; Klein 1991; Huggins et al. 1991; Nelson 1991). Closing some debates and excluding some topics from some people's intervention seem to run entirely counter to the ideal of free and open discussion as that has been understood in Western moral philosophy. I shall suggest, however, that a feminist conception of moral discourse may be able to justify such exclusions without denying that ideal and may even do so in its name.

Groups of women who have sought to remove their lives from the critical scrutiny of outsider feminists have offered a number of rationales for their desire. Prostitutes' groups have argued that middle-class feminists are ignorant of the real conditions of prostitute life and some North African women have argued that Western feminists do not understand the role of clitoridectomy and infibulation in African cultures. In both cases, the groups whose practices have been challenged by outsiders allege that the criticism is inadequately informed. Sometimes they also express concern that open discussion of certain issues may have deleterious consequences for their community; for instance, some lesbians worry that drawing attention to controversial lesbian practices may encourage attacks from homophobes and some African American women fear that their community may be divided by discussion of violence inflicted by African American men.

Outsider feminists whose interventions are rejected often remain unconvinced by these arguments.[3] Some may respond by asserting their familiarity with the cultures or subcultures in question; others may argue that first-person experience is not authoritative, noting that victims frequently rationalize their abuse, as well as their "choices" to remain in abusive situations. The outsiders may also object to what they perceive as misplaced concern for "the community" as a whole at the expense of some women within it. They may even argue that ignoring the plight of such women is racist or ethnocentric, insofar as it suggests a moral double standard according to which high levels of abuse and exploitation are regarded as "culturally acceptable" for some women but not for others.

In evaluating these difficult and complex issues, it is important to notice that these examples all share some significant features. In each of the foregoing cases, those who seek to protect their lives from scrutiny belong to a group that is socially stigmatized, and/or is a cultural minority, and/or has a history of colonization, while those whom they wish to exclude belong to more powerful or hegemonic groups. Each of the groups whose practices are in question is struggling under external pressure to maintain a sense of self-respect and cultural integrity; and each has been a frequent object of study by psychologists, sociologists, anthropologists, even criminologists from outside that group. These social scientists have typically assumed that their studies have made them experts on the lives of those studied, whom they have often presented as exotic, as victims, or as pathological.

In this context, some communities' resistance to opening their lives for critical feminist examination from the outside may be interpreted less as an attempt to limit the discursive autonomy of others than as a claim to discursive autonomy for themselves. Women from nonhegemonic groups have good reason to suppose that if their lives were to become the subject of feminist discussion, their own perspectives might be discounted. The views of feminists with professional credentials would likely be taken as authoritative, especially if they were published in scholarly journals, where authors are positioned as experts and those studied become "informants" whose opinions are merely data for expert analysis. One critic of the white Australian anthropologist Diane Bell observed that even though Bell's controversial article was officially co-authored with an Aboriginal woman, Topsy Napurrula Nelson, Nelson's words were placed in italics framed by Bell's prose, a device that distinguished Nelson's input from "the dominant White voice controlling the shape and tone of the academic text" (Larbalestier 1990, 147).

Objections to the discursive intervention of feminist outsiders do not necessarily depend on any particular hypothesis about the outsiders' motivation. Outsiders may wish to advance their professional reputations by becoming recognized as experts on some group of marginalized women; they may enjoy posing as the rescuers of victimized women; or they may care deeply for the welfare of the women about whose lives they speak. Regardless of the speakers' motivations, the structure and context of their discursive interventions may have the consequence of positioning the subjects of their discourse as less than equal. In these circumstances, discussion of some issues by some feminists may not only mute the voices of other women but even suggest that they are incapable of speaking for themselves. Ironically, it was precisely the recognition of these kinds of oppressive dynamics that led Western women to form the feminist groups in which they developed the sorts of discursive practices that I now call Feminist Practical Dialogue.

Reflection on the previous examples reveals that idealized understandings of practical discourses as politically innocuous exchanges of ideas occurring in some timeless domain are seriously misleading. To address the moral and political issues surrounding empirical discourse, feminists must recognize that practical discussions are historical events with real-life consequences, not all of which may be controlled or foreseen. In addition, we must never forget that empirical discussions are always infused with power, which influences who is able to participate and who is excluded, who speaks and who listens, whose remarks are heard and whose dismissed, which topics are addressed and which are not, what is questioned and what is taken for granted, even whether a discussion takes place at all. These aspects of moral discourse should be considered not only in feminist practice but also in philosophical theory. For instance, philosophers can appeal to them in explaining why inclusive participation and an open agenda may, on some occasions, impede rather than promote unconstrained discussion. Such considerations also help to explain the epistemological indispensability of closed communities of discourse.

THE EPISTEMOLOGICAL INDISPENSABILITY OF CLOSED COMMUNITIES

Themes of voice and silencing have been central to twentieth-century Western feminism and by now there exists an extensive feminist literature dissecting women's domination in or exclusion from discourse. One classic discussion is Gayatri Chakravorty Spivak's essay, "Can the Subaltern Speak?," in which the author details how "subaltern" Third World women have been represented in discourse in ways that have obscured their subjectivity while promoting the interests of the authors of the texts. (Spivak 1988) In Spivak's example, Indian widows immolated on their husbands' funeral pyres in the practice of *sati* were represented by some British colonizers as victims who must be saved from the slaughter of "backward practices" and by some Indian men as heroes loyal to "Indian" cultural traditions.[4] In both Marxist structuralist and post-structuralist accounts the widows' subjectivities were equally invisible. Meanwhile, Spivak asserts, the subaltern woman remains mute because she herself "cannot know or speak the text of female exploitation" (Spivak 1988, 288).

Why the subaltern woman cannot *speak* of her exploitation at first does not appear mysterious; perhaps this is Spivak's rhetorical way of saying that her indigenous language is incomprehensible to intellectuals or that she cannot produce "texts" because she is illiterate. But why can't she even *know* about her exploitation? Even if she is unfamiliar with classic texts of exploitation, such as Marxism, surely she must be aware that there is something wrong with her situation. How can she be content in her oppression? One answer to this puzzle is suggested by Indian feminist Uma Narayan:

> Girls (of my grandmother's background) were married off barely past puberty, trained for nothing beyond household tasks and the rearing of children, and passed from economic dependency on their fathers to economic dependency on their husbands to economic dependency on their sons in old age. Their criticisms of their lot were articulated, if at all, in terms that precluded a desire for any radical change. They saw themselves as personally unfortunate, but they did not locate the causes of their misery in larger social arrangements. (Narayan 1989, 267-68)

Narayan's words suggest that the subaltern woman's muteness is rooted not in slavish contentment but in her inability to conceptualize the injustice to which she is subjected. Like all diagnoses, this analysis implies the appropriate remedy: what the subaltern woman needs is a conceptual framework, a language capable of articulating her injuries, needs, and aspirations. The existing discourses or texts of exploitation do not provide such a language: even when they promise explicitly to liberate the subaltern, they obscure the distinctive nature of her oppression; indeed, by purporting to speak for her, they position her as mute. In order to articulate her specific exploitation, the subaltern woman must create her own language.

Language is a public construct and its absence is a public, not a private, deficit. Creating a new language is by definition a collective project, not something that can be accomplished by a single individual; if the subaltern woman seeks to enter practical discourse alone, therefore, her experience is likely to remain distorted and repressed. She can overcome her silence only by collaborating with other subaltern women in developing a public language for their shared experiences. She must become part of a group that explicitly recognizes itself as sharing a common condition of oppression—in Marxist terms, a group that constitutes itself as a class for itself as well as in itself. She must claim a collective identity distinct from her identification as the particular daughter, wife, and mother of particular others. Only by creating a collective identity with other women in similar situations, perhaps with other daughters, wives, and mothers, can the subaltern even come to see herself as subaltern and only in this way can she break through the barriers to her speech. Articulating women's distinctive interests requires a language and this, in turn, requires a community. Without either of these, the emergence of counterhegemonic moral perspectives remains impossible.

Small communities, whose members are known personally to each other, have been indispensable to the development of Western feminist moral perspectives. They have enabled Western feminism to offer alternative understandings of social phenomena expressed in a distinct vocabulary that includes expressions like "sexism," "womanism," "sexual objectification," "date rape," "othermother," "the double day," "sexual harassment," "the male gaze," "*mestizaje*," and "emotional labor." Such communities typically have focused on some specific aspect of what they have taken to be women's subordination and they have taken some beliefs for granted, as given within that group. They may have accepted as given the wrongness of militarism or rape or domestic violence or pornography, or they may have accepted as given the value of lesbianism or peer counseling or woman-produced music or erotica. Assuming some such beliefs as foundational for them, the members of the community then have gone on to explore the implications of these beliefs and to elaborate a distinctive moral perspective. For example, once the moral legitimacy of lesbianism was accepted, lesbians went on to raise questions about why people, especially women, are heterosexual, about the social and political consequences of a norm of heterosexuality, about the ways in which heterosexuality is implicated in Western conceptions of gender, and about prevailing definitions of sexuality and family.

It is not only feminists or even moral thinkers whose systems of ideas have been developed in the context of small personal communities united by adherence to certain beliefs or methods. The history of science is full of accounts of "invisible colleges" or groups of scientists working from shared assumptions. David L. Hull calls such groups "demes," by analogy with local populations of organisms sufficiently isolated that they play an important role in biological evolution (Hull 1988, 433-34). The notion of "schools" of artists, such as the Bauhaus, is commonplace and philosophers have frequently worked in groups such as the Jena Circle (to which Hegel belonged), the Vienna Circle, the Frankfurt School and the Oxford philosophers. All these small, usually face-to-face communities functioned as intellectual crucibles in which systems of ideas were explored and elaborated.

Helen Longino notes that progress in science would be impossible unless certain questions were closed to debate at least temporarily. She writes:

> The knowledge-extending mission of science requires that its
> critical mission be blocked. Were the critical dimension of
> science not controlled, inquiry would consist in endless testing;

> endless new proposals and new ideas would be subjected to
> critical scrutiny and rejected. (Longino 1990, 223)

Developing systems of moral and political ideas also requires that certain premises be held constant. By uniting around certain shared assumptions, moral and political communities provide intellectual space in which members are freed from pressure continually to defend their premises and explain their technical vocabulary. Because they are typically small and the members known personally to each other, communication within such communities is likely to be informal and rapid. Half-formed ideas may be tried out and sometimes may be developed by members literally thinking together.

When the ideas involved are heretical by the standards of the larger society, such communities provide emotional as well as intellectual support for their members. Patricia Hill Collins asserts that a "realm of relatively safe discourse, however narrow, is a necessary condition for Black women's resistance" (Collins 1990, 95). A single dissenting individual is likely to be labeled crazy, if not wicked, and, in the absence of support, she may even come to regard herself as wicked or crazy. María Lugones observes, "unless resistance is a social activity, the resister is doomed to failure in the creation of a new universe of meaning, a new identity, a *raza mestiza*. Meaning that is not in response to and looking for a response fails as meaning" (Lugones 1992, 36). When others share the dissenter's views or endorse her methods, the conditions exist for developing an oppositional identity that individuals often find validating, even emancipatory. Sarah Hoagland writes that "coming out (as a lesbian) was, for me, coming home. I experienced the sensation of landing and centering. It is lesbians who inspire me, lesbian energy which enlivens me. . . ." (Hoagland 1988, 3) Within the safety of her community, the dissenter may feel that finally she has the freedom to "be herself." She no longer has to be on guard or to dissemble. Finally, she is free to be "authentic," to say—and therefore discover—what she "really" thinks. Paradoxically, however, the same features that enable small moral communities to liberate the thinking of their members often simultaneously operate to limit that thinking.

MORAL AND EPISTEMOLOGICAL HAZARDS OF CLOSED COMMUNITIES

While it is liberating for the members of closed communities to be freed from having to defend their basic assumptions, their thought is also restricted by the constraints on what may be questioned within those communities. In scientific communities, shared assumptions often remain hidden and only idiosyncratic beliefs are challenged (Longino 1990, 233). The same is true in moral and political communities of right, left, and center, all of which appeal to foundational values often thought to be enshrined in documents taken as authoritative, such as the Bible, the Communist Manifesto or the U.S. Constitution. In consequence, intragroup disagreement is typically cast as debate over how to interpret the community's foundational values or texts.

Although it would be impossible to develop systems of moral and political ideas unless certain assumptions were temporarily taken for granted, it is equally true that, if those assumptions are never opened to challenge, the system based on them becomes a form of dogmatism. Members of the community find themselves forced to express questions and disagreements obliquely, perhaps even to suppress them entirely, at best to articulate them in the approved language, larded with references to the approved texts. People on the outside may regard the community as a cult, especially if the ideas to which it is committed are heretical or unorthodox.

All communities exert pressure on their members to conform to the prevailing interpretation of their unifying assumptions and values. These pressures are likely to be especially intense in small oppositional communities beleaguered by pressures from the larger society. Fearful of assimilation or defeat, such communities may regard internal conformity as a necessary condition of their survival and, in these circumstances, dissent may appear as betrayal. Community resistance to challenge and change is also likely to be stronger when the members' self-definitions are centrally bound up with the community as constituted, since dissent challenges more orthodox members of the community to modify their cherished beliefs and threatens values integral to their sense of who they are. When members regard their identities as inseparable from the community, they may also fear that change in the values of the community will not only affect the way the community is perceived by outsiders but also reflect on the members personally. If the community has a leader or leaders, they are likely to feel their authority threatened by dissenters, a challenge they are especially likely to resist if their work with the community is central to their life activity.

Most small communities encourage conformity through formal or informal sanctions, even if these are no more than chilliness toward or ridicule of certain ideas. Often, such communities also seek to strengthen group loyalty by developing a sense of superiority in relation to the larger society. Community members are encouraged to view themselves as an enlightened elite, dismissing those who disagree with them as sinful, ignorant, or victims of false consciousness. This perception may be used to justify different standards of behavior towards those within and those outside the community. The sense that the community comprises an in-group enjoying a privileged religious, scientific, political, or moral perspective also strengthens the community's ultimate weapon for enforcing conformity; namely, the threat of expulsion. Not merely excluded from the group, a nonconformist may be defined as unworthy to belong to it. She is labeled a heretic or a pagan, a quack or a charlatan, a traitor, a renegade or a counterrevolutionary, no longer a "true" feminist or communist, unprofessional, or un-American.

The threat of expulsion is the ultimate sanction enforcing conformity in most communities. How far the threat is successful in suppressing dissent depends on how much community members fear exclusion and this fear varies according to the type of community in question, its relationship to the larger society, the needs it satisfies for its members, and the dependence members feel on that community. If the members of a religious community believe that excommunication will result in an eternity of hellfire, they have an extremely powerful incentive to conform; so do members of a professional organization for whom expulsion will result in the loss of their occupational licenses. By contrast, the prospect of expulsion from a neighborhood swimming club is likely to be unpleasant but not especially frightening, because club membership does not represent the only way members can fulfil their needs for exercise and social affiliation.

When belonging to a particular community is central to a member's sense of her own identity, the threat of expulsion is likely to loom extraordinarily large. Leaving the community may represent losing connection with the religious, moral, political, or cultural values that have given meaning to her life. It may represent losing her emotional home, her sense of belonging, her colleagues, comrades, friends and lovers. Such fears are especially intense for members of racial/ethnic and oppositional communities, because no comparable alternatives are likely to be available. This is one reason why community loyalty and discipline are often especially strong among ethnic and cultural minorities and on both the right and the left of the political spectrum.

Some communities may seek to forestall challenges to their beliefs or values by limiting diversity among those they admit, excluding people thought likely to hold disruptive opinions or values or even people with an unacceptable image. Ethnic or cultural minorities may refuse to admit "half-bloods" or people who have been "Westernized"; lesbian communities may refuse to admit bisexuals; gay groups may exclude drag or leather queens. Conscious policies of exclusion reinforce the tendencies towards cultural homogeneity that exist in all small communities whose members rely on each other for emotional as well as intellectual support (Young 1990, 235). Policing the boundaries of the community serves to maintain the "purity" of its beliefs and values by insulating its members from the challenge of alternative thinking (Phelan 1989).

Endemic to closed communities are a number of closely related epistemological and moral dangers. They include the dangers of repression and denial of autonomy, dogmatism, intellectual dishonesty and self-deception, elitism, and partialism. For these reasons, I contend that, although temporarily closed communities are indispensable for the development of systematic alternatives to hegemonic moral systems, the alternatives they produce eventually must be subjected to wider moral evaluation. In order to increase the degree to which their moral agreements are justified, communities ultimately must open their basic commitments to critical scrutiny from the outside.

GLOBALIZING FEMINIST DISCOURSE

For contemporary Western feminists to open our basic commitments to critical scrutiny requires considering or reconsidering perspectives we have hitherto excluded. This may mean that we reconsider the views of those Western antifeminists who assert that a woman's place is in the home and that date rape and harassment are figments of paranoid feminist imaginations. It may also mean that we take account of Nonwestern perspectives, especially those ignored or demonized by Western media. Most immediately and urgently, however, it requires that Western feminists learn to hear and consider respectfully the views of Nonwestern women from the so-called Third World, including women whose voices are muted, even within their own nations.[5] Most especially, we should pursue critical engagement with those members of Nonwestern communities who share some of our own commitments but who may have disagreements or different perspectives on particular issues. Critical dialogue between members of communities that have significant differences but still share some basic concerns is likely to be more immediately useful in promoting reassessments of our own commitments and refinements of our own views than "dialogue" with those whose commitments and worldviews are far removed from our own. Dialogue with those who share many of our values and commitments is also practically indispensable for making social change within democratic contexts.

Some would challenge the possibility of global feminist dialogue on the grounds that feminism is not a worldwide movement. Such a view has often been held by Western feminists, who have assumed that the lot of Nonwestern women can be improved only through the introduction of Western feminist ideas. Chandra Talpade Mohanty observes that Western feminist images of the "average third world woman" have often portrayed her as leading "an essentially truncated life based on her feminine gender (read: sexually constrained) and her being 'third world' (read: ignorant, poor, uneducated, tradition-bound, family-oriented, victimized, etc.)." Mohanty contrasts this representation of Nonwestern women with the implicit self-representation of Western women "as educated, as modern, as having control over their own bodies and sexualities, and the freedom to make their own decisions" (Mohanty 1991b, 56).

Nonwesterners as well as Westerners have often portrayed feminism as an exclusively Western phenomenon. Kumari Jayawardena observes,

> The concept of feminism has . . . been the cause of much confusion in Third World countries. It has variously been

> alleged by traditionalists, political conservatives and even cer-
> tain leftists, that feminism is a product of "decadent" Western
> capitalism; that it is based on a foreign culture of no relevance
> to women in the Third World; that it is the ideology of women
> of the local bourgeoisie; and that it alienates or diverts women
> from their culture, religion and family responsibilities on the
> one hand, and from the revolutionary struggles for national
> liberation and socialism on the other. (Jayawardena 1986, 2)

The belief that feminism is primarily a Western phenomenon, ironically shared by both Nonwestern antifeminists and many Western feminists, is in fact mistaken. Kumari Jayawardena documents how women in Asia and the Middle East have fought collectively against their subordination from the late nineteenth century on, though Nonwestern women have been less likely than Western women to form autonomous women's organizations and have been more likely to express their feminism in the context of nationalist struggles, working-class agitation and peasant rebellions (Jayawardena 1986). Uma Narayan writes that the pain that motivated her Indian feminism "was earlier than school and 'Westernization,' a call to rebellion that has a different and more primary root, that was not conceptual or English, but in the mother-tongue" (Narayan 1997, 7).

Chandra Talpade Mohanty observes that "No noncontradictory or 'pure' feminism is possible" (Mohanty 1991a, 20) Today, the world beyond the industrialized West proliferates both small groups and large, government-sponsored organizations dedicated to improving the status of women and, in Nonwestern as in Western contexts, the beliefs of these groups reveal tensions between conservative and radical ideas. For instance, some Nonwestern movements assuming the label "feminist" have failed to address forms of domination affecting the lives of poor and peasant women or to challenge the ideology of the middle-class family; meanwhile, other Nonwestern movements concerned with increasing the self-reliance of poor women and enlarging their choices nevertheless refrain from direct challenges to male privilege (Newland 1991, 130) or eschew the label "feminist" because they perceive it as a white, middle-class movement narrowly defined as a struggle against gender discrimination (Johnson-Odim 1991, 313). Everywhere in the world, feminism is maligned and contested.

Whether or not they call themselves feminist, innumerable groups outside the West are currently working to promote what Maxine Molyneux calls women's "gender interests." Molyneux defines gender interests as "those that women (or men for that matter) may develop by virtue of their social positioning through gender attributes" (Molyneux 1985, 232). She distinguishes practical from strategic gender interests. Women's practical gender interests emerge directly from their concrete life situations and include such immediately perceived necessities as food, shelter, water, income, medical care, and transportation. Molyneux notes that demands for these "do not generally . . . challenge the prevailing forms of subordination even though they arise directly out of them" (1985, 232-3). Indeed, addressing women's practical gender interests may even reinforce the sexual division of labor by reinforcing the assumption that it is women's responsibility to provide for their families. By contrast, women's strategic gender interests are defined as necessary to overcoming women's subordination. According to Molyneux, they may include all or some of the following, depending on the social context:

> the abolition of the sexual division of labor; the alleviation of the burden of domestic labor and childcare; the removal of institutionalized forms of discrimination such as rights to own land or property, or access to credit; the establishment of political equality; freedom of choice over childbearing; and the adoption of adequate measures against male violence and control over women. (Molyneux 1985, 233)

It is groups working to promote women's strategic gender interests that are most likely to share the basic commitments held by many Western feminists.[6]

Because of their potentially challenging nature, local grassroots groups dedicated to addressing women's strategic gender needs in the Third World are largely unsupported either by national governments or bilateral aid agencies (Moser 1991, 109-10). They may be seen as communities of resistance comparable in many ways to Western feminist communities. Like some Western feminist groups, which may open women's health centers or run automobile or home maintenance workshops, many Nonwestern groups find that they can develop the skills and motivation necessary for addressing women's strategic gender interests by working immediately on women's practical gender interests. One example is the Forum Against Oppression of Women which, in 1979, began campaigning in Bombay to draw attention to issues such as rape and bride burning but soon shifted its focus to housing, which was an especially acute problem for women deserted or abused by their husbands in a culture where women by tradition had no access to housing in their own right. Organizing around homelessness raised awareness of the male bias in inheritance legislation, as well as in the interpretation of housing rights, and ultimately ensured that women's strategic gender needs related to housing rights were placed on the mainstream political agenda (Moser 1991, 109).

Even if we grant a significant base of similar commitments between Western feminists and Nonwestern women committed to advancing women's strategic gender interests, many obstacles exist to dialogue that is genuinely egalitarian, open, and inclusive.[7] Still, these are not insuperable obstacles to the possibility of global feminist discourse.

WHO MAY PARTICIPATE IN GLOBAL FEMINIST DISCOURSE?

If feminism is committed to inclusiveness, one might reasonably infer that everyone concerned about ending the subordination of all women is eligible to participate in global feminist discourse. To draw this inference, however, is to forget our earlier recognition that discourse is not an ahistorical abstraction but rather a series of discrete encounters that occur at specific places and times among specific individuals, who stand to each other in a variety of specific social, including power, relations. Even though I contend that equality, openness, and inclusiveness are central norms of feminist moral discourse, we have seen that they are not incompatible with limiting some people's access to some discussion about some topics on some occasions.

In putting the ideals of openness and inclusiveness into practice, it is necessary to remember both the social constitution of moral rationality and the vast power inequalities between the present Western and Nonwestern worlds. The first point entails that it is reasonable to exclude from specific moral discussions people who seem to share no common convictions on the basis of which rational discussion could occur; such people indeed exclude themselves. The second point suggests that it is sometimes reasonable for a beleaguered moral community to exclude members of more powerful communities, especially when the beleaguered community is addressing certain internal or domestic issues, such as the earlier example of Aboriginal violence against women. Members of subordinated groups may not wish to discuss problems affecting their community with members of more powerful communities, especially if the powerful communities already claim cultural superiority. Criticism of one's own cultural practices in the hearing of outsiders may be experienced as a form of betrayal, and the presence of outsiders who are perceived as more powerful may inhibit discussion among insiders. That the ideal of unconstrained discourse may sometimes permit or even require members of dominant groups to be excluded from the discourse of subordinated groups does not entail, of course, that it is equally legitimate for the members of dominant communities to exclude members of subordinated groups from their discussions, especially when the dominant groups are discussing practices that have a significant impact on the subordinated groups.

Even though there may be reasonable grounds for excluding members of dominant groups from specific occasions of discourse, outsiders' concerns about the situation of women in specific cultures are not necessarily illegitimate. When cultural relativism is espoused by the relatively powerless and impoverished, it may be a means of expressing resistance to cultural imperialism; when it is advocated by the wealthier and more powerful, however, cultural relativism is just as likely to express imperial arrogance as an ethnocentric insistence on the absolute superiority of the norms of the wealthier culture. For instance, it is certainly presumptuous for Western feminists to assume that they are already aware of the most important problems faced by women outside the West, or that they are experts on how those problems should be solved, but it does not manifest genuine cultural respect to assume without question that Nonwestern women are content with lives that Western women would find constraining, exhausting, or degrading. Conversely, it is equally legitimate for Nonwestern women to raise questions about the moral permissibility of practices widely accepted by Western feminists, practices that might include sex work or the integration of women into the military. Global feminism requires concern for women in other communities and nations and raising questions about the moral justifiability of foreign practices is very different from peremptorily condemning those practices, let alone intervening unilaterally to change them.

In an interesting discussion of the relative advantages and disadvantages of insiders and outsiders who engage in social criticism, David Crocker argues that insiders are not exclusively privileged in morally evaluating their own cultures. Insiders enjoy the advantages of understanding the cultural meaning of their own society's practices, of being able to express their evaluations in language accessible to their community, and of possessing undisputed standing for engaging in social criticism; but they also suffer characteristic disadvantages, such as possible ignorance of alternative ways of seeing and doing things and susceptibility to social pressures that may inhibit their freedom to express their criticisms. Outsiders suffer the disadvantages of unfamiliarity with cultural meanings, the perception that they are not entitled to intervene discursively in the affairs of another culture, and the possibility of ethnocentric arrogance or its inverse, romanticization of the culture in question. But they also enjoy the advantages of external perspectives, which may reveal things hidden from insiders, familiarity with novel moral ideas, and relative social freedom to say what needs to be said (Crocker 1991).

Despite the difficulties and dangers of cross-cultural moral discourse, it is not impossible for outsiders to participate in evaluating the internal practices of another culture. Advocates of women's strategic gender interests in both the West and the Third World therefore should not regard questions and criticisms of our own cultural practices by our foreign counterparts as inevitably presumptuous or unwarranted but should view them rather as moral resources. For feminism to become global does not mean that Western feminists should think of themselves as missionaries carrying civilization to primitive and barbarous lands, but neither does it mean that people concerned about the subordination of women in their own culture may dismiss the plight of women in others. At least on the level of morality, global feminism means that feminists in each culture must re-examine our own commitments in light of the perspectives produced by feminists in others, so that we may recognize some of the limits and biases of our own beliefs and assumptions. Of course, the moral evaluations of any cultural practice must always be "immersed" rather than "detached," taking account of "the practices, the perceptions, even the emotions, of the culture" (Nussbaum and Sen 1989, 308). Elsewhere, I suggest that a feminist conception of discourse, with its emphasis on listening, personal friendship, and responsiveness to emotion, and its concern to address power inequalities, is especially well suited to facilitate such an immersed evaluation.

We have seen already that the more conformist members of any community are likely to challenge dissenters' status as insiders; in a Third World context, attempts have sometimes been made to discredit the voices of African feminists or Western-trained medical personnel when they have been raised in opposition to traditional practices such as female genital surgery, portraying such critics as no longer authentic members of their communities. But community membership is partly, though not entirely, a matter of self-definition and it is rarely clear who is entitled to define others as inside or outside moral communities or by what process. All communities change and there is no reason to identify a community with its most conservative elements or to assume that individuals who dissent from some of their community's moral beliefs thereby renounce their membership in that community.

Recognizing the possibility, indeed the inevitability, of disagreement *within* as well as *among* moral communities complicates our hitherto simple model of insiders and outsiders. For instance, if we were to determine that issues that appeared to concern only a single group might be assessed solely by members of that group, so that only prostitutes could evaluate prostitution and only African women could discuss clitoridectomy and infibulation, we would immediately encounter new problems of identity, authorization, and legitimation. Who is entitled to speak for a group as a whole and whence derives her authority?[8] Can ex-prostitutes speak for prostitutes who are currently working? Can an African woman who has received a Western education fairly represent other African women? There is no reason to suppose that African women, or prostitutes, or lesbians, or African American women all think alike, and dissenters in these groups may be silenced by women who claim to speak for the whole. It is interesting to notice how the urban Aboriginal women who participated in the Bell controversy delegitimated the voice of Topsy Naparrula Nelson by labeling her "traditional," even though it could well be argued that Nelson was better qualified than her Western-educated challengers to speak for other Aboriginal women precisely by virtue of her traditional identity. Some Aboriginal women who had no opportunity to participate in the published debate might have agreed with Nelson in welcoming the intervention of an outsider whose professional credentials enabled her to be heard while their own voices were ignored.

Most people actually belong to more than one community and as the world becomes increasingly integrated through international trade, population migration, and electronic communication, communities are increasingly likely to overlap and individuals to be multicultural or multilingual. Poet Meena

Alexander, born in India, educated in North Africa and Britain, currently living in New York City, describes herself as a "woman cracked by multiple migrations."

> Everything that comes to me is hyphenated. A woman poet, a woman poet of color, a South Indian woman poet who makes up lines in English, a postcolonial language, as she waits for the red lights to change on Broadway. A Third World woman poet, who takes as her right the inner city of Manhattan, making up poems about the hellhole of the subway line. . . ." (Nair 1991, 71)

In the circumstances of the contemporary world, even women who never physically leave their communities of origin are increasingly likely to evaluate their own lives in light of what they know about the situation of women in other cultures—though it remains true that Nonwestern women are likely to know much more about Western cultures than Westerners about Nonwestern cultures. When external influences operate through a local response to things learned elsewhere, Nussbaum and Sen argue it is still an internal rather than an external evaluation of the practices of a given culture. They contend that "criticizing the position of women in, say, today's Iran by reference to freedom enjoyed by women elsewhere is no more 'external' than reference to the position of women in Iran's own past" (Nussbaum and Sen 1989, 321).

Although cultural communities are not fictions, they are set increasingly in a larger global context in which moral traditionalists often bemoan the impossibility of banishing external or foreign influences. Not only do many direct forms of economic and political intervention exist but, when global communications are so rapid and extensive, the sheer existence of alternative ways of life itself becomes a moral intervention. Once again, it must be noted that the external pressure for change is much stronger on Nonwestern than on Western cultures and that Western economies and politics inevitably will undermine some aspects of Nonwestern cultures while reinforcing others. Because nothing seems likely to prevent these eventualities, it is especially important for Western feminists to seek ways of being allies to Nonwestern women who are seeking to affect these developments so that they may promote rather than undermine the strategic gender interests of women in their communities.

WHAT IS ON THE GLOBAL FEMINIST AGENDA?

Western feminists have often assumed that priority in international feminist discourse must be given to what they perceive as horrific Nonwestern practices such as polygamy, the sex-selective abortion of female fetuses, female seclusion, arranged and child marriage, unilateral divorce, brideprice and bride burning, female infanticide and, currently the most popular topic of all, so-called female "circumcision" or female genital surgery. The last, in particular, has now become a stock example in Western classroom discussions of moral universalism versus cultural relativism and consideration of this issue has generated an extensive literature on topics such as discursive incommensurability and moral relativism.

Nonwestern women naturally resent what they regard as a sensationalized Western focus on non-Western marital and sexual practices.[9] Western discussions are typically predicated on the assumption that female genital surgery is morally unjustified, thus framing the issue as one of balancing the threats to the health and welfare of Third World women against the evils of maternalism or cultural imperialism. A related problem is that so much focus on these practices encourages Western feminists to regard themselves as missionaries spreading the civilizing word of feminism, while simultaneously positioning Nonwestern women as backward, barbarous, and victimized. Finally, Western discussions of female genital surgery and similar Nonwestern practices often misleadingly homogenize Nonwestern communities and ignore the existence of indigenous forms of dissent.[10]

Regardless of the circumstances in which it may become legitimate for outsiders to involve themselves in the domestic affairs of another community or nation, our increasingly integrated contemporary world does not lack issues that affect women more globally. Some cluster around the worldwide phenomenon of gendered violence against women; this phenomenon was explored at a global tribunal of nongovernmental women's organizations that met in Vienna in 1993 in conjunction with the Second World Conference on Human Rights to urge that violence against women be recognized as a violation of human rights, as well as to highlight the connections between the murder, torture and sexual coercion and abuse of women and their economic vulnerability. Many other issues are much less comfortable for Western feminists to address, since discussion may reveal that most Westerners are on the wrong rather than the right side of the moral divide. Central to these uncomfortable questions is the justice of the global system itself, a question that has been addressed directly by few Western feminists, especially feminist philosophers.

There are many ways in which what happens on one side of the world affects women on the other; even if Third World women's oppression cannot be reduced to imperialism, it nevertheless exists in a context of economic domination reinforced by Western military interventions, either directly or by proxy. Matters of international feminist concern therefore include not only explicitly gendered issues, such as efforts by Western agencies to include Third World women in "development" or to control their fertility by linking so-called aid with prohibitions on abortion or insistence on contraception; they also include less evidently gendered issues about the nature of development and the forces that currently define it.

Most pressing among these issues may be the debt owed by the Third World to the West. During the late 1960s and 1970s, when interest rates were low, the Third World engaged in massive borrowing to finance economic and social development. By the end of the 1970s, with interest rates rising, the Third World had increasing difficulty paying the interest on its loans and a world debt crisis resulted. Since 1982, severe "structural adjustment" policies have been imposed on the Third World by Western-controlled financial institutions such as the World Bank and the International Monetary Fund, whose primary concerns are to ensure that the debt to Western banks be serviced. These institutions' insistence on export-led development in the Third World and on sharp reductions in the economic and welfare functions of Third World states resulted, as early as 1986, in a net annual outflow from the Third World to the West three times as large as the amount received in aid from all Western sources. This hemorrhage of Third World wealth has inevitably had cata-strophic consequences for the living standards of most Third World women, though it has benefitted Third World elites (George 1988, 1992).[11] Related issues of global feminist concern include plant relocations by multinational corporations from the West to the Third World, multinational extraction of Third World resources and, even more generally, Western conceptions of development and patterns of consumption (Mies 1986; Shiva 1988; Mies et al 1988; Enloe 1990; Mies and Shiva 1993; Scott 1996). These provide a context for discussing issues such as environmental degradation in both the Third World and the West (Shiva 1988); the trade in heroin and cocaine (George 1992); militarism (Enloe 1990); tourism, including sex tourism (Enloe 1990); population control (Hartmann 1987; Jacobson 1990; Dixon-Mueller 1993); and the international traffic in women.

Western and Third World women are not affected equally by recent changes in the world economic order: Third World women are generally affected more adversely than Western women. A tiny minority of Third World women and a much larger proportion of Western women benefit from these changes, at least in some respects; but in both "worlds" the poorest women suffer most. In both "worlds," moreover, the contemporary structure of the world economic order affects the lives of women differently from—and generally more harshly than the way it affects men's lives. This is why these superficially ungendered matters actually are issues of the most urgent feminist concern.

Is There a Global Feminist Discourse Community?

Many Western accounts of moral rationality invoke idealized conceptions of moral community.[12] Idealizations offer simplified theoretical models that are often illuminating but may also mislead. My own project of developing a feminist conception of practical moral discourse is motivated by the convic-tion that the idealized communities postulated by many Western moral philosophers obscure several crucial features of empirical moral discourse, including considerations of social power.

Some authors have suggested that global feminism should be understood in terms of an "imagined community" (Mohanty 1991, 4; Ferguson 1995). This expression gained its contemporary currency from Benedict Anderson's book, *Imagined Communities*, which describes the myths and practices used by builders of modern nation-states to create a sense of common national identity and patriotism among disparate peoples (Anderson, 1983). Drawing on Anderson's insight that all communities are bound together by a shared conception of their history and traditions, ideals and values, Ann Ferguson suggests that thinking of global feminism in terms of an imagined community might inspire individual feminists to see themselves as part of a global sisterhood. Ferguson emphasizes that such identification must be more than a fantasy, requiring engagement in actual meaning- and value-making rituals with women who are not of one's own national origin (Ferguson 1995, 385). Margaret Walker, however, worries about the hazards of imagining a global feminist community. "Imagined communities are seductive because they yield real psychic comforts, powerful feelings of belonging and mattering; imagined communities are irrelevant or dangerous because they distract our attention from actual communities" (Walker 1994, 54).

Frequently overlooked features of actual communities include their fluidity and internal heterogeneity. The boundaries of empirical communities are shifting, permeable, and frequently contested; empirical communities are often riven by dissent and their members often belong simultaneously to other communities. Ignoring these aspects of empirical communities encourages what Uma Narayan calls "cultural essentialism," that is, images of national and cultural contexts as "sealed rooms, impervious to change, with a homogenous space 'inside' them inhabited by 'authentic Insiders' who all share a uniform and consistent account of their institutions and values" (Narayan 1997, 33). "Cultural essentialism" has often been used to serve colonial purposes but Narayan observes that today it is sometimes adopted uncritically by Western feminists in well-meaning efforts to recognize "Difference." Narayan argues that cultural essentialism is problematic not only because of its empirical inadequacy but because it promotes sharp oppositions which, like all binaries, over value one pole while disparaging the other. Cultural essentialism typically draws contrasts between Western and Nonwestern cultures. One version assigns to the "West" a commitment to such values as liberty and equality, despite innumerable examples of Western subjugation and inequality, while portraying such appalling but exceptional practices as *sati* as central to "Indian" culture (Narayan 1997); another version accepts a romanticized picture of Nonwestern cultures as spiritual and harmonious while representing Western culture as exclusively materialist and genocidal. Cultural essentialism reifies selected differences between "East" and

"West," and in doing so exaggerates the difficulties of discourse between feminists from each "world."

Other dangers of imagining a global feminist discourse community include the temptation to imagine some transnational feminist counterpublic, within which varying local interpretations of women's subordination receive final and authoritative adjudication. This could encourage acceptance of a model of moral rationality, according to which local communities generated distinct moral perspectives that would be assessed by "the" global community and perhaps finally ratified by a consensus of all feminists. Such a model would be misleadingly simple and mechanistic, relying on a neopositivist distinction between "discovery" and "justification" while ignoring the inevitably provisional nature of feminist agreements. Finally, the notion of imagined community might distract feminists from recognizing the real and continuing inequalities of power both within and among communities. Walker notes the danger of

> responding to an imagined (international or global) community of women or of feminists, while failing to take account of, and so responsibility for, the many ways our actual national and cultural communities make the imagined community simply impossible, and the invocation of it irrelevant, if not insulting. (Walker 1994, 54)

Despite the real dangers of imagining communities, I suggest that they be taken not as conclusive objections to any feminist imaginings of community but rather as warnings against inventing romanticized discursive utopias. If all communities are imagined, in the sense that they depend on a shared self-conception, then reinventing and reimagining communities becomes a crucial political task for feminists at the local, national, and global levels (Narayan 1997). In imagining a global feminist discourse community, however, we must avoid generating feminist versions of the naïvely apolitical idealizations produced in mainstream moral theory; for instance, we must avoid premature postulations of a global sisterhood. Instead, we must recognize that global feminist discourse communities are not philosophical or political fantasies but real entities that already have begun to exist. Innumerable feminists are engaged already in discussing issues that cross national borders and they are increasingly cooperating in working to address these issues. "The" global feminist discourse community is not singular, because global feminist discourse occurs in multiple and overlapping networks of individuals and communities and with varying and changing agendas. Indeed, it is a community in the making and, in this sense, it is not only both ideal and imagined but continually being reimagined. Feminist imaginings offer ideals toward which to aspire; imagining a global feminist discourse community that seeks constantly to be more inclusive, open, and equal may serve as a heuristic for feminist moral discourse and a basis for feminist political action.

NOTES

1. This paper draws on several sections of my book in progress, *Sex, Truth and Power: A Feminist Theory of Moral Reason*. I read the first version of this paper at an invited symposium of the Pacific Division of the American Philosophical Association in March 1997; the topic of the symposium was "Cultural Relativism and Global Feminism," and I thank its organizer, Dean Chatterjee. I read the second version at SOFPHIA and I thank all those who participated in the discussion, especially my introducer, Bat Ami Bar-On. Many people have offered valuable comments on the ideas presented here but in preparing this version I am grateful for help from Ann Ferguson, Sandra Harding, Jim Maffie, Linda Nicholson, and Margaret Walker. Special thanks go to Uma Narayan, who has discussed these issues with me over several years and who went carefully and sympathetically through an originally rambling draft, providing extremely helpful suggestions for organizing and focusing it.

2. For a first account of my conception of feminist practical discourse, see Jaggar 1995.

3. Some insiders also remain unconvinced. A good example of an insider critique of exclusionary views can to be found in Crenshaw 1997.

4. Spivak notes both that the British "grotesquely mistranscribed" the names of the women and that *sati* actually translates as "good wife" and is a common name for Indian girls.

5. Terminology is a problem. I am especially interested in the possibility of dialogue between feminists from the wealthy industrialized or postindustrial capitalist nations, located mainly in Western Europe, Australasia, and North America, on the one hand, and, on the other, women from the poor rural or industrializing nations, located mainly in Africa, Latin America, the Caribbean, South and Southeast Asia, and Oceania. Some people refer to each side of this divide as North and South respectively, but I avoid this usage here because "North" is often taken to include Japan and possibly Central and Eastern Europe and "South" to include Australasia. Instead, I choose to contrast Western feminisms—the Eurocentric feminist traditions of North America, Western Europe, and the Antipodes—either with Nonwestern feminisms, even though this usage linguistically privileges the West; or with Third World feminisms, even though the Second World no longer exists.

6. One recent study of global feminist activism is Amrita Basu's *Challenge of Local Feminisms: Women's Movements in Global Perspective* (Basu 1995).

7. One question confronting those who seek global feminist dialogue is whether conceptual and moral incommensurability make moral discourse impossible across cultural boundaries. I have no space here to address this question, but I argue elsewhere that incommensurability in moral perspectives does not entail mutual incomprehension sufficient to make moral dialogue impossible. Of course, that people can communicate with each other in principle does not at all guarantee that they understand each other in practice.

8. An excellent discussion of these issues is Alcoff 1991-92.

9. It has sometimes appeared to me that prurience is one factor encouraging this focus. For instance, a recent prize-winning "news" photograph portrayed a young woman examining herself after female genital surgery. She surely thought she was unobserved and the angle of the photograph suggested that the photographer was hiding in a tree with a telephoto lens. In my view, the photograph not only objectified and exoticized the young woman but grossly invaded her privacy.

10. In 1994, South Asian women's groups in Canada protested a Canadian doctor's willingness to abort female foetuses for Indian Canadians. The doctor defended himself by saying that he would be guilty of "cultural arrogance" if he criticized the practices of another ethnic community but his critics called his attitude racist, saying that sex selection was not inherent in South Asian cultures.

11. The social consequences of these policies may be summed up in a single figure from UNICEF (the United Nations Children's Fund) which estimates that half a million children die every year as a direct result of the debt crisis. The suffering and death of these children, a disproportionate number of whom are girls, obviously affects women's lives much more severely than men's; it is primarily women who struggle to care for these children, who cope with the malnutrition-caused disorders of the children who survive, and who bear more children at the cost of their own health and sometimes their lives.

12. For instance, Kant contends that a necessary condition of moral agency is membership in a community of equals, but he views this not as a specific empirical community but rather an idealization, an imagined transhistorical community comprising all rational beings. John Rawls's community of parties in the original position is also a thought experiment that is explicitly unrealizable. Habermas's communicative ethics is apparently more naturalistic in postulating an empirical discourse community but, because this community is defined in terms of conditions that are inevitably counterfactual, I would argue that it, too, turns out to be an idealized community. At first sight, communitarianism appears to be even more naturalistic than discourse ethics because it posits a variety of historically specific communities that have emerged organically and are characterized by adherence to distinctive moral traditions. I would contend, however, that communitarianism deals also in idealized communities because it works from a romanticized and essentialist vision of community.

REFERENCES

Alcoff, Linda. 1991-92. The problem of speaking for others. *Cultural Critique* 20: 5-32.

Anderson, Benedict. 1983. *Imagined communities: Reflections on the origins and spread of nationalism*. London: New Left Books.

Basu, Amrita, ed. 1995. *The challenge of local feminisms: Women's movements in global perspective*. Boulder, CO: Westview Press.

Bell, Diane. 1990. Reply [to Huggins et al.]. *Anthropological Forum* 6(2): 158-65.

———. 1991a. Intraracial rape revisited: On forging a feminist future beyond factions and frightening politics. *Women's Studies International Forum* 14(5): 385-412.

———. 1991b. Letter to the editor. *Women's Studies International Forum* 14(5): 507-13

Bell, Diane and Topsy Naparrula Nelson. 1989. Speaking about rape is everyone's business. *Women's Studies International Forum* 12(4): 403-16.

Collins, Patricia Hill. 1990. *Black feminist thought: Knowledge, consciousness and the politics of empowerment*. New York: Unwin Hyman.

Crenshaw, Kimberle. 1997. Intersectionality and identity politics: Learning from violence against women of color. In *Reconstructing political theory: Feminist perspectives*, ed. Mary Lyndon Shanley and Uma Narayan. University Park, PA: Pennsylvania State University Press.

Crocker, David A. 1991. Insiders and outsiders in international development. *Ethics and International Affairs* 5: 149-173.

Dixon-Mueller, Ruth. 1993. *Population policy and women's rights*. Westport, CT: Praeger.

Enloe, Cynthia. 1990. *Bananas, beaches and bases: Making feminist sense of international politics*. Berkeley: University of California Press.

Ferguson, Ann. 1995. Feminist communities and moral revolution. In *Feminism and Community*, ed. Penny A. Weiss and Marilyn Friedman. Philadelphia: Temple University Press.

George, Susan. 1988. *A fate worse than debt*. New York: Grove Press.

———. 1992. *The debt boomerang: How third world debt harms us all*. London: Pluto Press.

Hartmann, Betsy. 1987. *Reproductive fights and wrongs: The global politics of population control and contraceptive choice*. New York: Harper and Row.

Hoagland, Sarah Lucia. 1988. *Lesbian ethics: Toward new value*. Palo Alto, CA: Institute of Lesbian Studies.

Huggins, Jackie et al. 1991. Letter to the editor. *Women's Studies International Forum* 14(5): 506-7.

Hull, David L. 1988. *Science as a process: An evolutionary account of the social and conceptual development of science*. Chicago: University of Chicago Press.

Jacobson, Jodi L. 1990. *The global politics of abortion*. Washington DC: Worldwatch Institute.

Jaggar, Alison M. 1995. Toward a feminist conception of moral reasoning. In *Morality and social justice: Point/counterpoint*, ed. James P. Sterba. Lanham, MD: Rowman and Littlefield.

Jayawardena, Kumari, 1986. Feminism and nationalism in the third world. London: Zed Books Ltd.

Johnson-Odim, Cheryl. 1991. Common themes, different contexts: Third world women and feminism. In *Third world women and the politics of feminism*. See Mohanty, Russo, and Torres 1991.

Klein, Renate. 1991. Editorial. *Women's Studies International Forum* 14(5): 505-6.

Larbalestier, Jan. 1990. The politics of representation: Australian aboriginal women and feminism. *Anthropological Forum* 6(2): 143-157.

Longino, Helen E. 1990. *Science as social knowledge: values and objectivity in scientific inquiry*. Princeton: Princeton University Press.

Lugones, María C. 1992. On borderlands/La frontera: An interpretive essay. *Hypatia* 7(4): 31-37.

Mies, Maria. 1986. *Patriarchy and accumulation on a world scale: Women in the international division of labour*. London: Zed Books.

Mies, Maria, Veronika Bennholdt-Thomsen and Claudia von Werlhof. 1988. *Women: The last colony*. London: Zed Books.

Mies, Maria, and Vandana Shiva. 1993. *Ecofeminism*. London: Zed Books.

Mohanty, Chandra Talpade, Ann Russo and Lourdes Torres. 1991. *Third World Women and the Politics of Feminism*. Bloomington: Indiana University Press.

Mohanty, Chandra Talpade. 1991a. Cartographies of struggle: Third women and the politics of feminism. In *Third world women and the politics of feminism*. See Mohanty, Russo, and Torres 1991.

Mohanty. 1991b. Under western eyes: Feminist scholarship and colonial discourses. In *Third world women and the politics of feminism*. See Mohanty, Russo, and Torres 1991

Molyneux, Maxine. 1985. Mobilization without emancipation? Women's interests, the state, and revolution in Nicaragua. *Feminist Studies* 11(2): 227-54.

Moser, Caroline. O. N. Gender planning in the third world: Meeting practical and strategic needs. In *Gender and international relations*, ed. Rebecca Grant and Kathleen Newland. Bloomington, Indiana University Press.

Nair, Hema N. 1991. Bold type: The poetry of multiple migrations. *Ms*. January-February.

Narayan, Uma. 1989. The project of feminist epistemology: Perspectives from a Nonwestern feminist. In *Gender/Body/Knowledge: Feminist reconstructions of being and knowing*, ed. Alison M. Jaggar and Susan R. Bordo. New Brunswick: Rutgers University Press.

———. 1997. *Dislocating cultures: Identities, traditions, and third world feminism*. New York: Routledge.

Nelson, Topsy Napurrula. 1991. Letter to the editor. *Women's Studies International Forum* 14(5): 507.

Newland, Kathleen. 1991. From transnational relational relationships to international relations: Women in development and the International Decade for women. In *Gender and international relations*, ed. Rebecca Grant and Kathleen Newland. Bloomington: Indiana University Press.

Nussbaum, Martha and Amartya Sen. 1989. Internal criticism and Indian rationalist tradition. In *Relativism: Interpretation and confrontation*, ed. Michael Krausz. Notre Dame: University of Notre Dame Press.

Phelan, Shane. 1989. *Identity politics: Lesbian feminism and the limits of community*. Philadelphia: Temple University Press.

Scott, Catherine V. 1996. *Gender and development: Rethinking modernization and dependency theory*. Boulder, CO: Lynne Rienner.

Shiva, Vandana. 1988. *Staying alive: Women, ecology and development*. London: Zed Books.

Spivak, Gayatri Chakravorty. 1988. Can the subaltern speak? In *Marxism and the interpretation of culture*, ed. Cary Nelson and Lawrence Grossberg. Urbana: University of Illinois Press.

Walker, Margaret Urban. 1994. Global feminism: What's the question? *APA Newsletter on Feminism and Philosophy* 94(1): 53-54.

Young, Iris Marion. 1990. *Justice and the politics of difference*. Princeton, NJ: Princeton University Press.

2

Feminism, Women's Human Rights, and Cultural Differences

SUSAN MOLLER OKIN

The recent global movement for women's human rights has achieved considerable re-thinking of human rights as previously understood. Since many of women's rights violations occur in the private sphere of family life, and are justified by appeals to cultural or religious norms, both families and cultures (including their religious aspects) have come under critical scrutiny.

The recognition of women's rights as human rights has been taking place on the global stage—from the grassroots to the international conference levels—in the last two decades. This has required considerable rethinking of human rights. Many specific human rights that are crucial to women's well-being need to be identified and acted on to stop clearly gender-related wrongs. In this paper, I first show how many such rights cannot be recognized as human rights without some significant challenges both to that concept itself and to some institutions basic to the various human cultures, certainly families and religions. I then explore some of the interesting connections, and lacks of connection, between Western feminism—especially Western academic feminism—and the global movement for women's rights. Finally, I offer some thoughts about feminist critique (thoughts that have been stimulated by reading works by and attending meetings of feminist activists concerned with women's issues in other cultures), and also some thoughts about what kinds of support I think Western feminists can give to the global movement for women's rights.

Because some of women's most basic rights—to freedom of movement and to work outside of the home, and to bodily integrity and freedom from violence—have been very much in the international news lately, I shall refer to these examples fairly often. But by doing this I do not mean to downplay the importance of other crucial rights, such as rights to health care, to an adequate standard of living, and so on.

From the beginning of the post-World War II human rights movement, women have been formally included as holders of human rights. The Universal Declaration of Human Rights (1948) and many subsequent declarations, including the two United Nations International Covenants, that on Economic, Social and Cultural Rights (UNICESCR) and that on Civil and Political Rights (UNICCPR) proclaim the equal rights of human beings without regard to their sex. In practice, though, women are discriminated against in all of the world's countries, both in differing and in similar ways, and to a widely varying extent. Moreover, the grounds for this distinction have often been, and still are in many parts of the world (in some cultural or religious groups in all countries), seen as far more natural, inevitable, and benign than other grounds for distinction that human rights declarations prohibit—such as race, religion, or political opinion. Indeed, discrimination on the grounds of sex is frequently justified as being in accordance with many of the cultures—including religious aspects of these cultures—practiced in the world today.

It now seems quite startling that the Universal Declaration of Human Rights of 1948 should have so clearly repudiated distinctions of sex, given that there was not a country in the world at that time whose laws did not routinely make distinctions of sex, often on matters of basic rights. France and Italy had only just enfranchised women, and the Swiss did not do so (in national elections) until 1973. In most countries, sex discrimination in employment, family law, and many other areas of life remained routine for many years to come, and in many countries, violations of women's basic human rights are still commonplace (see, for example, Bunch 1994, 32-34). Nevertheless, the vast gap between declarations of rights and actual practice turns out to be a common pattern. This could make one quite cynical; for, as a few examples cited later will show, even declarations explicitly aimed at women's rights—such as the Universal Declaration of Women's Rights (1967) and the Convention on the Elimination of All Forms of Discrimination Against Women, or CEDAW (1979)—have been signed and even ratified by governments of countries whose laws or accepted practices are far from fulfilling the provisions of these conventions.

In general, the early universal human rights documents claim women's rights on a basis of equality with men and use gender-neutral language. This, however, as two feminist commentators have recently noted, can be "a double-edged instrument if it is used to punish women for failing to conform to the conventional norms expected of men" (Kaufman and Lindquist 1995, 121-22). The first declaration specifically aimed at women's human rights, the CEDAW, departs from gender-neutral language to address issues such as maternity leave, pregnancy-related health care, and affirmative action for women in education and employment. However, in the last twenty years it has been increasingly recognized that taking women seriously as equal human rights claimants with men requires considerable further rethinking of the concept of human rights.

It was especially during the preparations for the 1993 U.N. World Conference on Human Rights, held in Vienna, that a major worldwide petition drive was launched and "took off like a rocket" (Friedman 1995, 28). The petition urged that the conference should "comprehensively address women's human rights at every level of its proceedings" and recognize gender-based violence "as a violation of human rights requiring immediate action" (Friedman 1995, 28). As a result of this and a large strategic planning meeting bringing together women from many regions, women's human rights groups were by far the most organized of the NGO participants, and they had considerable impact on the Vienna Declaration and Program of Action. This was followed up and improved in significant ways at the Fourth World Conference on Women in Beijing in September 1995.

Why was it necessary to rethink human rights—as it was—in order to address many important women's rights?[1] Basically, because both the early conception of "the rights of man" in the seventeenth century and the original conception of international "human rights" in the mid-twentieth century were formulated with male household heads in mind. They were conceived as rights of such individuals against each other and, especially, against the governments under which they lived. It was generally recognized that there existed a sphere of privacy, protected by rights from outside intrusion, but not necessarily governed internally in accordance with the rights of its members. There can be little doubt that both Locke and his contemporaries and the framers of the Universal Declaration had male household heads foremost in mind when thinking about those who were to hold the "natural" and the "human" rights they respectively argued for and proclaimed (Bunch 1995; Okin 1989a, esp. 42-45; Pateman 1994). Locke gives, as an example of the private matters that no one would consider interfering with, a father's decision about whom his daughter should marry (Locke 1950, 28-29). Any rights the daughter may have claimed in the matter go unmentioned. Some similar twentieth-century examples of obliteration of women's rights in the private sphere will come up later.

A growing body of feminist human rights literature argues that the male bias of human rights thinking and its priorities had to change for women's rights to be fully recognized as human rights. The problem is not so much that men's claims to rights A, B, and C have been recognized, whereas women's claims to these exact same rights have not—which is not to say that this never happens. The problem is that existing theories, compilations, and prioritizations of human rights have been constructed after a male model. When women's life experiences are taken equally into account, these theories, compilations, and prioritizations change significantly. Examples of issues that come to the fore, instead of being virtually ignored, include rape (including marital rape and rape during war), domestic violence, reproductive freedom, the valuation of childcare and other domestic labor as work, and unequal opportunity for women and girls in education, employment, housing, credit, and health care. The aim has been—and it has largely been achieved, by the Vienna Human Rights Conference and then further by the Fourth World Conference on Women in Beijing—to incorporate into the center of the discourse of human rights issues that are often matters of life and death for women (and for children), but that were previously "perceived as part of the women's rights movement and hence of a special interest agenda . . . [and as] marginal to international law's more 'serious' responsibility for human rights" (Peters and Wolper 1995, 2).

Some generally recognized human rights abuses have specifically gender-related forms that were not typically recognized as human rights abuses. Frequently, these abuses are perpetrated by more powerful family members against less powerful ones. For example, slavery is generally recognized as a fundamental violation of human rights. But parents' giving their daughter in marriage in exchange for money or even selling her to a pimp has not typically been seen as an instance of slavery. If a husband pays a bride price for his wife or marries her without her adult consent; if he confines her to their home, forbids her to work for pay, or appropriates her wages; if he beats her for disobedience or mishap; these manifestations of slavery would not be recognized as violations of human rights in many parts of the world. In some parts, indeed, most of these acts would be regarded as quite within the limits of normal, culturally appropriate behavior in parents or husbands.[2] Also, there was little acknowledgement until recently of women's particular vulnerability to poverty and need for basic social services, such as health care, because of both their biological reproductive capacity and their assumption, in virtually all societies, of greater responsibility for children.

Even most human rights activists, until very recently, have been unwilling to recognize many culturally sanctioned abuses and instances of neglect of women as serious violations of human rights. Recently, though, especially over the last decade, this perception has been very strongly challenged. For example, it took until 1995 in Beijing for the international community to recognize women's right to say no to sexual intercourse. Even then, there was opposition from some quarters, including the Vatican, whose representatives "opposed the wording" of the clause (New York Times, 1995).

Those seeking to establish women's rights as human rights also point out that much earlier human rights thinking focuses on governments as violators of human rights. This is readily apparent from the wording of most of the international agreements. For example, "a central feature of the international legal definition of torture is that it takes place in the public realm: it must be 'inflicted by or at the instigation of or with the consent or acquiescence of a public official or other person acting in an official capacity.' " (Charlesworth 1994, 72, 83, n. 103). But whereas governments can often affect, and act to reduce or try to eliminate, many violations of women's human rights, the violations themselves are much more likely to be carried out by individual men (and sometimes women, too). Part of the reason for the "invisibility" of gender-based violations has been the neglect in human rights talk of the private or domestic sphere. For it is in this sphere that great numbers of the world's women live most (in some cases, virtually all) of their lives, and in which vast numbers of violations of women's human rights take place (Peters and Wolper 1995, 2).

In many countries—at least during peacetime—a woman's most dangerous environment is the home she lives in. So the public/private dichotomy, which leads to the assumption that the rights bearer is the head of a household and that an important one of "his" rights is the right to privacy in his personal and family life, places serious obstacles in the way of protecting the rights of women and children.[3] The problem is compounded by both the neglect and the denial of power differentials within households, and the assumption that families operate with a benignity never expected of the marketplace or the sphere of politics (Okin 1989b, 117-33; Pateman 1989). Promoting women's human rights clearly involves making changes in areas of life usually considered to be private, and "calling for government accountability in these areas requires a considerable reorientation of human rights law" (Friedman 1995, 20). Char-lotte Bunch, noting that violation of men's civil and political rights in the public sphere "has been privileged in human rights work," says that "they did not fear . . . violations in the private sphere of the home because they were the masters of that territory" (Bunch 1995, 13). By contrast, "by far the greatest violence against women occurs in the 'private' non-governmental sphere" (Charlesworth 1994, 72). Also, it is important to note that how things happen in the private realm of the household, including how decisions are made and how responsibilities and work are allocated, has a considerable impact on who can participate fully and effectively in the public spheres of politics, civil society, and markets (Bunch 1995, 13).

This situation of private rights violations is exacerbated by the fact that "respecting cultural differences" has increasingly become a euphemism for restricting or denying women's human rights. As feminist activist-scholars have been making clear, the relevance and even the sanctity of "cultural practices" is most often claimed when issues of sexuality, marriage, reproduc-tion, inheritance, and power over children are concerned (issues that play a larger part in most women's lives than they do in most men's). And this often happens in contexts where traditions or rules of that same culture or religion are *not* called on in other areas of life, such as commerce or crime (see, for example, Shaheed 1994; Mayer 1994). In India, for example, partly because of the history of violent religious intolerance, this distinction is built into the formal framework of the state; the different religious communities enforce their own "personal laws," and there is no uniform civil code of family law.[4] This can have grave consequences for women, who are differently (albeit usually unfairly) treated in divorce, and in custody and inheritance issues, depending on which religious group they belong to.

It is important to note, in this context, that the rise and the growth in political power of religious fundamentalism in many parts of the world are closely related to rejection of the imposition of "Western" or "white" culture and ideas. Women's freedom and equality are often understood as clear symbols of Western values, in contrast to which and in reaction against which religious, conservative, or nationalist movements define themselves (see, for example, Afkhami 1995, esp. the introduction and chap. 4; Moghadam 1994, esp. chaps. 1, 3, and 19; Narayan 1998).

The continuing and rising influence of cultural or religious justifications for women's inequality is one important reason why it is so significant for women's rights to be recognized as human rights. Many people fail to perceive what or how big the problems are, and many serious inequalities between the sexes are still regarded by many people as invisible, insignificant, natural, or culturally appropriate. This is true of some people in positions of power both inside and outside the cultures in which some of the most obvious and egregious violations of women's basic rights are taking place. For example, in Afghanistan in the fall of 1996, when the Taliban regime closed girls' schools, denied all women the right to go to work or to leave their homes without being completely covered up (rules enforced partly by beatings of those who broke them, by Taliban adolescent thugs), the (male) medical director of a hospital in Kabul said (and was regarded by *New York Times* reporter John F. Burns, as "typical" in saying) that the restrictions placed on women were "a small price to pay for the peace" that the Taliban victory had secured. Burns himself asked whether Amnesty Internationals's description of the situation as "a reign of terror" might not be "exaggerated" (*New York Times* 1996a).

Also in the fall of 1996, government officials in the Ivory Coast, when asked about the practice of clitoridectomy, were reported as conceding the "evils of genital cutting," or female genital mutilation, adding that, although they had a plan to educate people about the consequences of that practice, they had no budget or staff. The U.S. Embassy spokesman in Abidjan said, "it's a matter for local society to determine the extent to which these practices are to be tolerated." He was outdone in his cavalierness toward the girls and women harmed by the practice only by the French embassy spokesman, who said, "this is a marginal problem." Then, perhaps thinking again, this person added, "it's important, but to feed people is probably more important" (*New York Times* 1996b).

Such reactions shed some light on why it is important to fight the struggle for women's rights as a human rights struggle. It makes it *more difficult* for the old double standard, which obviously is still alive and well, to continue to convince people. It is difficult to imagine reactions similar to those just mentioned, to a situation in which all the men living under a given regime were kept under virtual house arrest. It is even more difficult to imagine such mild reactions to a sexual custom in which a man, in order to become marriageable and therefore able to survive economically, were allowed to ejaculate some sperm to be saved so that he could still reproduce, and then were pinned down by four or five people in order for his penis to be cut off with a knife. But this *would be* the closest male equivalent to female genital mutilation which, in its least invasive commonly practiced form, involves the removal of the clitoris, removing with it the possibility of female sexual satisfaction.[5] These are the kinds of parallels that become entirely plausible, once one draws attention to wrongs done to women as violations of human rights.

Again, in many societies (including Western industrialized ones until very recently), domestic violence against women has not been regarded as an issue for police and other appropriate authorities to report or to combat; it is seen as just part of domestic life, a normal—albeit regrettable—part of relations between the sexes (see, for example, Ofei-Aboagye 1994). Consider, too, how significant it is that not until the 1990s was rape in war treated as an indictable war crime. To many, until recently, rape was just "what some soldiers did" under wartime circumstances (Friedman 1995, 26).

It is also very striking that many countries in which forms of serious discrimination against women are practiced have signed and ratified the CEDAW, though in many instances with reservations. Mali, for example, a country in which 80 percent of the women have undergone female genital mutilation as children or adolescents, has signed and ratified both the Convention on the Rights of the Child and the CEDAW (Toubia 1995, 25). Many countries that have signed such international conventions and declarations do have laws against customs or cultural practices that can be very damaging to women, such as child marriage, or dowry. But these laws are almost never enforced, and the customs are allowed to prevail, in practice nullifying the women's rights to basic freedoms and bodily integrity.

One reaction to this might be to say: So what difference does it make to recognize abuses of women as human rights violations? My answer is that, especially now that the "no cultural exemptions" clause was adopted, after considerable struggle, in Beijing (see p. 45 below), it enables the international community to put these issues unambiguously on the table. Most governments do not like to be international pariahs, to have the eyes of the world focus on them only for their worst practices or their failure to prevent practices harmful to women and children. It has been clear from some of the recent news reports that ethnic and religious groups, too, can develop the same distaste for being seen as condoning serious harms done to women. Not surprisingly, Muslims in many countries—and even the governments of countries with strict Islamic laws—have distanced themselves from the particularly brutal fundamentalist types of behavior that the Taliban regime in Afghanistan has tried to justify as being in accordance with "Muslim principles" (*New York Times* 1996d).

Another reason for the importance of the recognition of women's rights as human rights is that it affects women's rights to asylum. It is no coincidence that, in the climate of international women's human rights generated by the series of U.N. conferences culminating in those in Vienna, Cairo, and Beijing, both Canada and the United States granted legitimate refugee status to women fleeing persecutions such as forced marriage or genital mutilation. This, in turn, has further consequences. For, once a violation of rights has earned a potentially *very* large group of people refugee status, the United States and other countries likely to be sought as places of asylum have a new incentive to try to use what influence they can to stop or reduce the violations where they happen.[6]

As we have seen, rights of great importance to women were long left off the human rights agenda because, as Charlotte Bunch, one of the prime movers to get them on this agenda, has said: "they have been largely invisible and/or are dismissed as private family, cultural or religious rather than political matters" (Bunch 1994, 33). Many violations of women's basic human rights both *occur within* families and are *justified by* reference to culture, religion, or tradition. So recognizing women's rights as human rights means looking at the institutions of family, religion, and culture or tradition in a new light. Let us look now at two examples, families and religions, comparing the changes that have already occurred from how they were addressed in earlier U.N. human rights documents, compared to how they are addressed in the recent Beijing Platform for Action.

Article 16 of the Universal Declaration of Human Rights is devoted to marriage and family. It specifies that "the family is the natural and fundamental group unit of society," that "marriage shall be entered into only with the free and full consent of the intending spouses," and that "men and women of full age, without any limitation due to race, nationality or religion, have the right to marry and to found a family . . . [and] are entitled to equal rights as to marriage, during marriage and at its dissolution" (United Nations, 1948). While they naturalize the heterosexual, two-parent family, these specifications—like many clauses in the declaration—are considerably more egalitarian about rights between the sexes than were laws and practices in virtually every country in the world at the time (and are in many countries now). Practices that violate them include arranged and coerced marriages, child marriages, unequal access to or terms of divorce, and, in some states of the U.S., along with other countries (until the Supreme Court declared them unconstitutional in 1967), legal prohibitions against interracial marriage (*Loving v. Virginia* 388 U.S. 1 [1967]).

The declaration, however, also includes an article that reminds us that it focused more on male heads of households than other family members. Article 12 reads: "No one shall be subjected to arbitrary interference with his privacy, family, home or correspondence, nor to attacks upon his honour and reputation." As well as the telling use of "his," in the current context of women's rights as human rights the mention of both "interference with his privacy" and "attacks upon his honour and reputation" sound far more ominous and objectionable than they probably did at the time. This is both because of our heightened awareness of violence in the "privacy" of family homes and because of the justification in some cultures of confinement, beating, and even murder of female household members if their sexual behavior (in some contexts, even their having been raped) is considered to have tainted their families' honor. The earlier treatment of families in the Beijing Platform for Action is far less abstract, definitely not constructed from the point of view of the male household head, and far more aware of what goes on and who does what in families. The clause most specifically on families *starts*: "Women play a critical role in the family . . . [which] is the basic unit of society and as such should be strengthened" (Covenant 1995, 15). It goes on to acknowledge that different forms of family exist in different cultural, political, and social systems. It specifically draws attention to women's greater contribution than men's to family care, to the social significance of this discrepancy, and to the desirability of shared responsibility for the upbringing of children among women, men, and society as a whole. It insists that women's family roles "must not be a basis for discrimination nor restrict the full participation of women in society" (Covenant 1995, 15).

Other clauses draw attention to the growing rate of female-headed households (about 25 percent globally in 1995), the causes of this phenomenon, and the greater likelihood of such families' being very poor (Covenant 1995, 13). Additional clauses point out that deprivation of and discrimination and violence against females in many parts of the world starts before birth and continues through the life cycle. These clauses imply that families play an active role in violating women's and girls' human rights. This is a very different, more critical, and much more complete picture of family life than the benign and rather abstract one in the Universal Declaration.

On the subject of religion, too, the recognition of women's rights as human rights has begun to change the perceptions of the U.N.'s proclamations, though here the changes have not progressed as far. In the Universal Declaration, Article 18 proclaims, "Everyone has the right to freedom of thought, conscience, and religion; this right includes freedom to change his religion or belief, and freedom . . , in public or private, to manifest his religion or belief in teaching, practice, worship and observance." However, in the UNICCPR what is *added* to this set of rights is "the liberty of parents and, when applicable, legal guardians, to ensure the religious and moral education of their children in conformity with their own convictions" (United Nations, 1966a, Article 18). Thus, it seems, children are distinctly not included among the "everyone" who has the right to choose and to change "his" beliefs. Rather, these must conform with those of the child's parents.

The Beijing Platform for Action takes, as it does on the subject of the family, a less abstract and also a less than totally positive approach to religion. Its statement on rights having to do with religion and conscience starts by asserting that "religion, spirituality and belief play a central role in the lives of millions of women and men, in the way they live and in the aspirations they have for the future." It goes on to proclaim the same universal and inalienable "right to freedom of thought, conscience and religion," including the rights to worship and to practice one's religion as the earlier human rights documents did. But the clause on religion ends, it is interesting to note, with a caution: "However, it is acknowledged that any form of extremism may have a negative impact on women and can lead to violence and discrimination" (Covenant 1995, 13-14).[7] No indication is given of what constitutes "extremism." But again, as in the case of families, it is significant that religions are recognized as not always unmitigated goods, at least from the point of view of women seeking equal rights.

Thus, international perceptions of both family and religion have begun to be affected by the recognition of women as full human rights holders. "Family" has become a highly contested concept, as actual families around the world have been changing rapidly. The idealized picture of the family as an environment with completely shared interests, and in which altruism (or benign paternalism) can be expected to dominate self-interest, has been very much challenged. It is recognized that many of the decisions that lead to the gender imbalance in population in some parts of the world, and other decisions that adversely affect girls' and women's well-being, are decisions made in families (Sen 1990b). Indeed, Amartya Sen has suggested that definitions of self in terms of family in some parts of the world may be so strong that persons may have no conception of their own personal welfare: "In some contexts the family identity may exert such a strong influence on our perceptions that we may not find it easy to formulate any clear notion of our own individual welfare." His example is "a typical rural Indian woman" (Sen 1990a, 126-27). Other social scientists too, questioning the previously assumed "unity of interests" of families, are opening up the "black boxes" as which families were often portrayed and showing what happens within. They argue that the new attention to families in the international economic development process may be a backward step for women and children unless what goes on within families—including "intrahousehold dynamics of gender and power" and "gender-equity issues"—are kept constantly in mind (see, for example, Jaquette 1993). Studies show, for example, that opportunities for women to earn money can have very significant effects on children's well-being, and that they also tend to improve women's bargaining position in their families.

It is also becoming clear, from evidence from many parts of the world and many religions, that fundamentalism of various kinds—many of which are clearly growing in power—is harsh on women and imposes rules irreconcilable with many of women's human rights. The days when religion was (for whatever mixture of reasons) regarded as unquestionably a good thing that needed only to be protected and taught to people, preferably at as young an age as possible, seem to be waning.

Now I come, not without some trepidation, to the subject of Western academic feminism's hesitant or ambivalent approach to the issue of violations of women's rights in other cultural contexts. I want to discuss the relationship, during these years of recognition of "women's rights as human rights," between much of Western feminist scholarship and Third World women's activism. During the 1980s and early 1990s, there was a striking divergence between, on the one hand, the activities, the discourse, and the preoccupations of many Western feminist theorists (including some feminists of Third World origins working in Western academic contexts) and, on the other hand, the activities and perceptions of feminist activists in the Third World (including some First World scholar-activists, like Charlotte Bunch, and other activists, like Fran Hosken, who were most in contact with Third World activists).

As has been by now well documented, one of the primary preoccupations of many Western feminist theorists during this period was the differences among women. Many earlier books and articles of Second Wave feminism that had made claims about "women" or "woman," about "motherhood" or "the family," about "sexuality" (and so on) were charged with being essentialist; making false generalizations; ignoring important differences among women, families, sexuality, and so on—differences associated with race or class, ethnicity or religion, sexual orientation, and other attributes. There was some important truth to many of these charges, and many of the criticisms have had a salutary effect. Some of early Second Wave feminism was undoubtedly marred by racist, class-prejudiced, and heterosexist elements. Largely because of critiques from within feminism, most more recent feminist scholarship has become more inclusive and less inclined to false overgeneralizations.

However, the critiques were at times exaggerated and carried to absurdity. Both aspects of them—the truth and the absurdity—have been discussed elsewhere by many feminists (see, for example, Martin 1994; Benhabib 1995; Okin 1994; Walby 1992). During the 1980s and the early 1990s, postmodernist scholarship was highly influential in Anglo-American academia; at the same time, African American, lesbian, and other critics of earlier feminism, were often rightly, critiquing it for ignoring their needs, interests, and perspectives. The feminist antiessentialist critique that often combined the two was at times carried to the extreme of asserting that no generalizations at all could or should be made about women, gender, mothering, or many other topics that some feminists thought it was still important to be able to discuss (see, for example, Spelman 1980; Kristeva 1981, esp. 137, 140).[8] In addition, it was sometimes claimed that, whatever the quality of the evidence presented or the strength of the argument made, the suggestion by any white, middle-class feminist that women and girls in cultures other than our own are disadvantaged or oppressed by elements of their own cultures amounted to offensive cultural imperialism (see, for example, Flax 1995; Moruzzi 1994).[9] After reading or experiencing these critiques, many feminists (whether First or Third World, but especially the former) might have felt more than somewhat inhibited about writing anything, especially about Third World women, that was not entirely contextualized and localized in its focus.

Chandra Talpade Mohanty's essay "Feminist Encounters: Locating the Politics of Experience," especially its critique of Robin Morgan's anthology *Sisterhood is Global*, exemplifies both of these types of critique. After conceding the "truly impressive" range of writing in the volume and disclaiming any intent "to lay blame or induce guilt," Mohanty critiques Morgan for being ahistorical, for erasing the effects of contemporary imperialism, for denying women's agency, for rendering invisible "the privilege of [her own] political 'location,'" and, above all, for generalizing about women's experience across cultures. Morgan is faulted for presuming to suggest that women share what she calls "universal sisterhood," " 'a common condition' . . . [which is] referred to at various points of her introductory essay as the suffering inflicted by a universal 'patriarchal mentality,' women's opposition to male power and androcentrism, and the experience of rape, battery, labour, and childbirth" (Mohanty 1992, 78-79, citing Morgan 1984, 1). Mohanty is clearly troubled by such generalization, even when the "white, western, middle-class privilege[d]" author of it has spent more than a decade communicating with women all over the world and inviting them to contribute to her anthology.

Mohanty is particularly critical of a passage in Morgan's introduction in which Morgan refers to a series of experiences related by women whose writing is included in the anthology, and then asks: "And do we not, after all, recognize one another?" (Mohanty 1992, 83 citing Morgan 1984, 35-36). The suggestion that women can recognize each other's experiences and problems across cultural, class, and ethnic lines seems both incredible and reprehensible to Mohanty, especially "in the context of the mass proletarianization of Third World women by corporate capital based in the U.S., Europe and Japan." With Morgan's notion of universal sisterhood, Mohanty says, her "middle-class, psychologized notion . . . effectively erases material and ideological power differences within and among groups of women" (Mohanty 1992, 83). Preferable to the pursuit of such a "reductive utopian vision," Mohanty suggests, is "uncovering alternative, non-identical histories which challenge and disrupt the spatial and temporal location of a hegemonic history" (Mohanty 1992, 84).[10] The timing of her critique is no less significant than its severity: first published in 1987, it was published in the revised version cited here in 1992. In these years, the "women's rights as human rights" movement was gathering steam and, in 1992, women all over the world were organizing and preparing the huge women's rights petition that was to have such impact at the 1993 Vienna conference.

The antiuniversalizing climate of much Western academic feminism was hardly conducive to the framing of women's rights as universal human rights. However, during the same decade-and-a-half in which feminists in academia who attempted to find, or claimed to have found, anything but differences between women were being taken to task for "essentialism;" Third World feminists and grassroots activists, as well as some Western feminists who were prepared to buck the tide, were working together to achieve the recognition by the international human rights community of women's rights as human rights. These women were having a very different experience and coming to very different conclusions than were postmodernist and other antiessentialist academic feminists. Holding hearings in their own countries, meeting and networking in regional and subregional groups, and then combining their knowledge at international meetings, groups from Africa, the Asia-Pacific region, and Latin America, as well as those from more economically developed parts of the world, were finding that women had a lot in common. They found that discrimination against women; patterns of gender-based violence, including domestic battery; and the sexual and economic exploitation of women and girls were virtually universal phenomena (Friedman 1995; Bunch 1994). At a time when many Western academic feminists were shrinking from making statements about women and gender and regarding "patriarchy" as an outdated overgeneralization, some 240 participants from 110 nongovernmental organizations (NGOs) in the Asia-Pacific region concluded the following:

> Patriarchy which operates through gender, caste, class and ethnicity, is integral to the problems facing women. Patriarchy is a form of slavery and must be eradicated. Womens' rights must be addressed in both the public and private spheres of society, in particular in the family. (Bunch 1994)

The Committee on the Elimination of All Forms of Discrimination Against Women issued such general statements as: "Women continue to be discriminated against all over the world as regards the recognition, enjoyment and exercise of their individual rights in public and private and are subject to many forms of violence" (quoted in Bunch 1994, 35). The Women's Caucus of the NGO-Coordination Group, in preparing for the 1993 Vienna conference, addressed "systematic gender discrimination" and said, "violence against women is closely linked to women's structural inequality and there is a critical need for reporting on gender discrimination in all countries" (quoted in Bunch 1994, 36).

At the same time, these groups were also loudly protesting the serious economic problems of many Third World women, and attributing many of them to the structural adjustment policies that were being enforced by the World Bank and other international financial powers, at the expense of social programs that directly affected women's well-being.[11] They did not contend that all of women's problems were identical from state to state, from culture to culture, from class to class, throughout the world. What was happening, though, was that through the channels of NGOs and other similar groups operating at many levels, many of the silent (or silenced) voices of women were finally being heard—voices that had been previously in no way represented by their male-dominated governments; voices that in many cases felt free to speak out, in the company of others concerned with women's rights, against what they experienced as abuses of women and girls. Many of them undoubtedly felt safe from the repercussions that they would probably suffer if they spoke out at home in their own countries.

As they spoke out, they recognized important general truths that affected the lives of many women around the globe. They recognized that women are greatly affected by laws and customs having to do with sexuality, marriage, divorce, child custody, and family life as a whole—laws and customs that often contribute to women's lesser power within their families. They recognized that women and girls are much more likely to be rendered sexually vulnerable than men and boys—far more likely to be sexually abused or exploited, and far more directly and drastically affected by their fertility than men, unless given the means and the power to control it. Third, they recognized that women and women's work tend to be valued considerably less highly than men and men's work—regardless of how productive or essential the actual work may be. In recognizing these things and thinking about how to counteract them, women achieved miracles, in the form of the international proclamations of women's rights achieved in Vienna, followed up in important ways in Cairo and then in Beijing.

One of the most significant innovations of the Program for Action that emanated from the Beijing Conference was its unprecedentedly strong rejection of "cultural" justifications for violating women's human rights. The statement reads as follows:

> While the significance of national and regional particularities and various historical, cultural and religious backgrounds must be borne in mind, it is the duty of states, regardless of their political, economic and cultural systems, to promote and protect all human rights and fundamental freedoms. (Covenant 1995, 9-10)

Further on, the document specifies, "Any harmful aspect of certain traditional, customary or modern practices that violates the rights of women should be prohibited and eliminated" (Covenant 1995, 112). It seems clear that thousands of Third World feminist activists were saying, "We want to be rid of these cultural excuses for women's oppression that have plagued us so long." If it was not clear earlier, surely it was clear now that bending over backward out of respect for cultural diversity could do great disservice to women and girls.

I shall finish with a few tentative words about some of the roles feminists (both Western and Third World) might play as social critics in the women's human rights arena. In particular, I shall focus on the question of how one can be sufficiently steeped in a culture and its social context to have any real depth of knowledge about it and, at the same time, have some critical distance from it. It seems that some of the best feminist social critics are "inside-outside critics"; that is, persons from within a culture who at some point in life have experience outside of that culture that makes them critical of at least some of its practices. The work of many such feminist critics is compelling, informed by detailed knowledge and understanding, and thought-provoking. These critics include Farida Shaheed, who cofounded and writes about the advocacy group Women Living under Muslim Laws; Rosemary Ofei-Aboagye, who has written from her adopted country, Canada, about domestic abuse in her native country, Ghana; Francis Kissling, the ex-nun who is director of Catholics for Free Choice, and who, though she still describes herself as a Catholic, is certainly "far out" in many of her beliefs and not much loved by her church's male hierarchy; Nahid Toubia, the Sudanese surgeon now living in the United States, who has become the leader of the struggle for global action against female genital mutilation; Fatima Mernissi, from Morocco, who, with other feminists from Muslim countries, is reinterpreting the *Qur'an*; and Mahnaz Afkhami, exiled from her native Iran to the United States and now director of the Washington D.C.-based Sisterhood is Global Institute, which has recently issued a manual aimed at translating the language of women's human rights so that they will be recognizable to and attainable in a variety of predominantly Muslim countries, from Jordan to Bangladesh and Malaysia.

But though these women are all undoubtedly, in a sense, particularly informed and effective as "inside-outside critics," being a critic so located is surely neither necessary nor sufficient for being an informed and effective feminist critic. Some people, on leaving their culture of birth, become perceptive critics of it, while others, who may have been similarly positioned in the same culture and then left it, remain ardent devotees rather than critics of it. Still others, who remain in their culture of origin develop deep and radical critiques of aspects of the practices and beliefs that surround them. How, otherwise, could Taslima Nasrin, who (I believe) had never been outside her native Bangladesh, become such an outspoken critic of its laws and customs oppressive to women that a *fatwah* (religious edict) was declared against her?

(And surely, to become this kind of feminist "critic from within" is even more unusual when one lives, as Nasrin did, in a society with little tolerance for dissent about its cultural practices concerning women.)

In addition, the very concept of "inside" and "outside" is problematic. For example, is an upper-class, British-educated, city-dwelling woman in India "inside" or "outside" the culture that makes rural poverty in India even more damaging and limiting for women than for men? And what of an immigrant in a European country who lives ghettoized, virtually without contact with the other culture(s) of her new country? It should also be taken into account that, as Uma Narayan has recently argued, being perceived even as partly an "outsider," especially if "Westernized," can be debilitating to Third World feminists trying to be effective within their cultures of origin (Narayan 1997, 1998).

There must surely be other ways of becoming, and dimensions to being, a good feminist critic than by being located both "inside" and "outside" of a given culture. For some persons, becoming unusually empowered in some way while remaining in their own culture can enable them to be effective critics. Having an unusual series of traumatic experiences resulting from an aspect of one's culture can also make one critical of it. Fauziya Kasinga, who was granted asylum in the United States in 1996 because she was in imminent danger of female genital mutilation and forced marriage in her native country, Togo, came from a family whose members became social critics out of a combination of these two circumstances. They had become relatively rich, and both parents had had sisters who had suffered or died from the procedure. Little did they, or their daughter—who was imprisoned in the United States until her lawyer found a judge who believed her story—expect it, but her case, which grew out of her family's critical stance toward an abuse of women commonly practiced in their own culture, has probably done more than any other event to bring this particular human rights violation to the forefront of the Anglo-American world's attention (*New York Times*, 1996e).[12]

There are other critics of their own country's and other countries' treatment of women whose effectiveness does not seem to be *caused by* deep contextual exposure to their original culture (though they may have this) followed by separation and a view from a distance. Think of Amartya Sen, whose power as a critic of abuses of women in many Third World countries comes in part from his concern for the sufferings of such women, but also from the particular combination of analytical and statistical skills he has developed as an economist and philosopher.[13]

It is also, surely, possible to become a good critic of some harms done within a culture by taking the anthropologist's route—going from outside to inside, where, if thorough and careful in one's listening and learning, one can become very knowledgeable about a culture without either becoming co-opted by it or losing the capacity to be critical of some aspects of it.

So, it seems, there is clearly no single criterion, nor any clear set of criteria, for what constitutes good feminist criticism and helps to get and to keep women's rights violations on the global agenda. However, listening to previously "silent voices" can play a very important role, and there seems to be little doubt that "inside-outside" critics can play an important role here (Parpart and Marchand 1995; Ackerly forthcoming). More than anything else, it seems, the grassroots-to-NGOs and NGOs-to-international fora contacts and discussions of the 1980s and 1990s, by which the previously silent voices of many women could be and can continue to be heard, have done much to change the way the world thinks about women's human rights.

At this point in history, when much has been "declared" but so much remains to be implemented, what can Western feminists do to help further women's rights internationally? Some would say there are so many abuses of women in our own society that we should just get on with trying to do something about these, and mind our own business with respect to the rest of the world. I think this is a reasonable answer for some. Yet it is clear that the movements for women's human rights—including some of the most basic—in many countries, are much helped by the international support they have been increasingly gaining and by the continued, if careful, criticism of women's rights violations from feminists outside the cultural context, as well as those within.

Women who are struggling against culturally or religiously sanctioned violations of women's rights most commonly say that they need, above all, three things. One that is essential is to be carefully listened to; to have the opportunities to engage in deliberation that can lead to the recognition of unmet needs and unrecognized rights and to the development of strategies for change (Ackerly forthcoming). Another is financial support; for many women's organizations formed for resistance from within have few and meager sources of funding. The third is the kind of intellectual and political support from Western feminists, and from the international community, that does not assault other cultures, but takes care to acknowledge their many valuable or neutral aspects while it criticizes those aspects that are harmful to women and girls.

NOTES

This paper has benefitted from the helpful comments of Uma Narayan and editorial and research assistance from Elizabeth Beaumont.
    1. There is substantial overlap between the material in the three following paragraphs and parts of my "Culture, Religion, and Female Identity Formation: Responding to a Human Rights Challenge," unpublished manuscript (n.d.).

2. For example, in March 1997, a court ruled in a pathbreaking case in Pakistan that the marriage of a twenty-one-year-old woman, though entered into without having been arranged by her father, was valid. Apparently, previously in Muslim Pakistan, much as in Locke's England, an adult woman could not enter into a valid marriage with the man of her choice. Some of the customs I mention, such as bride price, are sometimes justified as customs that honor the woman and her family. However, the practical effect of bride price is often to oppress women and to serve men. On the latter point, see Kaufman and Lindquist 1989, 131, citing Russell 1989.

3. A recent example of this attitude can be seen in the comment of the chief of pediatrics at a large hospital in Seattle, when interviewed about Congress's criminalizing of female genital mutilation. He said, "I think this is an issue that should be decided by a physician, the family and the child. Privacy should prevail and the brouhaha is inappropriate" (*New York Times* 1996c). On the arbitrariness of the public/private distinction where women's right to be free from violence is concerned, see Charlesworth 1994, 72-74.

4. For two different accounts of a case that focused international attention on such laws, see Das 1994, 117-58; Pathak and Rajan 1992, 257-79.

5. Nahid Toubia, Sudanese surgeon and expert on female genital mutilation, writes, "The male equivalent of clitoridectomy (in which all or part of the clitoris is removed) would be the amputation of most of the penis. The male equivalent of infibulation (which involves not only clitoridectomy, but the removal of or closing off of most of the sensitive tissues around the vagina) would be the removal of all of the penis, its roots of soft tissue, and part of the scrotal skin" (Toubia 1995, 9).

6. At the fall 1996 Association for Women in Development Conference in Washington, D.C., a "Listening Session" on the subject of female genital mutilation was hosted and attended by a half-dozen representatives from the U.S. Department of State, who came to listen to anyone who wanted to speak on the subject. The session drew about 150 women from many different countries, with very different extents of knowledge about and experience of the practice.

7. On conflicts between women's rights and cultural or religious rights, see also Charlesworth 1994, 74.

8. This tendency is also found, along with a lot of thoughtful insight and analysis, in some parts of Chandra Talpade Mohanty's essays, notably "Under Western Eyes: Feminist Scholarship and Colonial Discourse" (1991, 51-80, esp. 56-57, 66-69) and "Feminist Encounters: Locating the Politics of Experience" (1992).

9. See also the four references to the practice of clitoridectomy in *Third world women and the politics of feminism*, all of which focus not on the harm done to women by the practice but on the alleged harm done by Western feminists who oppose it (Mohanty et al. 1991, 57-58; 76 n. 7; 218-19; 322).

10. Ironically, Mohanty's own work was critiqued shortly thereafter for "overlook[ing] class in all its dimensions" and for "implicitly deny[ing] subject agency to 'Third World' women" (Marchand 1995, 57). This suggests that once one travels at all far down the critical path of postmodernism, there is no destination short of both scholarly and political paralysis.

11. It is clear that in some regions of the world, economic problems caused at least largely by these financial pressures played a part in the failure of more moderate governments and the rise of conservative or fundamentalist regimes that created harsher conditions for women.

12. The *New York Times* devoted approximately five full pages to the subject of female genital mutilation in 1996, much of them as a result of detailed and thorough investigative reporting in some of the African countries in which the practice is most common (see *New York Times* 1996b, 1996c).

13. If the number of times one sees it cited are any indication, Sen's article, "More than One Hundred Million Women are Missing" (1990b) must have raised many people's consciousness of the many forms of abuse—from before birth until premature death, from the obvious to the subtle—that women experience in many countries, but especially in Sen's native South Asian region.

REFERENCES

Ackerly, Brooke. N.d. *A feminist theory of social criticism*. Cambridge: Cambridge University Press.

Afkhami, Mahnaz. 1995. *Faith and freedom: Women's human rights in the Muslim world*. Syracuse: Syracuse University Press.

Benhabib, Seyla. 1995. Cultural complexity, moral interdependence, and the global dialogical community. In *Women, culture, and development: A study of human capabilities*, eds. Martha Nussbaum and Jonathan Glover. Oxford: Clarendon Press.

Bunch, Charlotte. 1994. Strengthening human rights of women. In *World conference on human rights, Vienna, June 1993: The contributions of NGOs: Reports and documents*, ed. Manfred Nowak. Vienna: Manzsche Verlag Universitatsbuchhandlung.

———. 1995. Transforming human rights from a feminist perspective. In *Women's rights, human rights: International feminist perspectives*. See Peters and Wolper 1995.

Charlesworth, Hilary. 1994. What are women's international human rights? In *Human rights of women: National and international perspectives*, ed. Rebecca J. Cook. Philadelphia: University of Pennsylvania Press.

Covenant for the new millennium: The Beijing declaration and platform for action. 1995. From the *Report of the fourth world conference on women*. U.N. Doc. A/CONF.177/20. Santa Rosa, CA: Freehand Books.

Das, Veena. 1994. Cultural rights and the definition of community. In *The rights of subordinated peoples*, eds. Oliver Mendelsohn and Upendra Baxi. Delhi: Oxford University Press.

Flax, Jane. 1995. Race/gender and the ethics of difference: A reply to Okin's "Gender inequality and cultural differences." *Political Theory* 23(3): 500-10.

Friedman, Elisabeth. 1995. Women's human rights: The emergence of a movement. In *Women's rights, human rights: International feminist perspectives*. See Peters and Wolper 1995.

Jaquette, Jane. 1993. The family as a development issue. In *Women at the center: Development issues and practices for the 1990s*, eds. Gay Young, Vidyamali Samarasinghe, and Ken Kusterer. West Hartford, CT: Kumarian Press.

Kaufman, Natalie Hevener, and Stefanie A. Lindquist. 1995. Critiquing gender-neutral treaty language: The convention on the elimination of all forms of discrimination against women. In *Women's rights, human rights: International feminist perspectives*. See Peters and Wolper 1995.

Kristeva, Julia. 1981. Excerpt from "Woman can never be defined." In *New French feminisms: An anthology*, eds. Elaine Marks and Isabelle de Courtivron. New York: Schocken.

Laqueur, Walter, and Barry Rubin. 1979. *The human rights reader*. Philadelphia: Temple University Press.

Locke, John. 1950. [1689] *A letter concerning toleration*. 1st ed. Indianapolis, IN: Bobbs Merrill.

Marchand, Marianne. 1995. Latin American women speak on development: Are we listening yet? In *Feminism, postmodernism, and development*. See Marchand and Parpart 1995.

Marchand, Marianne, and Jane Parpart. 1995. *Feminism, postmodernism, development*. New York: Routledge.

Martin, Jane Roland. 1994. Methodological essentialism, false difference, and other dangerous traps. *Signs* 19(3): 630-57.

Mayer, Ann Elizabeth. 1994. Universal versus Islamic human rights: A clash of cultures or a clash with a construct? *Michigan Journal of International Law* 15(2): 307-404.

Moghadam, Valentine, ed. 1994. Identity politics and women: Cultural reassertions and feminisms in international perspective. Boulder, CO: Westview Press.

Mohanty, Chandra Talpade. 1991. Under western eyes: Feminist scholarship and colonial discourses. In *Third world women and the politics of feminism*. See Mohanty, Russo, and Torres. 1991.

Mohanty, Chandra Talpade, Ann Russo, and Lourdes Torres, eds. 1991. *Third world women and the politics of feminism*. Bloomington: Indiana University Press.

———. 1992. Feminist encounters: Locating the politics of experience. In *Destabilizing theory: Contemporary feminist debates*, ed. Michele Barrett and Anne Phillips. Stanford: Stanford University Press.

Morgan, Robin. 1984. *Sisterhood is global: The international women's movement anthology*. New York: Anchor Press/Doubleday.

Moruzzi, Norma Claire. 1994. A problem with headscarves: Contemporary complexities of political and social identity. *Political Theory* 22(4): 653-72.

Narayan, Uma. 1998. Essence of culture and a sense of history: A feminist critique of cultural essentialism. *Hypatia* 13(2): 86-106.

———. 1997. Contesting cultures: 'Westernization,' respect for cultures, and third-world feminists. In Narayan, *Dislocating cultures: Identities, traditions, and Third-World feminism*. New York: Routledge.

New York Times. 1995. Women's meeting agrees on a right to say no to sex. 11 September.

———. 1996a. Walled in, shrouded and angry in Afghanistan. 4 October.

———. 1996b. African ritual pain: Genital cutting. 5 October.

———. 1996c. New law bans genital cutting in United States. 10 October.

———. 1996d. The many faces of Islamic law. 13 October.

———. 1996e. Woman's plea for asylum puts tribal ritual on trial. 9 November.

Ofei-Aboagye, Rosemary Ofeibea. 1994. Altering the strands of the fabric: A preliminary look at domestic violence in Ghana. *Signs* 19(4): 924-38.

Okin, Susan Moller. 1989a. Humanist liberalism. In *Liberalism and the moral life*, ed. Nancy Rosenblum. Cambridge: Harvard University Press.

———. 1989b. *Justice, gender, and the family*. New York: Basic Books.

———. 1994. Gender inequality and cultural differences. *Political Theory* 22(1): 5-24.

Parpart, Jane L., and Marianne H. Marchand. 1995. Exploding the canon: An intro-
duction/conclusion. In *Feminism, postmodernism, and development*. See Marchand
and Parpart 1995.

Pateman, Carole. 1989. Feminist critiques of the public/private dichotomy. In *The
disorder of women: Democracy, feminism, and political theory*. Stanford: Stanford
University Press.

———. 1994. The rights of man and early feminism. Frauen und Politik, *Swiss Yearbook
of Political Science*: 19-31.

Pathak, Zakia, and Rajeswari Sunder Rajan. 1992. Shahbano. In *Feminists theorize the
political*, eds. Judith Butler and Joan W. Scott. New York: Routledge.

Peters, Julie, and Andrea Wolper. 1995. *Women's rights, human rights: International
feminist perspectives*. New York: Routledge.

Russell, Diana E.H. 1989. *Lives of courage: Women for a new South Africa*. New York:
Basic Books.

Sen, Amartya. 1990a. Gender and cooperative conflicts. In *Persistent inequalities:
Women and world development*, ed. Irene Tinker. Oxford: Oxford University Press.

———. 1990b. More than one hundred million women are missing. In *New York
Review of Books* 37(20): 61.

Shaheed, Farida. 1994. Controlled or autonomous: Identity and the experience of the
network, women living under Muslim laws. *Signs* 19(4): 997-1019.

Spelman, Elizabeth V. 1980. *Inessential woman: Problems of exclusion in feminist thought*.
Boston: Beacon Press.

Toubia, Nahid. 1995. *Female genital mutilation: A call for global action*. New York:
Women, Inc.

United Nations. 1948. *Universal Declaration of Human Rights*. G.A. Res. 217A(III),
U.N. Doc. A/810. Adopted December 10, 1948.

United Nations. 1966a. *International Covenant on Civil and Political Rights*. G.A. Res.
2200(XXI), 21 U.N. GAOR, Supp. (No. 16) at 52, U.N. Doc. A/6316. Adopted
December 16, 1966.

United Nations. 1966b. *International Covenant on Economic, Social and Cultural Rights*.
G.A. Res. 2200(XXI), 21 U.N. GAOR, Supp. (No. 16), U.N. Doc. A/6316.
Adopted December 16, 1966.

United Nations. 1979. *Convention on the elimination of all forms of discrimination against
women*. G.A. Res. 34/180, U.N. Doc. A/Res/34/180. Adopted December 18, 1979.

Walby, Sylvia. 1992. Post—post-modernism? Theorizing social complexity. In *Destabilizing theory: Contemporary feminist debates*, eds. Michele Barrett and Anne Phillips.
Stanford: Stanford University Press.

3

Cultural Alterity: Cross-Cultural Communication and Feminist Theory in North-South Contexts

OFELIA SCHUTTE

How to communicate with "the other" who is culturally different from oneself is one of the greatest challenges facing North-South relations. This paper builds on existential-phenomenological and poststructuralist concepts of alterity and difference to strengthen the position of Latina and other subaltern speakers in North-South dialogue. It defends a postcolonial approach to feminist theory as a basis for negotiating culturally differentiated feminist positions in this age of accelerated globalization, migration, and displacement.

This essay will address the issue of understanding cultural differences in the context of cross-cultural communication and dialogue, particularly those cases in which such communication or attempted communication takes place between members of a dominant culture and a subaltern culture. From an examination of these issues we can perhaps draw some ideas that will permit us to reach a fuller understanding of cross-cultural feminist exchanges and dialogues. The reason for focusing on the topic of cross-cultural communication is that recently, I have become increasingly aware of the levels of prejudice affecting the basic processes of communication between Anglo-American and Latina speakers, as well as the difficulties experienced by many Latin American immigrants to the United States. It seems to me that in these times of massive prejudices against immigrants and of extraordinary displacements of people from their communities of origin, the question of how to communicate with "the other" who is culturally different from oneself is one of the greatest challenges facing North-South relations and interaction. If the question before us is how to frame the conditions for the possibility of a global feminist ethics—or whether such an ethics is indeed possible—I see no better place to start than to examine the conditions of possibility for cross-cultural communication as such.

My methodology for understanding what is at stake in cross-cultural and intersubjective communication will depend largely on an existential-phenomenological concept of alterity. In this tradition, the breakthrough in constructing the concept of *the other* occurs when one combines the notion of the other as different from the self with the acknowledgment of the self's decentering that results from the experience of such differences.[1] Moreover, the breakthrough involves acknowledging the positive, potentially ethical dimensions of such a decentering for interpersonal relations (as in Levinas 1979, Irigaray 1993, and Kristeva 1991), in contrast to simply taking the decentering one might experience in the light of the other's differences as a deficit in the individual's control over the environment. According to this understanding, interpersonal and social interactions marked by cultural (as well as sexual, racial, and other kinds of difference) allow us to reach new ethical, aesthetic, and political ground.

In other words, the other is not the one who passively confirms what I am predisposed to think about her; she is not the one who acts as the mirror to my self or the one whose image justifies my existing ego boundaries. If this were the case, the other would only be a stand-in for the self's narcissism. Just the contrary; the other is that person or experience which makes it possible for the self to recognize its own limited horizons in the light of asymmetrically given relations marked by sexual, social, cultural, or other differences. The other, the foreigner, the stranger, is that person occupying the space of the subaltern in the culturally asymmetrical power relation, but also those elements or dimensions of the self that unsettle or decenter the ego's dominant, self-enclosed, territorialized identity.

In addition to these presuppositions regarding otherness and difference derived from the phenomenological-existential and poststructuralist tradition, I will take into account recent methodological developments regarding the concept of cultural difference as represented in postcolonial feminist theory. Working against the background of the West's history of colonial enterprises and its exploitation of other societies and cultures, postcolonial theory, in its various manifestations, pays special attention to issues of language, class, racial, ethnic, sexual, and gender differences, and to the justification of narratives about the nation-state.[2] Postcolonial feminist theory, in turn, directs its attention to the lives of women and to the tensions affecting women whose voices appear in national narratives and accounts of diasporic migrations. At stake in these "post" theories is a certain loss of innocence with regard to narratives of identity because of a more critical awareness of the regulative power such narratives have in defining who we are, who we aren't, and who others are and aren't.[3] The regulative power of narratives of identity is something with respect to which we are, to some extent, complicit, but we are also able to examine these narratives from some distance. Postcolonial and feminist critics have therefore used psychoanalytic theory to investigate further and to elaborate aspects of the relation between self and other in the light of accepted narratives of cultural identity and difference. In particular, Kristeva has studied symbolic analogies between the foreign other and the Freudian concept of the uncanny in the self—what she has called the stranger within the self (Kristeva 1991). Postcolonial feminisms, problematizing the Western concept of self, question the regulative use of gender in national and postnational narratives, but also the Enlightenment concept of individualism that fails to notice the complex, multilayered, fragmented, contradictory aspects of the self.

Finally, and on a different note regarding issues of alterity and identity, one more presupposition guiding these reflections is the belief that what we hold to be the nature of knowledge is not culture-free but is determined by the methodologies and data legitimated by dominant cultures. In other words, the scientific practices of a dominant culture are what determine not only the limits of knowledge but who may legitimately participate in the language of science. In everyday practices, outside of university environments, women are seen as particularly illiterate when it comes to having scientific knowledge or being able to discuss scientific issues with experts in the field. One does not need to have read Foucault to realize how very interconnected is the relation of knowledge to power. My point is that cultural (not just scientific) knowledge involves a highly constraining form of power. This power involves constraints over oneself and constraints over others. The type of constraints I shall try to examine and deconstruct to some extent are those dealing with a dominant culture's understanding of cultural differences. In addition, my analysis tries to understand sociocultural differences without subjecting them to masculine-dominant, gender-normative categories and maxims.

There is a need to develop a model of ethical and philosophical understanding in which the meaning of sexual difference is not limited by a gender-normative bias regarding what constitutes "the female body" or the proper function of a woman's mental abilities. Similarly, there is a need to develop a model for the understanding of subaltern cultural differences. In other words, both the critique of gender-normative biases and the critique of cultural imperialism need to be taken into account. Nevertheless, given that quite a number of critiques of cultural imperialism are themselves based on masculinist (often highly authoritarian) models of liberation from imperialism, which in turn presuppose and reinforce the domination of men over women in liberation struggles, the critique of cultural imperialism should be tempered by some kind of pluricultural feminist perspective. All these considerations lead to a feminist postcolonial perspective that can balance the struggle against the legacy of colonial-imperial domination with the struggle for the creation of feminist and feminist-compatible societies.

THE DISPARITY IN SPEAKING POSITIONS

These reflections begin with some of my personal impressions regarding the difficulties of cross-cultural communication when one culture circumstantially holds the upper hand over another. The culture with the upper hand will generate resistance in the group that fails to enjoy a similar cultural status, while the culture of the subaltern group will hardly be understood in its importance or complexity by those belonging to the culturally dominant group unless exceptional measures are taken to promote a good dialogue. Even so, it is my view that no two cultures or languages can be perfectly transparent to each other. There is always a residue of meaning that will not be reached in cross-cultural endeavors, a residue sufficiently important to point to what I shall refer to more abstractly as a principle of (cross-cultural) incommensurability.[4]

The most common way to point to this excess of meaning is to refer to the untranslatable aspects of a language vis-à-vis another language. In this case, one might think of incommensurability arithmetically as a kind of minus effect to cross-cultural communication—what I get from the differently situated speaker is the conveyable message minus the specific cultural difference that does not come across. Theorized in this manner, the way to maximize intercultural dialogue would be to devise a way to put as much meaning as possible into the plus side of the exchange, so that as little as possible remains on the minus side of it. But although creating more effective means of communication between disparate groups can help reduce social conflict and tension, I don't believe much is understood about cultural difference if incommensurability is thought of in this predominantly quantitative manner.

Another way to think of incommensurability, and one that is much more relevant and fruitful for our discussion, is to look at nodes in a linguistic interchange or a conversation in which the other's speech, or some aspect of it, resonates in me as a kind of strangeness, as a kind of displacement of the usual expectation. Cultural alterity requires that one not bypass these experiences or subsume them under an already familiar category. Even the category of cultural diversity is called into question when diversity is institutionalized so as to mask a more radical view of differences. Postmodern postcolonial discourse looks for the possibilities of using nontotalizing concepts of difference rather than "the consensual, ethnocentric notion of the pluralistic existence of cultural diversity" (Bhabha 1994, 177). In the establishment's view of diversity, the rules controlling the representation of diversity usually reflect the will of the winners in political and military struggles. As Lyotard's debate with Habermas makes clear, the rationality of consensus is only a few steps from the desire for one system, one truth—in sum, one rationality—to dominate human civilization. In its extreme, the will to one truth has yielded the totalitarian Reign of Terror.[5] The representation of the one system as "pluralist" and favorable to cultural diversity must be called into question because of the sweeping power exercised by the system to harness the many into the yoke of the one (cf. Bhabha 1994, 152-55, 162-64). Even when the system is formulated as pluralist, the drawback is that only those differences are likely to enter the plural stage as are able to fit within the overall rationality that approves and controls the many as one.

Perhaps partly, though not exclusively, on account of this reason—because the new paradigm is born specifically out of the life experiences of many migrant and postcolonial peoples—some postcolonial critics have started to theorize the question of cultural difference in terms of what Homi Bhabha has called a "disjunctive temporality" (Bhabha 1994, 177) and Néstor García Canclini has labeled a "multitemporal heterogeneity."[6] These categories refer, in the first case, to the splitting, and in the second case, to the superimposition of temporalities marking off cultural differences, speaking positions, and narrative timeframes. In Latin American societies, as García Canclini's work demonstrates, African, indigenous, Spanish colonial, modern, and global narrative timeframes may intersect, simultaneously or disjunctively, a speaker's discourse. Taking this thought further, I would note that when such culturally situated speakers enter diasporic locations—as happens when they migrate from their original societies to the United States—they will bring with them these forms of cultural difference and hybridity. It is not exceptional for many Latin Americans to become acculturated as a result of sociocultural influences criss-crossed by two or more incommensurable cultures, sometimes in literal juxtaposition. For example, in the Caribbean, because of the effects of colonization, some of the Yoruba deities gained counterparts in the Spanish Catholic roster of saints. We could say the Catholic and the Yoruba figures inhabit two very different kinds of temporalities. From the standpoint of the worshipers' experiences, in some cases one of the temporalities would be superimposed on the other, while in other cases the two would become distinct.

In *Borderlands/La Frontera*, Gloria Anzaldúa, speaking as a Chicana-Tejana-lesbian-feminist writer, juxtaposes the temporality of ancient indigenous myths with her postcolonial North American existence. The shifts from English to Spanish to Nahuatl in Anzaldúa are not just shifts in languages or "codes," as she calls them, but in temporalities of perception and consciousness (Anzaldúa 1987, viii). These pluricultural temporalities create a disjunctive tension with the linear temporality of modernity governing the identities of producers and consumers in advanced capitalist societies. These multiple and disjunctive temporalities create a displacement in the relation between self and other, allowing the recognition of alterity both inside and outside the self. Their premise of selfhood begins with the acknowledging and appreciation of the nonidentical self. Anzaldúa's multihyphenated *mestiza* self reminds us of Kristeva's stranger within. More broadly, it exemplifies feminism's notion of the differences not only among but within women. These multiple layers within the self, responding to different perceptive fields and different, not necessarily commensurable temporalities, can predispose us psychologically to appreciate both the richness and the incommensurability of cultural differences. They lay the groundwork for cognitive, perceptual, and linguistically constituted relations between ourselves and others where the other's differences, even if not fully translatable into the terms of our own cultural horizons, can be acknowledged as sites of appreciation, desire, recognition, caring, and respect. I am speaking here of a psychological state in which the stranger is not abjected, derided, persecuted, shut out of view, or legalized out of existence, but—departing from the premise that the other is also human—neither is she subjected to the demand that she be the double, or reflected mirror image, of ourselves.

The question arises of how the principle of incommensurability applies to feminist ethics when feminist ethics is engaged in making and executing normative judgments cross-culturally. Will the feminist ethical claim or the normative judgment be impaired by the principle of incommensurability, and if so, to what extent? How are feminist ethical terms negotiated cross-culturally? Should they be negotiated at all? My first task is to try to explain how the principle of incommensurability works at the concrete level of everyday experience. I will address this issue from an existential standpoint based in part on my personal experience.

THE CULTURALLY DIFFERENT OTHER

What does it mean to be culturally different and to speak, at the level of culture, in a different voice? This question is generally answered by those with the power to mark others (or "the other") as different, rather than by those whose difference is in question in relation to the majority, or main members, of a given group. To be culturally different is not the same as being individually different or different by virtue of one's age or sex. If I am in a group among other women with roughly the same kind of education and occupational interests as myself and if we are roughly of the same age, what will mark me as culturally different is that I am, in today's terms, a Latina—a name that, while pointing to some aspects of my background, also erases important aspects of my individuality and the actual specificities of my cultural genealogy, which includes Caribbean, Latin American, and Western European background.

Latina casts me in a recognizable category, through which the meaning of my difference is delimited according to whatever set of associations this term may evoke. *Latina* is not simply a descriptive term referring to someone with a Latin American or Iberian ancestry currently residing in the United States. It is a signifier that both masks and evokes a range of associations—hot blooded, temperamental, submissive, defiant, illegal or illicit, sexually repressed or sexually overactive, oppressed, exploited, and so on. But the thread that draws together all the stereotypical associations is one of invisibility as a producer of culture. One reason for this is that women in masculine-dominant societies, including Anglo-American society, are viewed primarily as transmitters rather than producers of culture. They are viewed principally as caregivers whose function in culture is to transmit and conserve, not question and create, cultural values.

Latinas in the United States are also invisible as producers of culture because the term *Latina* lacks a specific national reference and, in the mind of Western modernity, nation and culture are still tightly interrelated. (For example, the great national museums of art and science exhibit those works that illustrate the cultural standards and the aesthetic and scientific power of various nations.) As a concept, *Latina* exceeds the category of the national. Because as Latinas we are not tied to a specifiable national culture (in contrast to members of a culturally dominant group), to be culturally visible in the dominant culture we have to show that we know how to incorporate two or more cultures into our way of being. Furthermore, we must demonstrate that the way we bring such cultures together can benefit the Anglo-American public. In order to receive recognition as a cultural agent, I must show that I can be both a Latina and a North American; that I can alternate between these identities, so much so that in extremely "tight" cultural situations, I can perform, in my North American voice, a public erasure of my Latina voice, if need be. My white, Anglo-American counterpart is not called on to perform such a feat with respect to her own cultural background. She does not have to erase her Anglo-American cultural background to be legitimated as a member of North American society. If she comes from a working-class background, she may have to erase her class background to be fully accepted in some strata of society; and if she is a lesbian, she may have to erase her sexual orientation (keep it closeted) to be acceptable in some groups. But to gain recognition as a cultural agent she does not have to erase or dilute her Anglo-American background as such. Moreover, she does not need to combine her cultural background with, say, that of Middle Eastern, Asian, African, or Latin American people before being accepted as an important contributor to society and culture. If she is Jewish, she will face special problems the farther she is removed from assimilating fully into the Protestant, Anglo-American, Western European tradition.

Returning to the problem of the culturally successful Latina woman, an interesting phenomenon can be observed. Once I am able to perform the feat of representing my culture in some distinctive way in the context of the dominant Anglo-American culture, I am no longer considered only a culturally marked "other." To my favor, I am now recognized as an accomplished handler and knower of cultures. In this capacity, I earn a special place in the group. I have stepped out of the "immanent" place of the other. I have, to some extent, transcended the "Latina" object-position and claimed my position as a cultural agent in terms recognized by the dominant cultural group. But in order to do this, I need to be knowledgeable in the language and epistemic maneuvers of the dominant culture, the same culture that in its everyday practice marks me as culturally "other" than itself. From a cultural standpoint as well as a psychoanalytical one, I have become a split subject. When I act as "myself" (in my reflexive sense of self, the "me" that includes and grows out of my early Cuban upbringing), my Anglo-American sociocultural environment will often mark me as "other." When, alternatively, I discursively perform the speaking position expected of a subject of the dominant culture, I am recognized as a real agent in the real world.

Still, something fundamentally important is missing in this latter recognition (a misrecognition, actually). What my interlocutor fails to recognize is that delimiting my capacity to speak in my culturally differentiated voice will have an effect on what I say in response. When one feels rejected, one switches tracks, as it were, and enters the dominant discourse, not without realizing what is lost. What my interlocutor recognizes is not what I would have liked—an encouragement to communicate insights I offer from a standpoint of cultural difference—but only my ability to enter a standard Anglo-American speaking position, a position that exists in negotiated tension with my culturally differentiated, reflexive sense of self. In other words, the local masternarrative exists in tension with what the Latina knows and experiences, and the former shuts out the latter. This is why sometimes, when some interlocutor responds to me (say, at the office) in reference to the self I perform there as a speaking subject, I get the sense that this colleague is not speaking to me at all; that my interlocutor is missing something, because the "me" that is culturally different is ignored, shut off, or bypassed.

There is a sense of frustration but also of missed opportunity in these mishaps in cross-cultural communication. What remains to be understood in the statements of the culturally differentiated other—that is, the incommensurable something not subject to perfect cultural translation—may actually be the most important part of the message my Anglophone interlocutor needs to receive. As I perceive it, my interlocutor takes in a fragment of the message and discards the rest. But one suspects it is precisely because the discarded part of the message would require the radical decentering of the dominant Anglophone speaking subject that it fails to reach such a subject's ears. Who or what is the other for the dominant, enlightened subject?[7] It is the one he would like to speak with occasionally, preferably in a foreign or distant location; it is the one he defends abstractly in arguments for democracy or against oppression. But let not the other (as other) make any demands in his everyday world, for in this case he might have to change his way of being. He might have to acknowledge his own split subjectivity, change his fixed way of life, welcome the stranger within, and perhaps alter his views and relations with others in ways he had not foreseen.

Cultural alterity therefore points to an ethics and to ways of knowing far deeper than the type of thinking wherein dominant cultural speakers perceive themselves to be at the epistemic and moral center of the universe, spreading their influence outward toward other rational speakers. Cultural alterity demands that the other be heard in her difference and that the self give itself the time, the space, and the opportunity to appreciate the stranger without and within. As Kristeva poignantly observes, "How could one tolerate a foreigner if one did not know one was a stranger to oneself?" (Kristeva 1991, 182).

If I may extrapolate from the kind of personal experience mentioned above to the situation of communication and dialogue among women North and South of the border, one sees how difficult it is for groups that are deeply entrenched in their own values, and that have the power to ignore the values of other groups, to attain any adequate understanding of cultural alterity. The reason for this is that people of different cultures do not speak the same (cultural) language and do not share the same cultural imaginary order. The science of anthropology has had to deal with the issue of cultural incommensurability for a long time. Why is this sense of incommensurability so hard to grasp for philosophy? Philosophers are often taught that philosophical claims can be stated in a language that is essentially outside of culture. This move essentializes philosophy, requiring an arsenal of conceptual weapons to police its boundaries, much as governments hire border patrols to keep illegal aliens outside the border. But isn't the language used to put forward philosophical claims—even the most formal and abstract language—already part of a culture? Aren't our conceptions of ethics, reason, and philosophy part of culture? Perhaps the issue should be put another way. Philosophers may acknowledge that incommensurability exists among various cultural formations and that it will impede the mapping of various cultural discourses exactly so that all of them match perfectly. The debate lies is whether such incommensurable elements should be assigned to what is irrelevant to philosophical meaning and knowledge, and thus irrelevant to the operations of reason; or whether, as I suggest, the incommensurable elements should be seen as inherent to the processes of reasoning itself.

In my view, cross-cultural (rational) discourse should be seen as limited by those elements of cultural difference that I have called incommensurable. That these elements of cultural difference cannot be fully apprehended in their "internal" intracultural meaning by outsiders, however, should not be taken as a sign that they are irrelevant to an understanding of cultural difference. Nor does it mean that acknowledging incommensurability will weaken the possibility of cross-cultural dialogue. Quite the contrary. Communication, including cross-cultural communication, involves two aspects, the second of which is often neglected. First, one must understand what is being said. Second, one must relate what is being said to a complex set of signifiers, denoting or somehow pointing to what remains unsaid. It is because of this very important (open-ended) dialectic between the said and the unsaid that the principle of incommensurability in cross-cultural communication assumes considerable importance.

In cross-cultural communication, each speaker may "say" something that falls on the side of the "unsaid" for a culturally differentiated interlocutor. Such gaps in communication may cause one speaker's discourse to appear incoherent or insufficiently organized. To the culturally dominant speaker, the subaltern speaker's discourse may appear to be a string of fragmented observations rather than a unified whole. The actual problem may not be incoherence but the lack of cultural translatability of the signifiers for coherence from one set of cultural presuppositions to the other.[8] Alternatively, the dominant speaker, relating only to fragments in the other's narrative, may believe that the whole message was transmitted, when only part of it was. This asymmetrical, nonreciprocal gap in communication can be tested, for example, if a third party interrupts the conversation and the subaltern speaker tries to resume it after the interval. The dominant speaker, lacking the sense that some element in the communication was still missing and believing that s/he has already heard the whole statement, does not perceive that the interlocutor should have the space to complete what was left unsaid. The subaltern speaker, in turn, is at a loss to explain that she had saved the most important part of the message for the end. Now she realizes that the interlocutor wants to move away from the subject of cultural difference, not toward it.

The speaker from the dominant culture is basically saying: communicate with me entirely on the terms I expect; beyond this, I am not interested. The ethical principle of cultural alterity must point to the inadequacy of such a speaker to engage in cross-cultural as well as interpersonal dialogue and conversation. Yet by the conventional norms of his own culture, the dominant speaker may never understand that he is silencing the culturally differentiated other because it never occurred to him to think that cross-cultural communication contains important, yet incommensurable, elements. Alternatively, he may be conscious of such incommensurable elements, but pay special attention to them only when the contrast between cultures involves a strong polarity, as in the cases of Asian or African cultures in contrast to Anglo-American culture. In this case, too, the Latina's subaltern message will not be heard, because her closer proximity to the West will disqualify her from the neoromanticized picture of the more culturally distant other.

It is incumbent on those speakers of the dominant cultural language not to foreclose the meaning of statements to only those meanings that are readily available to them. Assuming that one could map the statements of the culturally differentiated other according to three categories—readily understandable, difficult to understand, and truly incommensurable—one should never close the communication at the level of the first category, but should make the effort to let understanding reach into the other two domains. For example, if a Latina speaker alters the usual syntactical order normally used by English speakers, and if she also speaks with a heavy accent, these factors may make it harder for the native English speaker to understand what she is saying. With some effort, however, it is possible to figure out what is being said, if one is intent on paying attention and in engaging in followup questioning. Unfortunately, I have seen repeated cases of a Latina treated as if she were speaking nonsense, only because her accent, her sentence structure, and perhaps her vocabulary differ from that of ordinary English usage. Rather than taking the effort to listen to what the other is saying, the native speaker will treat the non-native speaker as if she were linguistically or intellectually incompetent. From the perception "I don't immediately understand what the other is saying," the dominant speaker will draw the invalid conclusion, "the other is speaking nonsense," "the other is incompetent," "the other does not belong here," and so on. The relegation of the culturally different "other" to a subordinate position, as this exemplary exercise shows, may itself be diagnosed as a lack of culture. Cultural prejudice of this sort is indeed a sign of a cultural deficit on the part of the dominant culture.

Furthermore, and with respect to the third category or level, placing a high stake on the incommensurable as that which requires recognition (rather than erasure or denigration in relation to a dominant culture) is fundamental to acquiring an understanding, even if only a partial understanding, of the culturally differentiated "other." If we hypothesize that incommensurability is largely manifested not only linguistically but in terms of disjunctive or heterogeneous temporalities, given the centrality of the concept of time in human existence, the very fabric of all social relationships will be affected by it. For example, intergenerational issues, productivity, leisure, and aging will not carry the same overall meaning for people of different cultural backgrounds.[9] Recognizing how culturally incommensurable clusters of meaning affect basic everyday interactions will bring culturally differentiated speakers one step closer to improved communication and understanding.

WOMAN AS "OTHER" OF ANOTHER WOMAN

Although in some of my examples I have been using the masculine pronoun to designate the culturally dominant speaker and the feminine to designate the subaltern, the relations of cultural dominance and subalternity can also obtain among speakers of the same gender or in the reverse combination. Basically, in coupled dualisms or binaries, the normative term "others" the nonnormative one (that is, the normative term subjects the nonnormative term to the subordinate position of "other"). This is one of the reasons why deconstructive feminist theory is so intent on moving beyond oppositional binaries and their corresponding forms of exclusion. For example, as Beauvoir and others have shown, in the man-woman binary, *man* is taken as normative for the human species, while *woman* is cast in the position of "other" of the normative. But take other examples: if the lady of the house is considered normative with respect to domestic authority and values, the female domestic worker will be seen as "other"; if the white woman is considered normative with respect to social status, the *mulata* will be other, and so on. Conversely, in popular culture, if the barrio is considered normative, high culture will be considered "other." In North-South and West-East binaries, if North and West are considered normative in terms of cultural standards, then South and East will be considered "other."

In antiimperialist politics, the terms are reversed. The Northern and the Western aggressors take on a lower cultural status while the Southern and Eastern cultures are hailed. When Western feminist theory fails to take into account the issues of colonialism and imperialism, the dangerous outcome will be that women from Eastern and Southern cultures will see in feminism the mark of Western colonization. Feminism in this instance will be tied symbolically to Western (capitalist) modernity and will not be dissociated from its values. In contrast, if feminism is seen as a movement of women in different parts of the world getting together and joining forces to overcome social, political, economic, and gender oppression, then this movement of emancipation becomes normative and the "other" becomes the outsider to, or obstructor of, this movement.

Herein lies the point of vulnerability for Western feminism, for if feminism is defined too narrowly, it will make an "other" of women whose path to emancipation it may fail to understand or recognize. In particular, it may relegate to the status of "other" many women in Eastern and Southern countries whose views do not fit squarely into Western feminist categories. Moreover, if Western feminism defines itself too narrowly or in terms that women in Eastern and Southern countries may not quite understand or appreciate—given the factor of cultural incommensurability—women in these countries may reject Western feminists as "other." This potential type of mutual exclusion takes us back to the impasse between feminism North and South, East and West. As Trinh Minh-ha notes in *Woman, Native, Other*, it is easy for conservative males in Third World countries to denounce feminism as a foreign, Western influence. When Western feminists try to denounce the conditions of women's oppression in Third World countries in "terms made to reflect or fit into Euro-American women's criteria of equality," this indirectly "serves the cause of tradition upholders and provides them with a pretext for muddling all issues of oppression raised by Third World women" (Mihn-ha 1989, 106).

Fortunately, thanks to the insistent voices of women from developing countries and ethnic minorities and to the growing sensitivities of Western feminists when it comes to conveying feminist messages in the light of cross-cultural differences, these difficulties are better handled now by feminists engaged in worldwide activism and politics.[10] What is less clear to me is whether Western feminists (as they pursue philosophy, for example) view themselves as one of many voices in the struggle for women's social, political, economic, and gender emancipation on a worldwide scale. It seems to me that Western feminism still harbors the hope that its own views of emancipation are universally valid for all the world's women, if only because Western thought generally does not mark itself as culturally specific. Instead, it engages in the discursive mode of a universal *logos*, which it takes to be applicable to all rational speakers. Here the issue of colonialism must be brought up, even if it is unpleasant and even if it interrupts the discussion about the criteria for recognizing rationally competent speakers across cultures. Without reference to the historic conditions of colonialism, it is impossible to understand fully the Western mind's presumption of speaking from the privileged position of universality.

The Western colonial enterprise and its impact on the Americas were such that there was no way to understand the disparity of Western and non-Western cultures in an ethically responsible, reciprocal way. The conquest of America offered no reciprocal way of accounting for the differences among Western and non-Western cultures and peoples. To those people who were judged "less developed" in Western European terms it brought the forces that colonized and enslaved them. While the racial composition of the Americas has changed since the conquest and colonization, the problem persists that the people who have not reached the West's level of material development are often considered inferior. The impoverished Mexican migrant to California and the Haitian migrant to South Florida become, more than five hundred years after the conquest, the targets of the combined historical effects of colonialist, racial, linguistic, class, and, where applicable, gender prejudices.

Is it possible for contemporary Western feminism to disentangle itself from the historical forces of Western colonialism and from the erasure of otherness that such forces entail? What are the points of contact today between feminists from developing countries and Western feminism? Is there reason to place hope in a new way of looking at things, the recently developed approach of *postcolonial feminisms*?

POSTCOLONIAL FEMINISMS

Postcolonial feminisms are those feminisms that take the experience of Western colonialism and its contemporary effects as a high priority in the process of setting up a speaking position from which to articulate a standpoint of cultural, national, regional, or social identity. With postcolonial feminisms, the process of critique is turned against the domination and exploitation of *culturally* differentiated others. Postcolonial feminisms differ from the classic critique of imperialism in that they try to stay away from rigid self-other binaries.[11] In addition, an intense criticism is directed at the gender stereotypes and symbolic constructs of the woman's body used to reinforce outdated masculinist notions of national identity.[12] Postcolonial feminisms call attention to the process of splitting the culturally dominant subject in terms of the demands placed on the dominant subject by culturally disadvantaged others. These feminisms hypothesize, at the psychosubjective level, that the unity of self or mind felt by the dominant subject is a totally artificial one, and that the oneness of his or her subjectivity (covering the fragments that make up his or her personality) is made possible only by adherence to a philosophy of colonialism, whether the adherence is owned up to or only enacted indirectly. In other words, postcolonial feminisms propose the view that we are not born a unified self, that the sense of being "one," of being a self, is something derived from language (becoming a competent speaker in a language), and that language itself is part of culture and reflects certain arrangements of cultural constructs with respect to how to understand cultural differences.

When a child is given a name, for example, Caroline, she is not told that the culture giving her this name is one that had a history of colonizing other people and of imposing its values on them. The psychological process of decolonization involves the attempt to unhinge the genealogy of one's name, of one's identity, from the inherited colonial culture. One must learn that one could not be oneself without a relationship to the other and that such a relationship ideally must not be wrought with injustices. While one cannot make time go backward, annulling Western culture's colonialist legacy, it is possible partially to deactivate this legacy by establishing alternative practices and values with the intent of reversing the effects of colonialism. A coordination of heterogeneous elements with a special emphasis on undermining colonialism's understanding of cultural difference becomes the alternative route to the construction of identity in what we would like to call a *postcolonial* perspective or context.

If the postcolonial perspective entails acknowledging the reality of colonialism (or the fight against it) in the construction of cultural values and personal identities, what does a postcolonial feminism entail regarding the problem of cross-cultural communication? Postcolonial identities put in question the belief in the neutrality of the sign and the separation of the subject and object of knowledge, as accepted by the Enlightenment. They point out that these semiotic and epistemic assumptions will ultimately have repercussions on women's bodies and on women's affective well-being. As literary critic Nelly Richard observes from Chile, feminist (postcolonial) criticism should be able to uncover the concerted interests of the dominant culture hidden behind "the supposed neutral transparency of signs and the model of mimetic reproduction propitiated by the market through a passive consumption" (Richard 1996, 744).

Moreover, as Gayatri Spivak aptly illustrates by allusion to the status of indebted families in India, the interests of transnational global capital hiding behind the purported neutrality of global consumption are not gender-neutral.

> In modern "India," there *is* a "society" of bonded labor, where the only means of repaying a loan at extortionate rates of interest is hereditary bond-slavery. . . . [Below family life at the level of survival] there is bonded prostitution, where the girls and women abducted from bonded labor or *kamiya* households are thrust together as bodies for absolute sexual and economic exploitation. (Spivak 1993, 82)

The deceptive transparency of signs, the growing expansion of passive consumption, the recourse to loans as the concrete mechanism for maintaining consumption, the exorbitant rates of interest imposed on already subaltern populations, and the woman's body as "the last instance in a [global] system whose general regulator is still the loan" (Spivak 1993, 82) are interconnected forms of exploitation that only postcolonial feminisms can fully address at this time. Whether in Chile, in India, or much closer to home, postcolonial feminisms alert us to the voices of split subjects deconstructing the logic of the totality in the light of cultural alterity.

FEMINIST AGENCY AND THE RESTRUCTURING OF THE IMAGINARY-SYMBOLIC ORDER

These comments on bonded labor illustrate a final and nevertheless familiar point for feminists; namely, that the ultimate oppression a human being can experience is to be bereft of any meaningful agency. African American feminist bell hooks has described oppression as the lack of choices.[13] I take this to mean that oppression involves conditions in which persons are deprived of agency, or that their options are limited to those that effectively fail to promote their own good.

If we look at the conditions that would empower women around the world to promote their own good, we see powerful interests set against women. There are powerful religious fundamentalisms all over the world and in various cultures that seek to define for women in categorical and absolutist terms what their own good is and to constrain women to act accordingly. These fundamentalisms also define the meaning of "nation" and "family" in categorical terms, promoting self-sacrifice and often war, while impeding those who are influenced by these ideologies from acting on their own desires for personal fulfillment and happiness. Some government and private institutions, moreover, derive enormous material benefits from women's cheap labor and from women's traditional family caregiving roles. There are forces in society that benefit from women ending up in prostitution, remaining illiterate, or being confined to economic and social conditions which, from girlhood on, subject them to recurrent violence and abuse. It seems that nothing could be more ethical than a universal feminist ethics designed to identify and correct such problems. How this is done, however, requires careful rethinking of how to employ the concepts of gender, identity, and oppression.

In my view, feminist ethical thinking needs to be "negotiated" cross-culturally. Such negotiation can be conducted on a case-by-case basis by individuals, or collectively by groups. The presence of so many mixed unions among people of different cultures offers some hope that effective cross-cultural communication in matters that pertain to intimate details of peoples' lives is not some sort of utopian fantasy. But people in mixed unions that are based on parity, as compared to the practices of dominant cultures with regard to subaltern cultures, are very strongly motivated to understand each other, as well as to communicate with each other so as to deepen and strengthen their understanding. Such individuals commit themselves to lifestyles in which giving of one's time to reach out to the other, as well as making space for the other's differences, are part of the very fabric of daily existence, neither a forced nor an occasional happening. People in mixed unions have also presumably experienced the positive benefits of their association to the extent that they would rather affirm what remains incommensurable in their distinct cultural horizons than shut the other out of their intimate life and feelings. No doubt, individuals who either work or live successfully with culturally differentiated others are highly skilled communicators, making optimum use of opportunities for cross-cultural, interactive engagements. The postcolonial feminist perspective highlights these interactive realities, deconstructing the traditional binarism of self-other paradigms, in which each side lays claim to either mutually exclusive or equal but separate realities.

Collectively, feminists can do much to promote cross-cultural understanding. Whether these groups are all-women groups or whether they include female and male feminists, perhaps their basic contribution is building and strengthening networks of solidarity. Although *solidarity* is an old term, long familiar to activists, the present circumstances at the turn of the century demand that we rethink and reawaken its meanings. Feminists from dominant global cultures and better-off economic sectors need to connect more closely with projects involving women and feminists from the periphery. We need to lobby actively for the inclusion of voices from the periphery so as to shake off the weight of colonialism and other oppressions that still mark the center's discourses. This is not to say that the voices from the periphery are not marked by the effects of colonialism, racism, and other oppressions, but that when such voices attempt to address these oppressions or engage in avant-garde cultural criticism, there is a common bond between us, despite our differences. It is up to us to recognize the centrality that this (other) bond represents and to help it assume its long overdue and legitimate place in the West's symbolic order and cultural imaginary. There is no other recourse but to destabilize and displace the subject of modernity from its conceptual throne and to sponsor alternative ways of relating and knowing that no longer shut out from "home" the realities of Latino, Asian, African, and other culturally marginalized peoples.

I believe that Western feminism cannot reach a point of maturity in this age of global, transnational, and diasporic ventures unless it openly adopts a postcolonial perspective. If it does, we will switch our identities away from subjects of a totalized notion of culture and will come to view ourselves as subjects of cultural difference. The West needs to learn how to step out of its colonial boots and start experiencing the reality of its subaltern environment and the cultures of the peoples it has disenfranchized and continues to disenfranchize. A challenging but not impossible task lies ahead. This is why the struggle continues.

NOTES

1. Although Sartre, Merleau-Ponty, Beauvoir, Heidegger, and Lacan function as key background figures for the concepts of the other and alterity, it is Levinas who is remembered primarily for formulating an ethics of alterity. With the advent of poststructuralism, important new perspectives have been offered by Irigaray's feminist ethics of sexual difference and Kristeva's psychoanalytic-semiotic studies.

2. For a concise overview of postcolonial theory see Sagar (1996). For classics from the Caribbean region see Fanon (1963) and Fernández Retamar (1989). For contemporary poststructuralist postcolonial criticism see Spivak (1990, 1993) and Bhabha (1993). For postcolonialism and Latin American literary criticism (in Spanish) see the special issue on Latin American cultural criticism and literary theory of *Revista Iberoamericana* (1996); for postmodern studies in Latin America see Beverley et al. (1995) and the special issue on "Postmodernism: Center and Periphery" of *South Atlantic Quarterly* (1993).

3. This point is made by Sagar (1996, 427) with specific reference to the work of Spivak, but it applies generally to deconstructive and poststructuralist feminisms.

4. I will not be using the term *incommensurability* in the Kuhnian sense of two incommensurable scientific theories that explain the same phenomena. By this term I try to designate the lack of complete translatability of various expressions or blocks of meaning between two or more linguistic-cultural symbolic systems. It may also refer to incommensurable ways of thinking insofar as the differences are culturally determined.

5. "We have paid a high enough price for the nostalgia of the whole and the one, for the reconciliation . . . of the transparent and the communicable experience" (Lyotard 1984, 81-82).

6. García Canclini (1995, 46-47). Using Latin America's elites as a reference point, García Canclini describes "multitemporal heterogeneity" as a feature of modern culture resulting from modernity's inability to superimpose itself completely on Latin America's indigenous and colonial heritages. I am using the term somewhat differently

because my primary references are neither to the perspective of modernity nor to that of the elites. My primary reference point is the existential-phenomenological sense of two or more experienced temporalities as manifested in the lived experiences of members of the population, including the economically disadvantaged, the popular sectors, the racial minorities, and, yes, extending to the middle and upper classes, where relevant.

7. I refer to the dominant enlightened subject in the masculine gender here because this account is based primarily on my concrete experience; in a later section, I address women's assumption of this voice.

8. It would help to be acquainted with the underrepresented culture in order to appreciate this point. For example, feminists know that all too often, the patterns of gender socialization and the power one gender (the masculine) holds in the overall legal-ethical system of thought over the feminine will make it appear that a woman's reasoning is fragmentary or insufficiently coherent in comparison to the reasoning of successfully socialized males. Asymmetrically given cultural differences can have a similar effect. A Latina feminist must communicate with her Anglo audience not only as a feminist but as a Latina, because she is already marked as such by the dominant culture. If she draws too heavily on her own cultural imaginary to explain her views, an account that is perfectly coherent to her may simply not carry over as such to her audience. The audience might complain that at times it could not follow the speaker or that the speaker was not sufficiently organized. This is not a matter of agreeing or disagreeing with the content of the speaker's message but of failing to connect the various aspects of the message into a fully coherent account. In my view, this could mean (though it does not necessarily have to mean) that the grounds for the speaker's reasoning are not readily available to speakers located in the dominant culture. Again, this could show how asymmetrical relations of power are reinforced between culturally differentiated speakers when one of the cultures is fully dominant over the other. Many different examples could be given of this phenomenon, not all of them similar. For especially racist dimensions of such asymmetry, consider Frantz Fanon's charge that a characteristic of the racism he encountered in France was the expectation that as a black person from the Caribbean, he could not speak French coherently (Fanon 1963, 35-36). Compare also Homi Bhabha's example of the Turk in Germany who feels he is being looked down on as an animal when he tries to use the first few words he has learned in the German language (Bhabha 1994, 165).

9. Obviously, there may be some overlap among people of different cultures regarding certain values, just as there may be differences in values among people of roughly the same cultural background. For example, political values can vary significantly among people of similar cultural backgrounds. Strong variations and disagreements can occur even among members of the same family just as, where such opportunities exist, a person can develop an affinity with the values of people from distant cultures. Agreement or disagreement on such *values* is a separate issue from the argument I am making about the principle of incommensurability as a factor to be reckoned with in cross-cultural communication between speakers from dominant and subaltern cultures.

10. Since the opening conference in Mexico City sponsored by the United Nations' Decade on Women (1975-85), Western feminists have learned that women from other parts of the world, including the West's own minority populations, have views of their own that require specific attention. These views cannot be assimilated into those of the Western feminisms, because the way a woman looks at her condition in the world will

depend on many factors, including her cultural and economic location. Theoretically, a helpful orientation toward greater acknowledgment of diversity came with the wave of "feminisms of difference" in the 1980s. Compare Olea (1995).

11. I offer a broad characterization of postcolonial feminisms so as to include different kinds of feminist critiques and my own voice in these debates. Racial, ethnic, class, and other differences are often incorporated, along with cultural and gender differences, into postcolonial feminist work. For some differences of opinion on the use of "postcolonial" as a category, see Sagar (1996). I read Anzaldúa's *Borderlands/La Frontera* as postcolonial, though it is not clear she would accept this term, given the Chicana practice of not subsuming this identification under others. But the fit is quite clear: she talks about the land of ancestors that has been taken over by several different countries, as well as the different cultural formations emerging there over time. Moreover, she states, "I grew up between two cultures, the Mexican (with a heavy Indian influence) and the Anglo (as a member of a colonized people in our own territory)" (Anzaldúa 1987, vii).

12. Grewal and Kaplan's *Scattered Hegemonies* (1994) addresses this point, as do Anzaldúa (1987) and Spivak (1993, 77-95).

13. "Being oppressed is the absence of choices" (hooks 1984, 5).

REFERENCES

Anzaldúa, Gloria. 1987. *Borderlands/La frontera: The new mestiza.* San Francisco: Aunt Lute Books.

Beauvoir, Simone de. 1952. *The second sex.* New York: Vintage.

Beverley, John, José Oviedo, and Michael Aronna, eds. 1995. *The postmodernism debate in Latin America.* Durham: Duke University Press.

Bhabha, Homi K. 1994. *The location of culture.* London: Routledge.

Fanon, Frantz. 1963. *Black skins, white masks.* New York: Grove Press.

Fernández Retamar, Roberto. 1989. *Caliban and other essays.* Minneapolis: University of Minnesota Press.

García Canclini, Néstor. 1995. *Hybrid cultures: Strategies for entering and leaving modernity.* Minneapolis: University of Minnesota Press.

Grewal, Inderpal, and Caren Kaplan, eds. 1994. *Scattered hegemonies: Postmodernity and transnational feminist practices.* Minneapolis: University of Minnesota Press.

hooks, bell. 1984. *Feminist theory: From margin to center.* Boston: South End Press.

Irigaray, Luce. 1993. *An ethics of sexual difference.* Ithaca: Cornell University Press.

Kristeva, Julia. 1981. Women's time. *Signs* 7(1): 13-35.

————. 1991. *Strangers to ourselves.* Trans. Leon S. Roudiez. New York: Columbia University Press.

Levinas, Emmanuel. 1979. *Totality and infinity.* Boston: Martinus Nijhoff.

Lyotard, Jean François. 1984. *The postmodern condition: A report on knowledge.* Trans. Geoff Bennington and Brian Massumi. Minneapolis: University of Minnesota Press.

Minh-ha, Trinh T. 1989. *Woman, native, other: Writing postcoloniality and feminism.* Bloomington: Indiana University Press.

Olea, Raquel. 1995. Feminism: modern or postmodern? In *The postmodern debate in Latin America.* See Beverley, John et al. 1995.

Richard, Nelly. 1993. The Latin American problematic of theoretical-cultural transference: Postmodern appropriations and counterappropriations. *South Atlantic Quarterly* 92(3): 453-59.

———. 1996. Feminismo, experiencia y representación. *Revista Iberoamericana*: Special issue on Latin American cultural criticism and literary theory, ed. Mabel Moraña. 62(176-77): 733-44.

Sagar, Aparajita. 1996. Postcolonial studies. In *A dictionary of cultural and critical theory*, ed. Michael Payne. Cambridge, MA: Blackwell.

Spivak, Gayatri Chakravorty. 1990. *The post-colonial critic.* Ed. Sarah Harasym. New York: Routledge.

———. 1993. *Outside the teaching machine.* New York: Routledge.

4

How to Think Globally:
Stretching the Limits of Imagination

LORRAINE CODE

Here I discuss some epistemological questions posed by projects of attempting to think globally, in light of the impossibility of affirming universal sameness. I illustrate one strategy for embarking on such a project, ecologically, in a reading of an essay by Chandra Talpade Mohanty. And I conclude by suggesting that the North/South border between Canada and the U.S.A. generates underacknowledged issues of cultural alterity.

The slogan "think globally, act locally" is inspirational for Western feminists, and challenging in the epistemological questions it poses. It is born of optimism and despair. The extent of optimism's warrant is apparent in the transformative effects of emancipatory projects that fall within the range of responsible local knowledge (with its negotiable limits) and the capacities of practitioners' imaginations to extend it into places less local. Local achievements enhance and refine practice-informing knowledge, strengthen or modify the content of governing conceptions of justice and right, tell optimistically in favor of feminism's global scope. Yet the risk of venturing too far is constant: of entering regions—discursive, geographical, cultural—where theorists and activists know not whereof they speak; where vigilance against epistemic imperialism and renewed colonization is a constant imperative. Thus pessimism is often in order when theorists-activists shift position, attempt to reenact local successes globally, confront the narrowness of their limits, despair about their translatability into other almost-local issues and their effects beyond the limits of locally-knowledgable imaginations. Such ideas infused the "think global, act local" slogan of the 1996 International Interdisciplinary Conference on Women in Adelaide, where the discussions ranged across optimism and despair.

Participants in the symposium "Cultural Relativism and Global Feminism" at the 1997 APA Pacific Division conference were asked in their letters of invitation to address "the apparent dilemma posed by the normative demands of cultural relativism when they clash with *our* firmly held moral belief of what is just and right" (my emphasis); and to propose a new "theoretical model" to counter the culturally imperialist threat implicit in "the global optimizing strategy of the utilitarian approach . . . reinforced by deontic rationalism." This threat takes on a special urgency in women's lives, where appeals to cultural relativism claim local immunity from global criticism, as in warnings to white affluent Western feminists to "back off" from condemning practices that enforce female degradation and exploitation in cultures, at home and abroad, that differ radically from "our own." Female genital mutilation is an obvious—if over-invoked—example of locally entrenched practices that violate (Western) feminist principles, and about which the cliché "one (wo)man's meat is another (wo)man's poison" is hard pressed to retain its political innocence.

In this discussion, I am assuming the urgency of knowing *whose* "firmly held moral belief" is at stake in these debates that permeate liberal political discourses of toleration. But I am not assuming, even tacitly (as the symposium's question appears to), that the goal is to escape cultural relativism, despite its contentious nature. Reading "global optimizing" as a project of achieving maximum (economic-social) homogeneity and uniformly "efficient" material productivity across human and "natural" global resources, I take it to be ineluctably complicit in promoting cultural imperialism, and thus in containing the limits of epistemic imagination within the self-certainties of the affluent world. I sketch a theoretical model for negotiating within the differences that cultural relativism and global feminism variously take as their starting points: an ecological model dependent for its global salience on stretching the limits of imagination(s) toward responsive and responsible local sensitivity, both close to and far from "home."

Addressing epistemological questions along a local-global spectrum raises timeworn questions about relativism versus absolutism. In the heyday of colonial imperialism, the myth prevailed, at least for those at the centers of colonial power—and thus the dominant voices on such issues—that local and global were virtually interchangeable. Knowledge produced and rightness enacted were informed by putatively universal conceptions of truth and justice: the colonial mission was to extend their reach into "unenlightened" regions where their self-evidence would be recognized accordingly. The rise of positivist-empiricist science at the height of colonialism's powers reinforced this pattern. The apparently universal validity of so much of natural science, its capacity to claim global pertinence and thus to override local superstition, coupled with a persistent unity-of-science presumption, fueled a conviction that all local truths—thus not just those of physical science—establish their truthfulness to the extent that they display their salience beyond merely local boundaries. Yet the connection with colonialism merits serious attention. Critics of relativism, both cultural and cognitive, often contend that relativism, too, is a presumption of the supremely privileged who are positioned to believe that they can make up the world at will, bypassing material constraints. But this argument's anti-relativist point is blunted, I believe, by the counterrecognition that it is precisely the supremely privileged who claim to have access to the one true story, presume to speak from nowhere and for everyone, and assume the material detachment that sustains the objectivist illusion in whose name relativism is condemned as irrational. Only they can imagine that "our" firmly held beliefs are direct descendants of Justice and Right.

Prompted by the impossibility of affirming universal sameness even in the name of sisterly solidarity, after the ethnocentrism, androcentrism, classism, Eurocentrism, heterosexism, and other "centrisms" that have shaped Western culture, and by the coercive, reductive effects of the utilitarian-positivistic social science that cooperates in legitimating "global optimizing," I am proposing that responsible global thinking *requires* not just cultural relativism but a *mitigated epistemological relativism* conjoined with a "healthy skepticism."[1] I am working with a deflated conception of relativism remote from the "anything goes" refrain which anti-relativists inveigh against it. It is "mitigated" in its recognition that knowledge-construction is always constrained by the resistance of material and human-social realities to just any old fashioning or making. Yet, borrowing Peter Novick's words, it is relativist in acknowledging "the plurality of criteria of knowledge . . . and deny[ing] the possibility of knowing absolute, objective, universal truth" (1988, 167).[2] Its "healthy skepticism" in this context manifests itself in response to excessive and irresponsible global pretensions, whose excesses have to be communally debated and negotiated with due regard to local specificities and global implications.

Few feminists positioned within the dominant regions of Anglo-American culture would presume, now, to speak for or about women situated elsewhere or otherwise as though they were "just like us," especially as there is no easily delineated "we" or "us" to claim homogeneity. Relativism's opponents have to assume that "we" are identically and, for epistemological purposes, only incidentally constrained and enabled by material-locational circumstances; that "we" all make sense of the world in the same way; that "knowledge" has a univocal, universal meaning.[3] I, however, take seriously Ofelia Schutte's claim that "what we hold to be the *nature of knowledge* is not culture-free but is determined by the methodologies and data legitimated by dominant cultures" (1998, 55 italics added). My purpose is not to enlist her as a participant in a relativist heresy, but to clarify my motivations. With Paul Feyerabend, I find in relativism "a weapon against intellectual tyranny" (1987, 19).

Like most weapons, there are limits to its effectiveness. Consider the law enacted by the Taliban of Afganistan requiring that lower windows of houses be fully screened and upper windows screened up to six feet, lest women be visible to inflame men's passions. A relativism that enjoins perfect tolerance would have no basis for condemnation. Yet I remain unrepentant even in the face of this reminder, not in order to "let a thousand tyrants flourish," but because even if relativism—critical cultural relativism—comes up against its own limits in such circumstances, it is demonstrably preferable to the imperialist alternatives that recognize no limits. Nor is the relativism I endorse a position of perfect tolerance: it is both critical and mitigated. The stark relativist-absolutist dichotomy, with its warnings against the impotence of tolerance or the political quietism of indecidability, is a historically contingent by-product of the objectivism of positivistic scientism. It sets up a conceptual trap whose effects are more rhetorical than praxis-effective, requiring feminists and other postessentialists to engage in ritualized disclaimers that divert attention from the interpretive sophistication that a well-thought-out, locally sensitive critical relativism yields.

My position resonates with the relativism Laurie Shrage endorses in *Moral Dilemmas of Feminism*, which is explicitly interpretive. One of its most active ingredients is a hermeneutic of suspicion wary of universally objective, neutral descriptions and judgments. It works principally with "cross-cultural comparisons" that enable "serious criticism" (Shrage 1994, 26-27). Feminisms at the end of this century have, I think, to operate in this territory between the local and the global (though neither on a middle ground nor in quietism or indifferent tolerance). Anti-relativists exaggerate the "slippery slope" effects of relativistic sympathies, whose logic rarely plummets knowledge-making into the depths of acritical irrationality. Thus I am less interested in resolving the dilemma posed for the APA symposiasts than in seeing how it can guide productive epistemic and moral-political practices that work between the local and global, the absolutely relative and the relatively absolute.

To focus my analysis methodologically and epistemologically, I am going to offer a reading of Chandra Talpade Mohanty's (1997) essay "Women Workers and Capitalist Scripts: Ideologies of Domination, Common Interests, and the Politics of Solidarity." The essay's title signals its multicultural and global engagement. It provides a point of entry into the epistemic demands generated by urgings to think globally, for several reasons: I read it as a piece of naturalistic epistemology of the best kind. I applaud its capacity to stretch the limits of its readers' imaginations *not* by homogenizing or aggregating the strange and the familiar, but by drawing cautiously circumscribed global conclusions out of sensitive local mappings in critical, cross-cultural comparisons. Mohanty sets out an impressive range of evidence that demonstrates the oppressive effects of global optimizing, especially for women's work. And I read her essay as offering a clear indication of how to proceed in developing an ecologically-modeled theoretical apparatus such as I am working to elaborate. I have chosen neither to engage in a critique of the detail of her analysis here, nor to interrogate its theoretical assumptions, but to read it specifically for its pertinence to developing methodological strategies for ecologically-framed global thinking.

In an article that addresses some feminist implications of Quinean and post-Quinean naturalized epistemology (Code 1996), I maintain that the laboratory is neither the only nor the best place for epistemologists to study "natural" human knowing in order to elaborate epistemologies that maintain clearer continuity with cognitive experiences—"natural knowings"—than orthodox *a priori*-normative epistemologies do. I advocate turning attention to how knowledge is made and circulated in situations with a greater claim to the elusive label "natural." My interests are in ways of gathering empirical evidence and in assumptions about the scope of evidence as it plays into regulative theories. My contention, briefly, is that evidence gathered from more mundane sites of knowledge production can afford better, if messier, starting points for naturalistic inquiry than much of laboratory evidence, for it translates more readily into settings where knowing matters in people's lives and the politics of knowledge are enacted. Yet this more everyday evidence does not yield "merely descriptive" conclusions, as anti-naturalists (Kim 1994) are wont to charge. Descriptions, mappings, and judgments that separate evidence from extraneous "noise" are always value-saturated, products of some one's or some group's location and choice; hence always contestable. Good descriptions are not self-announcing, nor are they final; for sedimented, taken-for-granted, common sense descriptions inform everyday and professional conceptions about how the world is, and how "we" may know it.[4] If orthodox epistemology has been working with misdescriptions of "natural" knowledge and epistemic subjectivity—as I think it has—then better descriptions are vital. They are the catalysts of good critique, the stuff of which normative principles are crafted, and the bases of policy and action.

I take the empirically informed, interpretively analyzed examples in Mohanty's essay as exemplary of local naturalistic inquiry that can enable global knowings within which (locally discerned) cultural relativism is indeed preserved, yet global strategies suggest themselves. Women's work, especially Third World women's work, is her focus. She maps ideologies and practices across four locations where women, at home or "abroad," are engaged in productive labor. Her purpose is to show how their work and their agency as laborers are represented, in each locale, within a conceptual frame that also exposes the sedimented conceptions of "the natural" that naturalize social and domestic divisions of labor in situations as diverse as the factories in the Silicon Valley, the lacemaking "homework" in Narsapur, and the situations of female migrant workers in Britain.

I am extracting an epistemological position that I find implicit in Mohanty's argument as an example, in practice, of naturalistic epistemology. It shows how received conceptions of knowledge are embedded in and partially constitutive of the "natural history of human beings"; it "exposes the uneven part played by [several] different social groups" in shaping and sustaining a highly gendered social-political economy; it reveals "the ideological character of [the] value-systems" that underwrite this economy from behind a posture of objectivity and universal validity.[5] Mohanty adduces sensitively-gathered evidence to show what these workers can and do know about themselves and about work, family, the social order, masculinity, and femininity within a hegemonic social imaginary that limits their possibilities of imagining beyond it. She proposes links, draws points of commonality out of how "the logic of capitalism in the contemporary global arena" (1997, 28) exploits both third- and first-world women. Yet she insists that the only way to understand local specificities is to "pay attention to the commonalities of their/our common *and* different histories" (28). Her work explicitly opposes "ahistorical notions of the common experience, exploitation, or strength of third-world women or between third- and first-world women, which serve to naturalize normative Western feminist categories of self and other" (28). She thus works deftly within cultural relativism and global feminism, giving neither hegemonic discursive power, yet demonstrating how effectively a relativism sensitive to across-the-board differences can map disparate knowings to establish links, affinities, and generalities, never absolute but always negotiable.

The knowings that circulate in this knowledge-gleaning process open out into informed comparison and critique, both epistemological and moral-political, across these links that are also neither assimilative nor divisive. Mohanty shows how, with local-situational variations, "women are . . . defined in relation to men and conjugal marriage," and work is "grounded in sexual identity, in concrete definitions of femininity, masculinity, and heterosexuality" (12). She produces compelling evidence to show that, again diversely, "women's bodies and labor are used to consolidate global dreams, desires, and ideologies of success and the good life" (10). Her mappings "delineate the interconnections between gender, race, and ethnicity, and the ideologies of work which locate women in particular exploitative contexts" (11). She exposes the conceptual frames that make it "possible to understand the *systematic* invisibility" of homework (21); and reports that "women internalize . . . the identities that define . . . them as nonworkers" (14). The *contingency*, variability, and local expediency of these "naturalized" definitions of work and workers emerge from Mohanty's analysis, together with traces of the complex ideological apparatus enlisted to sustain the exploitative structures that thrive on them.

But the stories convey as much optimism as despair. Mohanty affirms that "the predicament of poor working women and their experiences of survival and resistance in the creation of new organizational forms to earn a living and improve their daily lives . . . offers new possibilities for struggle and action" (23). And her mappings point toward a "geographically anchored" comparative methodology that can, she believes, show that "the local and the global are indeed connected through parallel, contradictory, and sometimes converging relations . . . which position women in different and similar locations as workers" (6). These analogies and disanalogies become the intersecting lines of critical evaluations of knowledge-in-circulation that abandon deductivism for an inductive, respectful relativism sensitive to particularities, even as they eschew reductivism to advocate a plurality of analyses and methods.

Thus Mohanty's essay also contributes to a larger theoretical project of showing that the relativism versus absolutism dichotomy is more forced than "natural" as a regulative epistemological frame. She shows by counterexample why working within its constraints thwarts reasonable deliberation about "what is just and right," and why choosing either "side" initiates a descent into injustice. Moreover, her studies expose global optimizing as one of the least viable routes toward justice and right precisely because of its reductivism, which requires no movement beyond the limits of imaginations rooted in the imperialism of illusory self-sameness. These are the essay's most powerful critical moments.

In the essay's creative dimension, these mappings are analogous to the bioregional narratives integral to the revisionary metaphorics of an *ecologically modeled* epistemology. Such an epistemology, which I am currently developing, will eschew the top-down rhetoric of mastery and domination that holds the relativism-absolutism dichotomy in place as a master censor: the rhetoric that sustains the dream (read: the nightmare) of global optimizing. Bioregional narratives play a constitutive part in ecological thinking for, in Jim Cheney's words, they are "grounded in geography rather than in a linear, essentialized narrative self" (1989, 126). They map local ecological relations by exposing the conditions, both physical and discursive, that sustain and/or threaten human lives and agency within the specificities of habitats, institutions, regions, environments, societies, and their interrelations separately traced and charted. Their strength is in the detail of their contextual sensitivity—their capacity to display the genealogical (power-focused) conditions of local knowledge-making and -circulating—and to expose analogous conditions across contiguous and more distant regions. Their dangers are in the pull of parochialism that they, like all local discourses, risk generating: the romanticism and aesthetic narcissism they risk endorsing. Mohanty's narratives evade these dangers, thus pointing to the promise of ecological thinking.

Concentrating on the detail of subjectivities, ideologies, practices, values, and on the links and breaks that separate and connect them, ecological thinking departs from the individualistic solipsism that drives the epistemologies and moralities of the philosophical mainstream. Whereas assumptions of homogenous sameness sanction the belief I mention above, that every locality can function as a stand-in for the global, ecological thinking is respectful of boundaries, yet committed to boundary-crossing in the interests of understanding the links, acknowledging the ruptures, translating responsibly across local differences to preserve and extend meanings at the same time.

In short, Mohanty's studies of women's work offer her readers ways of imagining, after all, how to think and act both locally and globally. And despite the pessimism that pervades my discussion here, I intend it, too, as a plea for the necessity of global thinking. Local-global comparisons are crucial contributors to the reflexivity that characterizes late twentieth-century thought. They highlight the contingency, the strangeness, of the familiar and local, even as they open out hitherto unthought possibilities rendered invisible by sedimented local assumptions and practices. Even the most minute and detailed concentration on the local risks losing sight of how its oppressive effects are often, in fact, global in the derivation of their power to exploit. Thus thinking globally is essential for understanding how power and privilege are maintained by corporations, systems, operations, and agendas that are by no means purely local. Jean Grimshaw reminds us of the "profound effects on women's lives" of "multinational corporations [which] are usually extremely remote from everyday experience" (1986, 102). Those effects have to be traced and interrogated in their widely diverse regional enactments.

Responsible bio-regional narratives are multistranded and selfcritical; none of them can stand as definitive tellings. Hence my focus on Mohanty's analysis here offers only a sketch of how such narratives might work. Constructed from the findings of many projects, they are ongoing, open to continuous revaluation, prepared to address the revisions that revealed incoherences require. Nor are final synthesis or ultimate convergence the aim, but preparations of the ground for better narratives that can be taken back to the site, redone if necessary, yet without paralyzing action in the meantime. Using such narratives as working hypotheses can make their effectiveness and inadequacies visible. All of this may sound like a tall order; but the experimental, evidence-responsive character of such "thoughtful practice" (Heldke 1992) attests to its possibility.[6]

Mohanty's global feminism extends beyond theorizing differences between-among-within "women" and operates differently, also, from a "politics of difference" in its emphasis on values, power, and meanings within hierarchically ordered sites of the production of worker and/or consumer subjectivities. Following Barnet and Cavanagh, she maps four intersecting "webs" of the global arena: the Global Cultural Bazaar, the Global Shopping Mall, the Global Workplace, and the Global Financial Network (1997, 10). In each, ideologies of masculinity, femininity, and sexuality perpetuate the psychic and social disenfranchisement of women. These proto-ecological mappings trace a finite number of threads across practices and ideologies to expose a network of links and breaks that is both thematically of a piece and yet—possibly—elastic enough in its explanatory power to stretch beyond the limits of its initially situated imaginings.

The ecologically modeled epistemology I envisage will work analogously: it cannot amount simply to a random, indiscriminate mapping that aims to record all of the knowings in a specific locale. Thus it is not before-the-fact neutral about what it is looking for: its hypotheses and the framings of its projects—its contexts of discovery and justification—are equally open to scrutiny. Whereas Mohanty maps women's work, labor-market exploitation, and poverty, another mapping would start from a different place. But such an acknowledgment invites critique only from theorists who believe that there can be agenda-free inquiry. In this revisioned project, agenda-free evidence-collection and interpretation are not the aim. Yet recognizing that an investigation is agenda-driven carries an imperative for vigilance against allowing that scheme to solidify, form rigid boundaries, so that it constrains and limits inquiry as much as it enables it. One of the methodological challenges is to keep inquiries both "on track" and open to surprises that could challenge or dislodge the agenda.

What I like about Mohanty's agenda is the manner of inquiry, the positioning of the inquirer's voice, how it lets the evidence speak—though neither naively nor without contest, nor by forcing it into ready-made boxes. It enjoins responsible listening, suggests connections and stops short of others, requires vigilance against pushing the limits even of imaginative knowing too far. These may seem like commonsensical admonitions. But such vigilant listening has not characterized utilitarian strategies of global optimizing, which manifest scant concern for ecological effects, whether local or global, literal or metaphorical. Such effects weave through the model I am developing: they argue forcibly against cultural imperialism.

And what do these thoughts enable me or "us" to say about activities, such as those of the Taliban, that violently disrupt this benign picture? It is hard to believe that "we" and "they" could enter a Western-orchestrated dialogue to generate the cross-boundary understandings that thinking globally requires. Why would they want to justify their actions to us? But the boundary is less rigid than it appears. There are striking continuities between the sexualization of women—"the hysterization of women's bodies" (Foucault 1978, 104)—that fuels the Taliban's prohibitions, and the global sexualizing of women's lives and labors that Mohanty details.[7] Yet does the hesitation she maintains—and I applaud—about proclaiming universal moral-political truths and a rigoristic moral stance, even through her documentation of invisible female labor and dire poverty, reach its limits with reference to such extremists? The answer must be yes, and no. Yes, because of the cruelty of their prohibitions, the horrors of their stonings to death, the impossibility even of imagining strategies of resistance such as Mohanty describes in other localities. No, because of continuities feminist and postcolonial theorists know too well, not just in distant parts of the globe but in localities too local to imagine with comfort. And no, because there are global mechanisms, however limited their power: organizations that bring pressure—often successfully—and that have to be kept in place and thinking globally, however optimistically or despairingly "we" may view their effectiveness. I remain caught, then, in the dilemma that framed the symposium: convinced that the relativism-or-absolutism dichotomy merely blocks productive debate. Yet also convinced, as Mohanty seems to be, that even where optimism is severely tested, immobilized despair cannot be a response to the "politics of hope and solidarity" (1997, 29) that she discerns in the midst of it.

POSTSCRIPT:

I return to the "think globally" slogan to conclude with a note about the location of *this* inquirer's voice—*my* voice. Writing as an anglophone Canadian for a U. S. philosophy conference and journal, hence as a member of a culture and society that often, to the world outside North America, appears indistinguishable from the United States of America, I find myself uneasily positioned, locally, on the "other" side of a different North-South border from the one that Ofelia Schutte (1998) refers to. I speak the language of the white, educated United States of America so well that I pass, almost always, as a native speaker (as long as I don't say "out" or "about"). Precisely because of my almost-complete fluency in the language, the "alterity" that inhibits my speaking about global feminism is difficult to articulate; and this cultural and linguistic fluency makes mentioning the differences, *making* an issue of them, sound like mere affectation. Yet it is not, I think, surprising that this sense of alterity obtrudes insistently in the discourses of global feminism, which have for me a foreign flavor, the flavor of a language that embeds a positional certainty in which I cannot participate. The incongruities are imperceptible on the surface, so resistant even to naming as "cross-cultural" that the conceptual apparatus for engaging with them is elusive. They do not make the striking difference in sustaining inequities and oppressions that differences of color, race, class, sexuality, age, and ability generate; in many circumstances they make no significant difference at all. Thus again, calling attention to them invites an impatient insistence that the similarities are so overwhelming as to erase the differences; that casting them as "cross-cultural" is equally excessive. Often they are mere variations in cultural *timbre*, inflection, intonation; at other times they invoke deep divisions in the histories that have made each of these two nations what they are, both locally and globally.

The apparent mutual transparency of most Canadian-U. S. feminist conversations creates the impression that there are no such divisions, that "we" all face the same issues and hold firmly to the same moral beliefs. Yet phenomenologically, matters are not so straightforward. It is not, I think, insignificant that I cannot, either in discomfort or in complacency, identify myself as part of a culture and a nation that counts as a global player. I do not live and think within a social imaginary for which there is no doubt, even at an unconscious level, that the events of which I am part simply by virtue of my place in that society have global import. Nor is Canada a global power, even though its membership in NAFTA confers a more-nearly global status and voice than sits easily with many Canadians; and though it increasingly takes up "neutral" positions in global events, in its role as a UN peacekeeper.[8] Thus my Canadian-ness, which is functionally so beside the point that it is imperceptible in most feminist debates, takes on a peculiar insistence in relation to global feminism. My thinking globally has to be more muted, less plainly continuous with my life as a citizen of a country that, globally, plays a minor and less influential part than the United States of America, whose status as a global power no one would question, even though by no means all of its citizens partake equally of that status.

Canada is not a globally dominant culture in the same way or to the same degree as the United States; nor are Canadian-U.S. relations symmetrical, as is clear from the impossibility of imagining a simple reversal of their dominant-subordinate positionings. On questions such as these, then, it is not a matter of course for a Canadian to believe that she needs to be "knowledgeable in the language and epistemic maneuvers" (Schutte 1998, 60) of a dominant culture whose epistemic standpoint tacitly embeds the self-knowledge of a global power. Thus thinking globally, for me, is a more tentative project than it seems to be for many affluent, educated, white Americans: a matter only of partial participation and uncertain voice.

I address this incongruence neither to identify it as a shortcoming nor to claim it as a virtue of being-Canadian, but to retain a place for the by-no-means-new thought that the very idea of global feminism must be differently inflected when the locality (in this instance, Canada) from which that idea is thought can be cast as an invisible colony of the new colonial power; when that locality risks disappearing into the global optimizing that permeates the agenda of North America's dominant culture. How do these thoughts recon-figure the imperatives to think globally, act locally? What renewed stretching of the limits of imagination do they require? These are the questions that this attempt to think through these issues leaves me to investigate further.

NOTES

1. For a fuller discussion see my "Must a Feminist Be a Relativist After All?" in Code 1995.

2. Thanks to a *Hypatia* reader for reminding me of this book's pertinence.

3. Himani Bannerji (1995, 54, 57-8) details an egregious example of imperialist anti-relativism: in writing his *History of British India*, James Mill eschewed "archival or empirical research, including the knowledge of local classical or vernacular languages and texts." He discounted the Orientalists' firsthand acquaintance with India, believing that "they lacked the necessary detachment . . . for a judge-historian, and he found himself eminently suitable for this task on the very ground of lack of knowledge of languages and lack of direct connections with or experiences of India."

4. For Hilary Kornblith (1990), naturalism's principal questions are: "What is the world that we may know it? And what are we that we may know the world?" He poses the questions differently in the Introduction to Kornblith (1994, 1): "1. How ought we to arrive at our beliefs? 2. How do we arrive at our beliefs? 3. Are the processes by which we do arrive at our beliefs the ones by which we ought to arrive at our beliefs?" I opt for the 1990 version for its more secular tone.

5. The phrases in quotation marks come from a passage I cite more fully in Code (1996) from Sabina Lovibond (1989, 12-13).

6. Lisa Heldke uses this phrase to characterize the epistemic practices central to the philosophy of John Dewey.

7. Michel Foucault claims that "the feminine body was analyzed—qualified and disqualified—as being thoroughly saturated with sexuality . . ." (1978, 104).

8. Thanks for this reminder to an anonymous referee for *Hypatia*.

REFERENCES

Bannerji, Himani. 1995. Beyond the ruling category to what actually happens: Notes on James Mill's historiography in *The History of British India*. In *Knowledge, experience, and ruling relations*, ed. Marie Campbell and Ann Manicom. Toronto: University of Toronto Press.

Cheney, Jim. 1989. Postmodern environmental ethics: Ethics as bioregional narrative. *Environmental Ethics* 11(2): 117-34.

Code, Lorraine. 1995. *Rhetorical spaces: Essays on (gendered) locations*. New York: Routledge.

———. 1996. What is natural about epistemology naturalized? *American Philosophical Quarterly* 33(1): 1-22.

Feyerabend, Paul. 1987. Notes on Relativism. In *Farewell to reason*. London: Verso.

Foucault, Michel. 1978. *The history of sexuality*, vol. 1. Trans. Robert Hurley. New York: Pantheon.

Grimshaw, Jean. 1986. *Philosophy and feminist thinking*. Minneapolis: University of Minnesota Press.

Heldke, Lisa. 1992. Foodmaking as a thoughtful practice. In *Cooking, eating, thinking: Transformative philosophies of food*, ed. Deane W. Curtin and Lisa M. Heldke. Bloomington: Indiana University Press.

Kim, Jaegwon. 1994. What is "naturalized epistemology"? In *Naturalizing epistemology*, ed. Hilary Kornblith. Cambridge: MIT Press.

Kornblith, Hilary. 1990. The naturalistic project in epistemology. Paper presented to the American Philosophical Association Pacific Division conference, March 1990.

———. ed. 1994. *Naturalizing epistemology*. Cambridge: MIT Press.

Lovibond, Sabina. 1989. Feminism and postmodernism. *New Left Review* 178: 5-28.

Mohanty, Chandra Talpade. 1997. Women workers and capitalist scripts: Ideologies of domination, common interests, and the politics of solidarity. In *Feminist genealogies, colonial legacies, democratic futures*, ed. M. Jacqui Alexander and Chandra Talpade Mohanty. New York: Routledge.

Novick, Peter. 1988. *That noble dream: The "objectivity" question and the American historical profession*. Cambridge: Cambridge University Press.

Schutte, Ofelia. 1998. Cultural alterity: Cross-cultural communication and feminist thought in North-South contexts. *Hypatia* 13(2): 53-72.

Shrage, Laurie. 1994. *Moral dilemmas of feminism: Prostitution, adultery, and abortion*. New York: Routledge.

5

Essence of Culture and a Sense of History: A Feminist Critique of Cultural Essentialism

UMA NARAYAN

Drawing parallels between gender essentialism and cultural essentialism, I point to some common features of essentialist pictures of culture. I argue that cultural essentialism is detrimental to feminist agendas and suggest strategies for its avoidance. Contending that some forms of cultural relativism buy into essentialist notions of culture, I argue that postcolonial feminists need to be cautious about essentialist contrasts between "Western" and "Third World" cultures.

In recent decades, feminists have stressed the need to think about issues of gender in conjunction with, and not in isolation from, issues of class, race, ethnicity, and sexual orientation, and have forcefully illustrated that differences among women must be understood and theorized in order to avoid essentialist generalizations about "women's problems" (Anzaldúa 1987; hooks 1981; Lugones and Spelman 1983). The feminist critique of gender essentialism does not merely charge that essentialist claims about "women" are over-generalizations, but points out that these generalizations are hegemonic in that they represent the problems of privileged women (most often white, Western, middle-class, heterosexual women) as paradigmatic "women's issues."

Such essentialist generalizations result in theoretical perspectives and political agendas that efface the problems, perspectives, and political concerns of many women who are marginalized in terms of their class, race, ethnicity, and sexual orientation. For instance, analyses that trace women's subordination to their confinement to domestic roles and the private sphere can constitute problematic essentialist generalizations if they ignore that the links between femininity and the private sphere are not trans-historical but have arisen in particular historical contexts. Thus, while the ideology of domesticity may have immured many middle-class women in the home, it also sanctioned the economic exploitation of women slaves and working-class women, whose most pressing problems did not result from their confinement to the private sphere.

In fora committed to the development of transnational and global feminist perspectives, feminists have often specifically reiterated the need to take account of national and cultural differences among women, in order to avoid essentializing analyses that pay inadequate attention to the concerns of women in Third World contexts. I am sympathetic to such feminist criticisms of gender essentialism and to the claim that feminist theories and political agendas need to be responsive to the diversity of women's lives, both within and across national contexts. However, I believe that this feminist injunction to attend to "differences among women" sometimes takes questionable forms. I will argue that feminist efforts to avoid gender essentialism sometimes result in pictures of cultural differences among women that constitute what I shall call "cultural essentialism." In the first section of this paper, I will describe some problematic similarities between "gender essentialism" and "cultural essentialism" and will try to uncover some reasons why analyses that try to avoid "gender essentialism" might end up subscribing to "cultural essentialism." In the second section, I will describe some important features of essentialist pictures of "cultures" and suggest some moves that facilitate feminist challenges to such pictures. In the third section, I will critically engage versions of cultural essentialism that arise from progressive segments of the political spectrum. In the fourth and final section, I will explore the implications of my critique of cultural essentialism for issues of cultural relativism. Throughout the essay, my goal is to argue that essentialist notions of "culture" pose particular problems for Third World feminist agendas.

GENDER ESSENTIALISM AND CULTURAL ESSENTIALISM

One important instance in which the injunction to attend to differences among women can lead to problems is when this project is carried out in a manner that avoids essentialism about women by replicating essentialist notions of "cultural differences" between "Western" and "Non-western" cultures. The project of attending to differences among women across a variety of national and cultural contexts then becomes a project that endorses and replicates problematic and colonialist assumptions about the cultural differences between "Western culture" and "Non-western cultures" and the women who inhabit them. Seemingly *universal* essentialist generalizations about "all women" are replaced by *culture-specific* essentialist generalizations that depend on totalizing categories such as "Western culture," "Non-western cultures," "Western women," "Third World women," and so forth.

Although often motivated by the injunction to take differences among women seriously, such moves fracture the universalist category "Woman" only slightly, because culture-specific essentialist generalizations differ from universalistic essentialist generalizations only in degree or scope, and not in kind. The resulting portraits of "Western women," "Third World women," "African women," "Indian women," "Muslim women," or the like, as well as the pictures of the "cultures" that are attributed to these various groups of women, often remain fundamentally essentialist. They depict as homogenous groups of heterogeneous people whose values, interests, ways of life, and moral and political commitments are internally plural and divergent. Numerous examples of such generalizations are criticized by Chandra Mohanty, who points out that each of the texts she analyzes

> assumes "women" have a coherent group identity within the different cultures discussed, prior to their entry into social relations. Thus, Omvedt can talk about "Indian women" while referring to a particular group of women in the State of Maharashtra, Cutrufelli about "women of Africa," and Minces about "Arab women," as if these groups of women have some sort of obvious cultural coherence. (Mohanty 1991, 70)

There are a number of similarities between gender essentialism and cultural essentialism. While gender essentialism often proceeds to assume and construct sharp binaries about the qualities, abilities, or locations of "men" and "women," cultural essentialism assumes and constructs sharp binaries between "Western culture" and "Non-western cultures" or between "Western culture" and particular "Other" cultures. In both cases, the discursive reiteration of such "essential differences" operates in a manner that helps construct the senses of gender identity and of cultural identity that shape the self-understandings and subjectivities of different groups of people who inhabit these discursive contexts. With both gender essentialism and cultural essentialism, discourses about "difference" often operate to conceal their role in the production and reproduction of such "differences," presenting these differences as something pre-given and prediscursively "real" that the discourses of difference merely describe rather than help construct and perpetuate.

While gender essentialism often conflates socially dominant norms of femininity with the problems, interests and locations of actual particular women, cultural essentialism often conflates socially dominant cultural norms with the actual values and practices of a culture. While gender essentialism often equates the problems, interests and locations of some socially dominant groups of men and women with those of "all men" and "all women," cultural essentialism often equates the values, worldviews, and practices of some socially dominant groups with those of "all members of the culture." For instance, Mary Daly's chapter on "Indian Suttee" (1978) reproduces an essentialist picture of "Indian culture" both by ignoring that *sati* was not a practice ever engaged in by "All Indians" and by effacing the history of criticisms and challenges posed to this practice by various groups of Indians (Narayan, 1997).

Given the similarities between cultural essentialism and gender essentialism, it is interesting to encounter culturally essentialist generalizations being generated as a result of self-conscious feminist attempts to avoid gender essentialism, something that happens not infrequently in classrooms and conferences, as well as in academic texts. Why is it that attempts to avoid gender essentialism sometimes generate rather than deter cultural essentialism? I believe that part of the explanation lies in the prevalence of an incomplete understanding of the relationship between "gender essentialism" and "cultural imperialism." The gender essentialism perpetuated by relatively privileged subjects, including Western feminists, is understood to be a form of "cultural imperialism," whereby privileged subjects tend to construct their "cultural Others" in their own image, taking their particular locations and problems to be those of "All Women." This account ignores the degree to which cultural imperialism often proceeds by means of an "insistence on Difference," by a projection of Imaginary "differences" that constitute one's Others as Other, rather than via an "insistence on Sameness." Failing to see that "cultural imperialism" can involve both sorts of problems, attempts to avoid the Scylla of "Sameness" often result in moves that leave one foundering on the Charybdis of "Difference."

Reducing "cultural imperialism" to the problem of "the imposition of Sameness" conceals the importance of the role that sharply-contrasting essentialist pictures of "cultural differences" between "Western culture" and its various "Others" played during colonial times, both in various justifications for colonial rule and in the scripts of various nationalist movements that challenged and sought to overthrow colonialism, pictures that resurface in postcolonial attempts at engaging with issues of cultural difference. A postcolonial feminist perspective that strives to be attentive to differences among women without replicating such essentialist notions of cultural differences needs to acknowledge the degree to which the colonial encounter depended on an "insistence on Difference"; on sharp, virtually absolute, contrasts between "Western culture" and "Other cultures." After all, Kipling's lines "Oh, East is East and West is West and never the twain shall meet" (Kipling 1944, 233) were written at a historical moment when East and West were engaged in a seriously protracted encounter.

This frequently reiterated contrast between "Western" and "Non-western" cultures was a politically motivated colonial construction. The self-proclaimed "superiority" of "Western culture" functioned as the rationale and mandate for colonialism. The colonial self-portrait of "Western culture" had, however, only a faint resemblance to the moral, political, and cultural values that *actually pervaded* life in Western societies. Thus liberty and equality could be represented as paradigmatic "Western values," hallmarks of its civilizational superiority, at the very moment when Western nations were engaged in slavery, colonization, expropriation, and the denial of liberty and equality not only to the colonized but to large segments of Western subjects, including women. Profound *similarities* between Western culture and many of its Others, such as hierarchical social systems, huge economic disparities between members, and the mistreatment and inequality of women, were systematically ignored in this construction of "Western culture."

The colonial picture of the sharp contrasts between "Western culture" and its Others also resulted in seriously distorted representations of various "colonized cultures," often as a result of the prejudiced and ideologically motivated stereotypes held by Western colonizers but *also* as a result of anti-colonial nationalist movements embracing and trying to revalue the imputed facets of their own "culture" embedded in these stereotypes. Thus, while the British imputed "spiritualism" to Indian culture to suggest lack of readiness for the this-worldly project of self-rule, many Indian nationalists embraced this definition in order to make the anticolonialist and national-ist argument that "our culture" was both distinctive from and superior to "Western culture." As a result of this colonial process, sharply contrastive essentialist pictures of "Western culture" and of various colonized "national cultures" were reiterated by both colonizers and the colonized, both of whom failed to register the degree to which their very constitution as "Western" or "Non-western" subjects resulted from these putative con-trasts between "cultures."

Given that many Third World countries are still subject to economic domination and political intrusion and control by Western powers in postcolonial times, political resistance to such domination and intrusion from a variety of points in the political spectrum is often articulated in terms that replicate problematically essentialist notions of "Western culture" and partic-ular "Third World cultures." Both Western and Third World feminists who often have legitimate worries about Western imperialism and valid concerns that feminist agendas pay attention to differences among women sometimes unfortunately tend to articulate these concerns in ways that replicate rather than challenge these essentialist notions of "Western culture" and "Third World cultures."

While culturally essentialist feminist representations of "Third World cultures" sometimes depict the practices and values of *privileged* groups as those of the "culture as a whole" (as Daly does in her discussion of *sati*), equally essentialist representations are produced when the "Representative Third World Woman" is modeled on *marginalized and underprivileged* Third World women. The latter sort of representation effaces Third World heterogeneity as effectively as the former, and bears the marks of a curious asymmetry, in that the most underprivileged of Western women are seldom cast as "Representa-tive of Western Culture." Chandra Mohanty accounts for this asymmetry

when she points to how several Western feminist texts work to produce the
image of an "average third world woman."

> This average third world woman leads an essentially truncated
> life based on her feminine gender (read: sexually constrained)
> and her being "third world" (read: ignorant, poor, uneducated,
> tradition-bound, domestic, family-oriented, victimized, etc.).
> This, I suggest, is in contrast to the (implicit) self-representa-
> tion of Western women as educated, as modern, as having
> control over their own bodies and sexualities, and the freedom
> to make their own decisions. (Mohanty 1991, 56)

Cultural essentialism often poses a pressing problem for feminist agendas in
Third World contexts, given that essentialist constructions of particular Third
World "cultures" often play a powerful ongoing role in political movements
that are inimical to women's interests in various parts of the Third World.
These essentialist portraits of culture often depict culturally dominant norms
of femininity, and practices that adversely affect women, as central components of "cultural identity." They often equate women's conformity to the
status quo with "the preservation of culture" and cast feminist challenges to
norms and practices affecting women as "cultural betrayals." In such essentialist constructions of culture, norms and practices affecting the social status and
roles of women are often represented as of central import to the task of
"resisting westernization" and "preserving national culture," reducing Third
World feminist contestations of local norms and practices pertaining to women
as "betrayals of Nation and Culture." When essentialist definitions of Third
World cultures are cloaked in the virtuous mantle of resistance to Western
cultural imperialism, Third World feminists and others who contest prevailing
norms and practices are discursively set up in the roles of "cultural traitors" and
"stooges of Western imperialism." In addition, essentialist pictures of "national
culture and traditions" often operate to justify the exploitation, domination,
and marginalization of religious and ethnic minorities, and members of socially
subordinate castes and the poor; and they are used to dismiss a variety of
political demands for justice, equality, rights, or democracy as symptoms of the
"cultural corruption" wrought by "Western ideas" (Mayer 1995, Howard
1993). These moves are often startlingly exemplified in the political rhetoric
and maneuvers of many Third World fundamentalist and conservative political movements.

Given that essentialist definitions of culture are often deployed in ways
that are detrimental to the interests of many members of the national
community, including various groups of women, I would argue that feminists have a serious stake in challenging such definitions. Viable postcolonial feminist perspectives need to engage in rethinking the prevailing portraits
of "Western culture" and of different Third World cultures, rather than assist-

ing in their replication and reification by conflating political resistance to Western domination and intrusion with essentialist notions of "cultural difference" and "cultural preservation."

In the previous section, I attempted to call attention to similarities between cultural essentialism and gender essentialism, and to analyze why some feminist attempts to avoid gender essentialism result in replicating cultural essentialism. I have also argued that essentialist notions of culture pose particular dangers for Third World feminist agendas. In this section, I shall focus on Third World contexts and present some of the "moves" that are predominantly (but not exclusively) deployed by fundamentalists to replicate essentialist representations of culture that are detrimental to the interests of women. I shall also delineate some "counter-moves" that might facilitate Third World feminist challenges to such essentialist pictures of culture. In so doing, I hope to point to anti-essentialist ways of thinking about "cultural differences" that would, I believe, better serve the interests of a progressive postcolonial feminist perspective.

A useful general strategy for resisting cultural essentialism is the cultivation of a critical stance that "restores history and politics" to prevailing ahistorical pictures of "culture." Essentialist pictures of culture represent "cultures" as if they were natural givens, entities that existed neatly distinct and separate in the world, entirely independent of our projects of distinguishing between them. This picture tends to erase the reality that the "boundaries" between "cultures" are human constructs, underdetermined by existing variations in worldviews and ways of life; representations that are embedded in and deployed for a variety of political ends. Essentialist representations of culture eclipse the reality that the labels or designations that are currently used to demarcate or individuate particular "cultures" themselves have a historical provenance, and that what they individuate or pick out as "one culture" often changes over time.

Antiessentialist feminists can counter this static picture of culture by insisting on a historical understanding of the contexts in which what are currently taken to be "particular cultures" came to be seen and defined as such. For example, while a prevailing picture of "Western culture" has its beginning in ancient Greece and perhaps culminating in the contemporary United States, a historical perspective would register that the ancient Greeks did not define themselves as part of "Western culture," an appellation that seems to have arisen only with the advent of European colonialism, and that "American culture" was initially as likely to be distinguished from "European culture" as assimilated to it qua "Western culture." The *Shorter Oxford English Dictionary* indicates that the term *Western* as used to refer to Europe in distinction to the

"Eastern" or "Oriental," begins around 1600, a testimony to its colonial origins. An antiessentialist perspective would also realize that many of the texts, artifacts, and practices ranging from ancient to modern times that are classified today as parts of "Indian culture" are "held together" by a label whose historical vintage is the British colonial period. This label is connected to the historical unification of an assortment of political territories into "British India," a union that enabled the nationalist challenge to colonialism to emerge as "Indian" and to stake its claim to self-government on the basis of a "national culture" (Narayan, 1995). Thus, an antiessentialist understanding of culture should emphasize that the labels that "pick out" particular "cultures" are not simple descriptions we employ to single out already distinct entities. Rather, they are fairly arbitrary and shifting designations, connected to various political projects that had different reasons for insisting upon the distinctiveness of one culture from another. Cultures are not pre-discursively individuated entities to which "names" are then bestowed as simple "labels," but entities whose individuation depends on complex discursive processes linked to political agendas.

Moreover, this historical sensibility also needs to be attentive to the historical and political processes by which particular values and practices have come to be imputed as *central* or *definitive* of a particular "culture." The "individuation" of a culture often proceeds precisely by casting certain values and practices as "constitutive and central elements" of the culture in order to distinguish it from "other cultures." Instead of seeing the centrality of particular values, traditions, or practices to any particular culture as *given*, we need to trace the historical and political processes by which these values, traditions, or practices have *come to be deemed* central constitutive components of a particular culture.

The feminist usefulness of both these moves is best illustrated by a concrete example. I will focus on the practice of *sati* (suttee), the immolation of widows on the funeral pyres of their husbands, which was constructed as a central component of "Indian culture" in colonial times, and is deployed in the political rhetoric of contemporary Hindu fundamentalists as an icon of the "Good Indian Woman," even as widow immolation has all but disappeared as a practice. An important question that feminists need to ask about *sati* is how and why this particular practice which is not engaged in by the vast majority of Hindu communities let alone all Indian ones, and which was the exceptional rather than routine fate of widows even in the few communities that practiced it, came to be regarded as a "Central Indian Tradition." The answer lies in complex nineteenth-century debates on the practice between British colonials and Indian elites that constituted *sati* as a "central and authentic Indian tradition," a process interestingly described in Lata Mani's "Contentious Traditions: The Debate on SATI in Colonial India" (1987). As a result of this debate, *sati* came to acquire, for both British and Indians, for its

supporters as well as opponents on both sides, an "emblematic status"—
becoming a larger-than-life symbol of "Indian Culture" in a way that *radically
transcended* the reality of its limited practice. Even for many Indian reformers
opposed to the actual practice, *sati* became a lofty symbol of "ideal Indian
womanhood," indicating a feminine nobility and devotion to family deemed
uncharacteristic of Western women.

This colonial history helps explain why *sati* has become a politically salient
symbol of "Indian culture" available for deployment by Hindu fundamentalists
today. However, this colonial history also operated in a manner that obscured
and concealed its role in the *production* of *sati* as a "Central Indian Tradition."
It operated so as to "naturalize" *sati's* status as a "core Indian tradition,"
implying that this status was obvious and pre-given and that the discursive
colonial contestation only *described and confirmed* its status rather than *created*
it. What resulted was an uncritical acceptance of *sati* as an "Authentic Indian
Tradition," which could then only be evaluated as either a "Morally Valuable
Good Tradition" or a "Morally Heinous Bad Tradition." This situation threatens to foreclose political challenges to *sati's very status* as a "Central Indian
Tradition." Feminists of Indian background have been among the few voices
to help call into question *sati's* very status as an "Indian tradition" by excavat-
ing the historical colonial context that "produced" this status (Mani 1987;
Kumar 1994, Oldenberg 1994).

Ahistorical essentialist pictures of cultures also obscure the degree to
which what is seen as constitutive of a particular "culture" and as central
to projects of "cultural preservation" *changes over time*. Thus, essentialist
notions of culture often rely on a picture that presents cultures not only as
"givens" but as "unchanging givens." Obscuring the reality of historical
change and the political contestations with which it is entwined promotes
a static and "fixed" picture of particular cultures, whereby their "values,
practices, and traditions," as well as their sense of what their culture
amounts to and what its "preservation" entails, appear immune to history.
I believe that a historically informed and antiessentialist feminist vision
requires that we learn to see cultures as less rigid and more suffused by change
than they are often depicted.

Many Third World feminist analyses are vitally useful in drawing attention
to how dominant members of a culture often willingly change or discard what
were previously regarded as "important cultural practices," and willingly
change or surrender various facets of such practices when it suits them, but
resist and protest other cultural changes. The changes that are resisted tend to
be changes that pose a threat to aspects of the dominant members' social
power, and are often changes pertaining to the status and welfare of women.
For instance, Olayinka Koso-Thomas's work reveals that in Sierra Leone,
virtually all the elaborate initiation rites and training that were traditional
preliminaries to female circumcision, and that lasted from one to two years,

have fallen by the wayside because people no longer have the time, money or social infrastructure for them. However, the practice of excision itself, abstracted from the whole context of practices in which it used to be embedded, is still seen as a crucial component of "preserving tradition," obscuring the degree to which other aspects of the tradition have been given up (Koso-Thomas 1987, 23). I believe that feminist contestations of what are designated as "traditional cultural practices" need to be alert to such *synecdochic moves* whereby "parts" of a practice come to stand in for a whole, because such substitutions invariably conceal various concrete social changes.

The synecdochic substitution that enables a radically changed cultural practice to masquerade as an "unchanging practice that is being culturally preserved" can also obscure relatively uncontested changes in "traditional practices" that have had substantial detrimental effects. For example, in the case of female circumcision in Sierra Leone, the disappearance of the initiation period seems to have modified the practice for the worse. The age at which excision is carried out has drastically decreased. It is now carried out on girl children rather than on teenagers, since girls no longer need to be old enough to learn the rituals and undergo the training which used to be constitutive facets of the practice (Koso-Thomas 1987, 23). Understanding and describing such facts of cultural change critically and politically is a crucial component of a feminist contestation of political agendas that rely on essentialist notions of "culture."

Feminist attention to such aspects of cultural change can help call attention to a general process that I call "selective labeling," whereby those with social power conveniently designate certain changes in values and practices as consonant with "cultural preservation" while designating other changes as "cultural loss" or "cultural betrayal" (Narayan, 1997). The deployment of "selective labeling" plays a powerful role in the facilitation of essentialist notions of culture because it allows changes that are approved by socially dominant groups to appear consonant with the preservation of essential values or core practices of a culture, while depicting changes that challenge the status quo as threats to "cultural preservation." Feminist attention to "selective labeling" can help underscore that those with social power often abandon or modify traditions when it suits them, and often do so in a manner that leaves these modifications unmarked as instances of "cultural change" and insulated from social debates about "cultural preservation." "Selective labeling" is at work in Third World contexts in which the conversion of many groups to Christianity does not raise qualms about "Westernization" or "cultural preservation," but where continuing adherence to female genital mutilation is represented as crucial to "preserving the culture." Similar arbitrariness is displayed by the Taliban in Afghanistan, which is obsessed with forcing women back to their "traditional place" but appears to have no qualms about the cultural effects of its massive reliance on foreign or Western-produced armaments to maintain state power.

Sensitivity to "selective labeling" can also enable feminists in different national contexts to draw attention to the extensive changes that have occurred *in the lives of women and in practices affecting women* that were once regarded as problematic but have come to be regarded as acceptable cultural modifications by large segments of the population. For instance, public education for women, initially seen as culturally problematic by various segments of the Indian elites, became transformed, in the course of roughly two generations, into something not only permissible but virtually the norm for the daughters of these families. A good proportion of the Indian bourgeoisie today no longer endorse the "tradition" of marrying off girls just past puberty, but still raise the specter of "cultural betrayal" when some of their daughters challenge the tradition of arranged marriages. These examples show how saddling women with the primary responsibility for "cultural preservation" might remain a relative constant, even as prevailing notions of what women need to do to "preserve culture" change over time. The examples illustrate how feminist perspectives are empowered when criticisms of the adverse effects of particular "traditions" on women combine with a critical stance toward ahistorical and essentialist pictures of those "traditions."

"PROGRESSIVE" VERSIONS OF CULTURAL ESSENTIALISM

Third World feminist struggles against various forms of political fundamentalisms often confront essentialist notions of culture that cast fundamentalists as "defenders of national culture and traditions" and represent Third World feminists as cultural traitors corrupted by the seduction of "Western values." However, fundamentalists are not the only ones who subscribe to and deploy essentialist pictures of culture. Essentialist notions of culture are held by people who occupy a wide range of places on the political spectrum. Progressive Western and Third World subjects, too, sometimes uncritically endorse essentialist notions of what "Western culture" or a particular "Third World culture" amounts to. Like many ideological notions, the widespread acceptance of essentialist ideas of culture results from how obvious these ideas appear to a great many people. These ideas can inform people's thought without actually being subject to thought. As a result, Third World feminists themselves have not necessarily been immune to essentialist pictures of culture, especially to essentialist notions of the differences between "Western culture" and particular "Third World cultures." I would argue, for instance, that feminist discourses that have asserted "women's equality" to be a "Western value" whose extension to Third World contexts is "a culturally imperialist theme imposed by the First World," (an assertion made by Non-western governments and feminist activists in the context of the 1975 International Women's Year conference) risk replicating essentialist notions of "culture."

Another example of cultural essentialism emanating from progressive parts of the political spectrum can be found in the contention, by feminists and others, that "human rights" are a "Western concept" whose extension to Third World contexts constitute an illegitimate "imposition of Western values." For instance, Adamantia Pollis and Peter Schwab have denied the legitimacy of employing Western cultural values to judge the institutions of non-Western cultures, insisting that the imposition on Third World societies of norms taken from the Universal Declaration of Human Rights amounts to moral chauvinism and ethnocentric bias (Pollis and Schwab, 1979). Such claims comprise problematic instances of cultural essentialism.

The assertion that "equality" and "human rights" are "Western values" is surely complicated by the historical reality that Western doctrines of equality and rights coexisted for decades with support for slavery and colonialism, and that equality and rights were denied to women; to racial, religious, and ethnic minorities within Western nations; and to virtually all subjects of colonized territories. It is only as a result of political struggles by these various excluded groups in both Western and Non-western contexts that doctrines of equality and rights have slowly come to be perceived as applicable to them, too. Thus, one could argue that doctrines of equality and rights, rather than being pure "products of Western imperialism" were often important products of such struggles *against Western imperialism*. Notions of equality and rights have often been significant in these struggles, and have long since embedded themselves in the vocabularies of Third World political struggles. Claims that "equality" and "rights" are "Western values" risk effacing the vital role that such notions have played and continue to play in those movements (Narayan 1993; Mayer 1995). In general, the *origins* of a practice or concept seldom limit its *scope of relevance*. Borrowing the ideas, practices, artifacts, and technologies of Others, assimilating them, and transforming them are ubiquitous processes, and hardly unique to Third World contexts. Entities of non-European origin that have been assimilated into "Western culture" over time include items as disparate as gunpowder, compasses, Christianity, and coffee.

Feminist claims that "equality" and "rights" are "Western values" also risk echoing the rhetoric of two groups of people who, despite their other differences, share the characteristic of being no friends of feminist agendas. The first are what I shall call "Western cultural supremacists," whose agenda of constructing flattering portraits of "Western culture" proceeds by claiming ideas of equality, rights, democracy, and so on as "Western ideas" that prove the West's moral and political superiority to all "Other" cultures (Bloom 1987; Schlesinger 1992). The second are Third World fundamentalists who share the views of Western cultural supremacists that all such notions are "Western ideas." Fundamentalists deploy these views to justify the claim that such ideas are "irrelevant foreign notions" used only by "Westernized and inauthentic" Third World subjects and to cloak their violations of rights and suppression of democratic processes in the mantle of cultural preservation (Howard 1993; Mayer 1995).

Certainly, Third World feminists have legitimate concerns about how some Western feminists understand and unpack notions of "women's equality." And they have legitimate worries that some Western feminist human rights agendas might ignore or slight the problems and concerns of various groups of women in their national contexts. However, such conflicts and differences are often not well captured by characterizing them as differences between "Western" and "Third World" understandings of these concepts. Sucheta Mazumdar succinctly characterizes the dangers of deploying such essentialist moves even when characterizing genuine conflicts and divergences between Western and Third World feminists.

> The U.N. Decade for Women was problematic for international women's solidarity. Many U.S. and European feminists with a poor understanding of class, ethnicity and international political realities simply replayed colonial stereotypes of Third World nations, were extremely patronizing of women from these nations, and often made no effort to separate the foreign policy objectives of their national governments from those of an internationalist women's movement. Third World women, for their part, rightly found this objectionable, and withdrew into a Third Worldist stance, replete with the rejection of feminism as a Western construct, omitting the fact that there is no such thing as "the Western woman". . . . This fed popular male perceptions, both the liberal and the left in Third World nations, that the women's movement was some concoction of female alienation in a commodity economy, and that it had no relevance in the collectivist ethos of Third World nations. (Mazumdar 1994, 268-69)

Interpretations of ideas such as rights and equality that are insensitive to the predicaments and vulnerabilities of members of socially marginalized groups, including women, do not emanate only from Western contexts; for instance, right-wing and fundamentalist movements in Third World contexts use notions of rights and equality for their own ends (Hasan 1994, xix). Today, a good many problematic political visions cut across national and geographical boundaries, as do valuable ones. I believe feminists are often better served by analyses that concretely show the particular ways that specific interpretations of rights or equality might be inadequate than by interpretations that criticize these notions for being "Western."

Furthermore, notions such as rights and equality are seriously contested within both Western and Third World contexts, with the result that there is hardly one "Western" or "Third World" or "Indian" vision of these concepts (Kiss 1997). Differences about the significance, implications, and applications of these terms exist within Western and Third World national contexts, as well as cut across them. Elsewhere in this issue of *Hypatia*, Susan Okin reveals the political struggles it has taken, and continues to take, to revise human rights doctrines to take account of women's gendered vulnerabilities, in *both* Western and Third World contexts (Okin 1998). Her analysis suggests that politically detrimental and politically valuable understandings of human rights have existed in both Western and Third World contexts.

I would strongly endorse Ofelia Schutte's desire, also expressed in this issue, for a postcolonial feminist perspective that acknowledges the reality of colonialism and the fight against it (Schutte 1998). Postcolonial feminists have good reason to oppose many of the legacies of colonialism, as well as ongoing forms of economic exploitation and political domination by Western nations at the international level. However, I do not think such an agenda is well served either by uncritically denigrating values and practices that appear to be in some sense "Western" or by indiscriminately valorizing values and practices that appear "Non-western." Political rhetoric that polarizes "Western" and "Non-western" values risks obscuring the degree to which economic and political agendas, carried out in collaboration between particular Western and Third World elites, work to erode the rights and quality of life for many citizens in both Western and Third World contexts. Such polarizations detract attention from realpolitik-driven collaborations that result in Western economic and military support for brutal and undemocratic Third World regimes, many of whom spout "anti-Western cultural preservation" rhetoric even as they remain deeply enmeshed in economic, political, and military collaboration with Western nations.

Political rhetoric that polarizes "Western" and "Non-western" values is dangerous in Third World contexts in which progressive and feminist agendas often contest policies that are backed not only by Western powers but by local elites and nation-states. Feminists must keep in mind that a value or practice's being "Non-western" (either in terms of its origin or its context of prevalence) does not mean that it is anti-imperialist or anti-colonial, let alone compatible with feminist agendas. Feminists must also remember that a value or practice's being "Western" in its origins does not mean that it can play no part in the service of anticolonial or postcolonial feminist agendas—as Okin's discussion of international human rights discourse demonstrates (Okin, 1998).

CULTURAL RELATIVISM AND CULTURAL ESSENTIALISM

Many feminists are tempted to regard relativism as "a weapon against intellectual tyranny" because they share Lorraine Code's sense that it is "demonstrably preferable to imperialist alternatives that recognize no limits" (Code 1998). Many feminists regard relativism as an antidote to "affirmations of universal sameness" that permits those who are privileged "to claim to have access to the one true story" (Code 1998). Relativism appears to be a useful deterrent to Western feminist inclinations to speak for or about women situated elsewhere or differently as though they were "just like us." I agree that one can continue to find feminist analyses in which inattention to differences among women facilitates the assumption that "they are just like us" and results in attempts to speak for or about "all women" without sufficient attention to their differences.

However, as my discussion in the first section of this essay indicates, I am reluctant simply to *equate* this problem that constitutes a central concern for contemporary feminist analysis, with the phenomenon of "cultural imperialism" as such. Part of what gives me pause in making this equation is my sense that "cultural imperialism" as it functioned in colonial times had a quite different logic, which *denied rather than affirmed* that one's Others were "just like oneself." I do not wish to deny that the agendas of the colonizing powers required some projection of "Sameness" on colonized peoples. The "civilizing mission" of colonialism, including the project of converting "the natives" to Christianity and the project of drawing colonized populations into European economic and political arrangements, did involve assumptions about forms of "Sameness" that would enable these populations to benefit from "becoming like Westerners" in these ways. However, even these projections of Sameness involved seeing Others as only "deficient examples of the same" (Lange 1998). Without this difference of "deficiency," the colonized populations' need for the colonial tutelage of Western nations would be undermined. The projected "Sameness" was merely an underlying *potential* in the colonized that signified their ability to benefit from the "progress" conferred by colonial rule.

The colonial willingness and eagerness to speak "for and about Others," and the colonialists' conviction that "theirs was the one true story," was, I believe, intimately interwoven with views that insisted on the colonized Others' *difference from*, and *inferiority to*, the Western Subject. While "assumptions of sameness" might well be the hallmark of one problematic tendency that haunts contemporary feminist analysis, I believe it is a serious mistake to take this "assumption of sameness" as the singular defining feature of "cultural imperialism" when "assumptions of difference" have played a substantial role as well. Once it is recognized that "assumptions of difference" have been deployed for cultural imperialist ends no less expeditiously than "assumptions of sameness," the temptation to relativism that is motivated by a desire to avoid cultural imperialism ought, I believe, to considerably weaken. An "insistence on cultural difference" was even more characteristic of the colonial project than gestures towards "sameness," an insistence that helped to cover over the sad similarities of ethnocentrism, androcentrism, classism, heterosexism, and other objectionable "centrisms" that often pervaded both sides of this reiterated "contrast" between "Western culture" and its several "Others."

My analysis underscores how much colonial mandates, as well as the political visions of contemporary Third World fundamentalisms, rely on a picture that focuses on "essential differences" between Western and particular Third World cultures. Insofar as versions of relativism subscribe to these colonial pictures of "essential differences" between cultures, relativism becomes a danger rather than an asset to feminist agendas. My previous analysis demonstrates how representations of particular Third World "cultures" that appeal to relativist notions that "our values and ways of life are distinct from those of Western Others, and constitute our national identity and authenticity" can be at least as detrimental to the interests of many Third World women as any "affirmations of universal sameness."

Many versions of relativism rely on a picture of "cultures" that I previously criticized as culturally essentialist, a picture in which cultures appear neatly, prediscursively, individuated from each other; in which the insistence on "Difference" that accompanies the "production" of distinct "cultures" appears unproblematic; and the central or constitutive components of a "culture" are assumed to be "unchanging givens." Such relativist pictures of cultural differences are, I believe, both empirically inaccurate and inimical to the interests of postcolonial feminists. Rather than embracing relativism, an anti-imperialist postcolonial feminism is better served by critically interrogating scripts of "cultural difference" that set up sharp binaries between "Western" and various "Non-western" cultures. Such interrogation will reveal both sides of the binary to be, in large measure, *totalizing idealizations*, whose Imaginary status has been concealed by a colonial and postcolonial history of ideological deployments of this binary.

For reasons suggested by the preceding remarks, I am not convinced by Lorraine Code's position that with respect to dismantling the master's house "relativism . . . may not be able to do it all, but it is demonstrably preferable to the alternatives" (Code 1998). Third World feminist political struggles are often painfully aware that there are a number of "master's houses." Some of these houses are owned not by "Western" masters but are part of the local real estate, while others have deeds so intricate that it is difficult to unravel how much they are the properties of "local" or "Western" masters. In their attempts to dismantle a number of these "master's houses," Third World feminists often discover that forms of cultural relativism have an important place in the tool-kits of local masters, leaving feminists susceptible to attacks as "Western-ized cultural traitors" who suffer from a lack of appreciation for "their traditions" and respect for "their culture." Forms of relativism have often enough functioned to strengthen the hand of a variety of masters. Feminists cannot afford only to be wary of "universal" claims, but must seek to under-stand the variety of dangerous ideological uses to which forms of both "universalist" and "relativist" claims can be put.

I would argue that what postcolonial feminists need to do is not to endorse "cultural relativism" but to resist various forms of cultural essentialism, *includ-ing relativist versions*. In addition to the strategies I previously mentioned, feminists need to resist cultural essentialism by pointing to the internal plural-ity, dissension and contestation over values, and ongoing changes in practices in virtually all communities that comprise modern nation-states. This critique of cultural essentialism would reject the idea that there is anything that can solidly and uncontroversially be defined as "Indian culture" or "African culture," or "Western culture" for that matter. It would proceed by challenging a "picture of the world" that some versions of cultural relativism assume to be true: that there are *neat packages called "different cultures," each of which is internally consistent and monolithic, and which disagrees only with "Other cultures."*

The position I am endorsing does not deny the existence of "cultural differences" *per se*. It would be foolish to deny that there are practices in certain contexts that are absent in others, and values that are endorsed in some quarters that are not endorsed in others. Rather, the position I endorse denies that "actual cultural differences" correspond very neatly to the "packages" that are currently individuated as "separate cultures" or manifest themselves as evenly distributed across particular "cultures." It insists that virtually all contemporary contexts are full of political debate and dissension about their practices and values, and it refuses to grant any of these perspectives the status of being the sole "authentic representative" of the views and values of a particular culture. It suggests that wariness about projected Imaginary "essen-tial differences" might better facilitate our taking account of the multiplicity of real differences in values, interests, and worldviews that traverse contempo-rary national and transnational contexts. I believe that the exchanges between various feminist discourse communities that Jaggar analyzes (Jaggar 1998) are crucial sites for clarifying the nature and import of a multiplicity of real differences that might mark feminist agendas in different national contexts, even as they provide spaces for contesting essentialist notions of "cultural differences."

While critical of particular pictures of "cultural differences" that underlie certain forms of cultural relativism, my counter-picture does not suffice to answer many important questions that arise in philosophical discussions about relativism. It remains agnostic, for instance, on the question of whether there is one neat and complete universal set of values that ought to command everyone's assent, but optimistic about the prospects for making many of the values that inform progressive politics and feminist agendas meaningful and efficacious in a variety of global contexts.

I would like to end by clarifying the connections between my critique of cultural essentialism and my stance on "generalizations" about cultures. Discussing the issue of gender essentialism, Okin argues that "the feminist anti-essentialist critique was at times carried to the extreme of asserting that no generalizations at all could be made about women" (Okin 1998). Does a commitment to opposing cultural essentialism entail a commitment to the extreme view that no generalizations at all can be made about "cultures?" It is my view that neither antiessentialism about gender nor antiessentialism about cultures entails an absolute prohibition on generalization, because all generalizations are not equally problematic. I would argue that there are significant differences between generalizations like "prostitution is still the main if not the only source of work for African women" cited critically by Mohanty (Mohanty 1991), and generalizations such as the statement of the Committee on the Elimination of All Forms of Discrimination Against Women, which asserts, "Women continue to be discriminated against all over the world as regards the recognition, enjoyment, and exercise of their individual rights in public and private and are subject to many forms of violence" (Bunch 1994, 35).

The former generalization is not only empirically false but also offensive and dangerous. The latter is both arguably true and politically useful in calling attention to human rights violations against women in a multiplicity of national contexts. The latter sort of generalization does not entail, and should not be taken to entail, the absence of variations within and across national contexts in the form of human rights violations that confront different groups of women. The claim that virtually every community is structured by relationships of gender that comprise specific forms of social, sexual, and economic subjection of women seems a generalization that is politically useful; it also leaves room for attention to differences and particularities of context with respect to the predicaments of different groups of women. I believe that the items on Martha Nussbaum's list of important human capabilities and functions are also generalizations of the latter sort, for she intends the list to "allow in its very design for the possibility of multiple specifications of each of the components" (Nussbaum 1995, 93).

I believe that antiessentialism about gender and about culture does not entail a simple-minded opposition to *all generalizations*, but entails instead a commitment to examine both their empirical accuracy and their political utility or risk. It is seldom possible to articulate effective political agendas, such as those pertaining to human rights, without resorting to a certain degree of abstraction, which enables the articulation of salient similarities between problems suffered by various individuals and groups. On the other hand, it seems arguably true that there is no need to portray female genital mutilation as an "African cultural practice" or dowry murders and dowry related harassment as a "problem of Indian women" in ways that eclipse the fact that not *all* "African women" or "Indian women" confront these problems, or confront them in identical ways, or in ways that efface local contestations of these problems.

The antiessentialist perspective I advocate does not endorse the view that the existence of cultural and other "differences" renders equally suspect each and every sort of generalization or universalistic claim. Kwame Anthony Appiah makes a useful point when he reminds us that "it is characteristic of those who pose as antiuniversalists to use the term universalism as if it meant *pseudouniversalism*. . . . What they truly object to—and who would not?—is Eurocentric hegemony posing as universalism" (Appiah 1992, 58). I would add that many of the essentialist pictures of "Indian culture" and the like that I critique are forms of what one might call "pseudoparticularism"—equally hegemonic representations of "particular cultures" whose "particularism" masks the reality that they are problematic generalizations about complex and internally differentiated contexts. Besides, even the injunction to attend to a variety of "differences" can hardly avoid the universalistic cast of a general prescription, and no political agenda can avoid general normative assessments of the salience and weight of particular kinds of "differences."

Given the significant dangers that varieties of cultural essentialism pose to feminist agendas, I believe that the development of a feminist perspective that is committed to antiessentialism both about "women" and about "cultures" is an urgent and important task for a postcolonial feminist perspective. Such a perspective must distinguish and extricate feminist projects of attending to differences among women from problematically essentialist colonial and postcolonial understandings of "cultural differences" between Western culture and its "Others." This essay is a contribution to the project of thinking about how contemporary feminists can resist reified and essentialist pictures of "cultures" and of "cultural contrasts" between "Western culture" and "Third World cultures," and submit them to critical interrogation.[1]

NOTE

1. I would like to thank Jennifer Church, Sandra Harding, Jim Hill, Tina Sheth and Susan Zlotnick for their generous assistance with various drafts of this paper.

REFERENCES

Anzaldúa, Gloria. 1987. *Borderlands/La frontera: The new mestiza.* San Francisco: Aunt Lute Books.

Appiah, Kwame Anthony. 1992. *In my father's house: Africa in the philosophy of culture.* New York: Oxford University Press.

Bloom, Allan. 1987. *The closing of the American mind.* New York: Simon and Schuster.

Bunch, Charlotte. 1994. Strengthening human rights of women. In *World conference on human rights Vienna 1993: The contributions of NGOs reports and documents,* ed. Manfred Nowak. Vienna: Manzsche Verlags und Universitatsbuchhandlung.

Code, Lorraine. 1998. How to think globally: Stretching the limits of imagination. *Hypatia* 13(2): 73-85.

Daly, Mary. 1978. Indian suttee: The ultimate consummation of marriage. In *Gyn/Ecology: The MetaEthics of radical feminism.* Boston: Beacon Press.

Hasan, Zoya, ed. 1994. *Forging identities: gender, communities and the state in India.* Boulder CO: Westview Press.

Hawley, John Stratton, ed. 1994. *Sati, the blessing and the curse.* New York: Oxford University Press.

hooks, bell. 1981. *Feminist theory: From margin to center.* Boston: South End Press.

Howard, Rhoda. 1993. Cultural Absolutism and the Nostalgia for Community. *Human Rights Quarterly* 15: 315-38.

Jaggar, Alison. 1998. Globalizing Feminist Ethics, *Hypatia* 13(2): 7-31.

Kipling, Rudyard. 1944. The Ballad of East and West. In *Rudyard Kipling's verse,* New York: Doubleday.

Kiss, Elizabeth. 1997. Alchemy or fool's gold: Assessing feminist doubts about rights. In *Reconstructing political theory: Feminist perspectives,* ed. Mary Lyndon Shanley and Uma Narayan. University Park: The Pennsylvania State University Press.

Koso-Thomas, Olayinka. 1987. *The circumcision of women: A strategy for eradication.* London: Zed Books.

Kumar, Radha. 1994. Identity politics and the contemporary Indian feminist movement. In *Identity politics and women: Cultural reassertions and feminisms in international perspective.* ed. Valentine Moghadam. Boulder CO: Westview Press.

Lange, Lynda. N.d. Burnt offerings to rationality: A feminist reading of the construction of indigenous peoples in Enrique Dussel's theory of modernity. *Hypatia* 13(3).

Lugones, María C., and Elizabeth V. Spelman. 1983. Have we got a theory for you! Feminist theory, cultural imperialism, and the demand for "The Woman's Voice" *Women's Studies International Forum,* 6(6): 573-81.

Mani, Lata. 1987. Contentious traditions: The debate on SATI in Colonial India. *Cultural Critique* Fall: 19-56.

Mayer, Ann Elizabeth. 1995. *Islam and human rights: Tradition and politics.* Boulder CO: Westview Press.

Mazumdar, Sucheta. 1994. Moving away from a secular vision? Women, nation, and the cultural construction of Hindu India. In *Identity politics and women: Cultural reassertions and feminisms in international perspective,* ed. Valentine Moghadam. Boulder CO: Westview Press.

Mohanty, Chandra Talpade. 1991. Under Western eyes: Feminist scholarship and colonial discourses. In *Third World women and the politics of feminism,* ed. Chandra

Talpade Mohanty, Ann Russo, and Lourdes Torres. Bloomington: Indiana University Press.

Narayan, Uma. 1993. What do rights have to do with it?: Reflections on what distinguishes "traditional non-Western" frameworks from contemporary rights-based systems. *Journal of Social Philosophy* 24(2): 186-99.

———. 1995. Eating cultures: Incorporation, identity and "Indian food." *Social Identities* 1(1): 63-88.

———. 1997. *Dislocating cultures: Identities, traditions and Third World feminism.* New York: Routledge.

Nussbaum, Martha C. 1995. Human capabilities, Female human beings. In *Women, Culture and Development,* ed. Martha Nussbaum and Jonathan Glover. Oxford: Clarendon Press.

Nussbaum Martha C. and Jonathan Glover, eds. 1995. *Women, culture and development.* Oxford: Clarendon Press.

Okin, Susan Moller. 1998. Feminism, women's human rights, and cultural differences. *Hypatia* 13(2): 32-52.

Oldenburg, Veena Talwar. 1994. The continuing invention of the Sati tradition. In *Sati, the blessing and the curse,* ed. John Stratton Hawley. New York: Oxford University Press.

Pollis, Adamantia and Peter Schwab. 1979. *Human rights: cultural and ideological perspectives.* New York: Praeger.

Schlesinger, Arthur M. Jr. 1992. *The disuniting of America: Reflections on a multicultural society.* New York: W.W. Norton.

Schutte, Ofelia. 1998. Cultural alterity: Cross-cultural communication and feminist thought in North-South contexts. *Hypatia* 13(2): 53-72.

6

"It's Not Philosophy"

ANDREA NYE

Women, Native, Other: Writing Postcoloniality and Feminism. By TRINH T. MINH-HA. Bloomington: Indiana University Press, 1989.

Black Feminist Thought: Knowledge, Consciousness, and the Politics of Empowerment. By PATRICIA HILL COLLINS. New York: Routledge, 1991.

Borderlands/La Frontera: The New *Mestiza.* By GLORIA ANZALDÚA. San Francisco: Aunt Lute Books, 1987.

Signs, Songs, and Memory in the Andes. By REGINA HARRISON. Austin: University of Texas Press, 1989.

"Have we got a theory for you! Feminist Theory, Cultural Imperialism and the Demand for 'The Woman's Voice.' " By MARÍA C. LUGONES and ELIZA-BETH V. SPELMAN. **Women's Studies International Forum** 6(6)(1983): 573-81.

"Structure/Antistructure and Agency under Oppression." By MARÍA C. LUGONES. **Journal of Philosophy** 87(10)(1990): 500-7.

"Playfulness, 'World'-Traveling, and Loving Perception." By MARÍA C. LUGONES. **Hypatia** 2(2)(1987): 3-19.

Many of the titles listed above require no review for feminist philosophers. Their value as additions to university curricula has been well proven in courses on feminist theory and feminist philosophy, as well as in interdisciplinary women's studies courses. At the same time, many philosophers, both men and women, continue to shrug off the suggestion that they be might be included as philosophical texts in courses on metaphysics, ethics, or epistemology with a dismissive "It's not philosophy."

It was with similar reservations that Aristotelians at Medieval universities discouraged their colleagues from discussing the work of the upstart Descartes, German academics ignored the Vienna Circle's logical positivism, and, at the present moment, some analytic philosophers discard feminist and multicultural thought as mere "politics." Far from illustrating a clear-cut disciplinary division between what is philosophy and what is not philosophy, however, such refusals mark a distinctive feature of philosophy as a body of thought constantly in the process of redefinition. Philosophy's very origin could be said to be in controversial self-questioning and self-renewal, as Socrates substituted for the Sophist's claim to "know" a more humble "love of knowledge." Often, self-questioning and redefinition have come from outside what is considered philosophy proper. Socrates, for example, introduced metaphors from the crafts and professions to illustrate the proper conditions for virtue. John Locke drew on Newtonian physics for a new approach to knowledge. More recently, post-World War II philosophers of mind have used theories of artificial intelligence to provide a model of the mind. In the grip of particular, strongly rooted philosophical paradigms, however, this history can be forgotten. And this may now be the case in English-speaking academic philosophy, where certain presuppositions as to the proper aim and methods of philosophy are sometimes held as dogma.

The purpose of this essay is not to bring new work to readers' attention but to reflect on the divide that continues to exist between materials that have inspired feminist philosophers to new insights and the currently established canon of philosophy. Even when ratified by a version of intellectual history that covers up personal or political sources of philosophical wisdom or that privileges science as the only knowledge, philosophy's parameters remain unstable. The very insistence on what is "real" or "hardcore" philosophy against what is "only" poetry, sociology, personal memoir, or politics itself renews the possibility of yet another philosophical reconstitution.

The work of the feminist thinkers reviewed here can be taken as illustrative of the way forms of thought position themselves in periods of intellectual change, not on the inside or the outside of a particular schism between philosophers and nonphilosophers, but on the cusp of a redefinition of "love of knowledge." At stake is more than an academic specialty. Philosophy, throughout its long, diverse, and contested history, has concerned itself with the basic themes of human life: the identity of the self, the nature of reality, the possibility of knowledge. Changes in philosophical paradigms often signal or reflect radical change in the way the human and the real are conceived. At the present moment, virtual realities, possible worlds, and artificial intelligence exercise analytic philosophers to revise and expand their logist and scientist assumptions. More radical and more historically significant, I would argue, are the revisions that the writers reviewed here envision from experiences as Asian, African American, or Hispanic women. Middle-class male college students may neglect their studies to stalk virtual women in multi-user domains; science fiction writers may imagine utopian universes operated by giant computers; cognitive scientists may conceive of the brain as a self-replicating program; but the information technology that inspires such speculation is only one facet of a deeper change in human life. In a world that is a global village, intellectual, racial, ethnic, or cultural enclaves are an impossibility. What it is to be human, what it is to think, what it is to know reality can no longer be defined according to one dominant cultural code. A Babel of tongues and ideas can no longer be dismissed as "barbarian," "primitive," "native." It is to this new real and not virtual international reality that Trinh, Collins, Anzaldúa, Harrison, Spelman, and Lugones speak.

Trinh Minh-Ha's work typifies the multidisciplinary interstices out of which new theory often emerges. Just as Socrates grafted ethics onto the rational forms of Euclidean geometry, or Descartes muddied the already tainted waters of Aristotle's metaphysics with Galilean physics, or the logical positivists used the methods of laboratory research to sweep aside centuries of idealist speculation, so Trinh in *Woman, Native, Other*, explores links between anthropology, literary criticism, psychoanalysis, philosophy, and local oral traditions of stories and narratives. In the forefront in her first chapter, "Commitment from the Mirror-Writing Box," is the imperative for theory of the Socratic "know thyself." Canonical styles of thought and expression can block self-reflection and create a theorizing that pretends to be pure assertion from no one and nowhere, subject only to refutation in its own terms. This, Trinh argues, is an illusion. A writer, whether of philosophy, anthropology, or fiction, writes as a subject with a history; whether it is acknowledged or not, she is conscious of herself as a writing subject. This reflective consciousness, ruled out in principle by the current philosophical establishment's truth-theoretic semantics, is the very essence of writing for Trinh. A writer who is not an automaton is conscious and questioning of her identity as writer. She is perpetually at odds with her language, critical of her relation to her own production, and concerned with the quality of her relation to her readers.

For Trinh the very essence of thoughtful writing and, by extension, thoughtful theorizing or philosophizing, is engagement with the dilemmas the above tangle of problematic interactions represent. As a writer, a woman experiences the freedom of a self-defining subject, but she also experiences the existential responsibility that goes along with that freedom. Her medium must be words, words whose grammar and diction are shaped in practices and motives often alien to her sense of herself and the world in which she lives. Even more difficult is the question of audience. The aim of writing, whether it is philosophy or poetry, is self-expression, but it is not clear how self-expression can be accomplished in a way that does not objectify or degrade those to whom or about whom one writes. How can a theorist write not just for a few colleagues in a closed, elitist academic circle, but to and for "the people"—for non-North

Americans, people of color, women as well as men? Trinh uses the example of a term popular in Marxist and other political theorizing. A Marxist theorist claims to write for the "masses," but what does this homogenizing of a "cadre" of docile workers indicate about relations between the middle-class leaders of a Bolshevik revolution and subjects who will be "reeducated" to their specifications?

Trinh continues to develop these questions in succeeding chapters on anthropology as a language of Western hegemony, the current "politics of difference" popular in feminist circles, and the ways that photographic images support and subvert textual motifs. She explores the various forms of negotiation that occur as the diverse voices of a postcolonial era gather strength and conviction in challenge to established authorities.

Interesting. But not philosophy. Or is it? Trinh meditates on the complex interrelations between individual selves speaking from unique and particular places in space and time, between the grammars and discursive forms that anchor meaning at particular moments in intellectual history, between speakers-writers and readers-hearers. I would argue that embedded in that meditation are the traditional philosophical issues of nature of self, reality, and knowledge. Most important, however, Trinh touches on what I take as the core essence of philosophy, the reinvention of thought adequate to a changing world.

Patricia Hill Collins addresses similar philosophical concerns in her *Black Feminist Thought* from the perspective of African American experience. How can African American women understand their situation, express it in meaningful terms, and construct knowledge necessary for solving problems in the black community? In her concluding chapter, "Toward an Afrocentric Feminist Epistemology," Collins summarizes her findings: while all might agree that knowledge of the multicultural societies in which virtually all of us must now live is absolutely necessary, the question is how that knowledge is to be obtained. The empiricist logicist epistemologies of the twentieth century are not adequate. Can one define concepts as the value ranges of countable, predetermined objects and then do measurable and verifiable statistical surveys? Can one define racism as a closed list of possible behaviors and then test for it? Can what is defined as black crime be correlated with the incidence of single-parent families to conclude that the answer to crisis in urban neighborhoods is to force black women into marriage and punish sexual promiscuity?

Collins suggests that the sort of knowledge developed by white social scientists and backed by current postpositivist philosophical epistemologies does not capture the reality of black women's "subjugated experience." Instead, she proposes other sources of knowledge: personal interviews, popular music and fiction, conversation, dialogue. Instead of constructing theory out of her or his own clear and distinct ideas, the scientist who draws knowledge from these sources will require new techniques, techniques that are beginning to be developed by feminist epistemologists such as Sandra Harding, Lorraine Code, Helen Longino, and Evelyn Fox Keller (Code 1987, 1991; Harding 1986, 1991; Keller 1985, 1992; Longino 1990). The techniques Collins seeks would not force categories on reality or preprogram the objects of human concern. They would require forms of validation and verification that do not allow stereotypes to slip by in the guise of facts, and that do not use convenient margins of error to escape anomalies. In the place of sterile academic debate between experts who assume common concepts, these techniques must bridge the distance between theory and concrete experience, and initiate dialogue between alternate and conflicting perspectives.

Not philosophy? Only sociology? And bad sociology at that? Again, I suggest a second look. Current philosophy of knowledge has shown surprising disinterest in what scientists actually do. In return, it is not surprising, perhaps, that scientists typically have found little of interest in academic philosophy of knowledge, although a few have noted how social metaphors shape concepts in science or how institutional factors can determine the methods of verification. Collins, like Trinh, opens possible critical intersections between science as a human production and human experience as expressed in stories, music, and conversation. Both point to the distinctive location of a new philosophy of knowledge that can critically reformulate our understanding of how to generate concepts to support remedies for conditions such as de facto segregation and black poverty.

The kind of knowledge that Collins calls for is not only negative diagnosis that condemns and criticizes existing theory. In the voices of the black women she studies is embedded knowledge of survival under oppression, dignity under duress, strength as intelligent communication. Such knowledge is outside the paradigm of naturalized epistemology now popular in philosophy, in which it is taken for granted that the human mind is a biological or information-processing mechanism developed as an aid to physical survival. In the experience of black women, survival without dignity or self-respect is worthless; experience as human is not understandable as an individual organism's competition for survival at all costs, but aims at a multifaceted, renegotiable life in common with others.

Gloria Anzaldúa and María Lugones treat similar themes from the contested borders between North American and Mexican, Spanish and Indian, Anglo and Chicano. In *Borderlands*, Anzaldúa identifies a faculty *la facultad*, a survival tactic of marginalized and oppressed peoples such as Chicano's struggling to survive in Anglo culture, indigenous people faced with Spanish overlords, and Mexicans negotiating with a vastly more powerful United States. People in these situations need to see beyond surface appearances, need to grasp deeper structures and patterns that motivate words and deeds, need a feeling-thinking awareness that bypasses preconceived ideas and may be representable initially only in images or symbols.

Anzaldúa relates this faculty of deeper insight and the "*mestiza*" consciousness that is its source to the condition of bilinguality or multilinguality. Traditionally, philosophers have been resolutely monolingual. Either they have insisted that Greek, Latin, German, or English is the preferred language of clear and rational thought, or they have taken the ingredients of thought as universal and assumed that insofar as it is rational and meaningful, any language must be understood in the terms of European semantics. Recalling the Spanish conquest of Peru in *Signs, Songs, and Memory in the Andes*, Regina Harrison makes clear the contested political and imperial history of such an assumption. With the aim of conquest and Christianization at any cost, Spanish-speaking missionaries and administrators struggled to communicate with indigenous Quechua people. Was the native language rich enough, rational enough to communicate the values and truths of Christianity? Or should priests and officials be trained in Quechua? Would Christian concepts expressed in Quechua be tainted with native superstition and animism? Should natives be taught and governed only in Spanish? Tracing misunderstandings and conceptual dissonance through actual, often violent interactions between Spanish speakers and native peoples, Harrison shows the naivete of any view of conceptual structure as universal. Time after time, Europeans failed to grasp the generative metaphysics of Quechua based on root metaphors of social symmetry and balance. Time after time, Quechua speakers insisted on understanding European doctrines in their own terms and were punished for it.

Those, like Anzaldúa, who live in the borderlands between cultures, and who must shuttle back and forth between linguistic worlds, cannot afford the illusion that there is a master metaphysics. They must constantly suffer the shock of collision between incompatible frames of reference, a collision which no longer can be avoided by cultural isolation and the violence of which only increases with opposition and confrontation. But it is at that very cultural crossroads, Anzaldúa argues, that a new kind of consciousness is possible. This is not the consciousness of a closed, self-consistent, unified logic based on a superior language or a master grammar, but a *mestiza* consciousness that works between conceptual worlds with divergent thinking that stretches concepts and tolerates ambiguity and contradiction. The thinking that will characterize what is prototypically human in the twenty-first century may not be that of the well-schooled cultural elite who travel to conferences and stay in first-class hotels. The relevant and privileged thought of the future may be the specialty of Anzaldúa's *mestizas* who move back and forth between cultures and languages, cultivating the deeper analyses necessary to bridge conceptual barriers.

But is this poetry, history, personal narrative, and not philosophy? Is the answer to that question so clear? Might the conceptual explorations of Anzaldúa and other women of color represent a new kind of philosophy, reunited to experience in the world? Instead of continuing to reflect the experience of an archaic ethnic or cultural hegemony, such a philosophy draws on the actual experience of human beings who move as a matter of course from one language to another and from one culture to another. If, as Hannah Arendt noted in *The Life of the Mind*, philosophers are the professionals among thinkers, perhaps the present experts are not those who adopt the fashionable fictions of artificial intelligence or the universal Turing machine brains of cognitive science, but Anzaldúa's *mestizas*, French-African, Indian-British, Asian-American, and Hispanic-American.

This suggestion has been pursued in a series of papers by the Hispanic philosopher María Lugones. In a 1983 dialogue with Elizabeth Spelman, "Have We Got a Theory for You!", Lugones explores forms of philosophizing that are not monovocal. Lugones's and the Anglo Spelman's voices combine, separate, intermingle in acknowledgment that perceptions differ, but also with the belief that in dialogue degrees of consensus, and therefore truth, are possible. In this early paper, Lugones addresses questions that she would continue to pursue in later work. What can be the motivation for dialogue between Anglo women from a dominant culture and Hispanic women? Why would an Anglo woman be willing to take the unsettling, even dangerous step of entering the world of women of color? Why would a Hispanic woman take the risk of dialogue with a culture she has every reason to distrust? Painstakingly, Lugones explores the ontological and metaphysical implications of these questions. Theory's purpose is to get at the meaning of experience, but how can one person get at the meaning of another's experience? Is there any possibility of theorizing across differences? Is there any kind of white feminist theorizing that could be useful or important to women of color? Such questions address practical problems in the feminist movement. They also involve the ontology of self and reality.

Lugones extends her meditation in the 1987 "Playfulness, 'World'-Traveling, and Loving Perception." An individual is identified by certain essential and accidental characteristics, or so rules the Aristotelian metaphysics of substance and attribute. But Lugones, as a woman who passes from her native Argentine culture to Anglo culture, finds that her characteristics change. At home she is playful; in the Anglo world, however, this is not a trait that anyone would attribute to her. Must this instability in identity be seen as the pathology of a split personality? In reality, concludes Lugones, to live in different "worlds of sense" and have different identities in those worlds is the normal state for those who travel between worlds.

But how, given what might be seen as a disfiguring fragmentation, is it possible to have agency, to think that one can bring about change in the world? Lugones addresses this further question in her contribution to the APA 1990 symposium on "Gender, Race, Ethnicity." Neither a structuralism that takes personal identity as constructed nor a poststructuralism that takes identity as necessarily fractured and partial can provide the answer to the problem of agency. A worker's experience of being paralyzed within the structures of capitalism or a woman's experience of being trapped in masculinist institutions is real enough. But when the "ontological pluralism" of different worlds of sense is taken into account, along with the personal pluralism that results, agency becomes possible. A woman who "travels" from world to world feels herself to be, and is, someone different in those worlds. She has intentions and desires that are not constant from world to world. This is not symptomatic of pathology, however, because she remembers herself in different worlds. This puts her in a position to conceive and even carry out actions foreign to established structures. At the moment when she passes from world to world, she has a freedom that is outside the paralyzing structures of one unitary culture.

How long it will be before such insights enter fruitfully into dialogue with establishment philosophical studies of identity across possible worlds, ontological relativity, and inscrutability of reference, is hard to determine. Worlds of sense, including academic worlds of sense, can be heavily barricaded. There are many reasons why those in positions of power may not want to move away from established paradigms. Throughout her writing, Lugones has insisted that the motivation for dialogue between worlds cannot be self-interest, that the risks in seeing yourself as others see you, the dangers of entering a world in which you are not protected by privileges of race or class, are prohibitive. She has insisted that the only conceivable reason for travel between worlds is friendship, friendship between individual women that overcomes the danger and self-interest that keep us safely at home.

Perhaps she is right. I would suggest, however, another reason might motivate women and men to participate in philosophizing in the style of Trinh, Collins, Anzaldúa, Harrison, Collins, Spelman and Lugones. The core motive for philosophizing has been variously described, but one very ancient suggestion is that the urge comes from awe, awe at the mystery and complexity of human existence. Philosophizing in the new global environment—philosophizing across languages and across cultures, philosophizing that accommodates a diversity of experience, philosophizing that refuses to sacrifice material fact for the simplicity of any virtual reality—has the compelling intellectual appeal of conceptual richness and experiential depth. This, one feels, with all its difficulty and messiness, is real life and real thought.

REFERENCES

Arendt, Hannah. 1978. *The life of the mind.* New York: Harcourt Brace Jovanovich.
Code, Lorraine. 1987. *Epistemic responsibility.* Hanover and London: University Press of New England for Brown University Press.

————. 1991. *What can she know?: Feminist theory and the construction of knowledge.* Ithaca: Cornell University Press.

Harding, Sandra. 1986. *The science question in feminism.* Ithaca: Cornell University Press.

————. 1991. *Whose Science? Whose Knowledge? Thinking From Women's Lives.* Ithaca: Cornell University Press.

Keller, Evelyn Fox. 1985. *Reflections on gender and science.* New Haven: Yale University Press.

————. 1992. *Secrets of life/Secrets of death: Essays on language, gender and science.* New York: Routledge.

Longino, Helen. 1990. *Science as social knowledge: Values and objectivity in scientific inquiry.* Princeton: Princeton University Press.

7

Chandra Mohanty and the Revaluing of "Experience"

SHARI STONE-MEDIATORE

Joan Scott's poststructuralist critique of experience demonstrates the dangers of empiricist narratives of experience but leaves feminists without a meaningful way to engage nonempiricist, experience-oriented texts, texts that constitute many women's primary means of taking control over their own representation. Using Chandra Mohanty's analysis of the role of writing in Third World feminisms, I articulate a concept of experience that incorporates poststructuralist insights while enabling a more responsible reading of Third World women's narratives.

Although early feminists raised feminist consciousness and countered male-centered worldviews with narratives of "women's experience," there is today a broad consensus among feminists that stories of "experience" are problematic. As Donna Haraway, Sandra Harding, and others have pointed out, appeals to experience risk naturalizing ideologically conditioned categories that structure our experiences of self and world. Joan Wallach Scott, in her widely cited essay "The Evidence of Experience," has articulated the strongest version of this critique. The very "selves" that "have" experiences, Scott argues, are constituted through discursive practices. Consequently, stories of marginalized persons' experiences (both personal narratives and the histories that draw on these) reinscribe the assumptions about identities, differences, and autonomous subjects that underlie available discourses.[1] Despite this critique, however, important postcolonial feminists, such as Gloria Anzaldúa, bell hooks, and Michelle Cliff, continue to write experience-oriented texts, for such texts play a key role in publicizing the contradictions of contemporary capitalist democracies. Scott's devaluation of experience leaves us without a way to engage these texts meaningfully. For if we dismiss stories of experience as positivist, then we refuse these leading theorists of race and gender—as well as all those excluded from official knowledge production—the power to offer critical perspectives on their worlds by narrating their experience. We may analyze their texts' rhetorical construction, but we forfeit learning from them any liberatory knowledge.

This essay investigates how, after Scott's critique, we can avoid naturalizing experience and yet still productively read, teach, and defend stories of "marginalized experience."[2] I argue that the more sophisticated of these narratives do intervene in the ideological processes that constitute experience; however, current concepts of experience—both empiricist and poststructuralist—unduly constrain our reading of these texts, allowing us to consider them only as reports of unreflective consciousness and obscuring the more subtle ways they emerge from and affect historical experience. After summarizing critiques of empiricist theories, I address the insights and the limits of Scott's poststructuralist concept of experience. I argue that while Scott helps us to approach "experience" critically, she ultimately forestalls an effective engagement with the more subtle marginal experience narratives (including Samuel Delany's memoir, a marginal experience text she considers paradigmatic) because her concept of experience as a discursive production oversimplifies the relations between experience and language.

In order to elucidate the subversive potential of the more nuanced, non-empiricist stories of experience, I turn to Chandra Talpade Mohanty's analysis of "Third World women's" writings.[3] In "Cartographies of Struggle," Mohanty engages, on their own terms, these women's life stories, testimonials, and personal essays. She reads these as creative responses to the tensions and contradictions of lived experience, when this experience is conditioned by local cultural practices, along with globally organized political and economic relations. Drawing on that essay, as well as Mohanty's more recent work, I propose an alternative account of "experience," one that neither naturalizes the latter nor reduces it to discourse but considers the complexities of historical experience and the reciprocal relations between experience and writing. Finally, I show how this Mohanty-inspired theory enables us to read the subtler marginal experience narratives in a way that foregrounds their interventions in hegemonic discourse and recognizes them as challenges to our own historical imaginations.

THE CRITIQUE OF "EXPERIENCE"

Since the 1980s, feminists have problematized attempts to ground knowledge or politics in women's experience. From feminist epistemology, we have learned that experience is not a truth that precedes culturally given representations of experience but is actually mediated by those representations. Haraway, for instance, has emphasized the discovery that visual experience is not mere reception of reality but an active process informed by expectations. This experience appears to us, however, as if it simply reflected external reality.

Furthermore, the world we perceive is itself a product of social and historical forces, yet experience tends to confront historical existence as mere fact. As Harding puts it, "our experience lies to us," presenting as natural culturally determined behavior and historically constructed social arrangements (1991, 287). Not only does the experiencing subject encounter the world through ideologically conditioned lenses, but the theorist who identifies experiences with a particular social group risks naturalizing exclusionary definitions of that group.

Feminist critics of identity politics, such as Elizabeth Weed and Mohanty, have addressed the dangers of building a politics around "women's experience." When "women's experience" is taken as the ground of a common interest, these theorists point out, we may reverse hierarchies, positing a different group as the subject of knowledge and politics. But we leave intact the categories for defining group identity, the exclusions those categories entail, and the broader structures of domination and exploitation.

While these analyses have made feminists wary of uncritical appeals to experience, Scott challenges the entire project of narrating experience. No writer or reader of experience-oriented texts can avoid the questions raised by Scott's radical critique. Drawing on Foucault and Lacan, Scott argues that it is only by virtue of the discursive practices that differentiate and regulate subjects that one attains awareness of one's identity, desires, interests, and distinct spheres of existence. Scott also employs Derrida's notion of discourse as a dynamic, variable system that creates meaning through differentiation. In view of these theories and of her own analysis of the historical force of gender constructs, Scott proposes that experience is an "epistemological phenomen[on]" that is "discursively organized in particular contexts or configurations" (1988, 5). Scott's notion of experience as a "linguistic event" (1991, 793) agrees with the aforementioned feminist critics insofar as it emphasizes the cultural biases affecting experience; but it goes further, to suggest that there is no experience at all outside of the discourses that delineate identities, naturalize desire, divide the personal from the political; in short, the discourses that "construct" identifiable, self-aware, and knowable subjects.

Others have sought more reflective or richer aspects of experience.[4] Scott, however, claims that the very assumption of individuals with internal, "experienced" truths reinforces the ideological processes constitutive of subjectivity, as well as the assumptions that have made experience into a supposed foundation of knowledge.[5]

Scott focuses on the ways experience-based epistemologies have limited historiography. According to Scott, historians seeking to document the experiences of underrepresented groups have treated experience as a "foundational concept," a category in which knowledge is articulated but the very emergence of which as a category of analysis remains unthematized. Failing to question the status of experience, these historians regard visual and visceral experience as previous historians regarded facts; that is, as the cornerstone of a prediscursive reality.[6] Their project of illuminating this "reality," Scott argues, can expose the existence of difference or of oppression but "precludes critical examination of the workings of the ideological system itself" (1991, 778).

Scott illustrates this argument with reference to Samuel Delany's memoir, *The Motion of Light in Water* (1988). Focusing on a passage in which Delany tries to communicate what he "sees" at a gay bathhouse, Scott claims that "the point of Delany's description, indeed of his entire book, is to document the existence of those [hitherto hidden gay] institutions" (Scott 1991, 775). This prevents him, she says, from problematizing the assumptions that inform his "vision," leading him to naturalize gay identity and desire, along with the "phallic economy" in which "gay" can only be the inverse of heterosexuality. This same project of writing in order to report visual experience, says Scott, "has long been the mission of historians documenting the lives of those omitted or overlooked in accounts of the past" (1991, 776). Like Delany, these historians conceive of their challenge to mainstream history as "a correction to oversights resulting from inaccurate or incomplete vision" (Scott 1991, 776). Just as Delany presumed that gay identity needed only to be unveiled to be understood, historians of "women's experience" or "workers' experience" place those identities and the logic underwriting them outside critical scrutiny. Consequently, Scott argues, marginal experience narratives not only obscure but also unwittingly perpetuate the discursive processes that "produce" experiencing subjects.

After Scott's critique, what can remain of the project of writing, reading, and defending marginal experience narratives? Some have responded to Scott by agreeing with her criticism of empiricist narratives but contending that many recent marginal experience narratives are not empiricist. Social historian Eleni Varikas, for instance, cites feminist histories that both narrate women's experiences and analyze the cultural processes by which definitions of gender have been constructed. Varikas speaks for many when she remarks that Scott's blanket criticism of histories of experience "risks throwing out the baby with the bathwater" (1995, 99).[7] In a different context, Elizabeth Weed also voices concern for "saving" certain narratives of experience. Despite the association of "experience" with traditional notions of the subject, says Weed, some feminists have nonetheless used experience "not to pin down the truth of the individual subject but as a critical effort to open up ideological contradictions" (1989, xxv). Such observations suggest that Scott has cast her net too wide, generalizing all stories of experience as positivist and overlooking the distinction between empiricist and nonempiricist texts.

I agree with efforts to limit the scope of Scott's charges to certain empiricist texts. Yet I also believe that Scott's critique presents a further challenge for proponents of marginal experience narratives. The ease with which Scott generalizes that all such narratives are empiricist belies a phenomenon that has impeded the effective reading of even the nonempiricist texts; namely, the absence of a theory of experience adequate to what the subtler marginal experience narratives are expressing. Without such an account of experience and narration, these narratives will continue to be read and evaluated on problematic, empiricist terms.[8] After Scott's critique, then, we need to clarify: How exactly do the more sophisticated marginal experience narratives treat experience, if not as evidence, and how can we read and defend these narratives without invoking a "completing the picture" empiricist epistemology?

THE LIMITS OF POSTSTRUCTURALIST "EXPERIENCE"

To answer these questions, we need to specify the limits of Scott's "poststructuralist" concept of experience for addressing these issues. To be sure, Scott points to fruitful areas for historical research. By thematizing language as a field where meanings are negotiated and constructed, she directs our attention toward the metaphors, oppositions, and exclusions by which representations of experience gain significance (for experiencing subjects and for theorists) and by which certain things (and not others) have come to count as experience. If Scott helps us to trace "experience" to some of the ideological processes behind it, her approach nonetheless becomes problematic when taken as a "definition of 'experience' that might work for historians" (Scott 1991, 773n). For when Scott defines experience as an epistemological phenomenon analyzable in terms of rhetorical mechanisms, she leaves historians without any notion of subjective existence distinct from representations of existence. In effect, in her effort to "refuse a separation between 'experience' and language" (Scott 1991, 793), Scott elides the distinction between the two, collapsing experience into language.

In the end, the empiricist approach to experience and Scott's poststructuralist approach constitute two polar opposite positions. The former assumes that, through experience, we gain access to a prediscursive reality; the latter assumes that our inquiry cannot go beyond discourse, that we can only analyze discursive mechanisms. Scott rightly criticizes the empiricist approach, but her own approach is also limited. Equating experience with representations of experience, she obscures the role of subjective experience in motivating and informing intervention in representational practices.

The problems with Scott's poststructuralist "experience" come to the fore in her attempt to reread Delany from this vantage point. In the second reading, Scott identifies Delany's bathhouse affirmation of his gay identity as a "discursive event"; that is, not the unveiling of his true self but "the substitution of one interpretation for another" (Scott 1991, 794). This theory, however, is inadequate to what Scott's closer attention to the text's language actually points toward. Although Scott does not theorize this, her second reading indicates paradoxical, mutually informing relations between Delany's experience and his writing, relations that make this text more than merely one discursive production among others. Scott's inability to confront the implications of her own reading manifests itself in an unresolved contradiction in that reading. On the one hand, Scott emphasizes that Delany's bathhouse "experience" is constituted in his interpretation of that event. Noting that the bathhouse is illuminated by a dim blue light, she says that what Delany calls his vision is really an interpretation of the blue light's multiple refractions, an interpretation informed by available discourses on sexuality. On the other hand, however, her analysis implies an experience distinct from language that prompts Delany to favor certain discourses over others and to use that discourse in an innovative, self-conscious manner. For instance, she observes that Delany's bathhouse reinterpretation of his gay identity was enabled by his "subjective perceptual clarity" (Scott 1991, 794). Furthermore, she suggests that Delany's own experience-motivated questioning of social categories was crucial to his innovative writing: on these reflections, Delany finds that "the available social categories aren't sufficient for [his] story" (Scott 1991, 795).

Scott's rereading of Delany leaves this paradox: Delany's experience is constituted in his interpretation of the experience, yet the interpretation is guided by his experiences and reflections on these. When Scott describes the memoir as a "discursive production of knowledge of the self," she recognizes one side of the paradox, the constitutive role of language. But she overlooks the experience that enables Delany to use language in the particular way he does. The short shrift that Scott gives to this motivating experience is evident in her failure to explicate "subjective perceptual clarity" or to explain the relation between Delany's subjective perceptual clarity and his text. Without paying attention to these relations between Delany's experience and his writing, Scott cannot distinguish the text's value from other representations of gay identity or of the sexual revolution; it is merely "the substitution of one interpretation for another."

If Scott intimates, but never fully confronts, the role of experience in Delany's rewriting of his identity, it is because "experience" in her theory can be nothing but a mirror of available discourses (whether these be ruling or oppositional discourses), with no excess. Ironically, such a theory reverses the empiricist privileging of subjective experience over language only to retain its one-dimensional, vision-oriented structure. Scott's insight is that vision is not immediate contact with an outside world but is always already mediated by discursive categories; yet she still considers this "seeing" of the world (now understood to be ideologically constituted) to be all of experience. In effect, experience for Scott is what Harding calls "spontaneous consciousness": the awareness one has of one's "individual experience" before any reflection on that experience or any consideration of the social construction of one's identity (Harding 1991, 269, 287, 295). As Harding suggests, we cannot call this experience "immediate," for it is thoroughly mediated by dominant cultural texts. It is, however, spontaneous, for it is experienced as if it were an immediate view of one's life and world. Empiricists naturalize this spontaneously conscious awareness; Scott recognizes this to be prefigured by discursive principles. For both, though, this exhausts experience. Indeed, this is why Scott is not concerned to distinguish between experience and language; in her view, experience can be nothing other than what codified categories enable one to conceptualize, and hence to "see."

Scott's unwitting narrowing of the realm of experience is also marked by her single reference to, and subsequent neglect of, the visceral domain. If she were to address the latter, she would confront aspects of experience that, while perhaps inextricable from language, are not mediated by language in the same way or to the same extent as perception.[9] Scott's inattention to visceral experience is symptomatic of her reduction of the many layers of experience to a spontaneous "vision."

To be sure, Scott is interested in the possibility of "seeing differently." Still, lacking a concept of experience distinct from discourse, she cannot explain the resources for creating or the motivations for employing oppositional discourses. Flattening experience into discursively constituted perception, Scott can recognize only two ways of treating experience: a naive empiricist presentation of experience as evidence, or an (objectifying) analysis of the language in which others have represented experience. The only critical project here is the theorist's analysis of language. Yet Scott's own reading of Delany indicates a text that fits into neither of these categories, but rather works within the tension between writing and experience and responds creatively to that tension.

REREADING "EXPERIENCE"

If we are to realize the critical potential of nonempiricist narratives of experience like Delany's, then we need a different concept of experience, one that does not treat experience as indubitable evidence but nevertheless recognizes experience to be a resource for critical reflection. We must also address the interrelations between experience and writing, treating these not as simple corresponding phenomena but still as phenomena that mutually inform each other. I find the outlines for such a concept of experience in Mohanty's commentary on Third World feminist writings. Like Scott, Mohanty criticizes narratives of "women's experience" that fail to examine the cultural processes that engender experiences and identities. Yet while Mohanty rejects homogenizing notions of identity and positivist appeals to experience, she recognizes that stories of experiences have been vital to Third World feminist praxis.

Concerned with engaging these feminisms, she does not dismiss the narration of experience as "epistemologically incorrect" and propose discourse analysis as the sole critical approach to experience. Instead, she investigates the force of those life stories, testimonials, and "histories from below" that have contributed to radical feminist praxis.

In addition to her focus on the most effective (as opposed to the most problematic) marginal experience narratives, Mohanty advances beyond Scott in two key respects. First, Mohanty not only addresses the role of discursive practices in constituting subjectivities; she also examines how subjects can be empowered as language users and knowledge producers. Second, Mohanty not only views social identities and social institutions, such as patriarchy, in terms of local discourses; she also situates these discourses within a global political-economic analysis. By combining her appreciation for the effects of local discourses with a concern for discursive agency and a global perspective, Mohanty discerns relations between experience, writing, and feminist struggles that Scott overlooks.

With respect to the relation between writing and oppositional consciousness, for instance, Scott tells us half the story: she explains how writing is performative of identity. If, however, we are to understand how women can deliberately and strategically reinterpret their lives, then we must also investigate the subjective resources for pursuing oppositional discourses. Mohanty foregrounds precisely this subjective input into rewriting identities, for she thematizes the creative process whereby those more powerful texts translate experience into radical political consciousness. Revaluing this creative work, Mohanty does not claim that marginalized experience needs simply to be expressed or unveiled. She argues, rather, that efforts to remember and to renarrate everyday experiences of domination and resistance, and to situate these experiences in relation to broader historical phenomena, can contribute to an oppositional consciousness that is more than a mere counterstance (Mohanty 1991a, 34-39).[10]

Mohanty identifies Gloria Anzaldúa's essay on "mestiza consciousness" as paradigmatic of the kind of radical rewriting of identity that is possible when we "rethink, remember, and utilize our lived relations as a basis of knowledge" (Mohanty 1991a, 34). Although Mohanty focuses on Anzaldúa's achievement, her articulation of a non-dualistic mestiza consciousness, Anzaldúa's own work shows how this mestiza consciousness takes shape as she remembers and rewrites specific lived experiences, in particular, painful experiences of cultural confusion. Driven to write by "internal strife," Anzaldúa recalls the sources of her suffering; for instance, being American, yet having her art and language devalued as "un-American"; seeing her father die from overwork as a farm laborer on originally Indian land; facing sexism from those who share her language and culture (Anzaldúa 1988, 37-39; 1990a, 203-08; 1990b, 377-79, 382, 388). Anzaldúa's emotional stress from being tricultural in a country that counterposes "American" to "Mexican," and female among a people who equate being "woman" with being defective, attests to Rosemary Hennessy's claim that the incoherences of ruling ideologies "comprise the very fabric of many women's lived reality" (Hennessy 1993b, 27). Insofar as Anzaldúa explores the connections between her personal trials and the contradictions of "Mexican-American" existence, her experiences serve not as mere evidence of oppression but as points of departure for radically renarrating "Mexican-American." For instance, her narrative problematizes the construction of this hyphenated identity as a mere addition to a self-sufficient "America," a "minority" defined in terms of an abstract, pluralist notion of difference. It thereby opens a space for redescribing her borderlands consciousness as an irrevocable part of America, a part that contains valuable knowledge for responding to cultural conflicts.

This Mohanty-inspired reading of Anzaldúa suggests that daily experience is not only shaped by hegemonic discourse but also contains elements of resistance to such discourses; elements that, when strategically narrated, challenge the ideologies that naturalize social arrangements and identities. Such a notion of experience—experience as a resource for confronting and renarrating the complex forces that constitute experience—allows us to return to Delany's text and to better understand what Scott can describe only vaguely as Delany's "subjective perceptual clarity." If we read Delany looking for experienced tensions that motivate creative responses, then we notice Delany's constant attempt to convey his experienced uneasiness with the labels "gay," "black," "artist," while also recognizing those categories' formative influence on his life. In a passage not unlike Anzaldúa's account of her cultural turmoil, Delany describes his discomfort with a language that defines his sexuality as a deviancy, a "private" problem (Delany 1988, 248). He responds to this not by positing an authentic, prediscursive self but by appropriating categories of identity into a narrative that problematizes those categories' naturalized status and "taken for granted" significance.

Delany's psychiatric interview dramatizes this approach. Delany begins by stating that he is homosexual, black, married, and a writer. Yet he resists letting those categories label him or provide an easy solution to how he should be treated, for he interrupts the logic of current discourses on sexuality as he confidently narrates the source of his anxieties: difficulties in bringing his homosexual relations into more standard social structures, problems in balancing those relations with his marriage (a marriage that was, for Marilyn, his wife, the only escape from her mother's legal custody), and compromises required in order to make a living from doing what he likes, writing, having to tailor his writing to a white, heterosexual audience (Delany 1988, 249). These problems cannot be explained by internal properties, such as "gayness." Rather, they are a function of Delany's multiple relations as they are conditioned and constrained by the social and political institutions regulating sexual and economic life.

Through telling his story, then, Delany defies basic tenets of our sexual discourses, including the essentializing of sexual roles and the compartmentalizing of sexual and economic life. The interviewing doctor's constant slips, calling him "Doctor Delany," indicate how this act empowers Delany as actor and knower. Like Anzaldúa, Delany demonstrates that such an experience-based renarrating of one's story does not require complete self-knowledge or a comprehensive social analysis. It requires only the courage to confront "the forces weighing on one's choices and actions" and the initiative to contribute to the terms in which these forces are represented.[11]

Mohanty's account of oppositional consciousness helps us to theorize this experience-motivated discursive agency. In addition, Mohanty disentangles the concept of experience from problematic notions of the private, discrete individual. Scott, in attempt to avoid naturalizing the private individual, eschews any narration of experience. Mohanty, however, suggests how narratives that skillfully contextualize personal struggles can contribute to a community consciousness that displaces the opposition between private and public life. For instance, Mohanty describes how the Jamaican life stories collected by Honor Ford-Smith cultivate a political consciousness through narrating everyday acts of resistance and encoding them in poetic images. In this way, the stories offer to their community images and narrative forms for remembering a history of struggle censored in colonialist narratives, a history whose operation in "peacetime" and in daily life resists given conceptions of political action (Mohanty 1991a, 35). Such texts do not simply privilege the personal over the political. Rather, they rewrite "personal experience" as part of common struggle, while contributing to the collective memory that sustains political community.

Mohanty's commentary thus suggests that critical knowledge and political consciousness do not follow automatically from living in a marginalized social location; they develop only with the struggle against oppression, when this struggle includes the work of remembering and renarrating obscured experiences of resistance to, or tension with, social and cultural norms. Such experiences are not transparent or prior to language, for they contain contradictions and take shape in reaction to culturally given images and stories. Therefore, the narration of such experience is no mere reporting of spontaneous consciousness. On the contrary, it involves rethinking and rearticulating obscured, often painful memories, and forging connections between those memories and collective struggle. Mohanty's insight is that this arduous and creative process of remembering, reprocessing, and reinterpreting lived experience in a collective context—and not the mere "substitution of one interpretation for another"—transforms experience, enabling one to claim subjecthood and to identify with oppositional struggles.

EXPERIENCE AND TRANSNATIONAL "REALITY"

Mohanty's global perspective is also crucial to advancing beyond Scott's reduction of experience to an effect of discourse. When Scott defines experience as an epistemological phenomenon constituted by local discursive practices, she abstracts knowledge practices from the broader political and economic systems in which knowledge circulates.[12] To be sure, Scott intends to "situate and contextualize language," and she sometimes acknowledges that discursive practices sustain and are sustained by an extradiscursive "reality" (1991, 783, 795). However, she stops short of specifying what it is that we "situate and contextualize" language in relation *to*, or explicating all that she lumps under "reality." Leaving this extradiscursive world vague, she can dismiss as "positivist" any attempt to associate experience or consciousness with a structurally determined social location.[13] Mohanty, by contrast, reads texts in relation to experienced struggles and locates these struggles within a global analytic. Her "transnational feminism" is not an internationalism that regards differences among women in an abstract sense of plurality and assumes patriarchy to mean the same thing for all women. Instead, Mohanty's globalism addresses the concrete social and political processes that cross national borders and that effect a complex of hierarchical relations among and within historically specific communities. From this vantage point, Mohanty sees that the global economy, with its transnational corporations, capital mobility, and international divisions of labor, has exacerbated (even while it has further complicated) race, class, sex, and gender hierarchies. She sees that (as Anzaldúa's and Delany's texts illustrate) global relations of labor, property, and state control profoundly affect people's daily choices and concerns—even if they are invisible to people and even if they do not define people's essential nature.

Other feminist theorists, including Harding, Hennessy, and Dorothy Smith, have also argued cogently for recognizing a structurally determined component of marginality and a radical potential for studying marginalized experience—even in the context of discursively constituted identities. Like Mohanty, these theorists value marginal experience narratives not because experience provides direct access to truth, or (at the other extreme) because "language is *the* site of history's enactment" (Scott 1991, 793, emphasis added), but because experience-oriented writing brings into public discussion questions and concerns excluded in dominant ideologies, ideologies which sustain and are sustained by political and economic hierarchies.

Mohanty's development of this argument offers a particularly effective response to Scott's critique. By thematizing the creative work that makes experience available for discussion, and by situating this work within her study of cross-border social institutions and social movements, Mohanty shows how narratives that reckon with historically specific experiences of domination and resistance need not (as Scott claims) merely add to given narratives a new group of ideologically produced subjects. On the contrary, such writing can help women facing multiple oppressions—oppressions sustained by globally organized powers—to develop the insights and agency necessary to resist those powers.

For instance, Mohanty's analysis, with Jacqui Alexander, of the "pedagogical dimension" of colonization indicates a crucial role for experience-oriented writing in the resistance to neocolonialism. According to Mohanty and Alexander, knowledge practices support subjugative relations by representing certain people in ways that objectify and dehumanize them (Alexander and Mohanty 1997, xxviii). In particular, such knowledge practices tend to reduce Third World women to victims or dependents, thus enabling political and cultural practices that exercise control over these women's bodies and sexuality (Alexander and Mohanty 1997, xxiii-xxiv). Scholarship participates (even if unwittingly) in this "discursive colonization" when it claims authority to speak for a certain group, suppresses the group's heterogeneity in order to fit people into neat social categories, or obfuscates the history and politics behind a definition of group identity (Mohanty 1991b, 52-54). This cultural colonization remains even after political colonization is dismantled, preventing Anglo feminists, anticolonial nationalists, and Third World women themselves from recognizing Third World women's agency. In this context, Third World women's self-conscious assumption of responsibility for how their identities and histories are represented constitutes an act of political agency, an act that—far from an illusion—is necessary in order for them to begin to define the terms of their own lives.

Mohanty's further insight is that marginal experience narratives can be a powerful means for Third World women to assert political and epistemic agency—even while challenging Enlightenment notions of the unified, autonomous subject. For Mohanty, these notions are pernicious because they disregard the ways that selfhood is constituted within multiple social relations and agency is gained only through political struggle. Unlike Scott, however, Mohanty does not simply debunk modernist concepts of agency but explores how Third World feminist agency can be redefined in terms of the coalitions that enable actual historical empowerment. In the present context of transnational power hierarchies, Mohanty argues, effective political agency requires forming alliances across class, race, and national boundaries (Mohanty 1991a, 2-4; Alexander and Mohanty 1997, xvii-xx, xl-xli). Moreover, if we want to rethink selfhood in these pluralist, collective terms, we cannot simply assert fragmented identities; we need to reckon with the complexities of marginalized people's historically specific struggles. Mohanty considers Anzaldúa's renarrating of "mestiza" exemplary of an identity "born of history and geography" (Mohanty 1991a, 37). Anzaldúa's mestiza consciousness responds to the particular situation of mixed-blood Mexicans living on land once colonized by Spain, later taken from Mexico by the United States. Because it grows out of an engagement with this history—a history of cultural collusions, mixing of genes, prejudices within communities that were victims of prejudice, and overlapping struggles—a mestiza consciousness implies an identity based on common goals rather than common essence (Anzaldúa 1990b, 380-85). A materially rooted identity, "mestiza" enables one to work in coalition with Native Americans, Mexicans, African Americans, and even males and whites who follow "our lead" (Anzaldúa 1990b, 384).

When experience-rooted rewritings of identity challenge discursive coloni-zation and suggest cross-border, cross-cultural solidarities, these narratives affirm the power to name, embrace, and shift between social positions strate-gically. In so doing, they not only renarrate the past but identify a historical location from which to imagine a different future. We could say that stories that reckon with and publicize contradictory, hitherto muted aspects of expe-rience are "between past and future," in Hannah Arendt's sense: they are grounded in the world we have inherited from the past; yet by offering a new, creative perspective on that past, they enrich our experience of the present, thereby interrupting the seeming momentum of history and enabling us to envision and work toward alternative futures.[14] Thus Anzaldúa links mestiza consciousness with a rewriting of the myth of progress, in which the latter is understood not in terms of racial purity but inclusivity (1990b, 377). Although it is an imaginative vision, it is not merely utopian, for it begins with her own everyday struggles as a lesbian, multilingual Chicana.

CONCLUSIONS: LEARNING FROM EXPERIENCE

In view of this analysis, I propose a Mohanty-inspired notion of experience. The experience that facilitates oppositional discourses consists of tensions between experience and language, tensions that are endured subjectively as contradictions within experience—contradictions between ideologically con-stituted perceptions of the world and reactions to these images endured on multiple psychological and bodily levels. Like Delany's "discomfort" with sexual roles and Anzaldúa's "psychic restlessness," somatic experience can contend with discursively organized perceptions even when it is constituted in relation to the latter. We need not rigidly enumerate or prioritize these layers of experience to recognize that it is the thickness, the multiplicity, and in particular, the tensions within experience that make experience a resource for "seeing" differently. Narratives that reckon with these tensions do not report spontaneous consciousness but create images and narrative forms for rearticulating experience in such a way that the narrated images enable the writer to confront those experienced tensions more constructively.

This account of experience allows readers to learn from experience-oriented texts in a way that both empiricist and poststructuralist epistemologies preclude. If an empiricist perspective allows readers to address these texts only to collect data within given narrative paradigms, Scott's approach is limited to authoritatively analyzing those paradigms. By contrast, a reading informed by a Mohantian notion of experience can attend to the relations between the text and the reader's own experience and can thereby hear the text's call to rethink the stories we tell of our own worlds.

For instance, if we read a text as a creative response to globally situated, experienced tensions, then we confront it neither as a representation nor a fiction but an invitation to reconsider the historical world from the perspective of that narrative. In effect, we can recognize such a text as an aid for what Harding calls "thinking from the standpoint of others' lives"; that is, interpreting the world in view of the insights of those who have struggled against oppression or exploitation (1991, chaps. 7, 10, 11). Mohanty's analysis indicates the importance of creatively produced narrative resources in this project. For if historical experience is complex and contradictory, and is conceptualized only through narrative work, then we can make sense of radically different perspectives on the historical world only if we can imagine different ways of organizing experience, ways that may be foreign to the basic narrative forms of dominant cultural texts. Those life stories that struggle to articulate and contextualize experienced contradictions can offer images and narrative matrices that help readers view the same world with a different focus; that is, to "see" their familiar world with greater sensitivity to elements unintelligible within hegemonic history.

When we recognize stories of experience to be resources for reordering experience, then we can avoid the "robot" repetition of others' views that Harding criticizes (1991, 291) and can approach those views as frameworks that facilitate our own exploration of the world from a different perspective, in which we must take responsibility for the frameworks we choose to employ. In addition, when we locate these narratives in a world of cross-cultural, cross-border processes, we recognize the urgency of considering the place of our own lives within other's narratives. From a global feminist approach, for instance, Anzaldúa's story not only affirms the insights of mestiza consciousness; it also challenges readers who are comfortable in a dominant culture to rethink their identities in light of her narrative, a narrative that situates Anglo-Americans in historically specific relations and obligations to other Americans. Read as a resource for exploring this perspective, Anzaldúa's text is not an endpoint but a point of departure for readers to pursue further understanding of that history and those obligations.

When we understand a narrative as an attempt to reckon with tensions within experience, tensions that reflect kinds of agency, community, or consciousness denied articulation in hegemonic discourse, then we also see that the text does not present self-evident data but only adumbrates inchoate phenomena. Read in this light, the text calls for our participation in exploring the meaning of those phenomena. Even Delany's bathhouse scene invites and facilitates such participation by his readers. Scott, criticizing Delany's alleged positivism, cites his assertion that a genuine sexual revolution requires "the infiltration of clear and articulate language into the marginal areas of human sexual exploration" (Delany 1988, 175). Neither Scott's first nor second reading, however, addresses the specific character of this "infiltration." Delany's "infiltration" is not realist reporting but, on the contrary, an explicitly personal and creative articulation of bits of memories. For instance, following the words cited above, Delany calls his account of the bathhouse "a fragment of an encounter." He does not report exactly what he sees or does but only intimates the scene (for example, "an orgy of a hundred or more") and tells us that he "moved forward into it."

Insofar as we respond to Delany's provocative, open-ended style, we do not find mere information, but promptings to imagine the bathhouse world, the kind of lifestyle, and the interpersonal relations that openly gay institutions make possible. When readers, aided by Delany's narrative, are encouraged to consider phenomena that defy simple opposition to a heterosexual norm or clear separation into "public" and "private" spheres, we become more aware of the social constructedness of the "real" and the "natural," less complacent about "taken for granted" sexual roles. We thereby gain an imaginative space to register our own discomfort with paradigms of sexual identity and to narrate additional stories that challenge them.

Finally, when we read a narrative as a response to tensions between experience and language, we can discern tensions and ambiguities within the text itself (for instance, Anzaldúa's simultaneous distancing from and embracing of "Mexican-American"). These tensions reflect the author's struggle to stretch or challenge her language's accustomed usage in order to reckon with phenomena that defy its logic. As such, these tensions indicate ways that our language may be vulnerable to further disruption or appropriation. Scott rightly points out that disruption is an inherent potential of discourse, for any discourse is indeterminate and conflicts with other discourses (1991, 793). To achieve this disruption, however, we must recognize that it is not discourse itself but our *experience of* discourse and our reckoning with that experience that propels discursive change. Discomfort with discourse exceeds what is represented in given discursive categories. It comes to language only through the struggle to rethink and remember the tensions between our experience and our received language and the work of articulating this by using language against the grain.

Mohanty emphasizes that "the point is not just 'to record' one's history of struggle, or consciousness, but how they are recorded; the way we read, receive and disseminate such imaginative records is immensely significant" (1991a, 34). In light of her analysis, I propose one guideline for responsible reading of stories of experience: we must not reduce these either to empirical evidence or to mere rhetorical constructions, but we must attend to the ways they can help us to discern contradictions in our own experience and can thereby facilitate our own further oppositional speaking and writing.

NOTES

I first presented this paper at the Fall 1996 meeting of the Midwest Society for Women in Philosophy. I thank the SWIP participants, Sandra Harding, the anonymous *Hypatia* reviewers, and especially John Stone-Mediatore for helpful comments on various versions of this essay.

1. Although there are important differences between historical and autobiographical texts, Scott's analysis, as well as Mohanty's, applies to both. Moreover, as Mohanty (1991a, 36) observes, much recent feminist work blurs the line between these two genres.

2. I define "marginalized experience" as kinds of experience that are systematically obscured or omitted in culturally dominant representations of the world. Such experiences are closely related to culturally, politically, and economically marginalized subject-positions, because people in these positions tend to endure the hidden costs and contradictions of social policies and because the subjectivity of these people is often denied in the dominant culture. Yet marginalized experience is not restricted to predefined positions, for anyone may endure a kind of experience that is systematically obfuscated in her culture. I hereafter abbreviate the phrase, *narratives of marginalized experience*, to *marginal experience narratives*.

3. "Third World women" is here understood as a political identity, a potential solidarity in concrete situations (Mohanty 1991a, 2-7; 1997, 7). In the course of this essay, I show how "Third World woman" is also a narrator-position in Carole Taylor's sense. As Taylor puts it, "certainly no fixed, foundational, essential, or unitary identity exists; but actual persons who narrate as women or Blacks or lesbians do exist and those narratives demand authority, dialogue, power" (1993, 73).

4. For instance, Harding values the experience that one gains by struggling against oppression (1991, 126-27, 282, 287); Mohanty values experience as a strategically chosen historical location (1982, 39-42); Weed refers to the possibility of using experience to critique ideologies of the subject (1989, xxv); and Haraway reclaims visual experience as an embodied, critically positioned, multidimensional phenomenon (1988, 582-87).

5. I should note that Scott does, at times, suggest the possibility of combining the narration of experience with discourse analysis (e.g., Scott 1988, 27), and some of her own histories work toward this. Nonetheless, her most developed critique of experience does not recognize any examples of nonpositivist narratives of experience. She argues here that the narration of experience "precludes" analysis of discursive mechanisms (Scott 1991, 778-79). On the opposition Scott establishes between these two projects, see also Canning 1994, 375.

6. Although Scott initially refers to historians' appeals to visual and visceral experience, her critique addresses only the former. I later discuss the significance of this.

7. Christine Stansell (1987) and Linda Alcoff (unpublished paper, cited in Moya 1997, 127) respond to Scott similarly.

8. An influential example here is Tilly, 1989. Despite their disagreement over future strategies, Tilly and Scott coincide in their sharp and sweeping criticisms of histories of experience as mere description that leave intact underlying paradigms.

9. Kathleen Canning (1994, 386-96) presents an illuminating example of what it could mean for historians to rethink "experience" in a way that attended to the body in "both its experiential and discursive dimensions."

10. Mohanty's argument draws on Dorothy Smith's analysis of the way that everyday life is structured by invisible relations of power (Smith 1987). Exceeding Smith, Mohanty focuses on the elements of daily life that resist these relations of power and the creative process whereby these elements are transformed into alternative accounts of subjectivity and agency.

11. This phrase is a paraphrase of Varikas's description of what is conveyed by Saint-Simonian feminists' narratives (1995, 99).

12. Scott's histories do treat some of the connections between discursive practices and political and economic arrangements; but my concern is that this is missing from her definition of experience as a product of discourse. This problem arises partly because Scott intends to include all aspects of social reality in her concept of discourse. "Discourse," she claims, encompasses "not only ways of thinking, but ways of organizing lives, institutions, societies" (1987, 40). However, she actually uses the term more narrowly to refer to knowledge practices that operate primarily on the conceptual level, as indicated in her identification of "discourse" with "rhetoric" (Scott 1988, 4). Thus, though Scott may not intend this, her definition of experience as a discursive production elides and ultimately obscures the reciprocal relations between language practices and labor, property, and state relations. On this latter point, see also Canning (1994, 379), Hennessy (1993a, 123-24), Stansell (1987, 26-29), and Varikas (1995, 95-98).

13. See, for instance, Scott's criticism of Christine Stansell, which, to my mind, caricatures Stansell's argument (Scott 1987, 43).

14. Hannah Arendt 1968 [1954], 7-15. Mohanty's discussion of experience as a strategically chosen location from which to envision alternative futures (Mohanty 1982, 30-31, 41-42) resonates with Arendt's account of "between-past-and-future" thinking as an activity that interrupts the momentum of a seemingly determined history.

REFERENCES

Alexander, M. Jacqui, and Chandra Talpade Mohanty, eds. 1997. *Feminist genealogies, colonial legacies, democratic futures*. New York: Routledge.

Alexander, M. Jacqui, and Chandra Talpade Mohanty. 1997. Introduction: Genealogies, legacies, movements. In *Feminist genealogies, colonial legacies, democratic futures*. See Alexander and Mohanty 1997.

Anzaldúa, Gloria. 1988. Tlilli, tlapalli: The path of the red and black ink. In *Multicultural literacy: Opening the American mind*, ed. Rick Simonson and Scott Walker. Saint Paul, MN: Graywolf Press.

———. 1990a. How to tame a wild tongue. In *Marginalization and contemporary cultures*, ed. Russell Ferguson, Martha Gever, Trinh Minh-ha, and Cornel West. Cambridge: New Museum of Contemporary Art and Massachusetts Institute of Technology.

———. 1990b. La conciencia de la mestiza: Towards a new consciousness. In *Making face, making soul hacienda caras: Creative and critical perspectives by feminists of color*, ed. Gloria Anzaldúa. San Francisco: Aunt Lute Books.

Arendt, Hannah. 1968 [1954]. *Between past and future: Eight exercises in political thought*. New York: Penguin.

Canning, Kathleen. 1994. Feminist history after the linguistic turn: Historicizing discourse and experience. *Signs* 19(2): 368-404.

Delany, Samuel. 1988. *The motion of light in water: Sex and science fiction writing in the East Village, 1957-1965*. New York: Arbor House.

Haraway, Donna. 1988. Situated knowledges: The science question in feminism and the privilege of partial perspective. *Feminist Studies* 14: 575-99.

Harding, Sandra. 1991. *Whose science? Whose knowledge? Thinking from women's lives*. New York: Cornell University Press.

Hennessy, Rosemary. 1993a. *Materialist feminism and the politics of discourse*. New York: Routledge.

———. 1993b. Women's lives/feminist knowledge: Feminist standpoint as ideology critique. *Hypatia* 8(1): 14-34.

Mohanty, Chandra Talpade. 1982. Feminist encounters: Locating the politics of experience. *Copyright* 1: 30-44.

———. 1991a. Cartographies of struggle: Third World women and the politics of feminism. Introduction to *Third World women and the politics of feminism*. See Mohanty, Russo, and Torres. 1991.

———. 1991b. Under Western eyes: Feminist scholarship and colonial discourses. In *Third World women and the politics of feminism*. See Mohanty, Russo, and Torres. 1991.

———. 1997. Women workers and capitalist scripts: Ideologies of domination, common interests, and the politics of solidarity. In *Feminist genealogies, colonial legacies, democratic futures*. See Alexander and Mohanty 1997.

Mohanty, Chandra, Ann Russo, and Lourdes Torres, eds. 1991. *Third World women and the politics of feminism*. Bloomington: Indiana University Press.

Moya, Paula. 1997. Postmodernism, "realism," and the politics of identity: Cherrie Moraga and Chicana feminism. In *Feminist genealogies, colonial legacies, democratic futures*. See Alexander and Mohanty 1997.

Scott, Joan Wallach. 1987. A reply to criticism. *International Labor and Working Class History* 32: 39-45.

———. 1988. *Gender and the politics of history*. New York: Columbia University Press.

———. 1991. The Evidence of experience. *Critical Inquiry* 17: 773-97.

Smith, Dorothy. 1987. *The everyday world as problematic: A feminist sociology*. Boston: Northeastern University Press.

Stansell, Christine. 1987. A response to Joan Scott. *International Labor and Working Class History* 32: 24-29.

Taylor, Carole Anne. 1993. Positioning subjects and objects: Agency, narration, relationality. *Hypatia* 8(1): 55-80.

Tilly, Louise. 1989. Gender, women's history, and social history. *Social Science History* 13: 439-62.

Varikas, Eleni. 1995. Gender, experience, and subjectivity: The Tilly-Scott disagreement. *New Left Review* 211: 89-101.

Weed, Elizabeth. 1989. Introduction: Terms of reference. In *Coming to terms: Feminism, theory, politics*, ed. Elizabeth Weed. New York: Routledge.

8

Sitios y Lenguas: Chicanas Theorize Feminisms

AÍDA HURTADO

Chicana feminist writers have written eloquently about the condition of women in their communities. Many of them have aligned themselves with and participated in various political movements. This practice has infused their theorizing with various influences which makes them similar to other feminist theorists but also different. This paper provides an overview of how Chicana feminist writings address the ethnic specific ways in which gender oppression is imposed on them and their proposals for liberation.

INTRODUCTION

Contemporary Chicana feminisms are truly children of the U. S. progressive political movements of the 1960s. Chicanas' activism on behalf of women's issues has a long, mostly undocumented history.[1] Contemporary writing by Chicana feminists, however, begins in substantive numbers in the late 1960s and is contemporaneous with the Chicano movement, free speech movement, Black power movement, Asian American movement, civil rights movement, and other progressive movements of the time. Unlike (mostly male) members of other progressive movements (Martínez, 1989), many Chicana feminists (as did other feminists of Color) participated simultaneously in more than one of these movements precisely because of their multiple stigmatized group memberships of class, race/ethnicity, gender, and sexuality (Sandoval 1990; Segura and Pesquera 1992; Pesquera and Segura 1993).[2] Many Chicanas participated in progressive political movements with the expectation that these movements would address women's issues as well—an expectation that many politically active women in the 1960s shared. Also shared was the disappointment in discovering that their comrades in struggle, both women and men, did not necessarily see gender as central to the political agenda or central to the analysis of oppression (García 1989; Segura and Pesquera 1992; Pesquera and Segura 1993).

Chicana feminisms were born out of acts of disruption, especially in the Chicano movement, to create spaces of resistance to patriarchy in general and patriarchy in their own ethnic/racial groups (García 1989). Disruption, that is, head-on confrontation, is one of the most powerful methods used by Chicana feminists to bring their issues to the political agenda. Many Chicana feminists disrupted all the movements they participated in: if working within the Chicano movement, they would argue for women's issues (Segura and Pesquera 1992, 78); if working with white feminists, they would argue for including ethnicity/race (Sandoval 1990); if working with Chicana women's organizations, they would argue for including lesbian and gay issues (Pesquera and Segura 1993, 107). As Córdova summarizes it: "Chicanas write in opposition to the symbolic representations of the Chicano movement that did not include them. Chicanas write in opposition to a hegemonic feminist discourse that places gender as a variable separate from that of race and class. Chicanas write in opposition to academics, whether mainstream or postmodern, who have never fully recognized them as subjects, as active agents" (1994, 194). In other words, Chicana feminisms are characterized by finding absences and exclusions and arguing from that standpoint (Collins 1991).

The authors of Chicana feminisms are informed by their participation in more than one political movement, which has benefitted their scholarship and artistic production by avoiding a false homogeneity in voicing their condition as women, as lesbians, as members of ethnic/racial groups, and as predominantly members of the working-class (Sandoval 1991; Pérez 1998). They have confronted their internal diversity earlier than many other groups (Zavella 1994), including the contemporary white women's movement. In other words, they recognize that there are many feminisms (Pesquera and Segura 1993). At the same time, their disruptive voices have been raised within the context of collaboration and political coalition with various progressive movements, such as Third World feminisms, white feminisms, the Chicano movement, socialist/Marxist movements, and revolutionary movements primarily in Latin America and the Caribbean (Puerto Rico, Cuba).

This article summarizes the contributions Chicana feminist scholars, creative writers, and artists have made to theorizing about gender subordination and the foundations for liberation. This review does not aim to be comprehensive, but rather focuses primarily on the writings of the last few years, because they have benefitted the most from feminist scholarship as well as other progressive scholarship. Also, Chicana scholars have made impressive analyses of the writings produced from the 1970s through the early 1990s (García 1989, 1997; Segura and Pesquera 1992; Pesquera and Segura 1993; Córdova 1994). A significant body of Chicana feminist literature exists now, and can inform our theorizing about the condition of Chicanas as well as the condition of all women in the United States.

METHODS FOR THEORIZING

Like all feminist scholars, Chicana feminists have struggled with methods that avoid erasing women's voices. Many of the methods they have developed are similar to those of other feminist scholars. However, unlike white and African American feminists, Chicana feminists strongly advocate and use different varieties of Spanish to increase the inclusion of all women. For many Chicanas, Spanish still remains the home language, which is critical in maintaining Chicano culture and which can, at times, serve as a barrier to keep the harshness of the outside world at bay.[3] For other Chicanas, who no longer speak Spanish, the reacquisition of the language is a political act (Cervantes 1981, 45-47; Moraga 1983, 55; Zavella 1994, 208).[4] Marisela Norte, a Chicana spoken word artist, explains how she writes on the bus ride from East Los Angeles (a predominantly Chicano area) to her office job downtown.[5] Her art reflects the images parading by her bus window. "I can write comfortably until someone looks over my shoulder and starts reading whatever it is that I'm writing. That's when I will switch languages depending on who's sitting next to me" (González and Habell-Pallan 1994, 94). Spanish is also the language of intimacy and resistance, and many Chicana feminists code-switch to Spanish to create a woman's space and discourse—*sitios y lenguas*, to quote Emma Pérez (1993).

The methods used by Chicana feminists include oral histories, adding the use of different varieties of Spanish (Ruiz, 1987, 1998; Romero 1992; Zavella 1997b; Pesquera 1997; Segura 1997); creative production, such as poetry, theatrical performance, painting, dance, music (Baca 1990, 1993; Cisneros 1994; Cantú 1995; Pérez 1996; Mora 1997); the documentation of creative production as evidence of feminism (Broyles 1986, 1989, 1994; Yarbro-Bejarano 1985, 1986, 1991, 1994); social science methods (Segura and Pesquera 1992; Pesquera and Segura 1993); and a variety of combinations of all these tools. Examples include the use of creative writing to see Chicanas as "their own ethnographers" (Quintana 1989, 189; 1996), the use of fables such as those proposed by Derrick Bell and his followers (Hurtado 1996a, 133), book-length essays drawing on a multidisciplinary literature to highlight Chicanas' condition (Castillo 1995), and multidisciplinary anthologies based on a mixing of genres (Moraga and Anzaldúa 1981, Moraga, 1983; Anzaldúa 1987, 1990; Del Castillo 1990; Trujillo 1991, 1998; Alarcón et al. 1993; De la Torre and Pesquera 1993).[6] As Sonia Saldívar-Hull advocates, "We have to look in nontraditional places for our theories: in the prefaces to anthologies, in the interstices of autobiographies, in our cultural artifacts, our *cuentos*, and if we are fortunate to have access to a good library, in the essays published in

marginalized journals not widely distributed by the dominant institutions"
(1991, 206). Regardless of the method, the struggle lies in documenting the
complexities of Chicanas' condition, which is highly influenced by their
gender but *not* independent of other historical material conditions.

Most Chicana feminist writers, methodologically and philosophically, are
very invested in distinguishing themselves from middle-class white feminists
(Cotera 1977; Saldívar-Hull 1991, 203-4; Segura and Pesquera 1992; Pesquera
and Segura 1993). Most Chicana theorists have never claimed unquestioned
allegiance to white feminisms, although they identify areas of agreement
(Segura and Pesquera 1992; Pesquera and Segura 1993; Segura and Pierce
1993; Cuadraz and Pierce 1994) and political coalitions (Hurtado 1996a,
41-43). For example, Segura and Pierce (1993) analyze how Nancy
Chodorow's work applies and does not apply to the Chicano family. Cuadraz
and Pierce (1994) poignantly describe their experiences as they journey
through an elite graduate program, including the similarities because of their
working-class backgrounds and gender, and the differences because of their
race/ethnicity. Hurtado (1996a) explores the different relationships women of
Color and white women have to white men; and Segura and Pesquera (1992)
examine the perceptions of Chicanas in higher education and in white-collar
jobs (Pesquera and Segura 1993) toward the white feminist movement.

Many Chicana feminists have a commitment to remaining loyal to the
working-class roots of their feminist struggle (Anzaldúa 1987; Gómez et al.
1983; Saldívar-Hull 1991, 204) but, at the same time, they face an inherent
tension between their commitment to these struggles and their own privilege
(Zavella 1994, 208). Although many Chicana feminists explicitly state their
own working-class origins (Cervantes 1981, 45; Anzaldúa 1987; Romero 1992,
4-5; Zavella 1994, 207-8; Hurtado 1996b, 383-84; Trujillo 1997, 268, among
others) as writers, academics, and successful artists, they have achieved a class
status higher than the constituencies they write about. Yet many of these
writers astutely use the tension between their attained class status and the class
status of their adopted constituencies to disrupt complacency and to push
concrete political action. For example, Judith Baca, a successful painter   ·
and muralist, recruits young people (some of them were former gang members) in the East Los Angeles area to help paint murals, thereby building
linkages between the themes of her creative production and the participation of the subjects of those themes (Neumaier 1990, 261). Similarly,
creative writers like Sandra Cisneros, Elba Sánchez, and Gloria Anzaldúa
(among others) are known for their work with high school students in
predominantly Chicano communities to expose their creative production
to the communities they write about. Regardless of the class origins of
Chicana feminists and their current class attainment, they have a strong
loyalty to working-class issues.

The literature produced by Chicana feminists is as diverse as the women they are attempting to describe and theorize about. Chicana feminists write from interdisciplinary perspectives in an attempt to encompass the diversity of Chicano communities. Although most Chicanas reside in the five Southwestern states (California, Texas, Arizona, New Mexico, and Colorado), a sizable number can be found in the Midwest, especially in the Chicago area. Chicanas' communities of origin vary from the southern borders of Texas to midwestern immigrant communities (Zavella 1994; 1997). The cornerstone of sexism experienced in these communities, however, has certain overarching dynamics regardless of their diversity. The similarities stem largely from the Catholic undergirding of Chicano culture (Castillo 1996; Espín 1984, 151, 1997) and the common history of conquest and subordination of Chicanos in the United States (Almaguer 1994). Chicanos' common history and material conditions produce similarities in U. S. Chicano culture, especially regarding gender ideology and practice. Although historically most Chicanas have resided in highly segregated neighborhoods, a small but growing number are moving away from predominantly Chicano areas. The writings on Chicana feminisms have not addressed this population of Chicanas.

In spite of the diversity of the population and of the writers, however, there are some convergences in their theorizing about the condition of women and their proposals for liberation. Nonetheless, because Chicana feminisms are rooted in the history of Chicanos as a group, many of their cornerstones are ethnic-specific. Chicana feminisms, as a body of work, offer an impressive theoretical framework from which to enhance feminist theory as a whole.

THE CONTRIBUTIONS OF CHICANA FEMINISMS

History and Material Conditions as the Basis for a Feminist Consciousness

A central project for many Chicana feminists has been to document the history of Chicanas and to debunk the stereotypes that portrayed them as nonagents in political struggles (Córdova 1994; Ruiz 1998). Chicana historians and social scientists are particularly interested in documenting women's struggles in the work place; for example, in maquiladoras and the garment industry (Mora and Del Castillo 1980), canneries (Ruíz 1987; Zavella 1987), and agricultural fields (Guerin-Gonzalez 1994). They record not only the struggles of women workers but also of women leaders (Pesquera and Segura 1993, 97; Méndez-Negrete 1995). The emphasis on labor issues (Pesquera 1991; Romero 1992; Segura 1994; Zavella 1987) stems not only from the intense participation of Chicanas in this sphere but also from the linkage between almost all Chicana feminist scholars and the Chicano movement (Segura and Pesquera 1992).

Most current Chicana feminist writings are produced by individuals who participated in the Chicano movement of the 1960s and 1970s (Segura and Pesquera 1992; Córdova 1994, 175, 188-89).[7] Ramón Gutiérrez (1993) describes the Chicano movement as encompassing the unionizing efforts of César Chávez with the farmworkers, the militant efforts of Reies López Tijerina to recapture the lands taken from Chicanos in the southwestern United States during the Mexican-American War of 1848, and the political mobilization of Chicano students on university campuses across this country. It was a movement that included students, labor organizers, agricultural workers, and cultural workers—mostly poets, singers, and actors in regional Chicano theater. Many of the writers of Chicana feminisms, regardless of the disciplinary affiliation, refer to their participation in the Chicano movement.

The political underpinnings of the Chicano movement were Marxist/socialist, infused with Chicano culture (Gutiérrez 1993, 46). They included a kind of secular Catholicism that was more cultural than religious in nature. The feminisms exposed by Chicanas are deeply rooted in the material conditions of Chicanos as a whole. As Saldívar-Hull states, "Chicana feminism, both in its theory and method, is tied to the material world" (1991, 220). Chicana feminisms proclaim the primacy of material conditions and advocate strongly the "basics" required for human existence, such as adequate jobs, decent wages, good working conditions, child care, health care, and public safety.[8] It is important to note, however, that even though many white feminists also claim some of these issues, the emphasis is somewhat different for many Chicana feminists. For example, even though reproductive rights have been central to the white feminist agenda, white feminists have emphasized the right to their bodies through birth control and abortion. For Chicana feminists, these two issues have also been central; but of equal concern has been the forced sterilization and forced birth control that some Chicanas have suffered through state intervention (Nieto 1974; Sosa Ridell 1993, 187).[9] Chicanas were writing about forced sterilization as early as the 1960s (Córdova 1994). Forced sterilization for white women has not been as central in their writing or in the white feminist political agenda; certainly not as central as abortion rights. Even those Chicana feminist writers who make incursions into more abstract topics like psychoanalysis (Pérez 1993) and cultural studies (Alarcón 1996; Chabram Dinersesian 1996; Fregoso 1993; Sandoval 1991, 1998) always proclaim the importance of material conditions in Chicanas' gender liberation and the liberation of Chicano communities as a whole.

Reclaiming Malinchismo and Rejecting Marianismo

Many Chicana feminists see links between the history of Chicanas in this country and Mexico as a centerpiece of their theorizing about the condition of women. For example, the origin of Chicanos as a group was an act of war and eventual conquest. The Treaty of Guadalupe Hidalgo of 1848, which ended the Mexican-American War, created Chicanos as a group. This treaty formalized Mexico's defeat and the loss of more than 50 percent of its territory. Overnight, the people residing in what has become the southwestern United States had a new government, which used a different language and a different culture and had the victor's power over them (Almaguer 1971; García 1973).

This, however, was not the first experience of conquest. For Chicana theoreticians, the conquest of the Americas included a woman, La Malinche, as a pivotal figure. Of course, Chicana feminists did not choose La Malinche as the defining figure in their feminisms. Yet because it was committed by a woman, many male writers have saddled all women with Mexico's initial betrayal (see Paz 1985 as a prime example of this tendency). Skepticism about women has its origins in the cultural and sexual violation of La Malinche. Historically, La Malinche, a woman, is the ultimate traitor of Mexico. La Malinche supposedly facilitated Hernán Cortés's conquest of the Aztec empire by acting as translator between the Spanish and the different Mixteca tribes. Norma Alarcón notes, "Malintzín [La Malinche] comes to be known as la lengua, literally meaning the tongue. La lengua was the metaphor used, by Cortés and the chroniclers of the conquest, to refer to Malintzín the translator" (1989, 59). From this betrayal, modern Mexico was born both figuratively and literally, because La Malinche converted to Catholicism and bore the children of Hernán Córtes's soldier Jaramillo. As Emma Pérez points out, Cortés did not feel Malintzín (or Malinche) was worthy of marriage because she was the "other, the inferior, disdained female;" when he was finished with her he passed her on to his soldier (1993, 61).

It is not surprising, therefore, that many feminists have engaged the polemics around La Malinche either to redeem her, to commiserate with her, or to appropriate her as a feminist hero (Alarcón 1989). But La Malinche is not the only historical figure to be engaged. Other female historical figures have also been embraced for their potential to illustrate a possible mapping for what can constitute a feminist consciousness that is specific to Chicanas. Examples are La Virgen de Guadalupe (Castillo 1996), Sor Juana Inés de la Cruz (González 1990; Gaspar de Alba 1998), La Llorona (Cisneros 1991; Mora 1996, 91; Viramontes 1985), and Frida Kahlo, among others (Córdova 1994, 193).[10] These historical figures also share an engagement with struggles that go beyond gender—mostly struggles around labor and social revolutions against repressive governments.

The other side of *Malinchismo* is *Marianismo*, or the veneration of the Virgin Mary. The Virgin Mary, especially her Mexican version, *La Virgen de Guada-lupe*, is the role model for Chicana womanhood: she is the mother, the nurturer, she has endured pain and sorrow, she is willing to serve (Nieto, 1974, 37). Chicanas are supposed emulate these same values and apply them in serving their husbands and children (Córdova 1994, 175). Although the root of these values is the Catholic church, they are nonetheless similar to the ideals of womanhood held by other ethnic and racial groups, including some whites, in U.S. society (members of the Christian Right come readily to mind). For many Chicanos, however, these same values have been a source of solace and strength to fight racism and resist oppression by the dominant group. The dedication that many women have for their families—and many men's commitment to uphold their side of the bargain by hard work in the agricultural fields, brutal work in factories, and low-paid, unskilled labor—has made it difficult for Chicana feminists to question these values. Consequently, the challenge for Chicana feminists has been simultaneously to critique the inherent sexism in dichotomizing their womanhood between *Malinchismo* and *Marianismo* and to recognize the courageous work of many women and men who have fought to preserve their families against brutal, racist state intervention. Chicana feminists have not always been successful in keeping all these issues in balance, nor have their challenges been met with open arms by most members of Chicano communities. Some Chicanas have not seen the advantages of challenging patriarchy and others have been afraid to betray their communities by joining *any* feminist cause (García 1989, 225).

It was not surprising, therefore, that when Chicana feminists questioned their roles in the Chicano movement, they were perceived by both men and women as not only attacking unequal gender practices but questioning the Catholic underpinnings of *all* Chicano culture. Consequently, many Chicano men in and outside the Chicano movement, as well as some women, called the emerging Chicana feminist consciousness a betrayal and labeled Chicana feminists "anti-family, anti-cultural, anti-man and therefore anti-Chicano movement" (Nieto-Gómez, 1974, 35). Ironically, they were called *Malinchistas* by the men in the movement signifying them as traitors to their communities and as sellouts to white feminism; they were also called lesbians because they supposedly were privileging their sex above the unity of the Chicano movement in its struggle for social justice (García 1989, 225-26). The accusation of lesbianism by homophobic Chicano nationalists of both genders was used to intimidate Chicana feminists into relinquishing their struggles on behalf of women's issues. In an effort to build solidarity, many contemporary Chicana theorists, both lesbian and heterosexual, defined their feminisms in allegiance with one another.

Sexuality

Chicana feminists have written eloquently of how *Marianismo* and *Malinchismo* dichotomize womanhood into the "good woman" and "bad woman," depending on how women exercise their sexuality (Hurtado 1998b). As Vásquez and González ask, "They say we are sometimes passionate, sexy, voluptuous, darkeyed, hot-tempered beauties; other times we are chaste and sexually pure; we are 'mamacitas': fat women surrounded by five or six little brown-skinned children, always cooking. This is what they say we are. Is that who we really are?" (1981, 50). To be a "good woman" is to remain a virgin until marriage and to invest devotion, loyalty, and nurturance in the family. Chicanos' definition of family, moreover, goes beyond the nuclear family to include extended networks of related kin, as well as friends (Baca Zinn 1975). As in all patriarchies, there are rewards for women who comply and punishments for those who rebel. As Anzaldúa laments, "Every bit of self-faith I'd painstakingly gathered took a beating daily. Nothing in my culture approved of me. *Había agarrado malos pasos* [I had taken the wrong path]. Something was 'wrong' with me. *Estaba más allá de la tradición* [I was beyond the tradition]" (quoted in Saldívar-Hull 1991, 213). But even among those who comply, patriarchal power, as in white, mainstream culture, has its prerogative of violence *at the discretion* of the father/husband with little or no accountability. Women who openly rebel pay the price. Again, as Anzaldúa declares: "*Repele, Hable pa' 'tras. Fuí muy hocicona. Era indiferente a muchos valores de mi cultura. No me deje de los hombres. No fuí buena ni obediente*" (1987, 15).[11] As a result of her rebellion, she was thought of as not being a "real woman."

The punishment and banishment from Chicano communities has been especially harsh for women who claim their lesbianism openly. To prefer women is the ultimate rejection of patriarchy; the strong Catholic underpinnings of Chicano culture make lesbianism a mortal sin (Trujillo 1991, 191). Many Chicana lesbians have found refuge in white lesbian and gay communities and in activism on behalf of lesbian and gay issues. Lesbian and gay activists, however, have never completely disengaged from their Chicano communities or from activism on behalf of Chicano issues (Trujillo 1997, 274). The political and theoretical sophistication gained from participation in this broader political base has infused much of the theorizing about Chicanas' gender issues.

Some of the most prolific Chicana feminist writers openly claim their lesbianism. They also are the best known in mainstream circles. Writers like Cherríe Moraga, Gloria Anzaldúa, and Emma Pérez have accomplished a great deal in making sexuality a central part of Chicana feminist theorizing. Chicano communities are as homophobic as white mainstream communities, and Chicana feminists who expose and defend lesbianism have profoundly challenged the status quo (Saldívar-Hull 1991, 214; Pérez 1998). It is important to acknowledge that progressive politics in Chicano communities are practiced by individuals deeply committed to maintaining the cultural integrity of Chicano culture as a challenge to the dominant hegemony of cultural, linguistic, and economic assimilation (Segura and Pesquera 1992). In that context, to propose that homophobia should be challenged even among working-class Chicanos is a deeply courageous act. At the same time, most of the lesbian Chicana writers have an intense loyalty to their communities of origin, to Chicano culture, to the Spanish language, and to working-class issues.

Many Chicana feminists have also written eloquently about their loyalty to their mothers (Cervantes 1981, 11-14; Moraga 1983; Córdova 1994, 193; Cantú 1995, 16-17; Mora 1997). The relationship they highlight in these writings is that of the intimacy, love, and caring provided by their mothers, grandmothers, and other mother figures such as aunts. That loyalty is born out of their shared condition as women, but also out of the writers' recognition of these women's class struggles to survive against all odds. Many Chicana writers speak of their mothers' fortitude and resilience on behalf of their families. Cantú describes the trials and tribulations of her grandmother or "mamagrande:"

> She holds her dreams in her heart. . . . The work, endless. From cooking daily meals—*sopa de arroz, guisados, postres* for lunch—and fancy festive meals—*cabrito, mole, tamales*—to keeping the linens whiter than white, fighting the dust and the grime of life on a ranch of a town. The keeping of appearances, of dignity, of what is right is even more tiring. . . . Her pains and her joys buried in her heart, her hands ever busy crocheting, embroidering, knitting, quilting. The work never stops, her handkerchief *a la mano* in her apron pocket ever ready for the tears of joy or of pain. Mamagrande.(1995, 17)

They see in their mothers unnamed feminists and unclaimed heroes who, through their daily lives, map what Chicana feminists want to capture in their writings. Pat Mora passionately describes the strength her mother gave her. Although her mother was one of the fortunate few of her generation to finish high school in the 1930s, she was unable to attend college. Nonetheless, her lack of higher education did not mean lack of assertiveness.

> I've never seen anyone intimidate my mother, who is about five feet tall. Without cheating and resorting to physical violence, I can't imagine anyone who could—not a president, prime minister, or pope. . . . When she's angry, I think her eyes can melt metal. She is assertively articulate in English or Spanish and has never hesitated to state her displeasure, whether at poor service, rude behavior, or injustice. She can be bilingually

fierce.... Articulate fire is wealth ... Ultimately, of course, she
was showing us the importance of expecting justice and of
clearly and forcefully stating objections to unfairness. (1993,
82-83)

Although not without tension, the relationship between mothers and
daughters in Chicana feminisms is overwhelming in its solidarity to political
struggle. Lesbian writers also speak of how the relationships with their mothers
flourished even when they disapproved of or did not understand their
daughters' commitment to lesbianism (Moraga 1983).

Chicana feminists committed to making sexuality central to Chicana feminisms have pushed all theoreticians to expand their frameworks beyond
race/ethnicity, gender, and class. The understanding of sexuality has not
developed separately from other Chicana feminist concerns. Sexuality, however, was not as dominant in Chicana feminists' early writings as it has become
since the publication of *This Bridge Called My Back* (Moraga and Anzaldúa
1981). Although lesbianism was the gateway to questions of sexuality,
Chicana feminists have also written about sexual pleasure and desire. Their
explicit treatment of sexuality has not been easy. Nonetheless, they have
taken the risk and exposed women's desires regardless of the normative
sanctions against explicitly speaking about, much the less experiencing,
pleasure through sex (Castillo, 1992; Sánchez 1992; Cisneros 1994; Zavella
1997b; Pérez 1998).

As part of the process of analyzing issues of desire and physical attraction,
some Chicana feminists have addressed the internal racism of their communities, based on skin color and Indian heritage as determined by phenotype
(Anzaldúa 1987, 21; Broyles 1994; Castañeda 1990, 228; Zavella 1994, 205).
Although male scholars have addressed these issues (Arce, Murguía and Frisbie
1987; Forbes 1968; Telles and Murguía 1990, 1992), and the issues were central
in the revisionist scholarship produced in the 1960s, Chicana feminists have
addressed how these issues relate to women specifically (Saldívar-Hull 1991,
214-15). In particular, Chicana feminists have addressed how skin color is used
to define desirable standards of beauty and womanhood (Anzaldúa 1981;
Zavella 1994, 205). As Zavella notes: "skin color in particular is commented
on, with *las gueras* (light-skinned ones) receiving appreciation, while *las prietas*
(dark-skinned ones) are devalued and admonished to stay out of the sunlight
so they won't get darker" (1994, 205).

Many Chicana feminists have reclaimed *mestizaje*, the mixture of European,
African, and Indian races, to resist the racist standards adopted in Chicano
communities of preferring lighter skin and European features, especially for
women. They have also exposed how negative racist judgments of darker-
skinned, Indian-looking women are related to the derogation of their womanhood and perceived desirability *as women*, even among otherwise progressive

men (Broyles 1994). As Norma Alarcón states: "It is worthwhile to remember that the historical founding moment of the construction of *mestiza(o)* subjectivity entails the rejection and denial of the dark Indian Mother as Indian which have compelled women to often collude in silence against themselves, and to actually deny the Indian position even as that position is visually stylized and represented in the making of the fatherland" (1990a, 252). By addressing the internal racism of Chicano communities and progressive Chicano men, Chicana feminists have turned the critical lens inward, illustrating how standpoint theory is extremely important to avoid essentializing any group as being above the dynamics of racism, sexism, and homophobia (Ochoa and Teaiwa 1994, ix). Furthermore, by including issues of beauty, sexual desirability, and construction of womanhoods, the analysis of *mestizaje* is *woman-centered* rather than relying on male scholars' paradigms for studying racism.

Commitment to Political Action

Regardless of the method used and the issues addressed, almost all Chicana feminists adamantly declare that their scholarship and artistic production should result in political action aimed at social change. Furthermore, regardless of their profession, whether academics, artists, creative writers, or performers, all ascribe to involvement in political action of some kind (Cuadraz 1997). They are also committed to progressive causes and publicly opposed to conservative political agendas, with a few exceptions (such as Linda Chavez [1991], who would not call herself a feminist anyway). The advocacy in many Chicana feminist writings of left-of-center political strategies by definition can exclude more politically moderate women (Pesquera and Segura 1993). Their commitment to working-class struggles can also exclude middle-class women who may not feel such affinity (Pesquera and Segura 1993). Neither question—politically moderate strategies and middle-class inclusion—has been addressed extensively by Chicana feminist writers.

The writings of Chicana feminists also suggest concrete organizing tools for political action. Foremost in their writings is an emphasis on the joys of struggle rather than on victimhood. Indeed, one area in which Chicana feminisms lack clarity is in delineating the human cost of oppression based on multiple group memberships. Once the oppression is acknowledged, most writers quickly proceed to highlight the resistance rather than the act of succumbing to brutal treatment (Anzaldúa 1987, 21; Hurtado 1996b). Many Chicana feminists have been critical of writings that do not highlight women's agency and therefore have tried to underscore survival rather than defeat (Mora and Del Castillo 1980). In emphasizing survival, they have also inadvertently mapped a set of strategies for resistance and for coalition building.

Chicana feminisms adhere to eclectic paradigms for political mobilization. Much of their theorizing about social change comes from everyday interactions with representatives of repressive institutions designed to control and oppress communities of Color, such as police, school officials, employers, and welfare workers (Hurtado 1989; Neumaier 1990; Pardo 1990, 1991; Sandoval 1991, 1998). Instead of proposing a grand theory of social change, the strategies proposed by Chicanas are context-dependent and largely the result of lessons gleaned from their daily lives and the daily lives of the women around them (Pardo 1990, 1991). As Sandoval reminds us,

> Any social order which is hierarchically organized into relations of domination and subordination creates particular subject positions within which the subordinated can legitimately function. These subject positions, once self-consciously recognized by their inhabitants, can become transformed into more effective sites of resistance to the current ordering of power relations. (1991, 11)

Scott (1990) has referred to these strategies as "weapons of the weak"; weapons that many Chicanas developed and used long before they were labeled (Pardo 1990, 1991). Nonetheless, the situationally based resistance is usually documented by Chicana feminists through *cuentos* (stories), myths (for example, *La Llorona*), *chistes* (jokes), or concrete actions that verge on performance art. For example, a colleague read her paper on colonization by printing it on a continuous computer paper that she unscrolled as she dramatically, and very effectively, deconstructed the myth of Cristóbal Colón (Christopher Columbus)—colón in Spanish meaning large ass. She chose to insert a dash in the word *colonizer* in Spanish as *Colón-ialista*, further adding to the play and resistance in her words. The combination of presenting a formal paper in a professional conference and simultaneously deconstructing the presentation and the medium of scholarly production created a consciousness-raising moment. It highlighted the effects of colonization on the descendants of its victims. Rather than assuming a scholarly distance from the topic, the professor's *enactment* clearly stated the political consequences of Columbus' voyage.[12]

Pardo provides another example of spontaneous political mobilization based on her research on the Mothers of East Los Angeles, a group formed to fend off the building of a prison and a toxic waste dump in their neighborhood. At one of their meetings, representatives of several oil companies attempted to gain their support for building an oil pipeline through the center of East Lost Angeles. The women asked one of the oil representatives about alternative routes for the pipeline.

"Is it going through Cielito Lindo [President Ronald Reagan's ranch]?" The oil representative answered, "No." Another woman stood up and asked, "Why not place it along the coastline?" Without thinking of the implications, the representative responded, "Oh no! If it burst, it would endanger the marine life." The woman retorted, "You value the marine life more than human beings?" His face reddened with anger and the hearing disintegrated into angry chanting. (Pardo 1990, 4)

There are countless other examples that will enrich our feminist theorizing as more Chicanas continue to write and experiment with words, genres, and politics.

Although not without tension, Chicana feminisms have addressed the inclusion of men in their efforts to mobilize politically. Chicana feminists fully acknowledge that although men in their communities hold patriarchal power over them, those same men are oppressed by white men and some white women because of their ethnicity or race (Moraga and Anzaldúa 1981). Since the writings of the late 1960s and early 1970s, few Chicana feminist writers have seen all men as having equal patriarchal power, a position similar to that of other feminists of Color and Marxist/socialist white feminists. Most Chicana feminists recognized the distinction very early in their lives as they interacted with white communities and were forced, as children, to make distinctions between different kinds of men according to race/ethnicity and class. The recognition of difference among men helped produce complex feminisms to explain why the writers kept their political allegiance to Chicanos while at the same time critically contesting these men's sexism and homophobia. However, Chicana feminists had to suspend strategically their critical views to join the men in fighting white men and white women on issues that affected their communities as a whole; for example, labor organizing, health benefits, affirmative action, and the environment. Pardo (1990) theorizes that the inclusion of fathers in the activities of the Mothers of East Los Angeles was not only politically astute but necessary for the preservation of the women's own political involvement. The more family members who participated in mobilizing against the building of a prison and a toxic dump in their neighborhood, the more political clout they could bring to the issues at hand. At the same time, they had to safeguard the group against men taking over by strategically subverting men's authority. For example, although they named a man president of the organization, the women had complete authority in the day-to-day activities; and when the president tried to exert his power by insisting that a fundraiser be held on Mother's Day, only the president and his wife showed up (Pardo 1990, 3). After this experience, the president did not try to impose his will again.

Coalition Building and the Recognition of Difference

Chicana feminists are tied to other feminisms and political struggles theoretically as well as practically. There are numerous attempts at coalition building with other feminists of Color for concrete political action (Ochoa and Teaiwa 1994). Coalition building is necessary because structural oppression is far from dismantled. As Angela Davis and Elizabeth Martínez put it, in response to the question of why we still have to categorize individuals according to their group memberships of race, class, gender, and sexuality,

> People ask: "Why can't we all see each other as human beings? Why do we have to emphasize these differences?" or "Why do we need feminism? Why can't we just have humanism? Doesn't talking about racism and the different races just perpetuate the problem?" This negates the structures of power that determine human relationships in this society in a way that is deadening for a great number of people, mostly, but by no means only people of color. You can't just say "Let's all get along" until we get rid of those structures. (Davis and Martínez 1994, 49)

The theoretical basis of Chicana feminisms is not consensus but contentious confrontation, and writers must be honest about how difficult it is to relate across differences. The frustrations experienced by many activists are clearly stated with very little glossing over or glorification of unity (Sifuentes and Williams 1994). It is from these spaces (sitios) of contention that many Chicana feminists make their contributions to our understanding of gender and political action.

Many Chicana feminists are adamant about not ranking oppressions, which might exclude causes perceived as not central to women's rights (for example, fighting for prisoners' rights, labor organizing, and environmental issues). Instead, Chicana feminisms struggle to incorporate diverse issues without losing the centrality of gender in all their battles. As Angela Davis and Elizabeth Martínez remind us,

> First of all, we have to reject any hierarchy of needs of different communities. . . . [We] don't mean that some communities or some groups on a campus or in any other community will not want to emphasize certain needs. . . . But we cannot be trapped in arguing about "My need is greater than yours," or "A women's center is more important than a Latino cultural center," or whatever. We have to fight together because there is a common enemy. Especially if you are up against an administration being divisive, [we] think everybody has to come together and form an alliance or a set of goals together. (1994, 43)

Davis and Martínez put it succinctly by stating, "the general idea is no competition of hierarchies should prevail. No 'Oppression Olympics.' " The hope is to accomplish "equality across difference" (1994, 44) without privileging only one way of relating to each other. Many Chicana feminists are committed to coalition politics from their knowledge that "women of Color" or "African American women" or "Chicana women" are racialized subjects that have been constructed through historical events and material conditions (1994, 46). Rather than adhering to an essentialist notion of identity, many Chicana feminists struggle with implementing standpoint theory through coalition building.

> One handy distinction is to think of coalitions being built around issues, and ideology being a worldview. An ideology is a set of ideas that explains what makes society tick and what its values are. We don't have to agree on that with other people in order to fight for health care, housing, affirmative action, or whatever. You do have to agree with somebody's ideology, I think, if you're going to join certain kinds of organizations . . . from the Boy Scouts to the Communist Party. But coalitions, networks, and alliances should never make the mistake of demanding ideological unity. (Davis and Martínez 1994, 47)

Along with recognizing the fluidity of social categories that constitute their social identities, many Chicana feminists also recognize the need to work for important political goals with individuals who do not have "ideological affinity" with them (Davis and Martínez 1994, 46). That is, in the expression of Chicana feminisms there is recognition that coalition work necessarily entails thoughtful compromise for the sake of political resistance and social change.

IMPLICATIONS OF THEORIZING IN LAS FRONTERAS

Chicana feminists have been at the forefront of theorizing from the borderlands—las fronteras—as their *sitios* (Mora 1993). The history of conquest, which basically layered one nation over an already existing one has given Chicana feminists the knowledge of the temporality of nation-states (Klahn 1994). The political line dividing the United States from Mexico does not correspond to the experiential existence on the border, where families live on both sides of the Rio Grande and where shopping, entertainment, and cultural expression do not abide by the legal line that separates both countries (Cantú 1995). Many Chicana feminists claim the borderlands as the *sitios* that provide the aperture for theorizing about subordination from an ethnically specific Chicana/*mestiza* consciousness (Anzaldúa 1987). It is at the border that Chicanas/mestizas learn the socially constructed nature of all categories. By standing on the U. S. side of the river they see Mexico and they see home; by standing on the Mexican side, they see the United States and they see home. Yet they are not really accepted on either side. The U.S.-Mexico border becomes the metaphor for all the "border crossings," both physical and psychological, that many Chicanas have had to endure.

The exposure to multiple borders allows many Chicanas to "see" the arbitrary nature of all categories and therefore the necessity nonetheless to take a stand. Many Chicana feminists struggle to construct paradigms that exclude while including, to reject while consenting, to struggle while accepting. Chicana feminists have named this *facultad* an "oppositional consciousness" (Sandoval 1991), "multiple realities" (Alarcón 1990b), or a state of *conscientización* (Castillo 1995, 171). The basic concept, however, involves the ability to hold multiple social perspectives while simultaneously maintaining a core center, around which revolve concrete material oppressions. More recently, some Chicana feminists have been quick to point out that the ability or *facultad* to cross "borders" is not easy to exercise—at least, not without enormous pain and retribution from authority figures who require a "false" unified self (Lamphere, et al. 1993). True enough—those who exercise *la facultad*, especially in writing, are the outliers (Hurtado 1996b) who run the risk of expulsion from their communities. There are, however, women who exercise *la facultad* without writing about it and without calling it a feminist consciousness, who impart their lessons to younger women around them, and who resist gender subordination through everyday acts of rebellion (Steinem 1983) and guerrilla warfare of the mind (Hurtado 1989; Pardo 1990; Sandoval 1991).

Many Chicana feminists work across differences finding dimensions of similarity through strategic suspensions (Hurtado 1996b) and produce feminisms that defy "geopolitical borders" (Saldívar-Hull 1991, 211). Chicana feminists have also made enormous contributions to theorizing *nonhierarchical* relationships with Third World feminists all over the world and with U. S. feminists of Color (Saldívar-Hull 1991, 208-29). Their theorizing averts the obstacle of race privilege faced by white feminisms. Many Chicana feminists' working-class commitments, however fraught with tensions, have also been a bridge to women of Color in the United States and in Third World countries. Many of the cornerstones of Chicano culture based on Catholicism and on a rural, working-class culture find their echo in some Third World feminisms, especially in Latin America (Sternbach, et al. 1992). Moreover, Chicana feminists' commitment to the liberation of their communities as a whole is much more common among Third World feminists than is the Western view of freedom based on *individual* rights that has highly influenced white feminists in the United States (Brown 1992). Inevitably, white feminists' position in relation to white men as fathers, lovers, siblings, husbands, and brothers interferes with how much Third World feminists can trust them as individuals or see themselves reflected in many white feminist writings. These barriers are significant for many Chicana feminists, who feel that they are a politically colonized group within the United States (Saldívar-Hull 1991) because of the history of conquest and labor exploitation their group has suffered at the hands of the dominant white group. The exploitation, moreover, has benefitted white women directly and indirectly because of their race (Ostrander 1984; Sturgis 1988; McIntosh 1992; Frankenberg 1993; Fine 1997; Hurtado 1998a) and because of their familial relationship to white men (Hurtado 1996a).

The frameworks proposed by Chicana feminisms for liberation are reflexive in nature—there is a constant self-scrutiny to ensure not to oppress others (Zavella 1997a). As Emma Pérez contends, "Within capitalist patriarchal ideology, there is no place for the sensitive human being who is willing to transform the world . . . each member of the collective taking responsibility for her/his contradictions within the collective, willing to grapple with the question, 'Who am I exploiting?' " (1991, 173). Even though their group memberships place Chicanas, especially lesbians, at great risk (Trujillo 1997), they thereby assume agency. They know that within specified, restrictive contexts, they, too, can act in prejudicial and racist ways. As a whole, Chicana feminisms are theories about liberation for all.

Throughout many of the writings by Chicana feminists, there is a commitment to Chicano culture and to their communities. As Amalia Mesa-Bains, artist and cultural worker, declares, "My work, with rare exception, is always rooted in my culture" (quoted in González and Habell-Pallan 1994, 86). As part of this cultural engagement, Chicana feminists adhere to a secular Catholicism that appropriates certain cornerstones of this religion because they are an integral part of Chicano culture. For example, Chicanas invoke the spirituality of religious practice (baptisms, masses, weddings), liberation theology (labor organizing and political mobilization through religious participation), and religious figures like the Virgin of Guadalupe to raise feminist consciousness (Castillo 1996). Commitment to the Spanish language is another refusal to assimilate. The use of different varieties of Spanish by many Chicana feminists establishes their distinctiveness from white mainstream culture and asserts another cultural space through their *lenguas* (languages). Spanish can also serve as a bridge to coalition with Latin American feminists and to common *sitios* through common *lenguas* (Lugones 1990, 396-97; Sternbach et al. 1992, 419).

FUTURE DIRECTIONS IN CHICANA FEMINISMS

In the next fifteen years, the challenge for Chicana feminist scholars will be similar to that faced by current white feminisms: how to engage young women, when many of the barriers that were the impetus for theorizing are slowly melting away. For Chicana feminists, the common working-class origins, the predominance of Spanish in their backgrounds, and the persistence of sexism, heterosexism, and racism have fueled much of their passion and vitality. Younger Chicanas will have had much more varied social and class experiences than the current writers, and their gender consciousness will necessarily be different. The question is whether current feminist frameworks will be relevant to these young women. The question is especially relevant when these young women have been exposed to much more interethnic contact than twenty years ago, when the Chicano movement advocated a nationalist position that scorned interethnic relations, especially of the intimate kind. Increasingly, the children of the intermarriages of the 1960s require us to rethink what constitutes Chicana identity (González and Habell-Pallan 1994, 81-82). Unlike intermarriages of the more distant past, which were not only few but primarily between Chicanos and whites, the 1960s provided a broader context for intergroup contact, and "mixed" heritage now means every possible combination of ethnicities and races. Many of these unions occurred between members of subordinate groups, such as African Americans, Asian Americans, and Latinos. Especially important for Chicana feminist theorizing, which is based on Mexican history and nationality, is the increase of intermarriage between different Latino groups whose children will increasingly identify with a Latino "pan-ethnicity" rather than a specific Latino national group (Padilla 1985; López and Espíritu 1990).

These emerging social formations will also be characterized by an increase in social and economic mobility. This change is, of course, still very small, but nonetheless it will increase class diversity, which will also affect Chicana feminisms. To be sure, those with increased economic and educational opportunities are the ones most likely to join the academy and most likely to be the next generation of writers.

At the same time, we are experiencing the dismantling of affirmative action, attacks on abortion rights, and the backlash against immigration. The Chicana feminisms of the future will have to address the contradictions of advances in the context of repression. In many ways, the terms of the debates of the progressive movements in the 1960s and 1970s were much clearer, because the political and economic lines were well drawn (Gutiérrez 1993; Fernández 1994). The challenge for younger feminists will be to develop paradigms that are complex enough to encompass contradictions and subtleties that many earlier Chicana feminists could not possibly have envisioned.

Chicana feminisms have eloquently addressed issues of sexuality insofar as they affect lesbian concerns, but certainly there is much more to be done. Less often addressed is the explicit study of the range of sexualities and their relationship to patriarchy in Chicano communities. There have been some promising starts (most notably Zavella 1997b) but not a well-developed literature. Intimately tied to women's sexuality is the study of gay issues for Chicano men. How do Chicano gays subvert the power of patriarchy in

Chicano communities, and how is this "betrayal" handled by members of those communities? There are also some promising starts in this area, most notably Almaguer (1991). Exposing sexuality issues in Chicano communities is an especially delicate subject for exactly the same reasons that exposing women's issues was delicate in the early 1970s. These issues threaten to divide the political struggle to gain some of the basic necessities of life; focusing on sexuality threatens to subvert the Catholic underpinnings of Chicano culture, that important source of strength in fending off racist attacks on Chicano communities. Scholars writing about sexuality confront the next frontier in Chicana/o studies. They take an important step in expanding the paradigms of gender issues from a feminist perspective. Saldívar-Hull summarizes the premises on which Chicana feminisms currently exist.

> From Anzaldúa's important revision of Texas history to the theoretical proclamations by the collective voices of Moraga, Gómez, and Romo-Carmona to Viramonte's questioning the constitution of family, Chicana feminism challenges boundaries defined by the hegemony. . . . Chicana feminism, both in its theory and method, is tied to the material world. When feminist anthologizers . . . cannot recognize Chicana theory, it is because Chicanas ask different questions which in turn ask for a reconstruction of the very premise of "theory." Because the history of the Chicana experience in the United States defines our particular *mestizaje* of feminism, our theory cannot be a replicate of white feminism nor can it be only an academic abstraction. The Chicana feminist looks to her history (to paraphrase Bourne's plea for feminist praxis) to learn how to transform the present. For the Chicana feminist it is through our affiliation with the struggles of the other Third World people that we find our theories and our methods. (1991, 220)

It is on these lived experiences that the next phase of Chicana feminisms will have to be built.

NOTES

My sincerest appreciation to the following colleagues for their thoughtful comments and guidance on this paper: Hale Bolak, Norma Cantú, Gloria Cuadraz, Rosa Linda Fregoso, Norma Klahn, Josie Méndez-Negrete, Elba Sánchez, Patricia Zavella. Also my gratitude to my undergraduate research assistant Christina Santana.

Correspondence regarding this article should be addressed to Aída Hurtado, Psychology Department, University of California, Santa Cruz, Social Science II, Santa Cruz, CA 95064. Electronic mail should be sent via Internet to aida@cats.ucsc.edu.

1. The epigram is taken from Emma Pérez's article "Speaking from the margin: Uninvited discourse on sexuality and power" (1993). In her writing, Emma Pérez advocates Chicanas' reacquisition of that part of themselves that is *india* and that has been "plundered through conquest and colonization." She declares "we reclaim the core for our women-tempered *sitios y lenguas* [spaces and languages/tongues]" (Pérez 1993, 62).

2. A word about ethnic labels. I use *people of Color* to refer to Chicanos, Asians, Native Americans, and Blacks, all of whom are domestic minorities. Therefore, I capitalize *Color* because it refers to specific ethnic groups. I also capitalize *Black* following the argument that it refers not merely to skin pigmentation but also to a "heritage, an experience, a cultural and personal identity, the meaning of which becomes specifically stigmatic and/or glorious and/or ordinary under specific social conditions. It is socially created as, and at least in the American context no less specifically meaningful or definitive than, any linguistic, tribal, or religious ethnicity, all of which are conventionally recognized by capitalization" (MacKinnon 1982, 516). On the other hand, *white* is left lowercase because it refers not to one or specified ethnic groups but to many.

3. Pat Mora writes about her grandfather's refusal to allow English to be spoken in his home: "Cuando entras a esta casa, hija, pisas México." (When you enter this house, daughter, you are in Mexico) (1993, 81).

4. Patricia Zavella relates how her parents' experience of language repression in their childhood convinced them not to teach her Spanish. Like others, she "eventually took Spanish classes and attempted to regain 'our' language" (1994, 208).

5. González and Habell-Pallan define the spoken word genre as characterized by "crossing of prose with poetry and song with rap, and is circulated by live performance and by cassette and compact disk" (1994, 103).

6. Sonia Saldívar-Hull states, "Anzaldúa's text is itself *mestizaje*; a postmodernist mixture of autobiography, historical document, and poetry collection. Like the people whose lives it chronicles, *Borderlands* resists boundaries as well as geopolitical borders" (1991, 211).

7. There is a growing number of younger Chicana feminist writers, most still in graduate school, who will not have had direct experience with the Chicano movement of the 1960s and 1970s. Their academic and artistic production will undoubtedly infuse Chicana feminist writings with vital new voices and insights. See González and Habell-Pallan (1994) as an example of this emergent literature.

8. From Chicana feminist writings in the 1970s, Córdova (1994) includes the following issues: "welfare rights, childcare, health, birth control, sterilization, legal rights, prison experience of Chicanas, sex roles, images of Chicanas, heroines of history, labor struggles (mostly historical), and organizing themselves as Chicanas" (178).

9. Sosa Ridell (1993) makes a plea for Chicanas to address the political and cultural issues raised by the new reproductive technologies, such as in vitro fertilization, surrogate motherhood, and artificial insemination. She perceives Chicanas and other women of Color to be particularly vulnerable to abuses of these technologies because: "the lack of control Chicanas/Latinas may experience over their reproductive lives must be linked to their material conditions. These material conditions include a socioeconomic status which places them in a high-risk category for continued reproductive victimization, increased health risks due to their occupational segregation, and exclusion from access to information, services, and decision-making in the area of reproductive technology policy making" (190).

10. The Virgin of Guadalupe is the patron saint of Mexico and, for many, the Catholic version of the Aztec goddess Tonanztín. She has special significance because she is Indian, and for Chicana feminists, she symbolizes the redemption of *mestizaje* (the mixture of European and Indian races). For an extensive analysis of *La Virgen de Guadalupe* see Castillo (1996). Sor Juana Inés de la Cruz (1648-1695) was a seventeenth-century Mexican nun, a scholar, poet, playwright, and intellectual who addressed in her work the unfair condition of women. *La Llorona*, (or the weeping woman), a sixteenth-century Mexican legend, wanders the streets at night howling for the loss of her children, whom she killed by drowning them after her husband betrayed her with another woman (Limón 1990, 414-15). Frida Khalo (1907-1954) was a famous Mexican painter who also was a committed Marxist and political activist (Herrera 1983).

11. Quoted in Saldívar-Hull (1991, 213), wherein she translates it as "I argued. I talked back. I was quite a bigmouth. I was indifferent to many of my culture's values. I did not let the men push me around. I was not good nor obedient."

12. My colleague Patricia Zavella related this story with great gusto to a group of Chicana scholars. For the published version of this paper see Chabram-Dernersesian 1996.

REFERENCES

Alarcón, Norma. 1989. Traductora, traidora: A paradigmatic figure of Chicana feminism. *Cultural Critique* 13(Fall): 57-87.
———. 1990a. Chicana's feminism: In the tracks of the "the" native woman. *Cultural Studies* 4(3): 248-56.
———. 1990b. The theoretical subject(s) of "This bridge called my back" and Anglo-American feminism. In *Making face, Making soul/Haciendo caras/Creative and critical perspectives by women of Color*. See Anzaldúa 1990.
———. 1996. Conjugating subjects in the age of multiculturalism. In *Mapping multiculturalism*, ed. Avery F. Gordon and Christopher Newfield. Minneapolis: University of Minnesota Press.
Alarcón, Norma, Rafaela Castro, Emma Pérez, Beatríz Pesquera, Adaljiza Sosa Riddell, and Patricia Zavella, eds. 1993. *Chicana critical issues*. Berkeley: Third Woman Press.
Almaguer, Tomás. 1971. Toward the study of Chicano colonialism. *Aztlán: Chicano Journal of the Social Sciences and Arts* 2(2): 7-21.
———. 1991. Chicano men: A cartography of homosexual identity and behavior. *differences: A Journal of Feminist Cultural Studies* 3(2): 75-100.
———. 1994. *Racial fault lines: The historical origins of white supremacy in California*. Berkeley: University of California Press.
Anzaldúa, Gloria. 1981. *La prieta*. In *This bridge called my back: Writings by radical women of color*. See Moraga and Anzaldúa 1981.
———. 1987. *Borderlands/la Frontera: The new mestiza*. San Francisco: Spinsters/Aunt Lute.
Anzaldúa, Gloria, ed. 1990. *Making face, making soul/Haciendo caras/Creative and critical perspectives by women of Color*. San Francisco: Aunt Lute Books.

Arce, Carlos H., Edward Murguía, and W. Parker Frisbie. 1987. Phenotype and life chances among Chicanos. *Hispanic Journal of Behavioral Sciences* 9: 19-32.

Baca, Judith. 1990. World wall: A vision of the future without fear. *Frontiers* 14(2): 81-5.

————. 1993. Uprising of the mujeres. In *Chicana critical issues*. See Alarcón et al. 1993.

Baca Zinn, Maxine. 1975. Political familism: Toward sex role equality in Chicano families. *Aztlán* 6(1): 13-26.

Brown, Wendy. 1992. Finding the man in the state. *Feminist Studies* 18(1): 7-34.

Broyles, Yolanda Julia. 1986. Women in El Teatro Campesino: ¿Apoco estaba molacha la virgen de Guadalupe? In *Chicana Voices: Intersections of Class, Race and Gender*, ed. Ricardo Romo. Austin: Center for Mexican-American Studies, University of Texas.

————. 1989. Toward a re-vision of Chicano theater history: The women of El Teatro Campesino. In *Making a spectacle: Feminist essays on contemporary women's theater*, ed. Linda Hart. Ann Arbor: University of Michigan Press.

————. 1994. *El Teatro Campesino: Theater in the Chicano movement*. Austin: University of Texas Press.

Cantú, Norma Elia. 1995. *Canícula: Snapshots of a girlhood en la frontera*. Albuquerque: University of New Mexico Pres.

Castañeda, Antonia I. 1990. The political economy of nineteenth-century stereotypes of californianas. In *Between borders: Essays on Mexicana/Chicana history*. See Del Castillo 1990.

Castillo, Ana. 1992. The Mixquiahuala letters. New York: Doubleday.

————. 1995. *Massacre of the dreamers*. New York: Plume Book. ·

Castillo, Ana, ed. 1996. *Goddess of the Americas/ La Diosa de las Americas: Writings on the virgin of Guadalupe*. New York: Riverhead Books.

Cervantes, Lorna Dee. 1981. *Emplumada*. Pittsburgh: University of Pittsburgh Press.

Chabram-Dernersesian, Angie. 1996. The Spanish colón-ialista narrative: Their prospectus for us in 1992. In *Mapping Multiculturalism*, eds. Avery F. Gordon and Christopher Newfield. Minneapolis: University of Minnesota Press.

Chavez, Linda. 1991. *Out of the barrio: Toward a new politics of Hispanic assimilation*. New York: Basic Books.

Cisneros, Sandra. 1991. *Woman hollering creek and other stories*. New York: Random House.

————. 1994. *Loose woman*. New York: Alfred A. Knopf.

Collins, Patricia Hill. 1991. *Black feminist thought/Knowledge, consciousness, and the politics of empowerment*. New York: Routledge.

Córdova, Teresa. 1994. The emergent writings of twenty years of Chicana feminist struggles: Roots and resistance. In *The handbook of Hispanic cultures in the United States*, ed. Félix Padilla. Houston: Arte Público Press.

Cotera, Marta. 1977. *Chicana feminism*. Austin, Texas: Information Systems Development.

Cuadraz, Gloria Holguín. 1997. Chicana/o generations and the Horatio Alger myth. *Thought and Action: NEA Journal of Higher Education*, 13(1): 103-120.

Cuadraz, Gloria Holguín, and Jennifer Pierce. 1994. From scholarship girls to scholarship women: Surviving the contradictions of class and race in academe. *Explorations in Ethnic Studies* 17(1): 1-23.

Davis, Angela, and Elizabeth Martínez. 1994. Coalition building among people of color. *Inscriptions* 7: 42-53.

De la Torre, Adela, and Beatríz M. Pesquera, eds. 1993. *Building with our hands: New directions in Chicana studies.* Berkeley: University of California Press.

Del Castillo, Adelaida, ed. 1990. *Between borders: Essays on Mexicana/Chicana history.* Encino, CA: Floricanto Press.

Espín, Oliva M. 1984. Cultural and historical influences on sexuality in Hispanic/Latin women. In *Pleasure and danger: Exploring female sexuality,* ed. Carol S. Vance. London: Routledge and Kegan Paul.

Fernández, R. 1994. Abriendo-caminos in the brotherland: Chicana writers respond to the ideology of literary nationalism. *Frontiers—A Journal of Women's Studies* 14(2): 23-50.

Fine, Michelle. 1997. Witnessing whiteness. In *Off white: Readings on race, power, and society,* eds. Michelle Fine, Lois Weis, Linda C. Powell, and Mun Wong. New York: Routledge.

Forbes, Jack. 1968. Race and color in Mexican-American problems. *Journal of Human Relations* 16(1): 55-68.

Frankenberg, Ruth. 1993. *White women, race matters: The social construction of whiteness.* Minneapolis: University of Minnesota Press.

Fregoso, Rosa Linda. 1993. The mother motif in *La Bamba* and *Boulevard Nights.* In *Building with our hands: New directions in Chicana studies.* See De la Torre and Pesquera 1993.

García, Alma. 1989. The development of Chicana feminist discourse, 1970-1980. *Gender and Society* 3(2): 217-38.

García, Alma, ed. 1997. *Chicana feminist thought. The basic historical writings.* New York: Routledge.

García, Chris F. 1973. *Political socialization of Chicano children: A comparative study with Anglos in California schools.* New York: Praeger Press.

Gaspar de Alba, Alicia. 1998. The politics of location of the tenth muse of America: An interview with Sor Juana Inés de la Cruz. In *Living Chicana theory.* See Trujillo 1998.

González, Jennifer A., and Michelle Habell-Pallan. 1994. Heterotopias and shared methods of resistance: Navigating social spaces and spaces of identity. *Inscriptions* 7: 80-104.

González, María R. 1990. El embrín nacionalista visto a través de la obra de Sor Juana Inés de la Cruz. In *Between borders: Essays on Mexicana/Chicana history.* See Del Castillo 1990.

Gómez, Alma, Cherríe Moraga, and Romo-Carmona, Mariana, eds. 1983. *Cuentos: Stories by Latinas.* New York: Kitchen Table Women of Color Press.

Guerin-Gonzalez, Camille. 1994. *Mexican workers and American dreams: Immigration, repatriation, and California farm labor, 1900-1930.* New Brunswick: Rutgers University Press.

Gutiérrez, Ramón A. 1993. Community, patriarchy and individualism: The politics of Chicano history and the dream of equality. *American Quarterly* 45(1): 44-72.

Herrera, Hayden. 1983. *Frida: A biography of Frida Kahlo.* New York: Harper and Row.

Hurtado, Aída. 1989. reflections on white feminism: A perspective from a woman of Color. In *Social and gender boundaries in the United States,* ed. Sucheng Chan. Lewiston: Edwin Mellen Press.

———. 1996a. *The color of privilege: Three blasphemies on race and feminism.* Ann Arbor: University of Michigan Press.

————. 1996b. Strategic suspensions: Feminists of Color theorize the production of knowledge. In *Knowledge, difference, and power: Essays inspired by women's ways of knowing*, ed. Nancy Rule Goldberger, Jill Mattuck Tarule, Blythe McVicker Clinchy, and Mary Field Belenky. New York: Basic Books.

————. 1998a. The Trickster's play: Whiteness in the subordination and liberation process. In *Theorizing race and ethnicity*, eds. Rodolfo D. Torres and Louis F. Miron. Oxford, UK and Cambridge, MA: Blackwell Publishers.

————. 1998b. The politics of sexuality in the gender subordination of Chicanas. In *Living Chicana theory*. See Trujillo 1998.

Klahn, Norma. 1994. Writing the border: The languages and limits of representation. *Journal of Latin American Cultural Studies* 3(1-2): 29-55.

Lamphere, Louise, Patricia Zavella, Felipe González, with Peter B. Evan. 1993. *Sunbelt working mothers: Reconciling family and factory*. Ithaca: Cornell University Press.

Limón, José E. 1990. *La Llorona*, the third legend of greater Mexico: Cultural symbols, women, and the political unconscious. In *Between borders: Essays on Mexicana/Chicana history*. See Del Castillo 1990.

López, David, and Yen Espiritu. 1990. Panethnicity in the United States: A theoretical framework. *Ethnic and Racial Studies* 13(2): 198-224.

Lugones, María C. 1990. Playfulness, "world"-travelling and loving perception. In *Making face, making soul/Haciendo caras/Creative and critical perspectives by women of Color*. See Anzaldúa 1990.

MacKinnon, Catherine A. 1982. Feminism, Marxism, method, and the state: An agenda for theory. *Signs: Journal of Women in Culture and Society* 7(31): 515-44.

Martínez, Elizabeth. 1989. That old (white) male magic. *Z Magazine* 27(8): 48-52.

McIntosh, Peggy. 1992. White privilege and male privilege: A personal account of coming to see correspondences through work in women's studies. In *Race, class, and gender*, ed. Margaret L. Andersen and Patricia Hill Collins. Belmont: Wadsworth.

Méndez-Negrete, Josephine. 1995. ". . . Es lo que haces!": A sociohistorical analysis of relational leadership in a Chicano/Latino community. Ph.D. diss., Sociology Department, University of California, Santa Cruz.

Mora, Magdalena, and Adelaida R. Del Castillo. 1980. *Mexican women in the United States: Struggles past and present*. Los Angeles: Chicano Studies Research Center, University of California.

Mora, Pat. 1993. *Nepantla: Essays from the land in the middle*. Albuquerque: University of New Mexico Press.

————. 1996. Coatlicue's rules: Advice from an Aztec goddess. In *Goddess of the Americas/ La Diosa de las Americas: Writings on the virgin of Guadalupe*. See Castillo 1996.

————. 1997. *House of houses*. Boston: Beacon Press.

Moraga, Cherríe. 1983. *Loving in the war years: Lo que nunca pasó por sus labios*. Boston: South End Press.

Moraga, Cherríe, and Gloria Anzaldúa, eds. 1981. *This bridge called my back: Writings by radical women of color*. Watertown, MA: Persephone Press.

Neumaier, Diane. 1990. Judy Baca: Our people are the internal exiles. (from an interview with the Chicana muralist Judy Baca). In *Making face, making soul/Haciendo ccras/Creative and critical perspectives by women of Color*. See Anzaldúa 1990.

Nieto, Consuelo. 1974. The Chicana and the women's rights movement: A perspective. *Civil Rights Digest* 6(3): 36-42.

Nieto-Gómez, Anna. 1974. La feminista. *Encuentro Femenil* 1(2): 34-37.

Ochoa, María, and Teresía Teaiwa, eds. 1994. Enunciating our terms: Women of Color in collaboration and conflict. *Inscriptions* 7: 1-155.

Ostrander, Susan. 1984. *Women of the upper class.* Philadelphia: Temple University Press.

Padilla, Félix M. 1985. *Latino ethnic consciousness: The case of Mexican Americans and Puerto Ricans in Chicago.* Notre Dame: University of Notre Dame Press.

Pardo, Mary. 1990. Mexican American women grassroots community activists: Mothers of East Los Angeles. *Frontiers* 21(1): 1-7.

———. 1991. Creating community: Mexican American women in Eastside Los Angeles. *Aztlán* 20(1-2): 39-71.

Paz, Octavio. 1985. *The labyrinth of solitude.* Trans. by Lysander Kemp, Yara Milos, and Rachel Phillips Belash. New York: Grove Press.

Pérez, Emma. 1991. Sexuality and discourse: Notes from a Chicana survivor. In *Chicana lesbians: The girls our mothers warned us about.* See Trujillo 1991.

———. 1993. Speaking from the margin: Uninvited discourse on sexuality and power. In *Building with our hands: New directions in Chicana studies.* See De la Torre and Pesquera 1993.

———. 1996. *Gulf dreams.* Berkeley: Third Woman Press.

———. 1998. Irigaray's female symbolic in the making of Chicana lesbian *sitios y lenguas* (sites and discourses). In *Living Chicana theory.* See Trujillo 1998.

Pesquera, Beatríz M. 1991. "Work gave me a lot of confianza": Chicanas' work commitment and work identity. *Aztlán* 20(1-2): 97-118.

———. 1997. In the beginning he wouldn't lift even a spoon. In *Situated lives,* eds. Louise Lamphere, Helena Ragoné, and Patricia Zavella. New York: Routledge.

Pesquera, Beatríz M., and Denise A. Segura. 1993. "There is no going back": Chicanas and feminism. In *Chicana critical issues.* See Alarcón et al. 1993.

Quintana, Alvina E. 1989. Challenge and counter-challenge: Chicana literary motifs. In *Social and gender boundaries in the United States,* ed. Sucheng Chan. Lewiston: Edwin Mellen Press.

———. 1996. *Home girls: Chicana literary voices.* Philadelphia: Temple University Press.

Romero, Mary. 1992. *Maid in the U.S.A.* New York: Routledge.

Ruiz, Vicki L. 1987. *Cannery women, cannery lives: Mexican Women, unionization, and the California food processing industry, 1980-1950.* Albuquerque: University of New Mexico Press.

———. 1998. *From out of the shadows/Mexican women in twentieth-century America.* New York: Oxford University Press.

Saldívar-Hull, Sonia. 1991. Feminism on the border: From gender politics to geopolitics. In *Criticism in the borderlands: Studies in Chicano literature, culture, and ideology,* eds. Hector Calderón and José David Saldívar. Durham: Duke University Press.

Sánchez, Elba. 1992. *Tallos de luna/Moon shoots.* Santa Cruz, CA: Moving Parts Press.

Sandoval, Chéla 1990. The struggle within: A report on the 1981 N.W.S.A. conference. In *Making Face, Making Soul/Haciendo Caras/Creative and critical perspectives by women of Color.* See Anzaldúa 1990.

———. 1991. U.S. third world feminism: The theory and method of oppositional consciousness in the postmodern world. *Genders* 10(Spring): 1-24.

————. 1998. Mestisaje as method: Feminists-of-color challenge the canon. In *Living Chicana theory*. See Trujillo 1998.

Scott, James C. 1990. *Domination and the arts of resistance*. New Haven: Yale University Press.

Segura, Denise A. 1994. Inside the work worlds of Chicana and Mexican immigrant women. In *Women of color in U. S. society*, eds. Maxine Baca Zinn and Bonnie Thornton Dill. Philadelphia: Temple University Press.

————. 1997. Chicanas in white collar jobs. "You have to prove yourself more." In *Situated lives*, ed. Louise Lamphere, Helena Ragoné, and Patricia Zavella. New York: Routledge.

Segura, Denise A., and Pesquera, Beatríz. 1992. Beyond indifference and antipathy: The Chicana movement and Chicana feminist discourse. *Aztlán: A Journal of Chicano Studies* 19(2): 69-93.

Segura, Denise A., and Jennifer L. Pierce. 1993. Chicana/o family structure and gender personality: Chodorow, familism, and psychoanalytic sociology revisited. *Signs: Journal of Women in Culture and Society* 19(1): 62-91.

Sifuentes, Alma, and Kim D. Hester Williams. 1994. Private parts: Battling barriers, forging friendships. *Inscriptions* 7: 105-22.

Sosa Ridell, Adaljiza. 1993. The bioethics of reproductive technologies: Impacts and implications for Latinas. In *Chicana critical issues*. See Alarcón et al. 1993.

Steinem, Gloria. 1983. *Outrageous acts and everyday rebellions*. New York: Holt, Rinehart, and Winston.

Sternbach, Nancy Saporta, Marysa Navarro-Aranguren, Patricia Chuchryk, and Sonia E. Alvarez. 1992. Feminisms in Latin America: From Bogotá to San Bernardo. *Signs: Journal of Women in Culture and Society* 17(2): 393-434.

Sturgis, Susanna J. 1988. Class/Act: Beginning a translation from privilege. In *Out the other side: Contemporary lesbian writing*, eds. Christian McEwan and Sue O'Sullivan. London: Virago.

Telles, Edward E., and Edward Murguía. 1990. Phenotypic discrimination and income differences among Mexican Americans. *Social Science Quarterly* 71(4): 682-93.

————. 1992. The Continuing significance of phenotype. *Social Science Quarterly* 73(1): 120-22.

Trujillo, Carla, ed. 1991. *Chicana lesbians: The girls our mothers warned us about*. Berkeley, CA: Third Woman Press.

Trujillo, Carla. 1997. Sexual identity and the discontents of difference. In *Ethnic and cultural diversity among lesbians and gay men*, ed. Beverly Greene. Thousand Oakes: Sage Publications.

————. 1998. *Living Chicana theory*. Berkeley: Third Woman Press.

Vásquez, Melba J., and Anna M. González. 1981. Sex roles among Chicanos: Stereotypes, challenges, and changes. In *Explorations in Chicano psychology*, ed. Augustine Baron Jr. New York: Praeger.

Viramontes, Helena María. 1985. *The Moths and other stories*. Houston: Arte Público Press.

Yarbro-Bejarano, Yvonne. 1985. Chicanas' experience in collective theater: Ideology and form. *Women and Performance* 2(2): 45-58.

————. 1986. The female subject in Chicano Theater: Sexuality, "race," and class. *Theater Journal* 38(1): 389-407.

————. 1991. De-constructing the lesbian body: Cherríe Moraga's *Loving in the war years*. In *Chicana lesbians: The girls our mothers warned us about*. See Trujillo 1991.

————. 1994. Gloria Anzaldúa's "Borderlands/La frontera": Cultural studies, "difference," and the non-unitary subject. *Cultural Critique* 28(Fall): 5-28.
Zavella, Patricia. 1987. *Women's work and Chicano families: Cannery workers of the Santa
Clara Valley.* Ithaca: Cornell University Press.
————. 1994. Reflections on diversity among Chicanas. In *Race*, eds. Steven Gregory
and Roger Sanjek. New Brunswick: Rutgers University Press.
————. 1997a. Constructing identity with "Chicana" informants. In *Situated lives:
Gender and culture in everyday life*, eds. Louise Lamphere, Helena Ragoné, and
Patricia Zavella. New York: Routledge.
————. 1997b. "Playing with fire": The gendered construction of Chicano/Mexican
sexuality. In *The gender/sexuality reader: Culture, history, political economy*, eds.
Roger N. Lancaster and Micaela di Leonardo. New York: Routledge.

9

It's All in the Family: Intersections of Gender, Race, and Nation

PATRICIA HILL COLLINS

Intersectionality has attracted substantial scholarly attention in the 1990s. Rather than examining gender, race, class, and nation as distinctive social hierarchies, intersectionality examines how they mutually construct one another. I explore how the traditional family ideal functions as a privileged exemplar of intersectionality in the United States. Each of its six dimensions demonstrates specific connections between family as a gendered system of social organization, racial ideas and practices, and constructions of U.S. national identity.

When former vice president Dan Quayle used the term *family values* near the end of a speech at a political fundraiser in 1992, he apparently touched a national nerve. Following Quayle's speech, close to three hundred articles using the term *family values* in their titles appeared in the popular press. Despite the range of political perspectives expressed on "family values," one thing remained clear—"family values," however defined, seemed central to national well-being. The term *family values* constituted a touchstone, a phrase that apparently tapped much deeper feelings about the significance of ideas of family, if not actual families themselves, in the United States.

Situated in the center of "family values" debates is an imagined traditional family ideal. Formed through a combination of marital and blood ties, ideal families consist of heterosexual couples that produce their own biological children. Such families have a specific authority structure; namely, a father-head earning an adequate family wage, a stay-at-home wife, and children. Those who idealize the traditional family as a private haven from a public world see family as held together by primary emotional bonds of love and caring. Assuming a relatively fixed sexual division of labor, wherein women's roles are defined as primarily in the home and men's in the public world of work, the traditional family ideal also assumes the separation of work and family. Defined as a natural or biological arrangement based on heterosexual attraction, this monolithic family type articulates with governmental structures. It is organized not around a biological core, but a state-sanctioned, heterosexual marriage that confers legitimacy not only on the family structure itself but on children born into it (Andersen 1991).[1]

The power of this traditional family ideal lies in its dual function as an ideological construction and as a fundamental principle of social organization. As ideology, rhetoric associated with the traditional family ideal provides an interpretive framework that accommodates a range of meanings. Just as reworking the rhetoric of family for their own political agendas is a common strategy for conservative movements of all types, the alleged unity and solidarity attributed to family is often invoked to symbolize the aspirations of oppressed groups. For example, the conservative right and Black nationalists alike both rely on family language to advance their political agendas.

Moreover, because family constitutes a fundamental principle of social organization, the significance of the traditional family ideal transcends ideology. In the United States, understandings of social institutions and social policies are often constructed through family rhetoric. Families constitute primary sites of belonging to various groups: to the family as an assumed biological entity; to geographically identifiable, racially segregated neighborhoods conceptualized as imagined families; to so-called racial families codified in science and law; and to the U.S. nation-state conceptualized as a national family.

The importance of family also overlaps with the emerging paradigm of intersectionality. Building on a tradition from Black Women's Studies, intersectionality has attracted substantial scholarly attention in the 1990s.[2] As opposed to examining gender, race, class, and nation, as separate systems of oppression, intersectionality explores how these systems mutually construct one another, or, in the words of Black British sociologist Stuart Hall, how they "articulate" with one another (Slack 1996). Current scholarship deploying intersectional analyses suggests that certain ideas and practices surface repeatedly across multiple systems of oppression and serve as focal points or privileged social locations for these intersecting systems.[3]

The use of the traditional family ideal in the United States may function as one such privileged exemplar of intersectionality.[4] In this paper, I explore how six dimensions of the traditional family ideal construct intersections of gender, race, and nation. Each dimension demonstrates specific connections between family as a gendered system of social organization, race as ideology and practice in the United States, and constructions of U.S. national identity. Collectively, these six dimensions illuminate specific ways that ideological constructions of family, as well as the significance of family in shaping social practices, constitute an especially rich site for intersectional analysis.

While I provide a preliminary framework of how gender, race, and nation intersect in family rhetoric and practices, more comprehensive analyses might reveal how other systems of inequality operate via similar processes. Social class is certainly important across multiple social hierarchies. Ethnicity and religion also constitute categories of belonging that invoke family rhetoric (Anthias and Yuval-Davis 1992). Politicizing ethnicity and religion requires manipulating understandings of group loyalty conveyed by family rhetoric. Instead of viewing this process as solely confined to ethnicity or religion, intersectional analyses would join studies of ethnicity and religion more closely to intersections of gender, race, class, and nation. Similarly, because it is so closely linked to issues of gender identity and reproduction, sexuality remains important in constructions of family, and actual families remain deeply implicated in reproducing heterosexism. Age provides yet another suggestive link to the richness of the root metaphor of family. While I allude to class, ethnicity, sexuality and age in the following discussion, I place greater emphasis on how family links social hierarchies of gender, race, and nation. A comprehensive and more nuanced discussion of family as a site of inter-sectionality would encompass these and other hierarchies.

MANUFACTURING NATURALIZED HIERARCHY

One dimension of family as a privileged exemplar of intersectionality lies in how it reconciles the contradictory relationship between equality and hierar-chy. The traditional family ideal projects a model of equality. A well-function-ing family protects and balances the interests of all its members—the strong care for the weak, and everyone contributes to and benefits from family membership in proportion to his or her capacities. In contrast to this idealized version, actual families remain organized around varying patterns of hierarchy. As Ann McClintock observes, "the family image came to figure *hierarchy within unity* [emphasis in original] as an organic element of historical progress, and thus became indispensable for legitimating exclusion and hierarchy within nonfamilial social forms such as nationalism, liberal individualism and imperialism" (McClintock 1995, 45). Families are expected to socialize their members into an appropriate set of "family values" that simultaneously rein-force the hierarchy within the assumed unity of interests symbolized by the family and lay the foundation for many social hierarchies. In particular, hierarchies of gender, wealth, age, and sexuality within actual family units correlate with comparable hierarchies in U.S. society. Individuals typically learn their assigned place in hierarchies of race, gender, ethnicity, sexuality, nation, and social class in their families of origin. At the same time, they learn to view such hierarchies as natural social arrangements, as compared to socially constructed ones. Hierarchy in this sense becomes "naturalized" because it is associated with seemingly "natural" processes of the family.

The "family values" that underlie the traditional family ideal work to naturalize U.S. hierarchies of gender, age, and sexuality. For example, the traditional family ideal assumes a male headship that privileges and naturalizes masculinity as a source of authority. Similarly, parental control over dependent children reproduces age and seniority as fundamental principles of social organization. Moreover, gender and age mutually construct one another; mothers comply with fathers, sisters defer to brothers, all with the understanding that boys submit to maternal authority until they become men. Working in tandem with these mutually constructing age and gender hierarchies are comparable ideas concerning sexuality. Predicated on assumptions of heterosexism, the invisibility of gay, lesbian, and bisexual sexualities in the traditional family ideal obscures these sexualities and keeps them hidden. Regardless of how individual families grapple with these hierarchical notions, they remain the received wisdom to be confronted.

In the United States, naturalized hierarchies of gender and age are interwoven with corresponding racial hierarchies, regardless of whether racial hierarchies are justified with reference to biological, genetic differences or to immutable cultural differences (Goldberg 1993). The logic of the traditional family ideal can be used to explain race relations. One way that this occurs is when racial inequality becomes explained using family roles. For example, racial ideologies that portray people of color as intellectually underdeveloped, uncivilized children require parallel ideas that construct Whites as intellectually mature, civilized adults. When applied to race, family rhetoric that deems adults more developed than children, and thus entitled to greater power, uses naturalized ideas about age and authority to legitimate racial hierarchy. Combining age and gender hierarchies adds additional complexity. Whereas White men and White women enjoy shared racial privileges provided by Whiteness, within the racial boundary of Whiteness, women are expected to defer to men. People of color have not been immune from this same logic. Within the frame of race as family, women of subordinated racial groups defer to men of their groups, often to support men's struggles in dealing with racism.

The complexities attached to these relationships of age, gender, and race coalesce in that the so-called natural hierarchy promulgated by the traditional family ideal bears striking resemblance to social hierarchies in U.S. society overall. White men dominate in positions of power, aided by their White female helpmates, both working together to administer to allegedly less-qualified people of color who themselves struggle with the same family rhetoric. With racial ideologies and practices so reliant on family for meaning, family writ large becomes race. Within racial discourse, just as families can be seen naturally occurring, biologically linked entities who share common interests, Whites, Blacks, Native Americans, and other "races" of any given historical period can also be seen this way. The actual racial categories of any given period matter less than the persistent belief in race itself as an enduring principle of social organization that connotes family ties. Thus, hierarchies of gender, age, and sexuality that exist *within* different racial groups (whose alleged family ties lead to a commonality of interest) mirrors the hierarchy characterizing relationships *among* groups. In this way, racial inequality becomes comprehensible and justified via family rhetoric.

This notion of naturalized hierarchy learned in family units frames issues of U.S. national identity in particular ways. If the nation-state is conceptualized as a national family with the traditional family ideal providing ideas about family, then the standards used to assess the contributions of family members in heterosexual, married-couple households with children become foundational for assessing group contributions to overall national well-being. Naturalized hierarchies of the traditional family ideal influence understandings of constructions of first- and second-class citizenship. For example, using a logic of birth order elevates the importance of time of arrival in the country for citizenship entitlements. Claims that early-migrating, White Anglo-Saxon Protestants are entitled to more benefits than more recent arrivals resemble beliefs that "last hired, first fired" rules fairly discriminate among workers. Similarly, notions of naturalized gender hierarchies promulgated by the traditional family ideal—the differential treatment of girls and boys regarding economic autonomy and free-access to public space—parallel practices such as the sex-typing of occupations in the paid labor market and male domination in government, professional sports, the streets, and other public spaces.

As is the case with all situations of hierarchy, actual or implicit use of force, sanctions and violence may be needed to maintain unequal power relations. However, the very pervasiveness of violence can lead to its invisibility. For example, feminist efforts to have violence against women in the home taken seriously as a bona fide form of violence and not just a private family matter have long met with resistance. In a similar fashion, the extent of the violence against Native American, Puerto Rican, Mexican-American, African-American, and other groups who were incorporated into the United States not through voluntary migration but via conquest and slavery remains routinely overlooked. Even current violence against such groups remains underreported unless captured in a dramatic fashion, such as the videotaped beating of motorist Rodney King by Los Angeles police officers. Despite their severity and recent increase, hate crimes against gays, lesbians, and bisexuals also remain largely invisible. Through these silences, these forms of violence not only are neglected, they become legitimated. Family rhetoric can also work to minimize understandings of violence in groups that self-define in family terms. In the same way that wife battering and childhood physical and sexual abuse become part of the "family secrets" of far too many families, so does the routine nature of violence targeted against women, gays, lesbians, and children within distinctive racial and ethnic groups.

Subordinated groups often face difficult contradictions in responding to such violence (Crenshaw 1991). One response consists of analyzing one or more hierarchies as being socially constructed while continuing to see others as naturalized. In African-American civil society, for example, the question of maintaining racial solidarity comes face-to-face with the question of how naturalized hierarchies construct one another. Maintaining racial solidarity at all costs often requires replicating hierarchies of gender, social class, sexuality, and nation in Black civil society. Consider, for example, typical understandings of the phrase "Black on Black violence." Stressing violence among Black men permits patterns of Black male violence targeted toward Black women—domestic abuse and sexual harassment in the workplace—to remain hidden and condoned. In the face of sexual harassment, especially at the hands of Black men, African-American women are cautioned not to "air dirty laundry" about internal family problems. The parallel with victims of domestic violence who are encouraged to keep "family secrets" is startling. In general, whether it is family as household, family as a foundation for conceptualizing race, or the national family defined through U.S. citizenship, family rhetoric that naturalizes hierarchy inside and outside the home obscures the force needed to maintain these relationships.

LOOKING FOR A HOME: PLACE, SPACE, AND TERRITORY

The multiple meanings attached to the concept of "home"—home as family household, home as neighborhood, home as native country—speak to its significance within family as a privileged exemplar of intersectionality. In the United States, the traditional family ideal's ideas about place, space, and territory suggest that families, racial groups, and nation-states require their own unique places or "homes." Because "homes" provide spaces of privacy and security for families, races, and nation-states, they serve as sanctuaries for group members. Surrounded by individuals who seemingly share similar objectives, these homes represent idealized, privatized spaces where members can feel at ease.

This view of home requires certain gendered ideas about private and public space. Because women are so often associated with family, home space becomes seen as a private, feminized space that is distinct from the public, masculinized space that lies outside its borders. Family space is for members only—outsiders can be invited in only by family members or else they are intruders. Within these gendered spheres of private and public space, women and men again assume distinctive roles. Women are expected to remain in their home "place." Avoiding the dangerous space of public streets allows women to care for children, the sick, and the elderly, and other dependent family members. Men are expected to support and defend the private, feminized space that houses their families. Actual U.S. families rarely meet this ideal. For example, despite feminist analyses that discredit the home as a safe place for women, this myth seems deeply entrenched in U.S. culture (Coontz 1992).

A similar logic concerning place, space, and territory constructs racialized space in the United States.[5] Just as the value attached to actual families reflects their placement in racial and social class hierarchies, the neighborhoods housing these families demonstrate comparable inequalities. Assumptions of race- and class-segregated space mandate that U.S. families and the neighborhoods where they reside be kept separate. Just as crafting a family from individuals from diverse racial, ethnic, religious or class backgrounds is discouraged, mixing different races within one neighborhood is frowned upon. As mini-nation-states, neighborhoods allegedly operate best when racial and/or class homogeneity prevails. Assigning Whites, Blacks, and Latinos their own separate spaces reflects efforts to maintain a geographic, racial purity. As the dominant group, Whites continue to support legal and extra-legal measures that segregate African-Americans, Native Americans, Mexican-Americans, Puerto Ricans, and other similar groups, thereby perpetuating cultural norms about desirability of racial purity in schools, neighborhoods, and public facilities. For example, tactics such as the continual White flight out of inner cities, deploying restrictive zoning in suburban communities in order to restrict low-income housing, and shifting White children into private institutions in the face of increasingly colored schools effectively maintain racially segregated home spaces for White men, women, and children. This belief in segregated physical spaces also has parallels to ideas about segregated social and symbolic spaces. For example, lucrative professional categories remain largely White and male, in part, because people of color are seen as less capable of entering these spaces. Similarly, keeping school curricula focused on the exploits of Whites represents another example of ideas about segregated spaces mapped on symbolic space. Overall, racial segregation of actual physical space fosters multiple forms of political, economic, and social segregation (Massey and Denton 1993).

Securing a people's "homeland" or national territory has long been important to nationalist aspirations (Anthias and Yuval-Davis 1992; Calhoun 1993). After its successful anticolonial struggle against England and its formation as a nation-state, the United States pursued a sustained imperialist policy in order to acquire much of the land that defines its current borders. This history of conquest illustrates the significance of property in relations of space, place, and territory. Moreover, just as households and neighborhoods are seen as needing protection from outsiders, maintaining the integrity of national borders has long formed a pillar of U.S. foreign policy. Because the United States has operated as a dominant world power since World War II, shielding its own home "soil" from warfare has been a minor theme. Instead, protecting so-called American interests has been more prominent. Individuals and businesses who occupy foreign soil represent extensions of U.S. territory, citizens of the national family who must be defended at all costs.

Overall, by relying on the belief that families have assigned places where they truly belong, images of place, space, and territory link gendered notions of family with constructs of race and nation (Jackson and Penrose 1993). In this logic that everything has its place, maintaining borders of all sorts becomes vitally important. Preserving the logic of segregated home spaces requires strict rules that distinguish insiders from outsiders. Unfortunately, far too often, these boundaries continue to be drawn along the color line.

ON "BLOOD TIES": FAMILY, RACE, AND NATION

Presumptions of "blood ties" that permeate the traditional family ideal reflect another dimension of how family operates as a privileged exemplar of intersectionality. In the United States, concepts of family and kinship draw strength from the flow of blood as a substance that regulates the spread of rights (Williams 1995). While the legal system continues to privilege heterosexual married couples as the preferred family organization, the importance given to bonds between mothers and children, brothers and sisters, grandmothers and grandchildren, illustrates the significance of biology in definitions of family. Representing the genetic links among related individuals, the belief in blood ties naturalizes the bonds among members of kinship networks. Blood, family, and kin are so closely connected that the absence of such ties can be cause for concern. As the search of adoptees for their "real" families or blood relatives suggests, blood ties remain highly significant for definitions of family.

Given the significance attached to biology, women of different racial groups have varying responsibilities in maintaining blood ties. For example, White women play a special role in keeping family bloodlines pure. Historically, creating White families required controlling White women's sexuality, largely through social norms that advocated pre-marital virginity. By marrying White men and engaging in sexual relations only with their husbands, White women ensured the racial purity of White families. Thus, through social taboos that eschewed pre-marital sexuality and interracial marriage for White women, White families could thereby avoid racial degeneration (Young 1995). When reinserted into naturalized hierarchies of gender, race, class, and nation, and institutionally enforced via mechanisms such as segregated space and state-sanctioned violence, efforts to regulate sexuality and marriage reinforced beliefs in the sanctity of "blood ties."

Historically, definitions of race in U.S. society also emphasized the importance of blood ties.[6] Biological families and racial families both rely on similar notions. The connections between the race and blood ties were so self-evident that nineteenth-century Black nationalist thinker Alexander Crummell claimed, "races, like families, are the organisms and ordinances of God; a race feeling is of divine origin. The extinction of race feeling is just as possible as the extinction of family feeling. Indeed, a race *is* a family" (quoted in Appiah 1992, 17). Definitions of race as family in the United States traditionally rested on biological classifications legitimated by science and legally sanctioned by law. By grouping people through notions of physical similarity, such as skin color, facial features, or hair texture, and supported by law and custom, scientific racism defined Whites and Blacks as distinctive social groups (Gould 1981). Just as members of "real" families linked by blood were expected to resemble one another, so were members of racial groups descended from a common bloodline seen as sharing similar physical, intellectual, and moral attributes. Within this logic, those lacking biological similarities became defined as family outsiders, while racially different groups became strangers to one another.

A similar logic can be applied to understandings of nation. One definition views a nation as a group of people who share a common ethnicity grounded in blood ties. Cultural expressions of their peoplehood—their music, art, language, and customs—constitute their unique national identity. Under this ethnic nationalism model, each nation should have its own nation-state, a political entity where the ethnic group can be self-governing. While this understanding of nation has a long history in European cultures (Anthias and Yuval-Davis 1992; Yuval-Davis 1997, 26-29), it is less often applied to questions of U.S. national identity. Instead, the United States is often seen as an important expression of civic nationalism where many different ethnic groups cooperate within the boundaries of one nation-state (Calhoun 1993). In contrast to nation-states where ethnic or tribal membership confers citizenship rights, the democratic principles of the U.S. Constitution promise equality for all American citizens. Regardless of race, national origin, former condition of servitude, and color, all citizens stand equal before the law. Via these principles, the United States aims to craft one nation out of many and to transcend the limitations of ethnic nationalism.

Despite this portrayal, U.S. national identity may be grounded more in ethnic nationalism than is typically realized. Notions of U.S. national identity that take both family and race into account result in a view of the United States as a large national family with racial families hierarchically arranged within it. Representing the epitome of racial purity that is also associated with U.S. national interests, Whites constitute the most valuable citizens. In this racialized nation-state, Native Americans, African-Americans, Mexican-Americans, and Puerto Ricans become second-class citizens, whereas people of color from the Caribbean, Asia, Latin America, and Africa encounter more difficulty becoming naturalized citizens than immigrants from European nations. Because all of these groups are not White and thereby lack appropriate blood ties, they are deemed to be less-worthy actual and potential U.S. citizens.

When seen in this framework that links family, race, and nation, public policies of all sorts take on new meaning. An example is the historical similarity between the adoption of children and the process of acquiring citizenship. When children are screened for their suitability for adoption, factors such as their racial, religious, and ethnic background carry a prominent weight. Younger children, who allegedly are less socialized, are typically preferred over older ones. When adoptions are finalized, such children become "naturalized" and legally indistinguishable from children born into the family unit. In a similar fashion, immigration policies screen potential citizens in terms of how well they match the biological make-up of the U.S. national family. Historically, immigration policies have reflected the perceived racial, ethnic, and labor needs of a domestic political economy that routinely discriminated against people of color (Takaki 1993). Those who wish to become adopted citizens must undergo a socialization process whereby they study important elements of U.S. culture. This socialization process aims to transform so-called aliens into bona fide U.S. citizens who are indistinguishable from those born in the United States.

MEMBERSHIP HAS ITS PRIVILEGES: RIGHTS, OBLIGATIONS AND RULES

By suggesting an ideal relationship between the rights and responsibilities of family membership, the traditional family ideal operates as a privileged exemplar of intersectionality in yet another way. In a situation in which notions of belonging to a family remain important to issues of responsibility and accountability, individuals feel that they "owe" something to, and are responsible for, members of their families. For example, people within family units routinely help their family members by babysitting, lending money, helping relatives find employment and housing, or caring for the elderly. Family members linked by blood are entitled to these benefits merely by belonging. Even when family members lack merit, they are entitled to benefits simply because they belong. Beyond this issue of access to entitlements, individuals incur differential responsibilities that depend on their placement in family hierarchies. For example, women are expected to perform much of the domestic labor that keeps the family going, whereas men's duties lie in providing financial support.

In a similar fashion, U.S. citizens by birth or naturalization acquire certain rights and responsibilities that accrue from membership. Citizens are promised entitlements such as equal protection under the law, access to unemployment insurance, old age pensions, free public education, and other social welfare benefits. Citizens are also expected to fulfill certain obligations to one another. U.S. citizens are expected to pay taxes, observe the law, and engage in military service when required. In contrast to the rights and responsibilities provided insiders, outsiders lack both the entitlements provided group members and the obligations attached to belonging. Similar to non-family members, non-U.S. citizens are neither entitled to citizenship benefits nor responsible for national duties.

In the United States where race is constructed via assumed blood ties, race influences the differential distribution of citizenship rights and responsibilities. Taxation policies illustrate how ideas about family and race reinforce differences in entitlements and obligations. Despite the 1954 *Brown vs. Board of Education* decision outlawing racial segregation in public schools, large numbers of African-American children remain warehoused in poorly funded, deteriorating, racially segregated inner city schools. These children are seen as lacking merit and therefore unworthy of public support. Contrasting their lot with the often lavish school facilities and services provided to children attending overwhelmingly White suburban schools, especially in affluent districts, reveals substantial racial differences. Even though many of these suburban children lack merit, the location of their homes entitles them to superior public services. It is important to remember that these patterns of racial segregation and differential obligations and entitlements experienced by all U.S. children are far from random. Governmental policies helped create these patterns of racially segregated spaces that reproduce social inequalities (Massey and Denton 1993; Oliver and Shapiro 1995).

In a situation of naturalized hierarchy, conceptualizing U.S. national identity as composed of racial groups that collectively comprise a U.S. national family fosters differential patterns of enforcement of the rights and obligations of citizenship. Members of some racial families receive full benefits of membership while others encounter inferior treatment. Gender hierarchies add additional complexity. African-American women's experiences with entitlement criteria for 1930s Social Security programs, for example, illustrate how institutionalized racism and gender-specific ideology public policies shaped national public policy. Race was a factor in deciding which occupations would be covered by Social Security. Two occupational categories were expressly excluded from coverage: agricultural and domestic workers, the two categories that included most African-American women. Also, by providing differential benefits to men and women through worker's compensation (for which Black women did not qualify) and mothers's aid, from its inception, Social Security encompassed ideas about gender. Eligibility rules rewarded women who remained in marriages and were supported by their husbands but penalized women who became separated or divorced or who remained single and earned their own way. Black women who were not in stable marriages lacked access to spousal and widows benefits that routinely subsidized White women. In this case, the combination of race-targeted polices concerning occupational category and gender-targeted policies concerning applicants' marital status worked to exclude Black women from benefits (Gordon 1994). On paper, Black women may have been first-class U.S. citizens, but their experiences reveal their second-class treatment.

FAMILY GENEALOGY:
INHERITANCE AND THE FAMILY WAGE

Naturalized hierarchies embedded in the traditional family ideal articulate not only with hierarchies of race and nation but also with hierarchies of economic or social class (Collins 1998, chapter 6). The traditional family ideal may be more heavily implicated in social class organization in the United States than previously imagined. Using the individual as the unit of analysis, social class analyses have traditionally examined men's incomes as central to family organization. However, moving from individuals to families as the basic unit of social class analysis, and from income to wealth as a measure of class, illustrate yet another way that family serves as a privileged exemplar for intersectionality. Shifting to wealth as a measure of social class status suggests that families serve as important social units for wealth's intergenerational transmission. As Oliver and Shapiro observe, "private wealth thus captures inequality that is the product of the past, often passed down from generation to generation" (Oliver and Shapiro 1995, 2).

Focusing on wealth not only references contemporary economic inequality but also incorporates the historical origins and reproduction of class differences over time. Despite ideas that social mobility is widespread, U.S. children routinely enjoy or suffer the economic status of their parents. Families constitute important sites for inheritance, not solely of cultural values, but of property. Families use wealth to create opportunities, secure a desired standard of living, and pass their social class status to their children. In this process, the family home becomes more than a private respite from the demands of the public sphere. When "family values" and "property values" become intertwined, homes in racially segregated neighborhoods become important investments. The traditional family ideal shows the family not only occupying a home, but owning it. Ensconced in tax policies that provide lucrative benefits for homeowners, for many Americans, the single-family home as a tangible symbol of wealth remains central to the American dream (Coontz 1992). Wealth matters because, if one adheres to rules of marriage and childbearing, it is directly transferable from generation to generation.

It would be a mistake to view the intergenerational transmission of property as primarily a phenomenon affecting middle-class and affluent families. Certainly property-owning families at the founding of the United States enjoyed an immense advantage that many were able to broker into persistent economic and political power. The wealth of these families stood in stark contrast to the situation of Native Americans who lost land and livelihood in wars of conquest, or to that of African-Americans whose enslavement rendered them the property that was inherited. Despite the historical concentration of wealth among a small percentage of families, the intergenerational transmission of wealth through family also operates among working-class families. Traditional analyses view working-class families in purely wage-earning terms. Such families are thought to have no property to pass on to their children, and are seen as mere employees of other more wealthy families. However, the notion of working-class men being entitled to a "family wage" emerges at the intersection of expectations of family inheritance and a naturalized gender hierarchy. In this situation, working-class men inherit opportunities to earn a wage and are expected to use that wage to support their families. According to this logic, women's and children's social class status derives from that of men.

When these relationships regulating intergenerational property transmission are racialized, as they are in the United States, another level of complexity emerges. In her analysis of how racism undermined the War on Poverty program, Jill Quadagno describes the resistance that craft unions put forth when pressured to change entrenched patterns of racial discrimination. As Quadagno points out, the right of unions to select their own members was seen as a "property right of the working class. This was a most compelling argument for nepotism—the tradition of passing on the craft from fathers to sons" (Quadagno 1994, 65). Among Philadelphia plumbers, 40 percent of the apprentices were sons of members. Fathers wanted their sons to be trained as plumbers and to continue in the business. Practices such as these virtually ensured that African-Americans and other groups were excluded from lucrative positions. Quadagno quotes one construction worker who explains the concept of property rights and property transmission in White working-class families:

> Some men leave their sons money, some large investments, some business connections and some a profession. I have none of these to bequeath to my sons. I have only one worthwhile thing to give: my trade. . . . For this simple father's wish it is said that I discriminate against Negroes. Don't all of us discriminate? Which of us when it comes to choice will not choose a son over all others? (quoted in Quadagno 1994, 65)

In effect, racial discrimination in education, employment, and housing historically reflected White working-class understandings of these social locations as "private property" to be disposed of as inherited wealth. While such attitudes certainly may reflect personal prejudice, racial discrimination thus may be more closely attached to property rights and concerns about the value of inheritable property than actual attitudes toward African-Americans.

FAMILY PLANNING

The significance of the family as an exemplar of intersectionality can also be seen in one final dimension of family rhetoric. Family planning comprises a constellation of options, ranging from coercion to choice, from permanence to reversibility regarding reproduction of actual populations. In the case of individual families, decision-making lies with family members; they decide whether to have children, how many children to have, and how those children will be spaced. Feminist scholars in particular have identified how male control over women's sexual and reproductive capacities has been central to women's oppression (see, for example, Raymond 1993). However, just as women's bodies produce children who are part of a socially constructed family grounded in notions of biological kinship, women's bodies produce the population for the national "family" or nation-state, conceptualized as having some sort of biological oneness. In this sense, family planning becomes important in regulating population groups identified by race, social class, and national status (Heng and Devan 1992; Kuumba 1993).

Social policies designed to foster the health of the United States conceptualized as a national family follow a family planning logic, as demonstrated via eugenic thinking. Early twentieth century "racial hygiene" or eugenic movements compellingly illustrate the thinking that underlies population policies designed to control the motherhood of different groups of women for reasons of nationality and race (Haller 1984; Proctor 1988). Eugenic philosophies and the population policies they supported emerged in political economies with distinctive needs, and in societies with particular social class relations. Common to eugenic movements throughout the world was the view that biology was central to solving social problems. Societies that embraced eugenic philosophies typically aimed to transform social problems into technical problems amenable to biological solutions effected via social engineering. Eugenic approaches thus combined a "philosophy of biological determinism with a belief that science might provide a technical fix for social problems" (Proctor 1988, 286).

Three elements of eugenic thinking seem remarkably similar to themes in American public policy. Those embracing eugenic thinking saw "race and heredity—the birth rates of the fit and the unfit—as the forces that shape[d] . . . political and social developments" (Haller 1984, 78). First, eugenic thinking racializes segments of a given population by classifying people into mutually exclusive racial groups. Because the United States has operated as a racialized state since its inception, race remains a fundamental principle of U.S. social organization. While racial meanings change in response to political and economic conditions, the fundamental belief in race as a guiding principle of U.S. society remains remarkably hardy. Associating diverse racial groups with perceived national interests, a second element of eugenic thinking, also has a long history in the United States. The third feature of eugenic thinking, the direct control of different racial groups through various measures also is present in U.S. politics. So-called positive eugenic—efforts to increase reproduction among the better groups who allegedly carried the outstanding qualities of their group in their genes—and negative eugenic—efforts to prevent the propagation by less desirable groups—also have affected U.S. public policy.

While now seen as an embarrassment, past ideas concerning eugenic gained considerable influence in the United States. As Haller points out, Francis Galton, the founder of the eugenic movement in England, believed that "Anglo-Saxons far outranked the Negroes of Africa, who in turn outranked the Australian aborigines, who outranked nobody. Because he believed that large innate differences between races existed, Galton felt that a program to raise the inherent abilities of mankind involved the replacement of inferior races by the superior" (Haller 1984, 11). Galton's ideas proved popular in the racially segregated United States. U.S. eugenic laws preceded by twenty years the sterilization laws of other countries, and were seen as pioneering ventures by eugenicists abroad. The U.S. Supreme Court's 1927 *Buck vs. Bell* decision held that sterilization fell within the police power of the state. Reflecting the majority opinion, Oliver Wendell Holmes wrote,

> It would be strange if it could not call upon those who already sap the strength of the state for these lesser sacrifices, often not felt to be such by those concerned, in order to prevent our being swamped by incompetence. It is better for all the world, if instead of waiting for their imbecility, society can prevent those who are manifestly unfit from continuing their kind. The principle that sustains compulsory vaccination is broad enough to cover cutting the Fallopian tubes. . . . Three generations of imbeciles is enough. (Haller 1984, 139)

Given this intellectual context, differential population policies developed for different segments of the U.S. population emerge in direct relation to any group's perceived value within the nation-state.[7] In periods of profound social change, such as the massive European migration that preceded the *Buck vs. Bell* decision, eugenic philosophies can reemerge. With the civil rights, women's, anti-war, and other social movements of the 1950s and 1960s, as well as the growing nonwhite immigrant population of the 1970s and 1980s, the United States experienced profound change. Omi and Winant (1994) interpret the expanding conservative social projects that emerged during this period as a direct response to the perceived gains of Blacks and women. One core feature characterizing the rhetoric of social projects of the Right was a return to the family values of the traditional U.S. family. By associating the ideal family with U.S. national interests, these movements linked those interests to their own political agendas concerning race and gender. Returning to "family values" not only invoked racial and gendered meanings, it set the stage for reviving a logic of eugenic that could be applied to adolescent pregnancy, women's poverty, street crime, and other social issues.

In this context, contemporary American social policies from the 1960s through the "family values" debate of the 1990s become more comprehensible. When attached to state policy in a racialized nation-state, questions of controlling the sexuality and fertility of women from diverse race, social class, and citizenship groups become highly politicized. For example, White women, especially those of the middle class, are encouraged to reproduce. In contrast, women of color, especially those lacking economic resources or not in state sanctioned marriages, are routinely discouraged from having children (Raymond 1993). Population policies such as providing lavish services to combat infertility for White, middle class women, while offering a limited range of Norplant, Depo Provera, and sterilization to poor African-American women constitute contemporary reflections of the logic of eugenic thinking (Davis 1981; Nsiah-Jefferson 1989).

In the logic of the family as a privileged exemplar of intersectionality, viewing race- and gender-based policies as regulating different forms of social relations is fallacious. Current assumptions see African-Americans as having race, White women as having gender, Black women as experiencing both race and gender, and White men experiencing neither. These assumptions dissipate when confronted with actual population policies designed to regulate the childbearing patterns of different racial and ethnic groups generally, and the mothering experiences of different groups of women in particular.

RECLAIMING FAMILY

Family occupies such a prominent place in the language of public discourse in the United States that rejecting it outright might be counterproductive for groups aiming to challenge hierarchies. Because the family functions as a privileged exemplar of intersectionality in structuring hierarchy, it potentially can serve a similar function in challenging that hierarchy. Just as the traditional family ideal provides a rich site for understanding intersectional inequalities, reclaiming notions of family that reject hierarchical thinking may provide an intriguing and important site of resistance.

Many groups aim to dismantle social hierarchy, yet use unexamined ideas about family in crafting their political programs. Consider how Black nationalist-influenced projects within African-American civil society invoke family rhetoric. Sociologist Paul Gilroy (1993) notes that the "trope of kinship" permeates Black understandings of culture and community to the point that African-Americans largely accept the notion of race as family and work within it. In Black-influenced projects, families are seen as building blocks of the nation. The Afrocentric yearning for a homeland for the Black racial family and the construction of a mythical Africa to serve this purpose speaks to the use of this construct. Family language also shapes everyday interactions: African-American strangers often refer to one another as "brother" and "sister"; some Black men refer to each other as "bloods." In hip-hop culture, "homies" are Black males from one's neighborhood, or home community. Within this political framework, Whites remain the strangers, the outsiders who are castigated in Black political thought. Ironically, though the popular press often associates the traditional family ideal with conservative political projects, this rhetoric finds a home in what many African-Americans consider to be the most radical of Black political theories (Appiah 1992; Gilroy 1993).

Feminist politics can contain similar contradictions regarding family. U.S. feminists have made important contributions in analyzing how the traditional family ideal harms women. However, feminism's longing for a sisterhood among women has proved difficult to sustain in the context of U.S. race and class politics. Assumptions of an idealized sisterhood floundered because women of color, among others, questioned their place in the feminist family. Even more significant is the U.S. media's routine characterization of feminism as anti-family. Although much of the backlash against feminism claims that U.S. feminists are anti-family, many women who are not part of this backlash probably remain suspicious of any political movement that questions such an important social institution by appearing to dismiss it. This is unfortunate, because family rhetoric often forms a powerful language to organize people for a variety of ends.

Given the power of family as ideological construction and principle of social organization, Black nationalist, feminist, and other political movements in the United States dedicated to challenging social inequality might consider recasting intersectional understandings of family in ways that do not reproduce inequality. Instead of engaging in endless criticism, reclaiming the language of family for democratic ends and transforming the very conception of family itself might provide a more useful approach.

NOTES

I would like to thank the editors of this volume and four anonymous reviewers for their helpful comments on an earlier draft of this essay. I also thank the students at the University of Cincinnati in my graduate seminar "Gender and Intersectionality" for their insightful ideas.

1. By dislodging beliefs in the naturalness or normality of any one family form, feminist scholarship analyzes the significance of specific notions of family to gender oppression (Thorne 1992). As Stephanie Coontz (1992) reports, this traditional family ideal never existed, even during the 1950s, a decade that is often assumed to be the era of its realization. Feminist anthropologists also challenge the traditional family ideal by

demonstrating that the heterosexual, married couple form in the United States is neither "natural," universal, nor cross-culturally normative (Collier et al. 1992). Recent family scholarship suggests that large numbers of U.S. families never experienced the traditional family ideal, and those who may have once achieved this form are now abandoning it (Coontz 1992; Stacey 1992).

2. In the early 1980s, several African-American women scholar-activists called for a new approach to analyzing Black women's lives. They claimed that African-American women's experiences were shaped not just by race but also by gender, social class, and sexuality. In this tradition, works such as *Women, Race, and Class* by Angela Davis (1981), "A Black Feminist Statement" drafted by the Combahee River Collective (1982), and Audre Lorde's (1984) classic volume *Sister Outsider* stand as groundbreaking works that explore interconnections among systems of oppression. Subsequent work aimed to name this interconnected relationship with terms such as *matrix of domination* (Collins 1990), and *intersectionality* (Crenshaw 1991). Because Black lesbians were at the forefront in raising the issue of intersectionality, sexuality was one of the emphases in early work by African-American women. However, pervasive homophobia in African-American communities, as evidenced by the reaction to the works of Alice Walker, Ntosake Shange, Michele Wallace and other early modern Black feminists, diverted attention from intersectional analyses that emphasized sexuality. The absence of a developed tradition of queer theory in the academy also worked against more comprehensive intersectional analyses. For early intersectional analyses that included sexuality, see the essays in Barbara Smith's (1983) edited volume *Home Girls: A Black Feminist Anthology*.

3. A wide range of topics, such as the significance of primatology in framing gendered, raced views of nature in modern science (Haraway 1989); the social construction of Whiteness among White women in the United States (Frankenberg 1993); race, gender, and sexuality in the colonial conquest (McClintock 1995); and the interplay of race, class, and gender in welfare state policies in the United States (Brewer 1994; Quadagno 1994) have all received an intersectional treatment. Moreover, the initial emphasis on race, social class, and gender has expanded to include intersections involving sexuality, ethnicity, and nationalism (Anthias and Yuval-Davis 1992; Parker et al. 1992; Daniels 1997).

4. Theoretical and empirical work on women of color's location in work and family not only challenges the traditional family ideal, but paves the way for the more general question of family as a privileged site of intersectionality. For work in this tradition, see Dill 1988, Zinn 1989, and Glenn 1992.

5. In this section, I emphasize land as literal space. However, symbolic space, or the terrain of ideas, is organized via similar principles. Foucault's (1979) idea of disciplinary power in which people are classified and located on a knowledge grid, parallels my discussion of the mapping of symbolic space.

6. By tracing the changing meaning of race in the sixteenth-century *Oxford English Dictionary*, David Goldberg identifies the foundational meanings that subsequently link race with family. Goldberg notes, "in general, 'race' has been used to signify a 'breed or stock of animals' (1580), a 'genus, species or kind of animal' (1605), or a 'variety of plant' (1605). It refers at this time also to 'the great divisions of mankind' (1580) and especially to 'a limited group of persons descended from a common ancestor' (1581), while only slightly later to a 'tribe, nation or people considered of common stock' " (1600) (Goldberg 1993, 63). Note the connections between animals, nature, family, tribe, and nation.

7. For extended discussions of this concept, see the essays in Bridenthal et al. (1984) *When Biology Became Destiny: Women in Weimar and Nazi Germany*. This volume contains one of the best discussions I have encountered of the links between gender, social class, race, and nation, when policies were actually implemented in one nation-state.

REFERENCES

Andersen, Margaret L. 1991. Feminism and the American family ideal. *Journal of Comparative Family Studies* 22(2)(Summer): 235-46.

Anthias, Floya, and Nira Yuval-Davis. 1992. *Racialized boundaries: Race, nation, gender, colour and class in the anti-racist struggle*. New York: Routledge.

Appiah, Kwame Anthony. 1992. *In my father's house: Africa in the philosophy of culture*. New York: Oxford University Press.

Brewer, Rose. 1994. Race, gender and US state welfare policy: The nexus of inequality for African American families. In *Color, class and country: Experiences of gender*, ed. Gay Young and Bette Dickerson. London: Zed Books.

Bridenthal, Renate, Atina Grossmann, and Marion Kaplan, eds. 1984. *When biology became destiny: Women in Weimar and Nazi Germany*. New York: Monthly Review Press.

Calhoun, Craig. 1993. Nationalism and ethnicity. *Annual Review of Sociology* 19: 211-39.

Collier, Jane, Michelle Z. Rosaldo, and Sylvia Yanagisako. 1992. Is there a family?: New anthropological views. In *Rethinking the family*. See Thorne and Yalom 1992.

Collins, Patricia Hill. 1990. *Black feminist thought: Knowledge, consciousness, and the politics of empowerment*. New York: Routledge, Chapman and Hall.

———. 1997. African-American women and economic justice: A preliminary analysis of wealth, family, and Black social class. *University of Cincinnati Law Review* 65(3)(Spring): 825-52.

———. 1998. *Fighting words: African-American women and the search for justice*. Minneapolis: University of Minnesota Press.

Combahee River Collective. 1982. A Black feminist statement. In *But some of us are brave*, ed. Gloria T. Hull, Patricia Bell Scott, and Barbara Smith. Old Westbury, NY: Feminist Press.

Coontz, Stephanie. 1992. *The way we never were: American families and the nostalgia trap*. New York: Basic Books.

Crenshaw, Kimberle. 1991. Mapping the margins: Intersectionality, identity politics, and violence against women of color. *Stanford Law Review* 43(6): 1241-99.

Daniels, Jessie. 1997. *White lies*. New York: Routledge.

Davis, Angela Y. 1981. *Women, race, and class*. New York: Random House.

Dill, Bonnie Thornton. 1988. Our mothers' grief: Racial ethnic women and the maintenance of families. *Journal of Family History* 13(4): 415-31.

Foucault, Michel. 1979. *Discipline and punish: The birth of the prison*. New York: Schocken.

Frankenberg, Ruth. 1993. *The social construction of whiteness: White women, race matters*. Minneapolis: University of Minnesota Press.

Gilroy, Paul. 1993. It's a family affair: Black culture and the trope of kinship. In *Small acts: Thoughts on the politics of Black cultures*. New York: Serpent's Tail.

Glenn, Evelyn Nakano. 1992. From servitude to service work: Historical continuities in the racial division of paid reproductive labor. *Signs* 18(1): 1-43.

Goldberg, David Theo. 1993. *Racist culture: Philosophy and the politics of meaning*. Cambridge, MA: Blackwell.

Gordon, Linda. 1994. *Pitied but not entitled: Single mothers and the history of welfare*. Cambridge: Harvard University Press.

Gould, Stephen Jay. 1981. *The mismeasure of man*. New York: W. W. Norton.

Haller, Mark H. 1984 [1963]. *Eugenics: Hereditarian attitudes in American thought*. New Brunswick: Rutgers University Press.

Haraway, Donna. 1989. *Primate visions: Gender, race, and nature in the world of modern science*. New York: Routledge, Chapman and Hall.

Heng, Geraldine, and Janadas Devan. 1992. State fatherhood: The politics of nationalism, sexuality and race in Singapore. In *Nationalisms and sexualities*, ed. Andrew Parker, Mary Russo, Doris Sommer and Patricia Yaeger. New York: Routledge.

Jackson, Peter, and Jan Penrose. 1993. Introduction: Placing "race" and nation. In *Constructions of race, place and nation*, ed. P. Jackson and J. Penrose. Minneapolis: University of Minnesota Press.

Kuumba, Monica Bahati. 1993. Perpetuating neo-colonialism through population control: South Africa and the United States. *Africa Today* 40(3): 79-85.

Lorde, Audre. 1984. *Sister outsider*. Trumansberg, NY: Crossing Press.

Massey, Douglas S., and Nancy A. Denton. 1993. *American apartheid: Segregation and the making of the underclass*. Cambridge: Harvard University Press.

McClintock, Anne. 1995. *Imperial leather*. New York: Routledge.

Nsiah-Jefferson, Laurie. 1989. Reproductive laws, women of color, and low-income women. In *Reproductive laws for the 1990s*, ed. Sherrill Cohen and Nadine Taub. Clifton, NJ: Humana Press.

Oliver, Melvin L., and Thomas M. Shapiro. 1995. *Black wealth/ White wealth: A new perspective on racial inequality*. New York: Routledge.

Omi, Michael, and Howard Winant. 1994. *Racial formation in the United States: From the 1960s to the 1990s*. New York: Routledge.

Parker, Andrew, Mary Russo, Doris Sommer, and Patricia Yaeger, eds. 1992. *Nationalisms and sexualities*. New York: Routledge.

Proctor, Robert N. 1988. *Racial hygiene: Medicine under the Nazis*. Cambridge: Harvard University Press.

Quadagno, Jill. 1994. *The color of welfare: How racism undermined the war on poverty*. New York: Oxford University Press.

Raymond, Janice. 1993. *Women as wombs: Reproductive technologies and the battle over women's freedom*. San Francisco: Harper San Francisco.

Slack, Jennifer Daryl. 1996. The theory and method of articulation in cultural studies. In *Stuart Hall: Critical dialogues in cultural studies*, ed. David Morley and Kuan-Hsing Chen. New York: Routledge.

Smith, Barbara, ed. 1983. *Home girls: A Black feminist anthology*. New York: Kitchen Table Press.

Stacey, Judith. 1992. Backward toward the postmodern family: Reflections on gender, kinship, and class in the Silicon Valley. In *Rethinking the family*. See Thorne and Yalom 1992.

Takaki, Ronald. 1993. *A different mirror: A history of multicultural America*. Boston: Little Brown.

Thorne, Barrie. 1992. Feminism and the family: Two decades of thought. In *Rethinking the family: Some feminist questions*. See Thorne and Yalom 1992.

Thorne, Barrie, and Marilyn Yalom, eds. 1992. *Rethinking the family: Some feminist questions*. Boston: Northeastern University Press.

Williams, Brackette F. 1995. Classification systems revisited: Kinship, caste, race, and nationality as the flow of blood and the spread of rights. In *Naturalizing power: Essays in feminist cultural analysis*, ed. Sylvia Yanagisako and Carol Delaney. New York: Routledge.

Young, Robert J. C. 1995. *Colonial desire: Hybridity in theory, culture and race*. New York: Routledge.

Yuval-Davis, Nira. 1997. *Gender and nation*. Thousand Oaks, CA: Sage.

Zinn, Maxine Baca. 1989. Family, race, and poverty in the eighties. *Signs* 14(4): 875-84.

10

Dualisms, Discourse, and Development

DRUCILLA K. BARKER

This essay reviews a body of literature on feminism, development, and knowledge construction. This literature rejects essentialist constructions of women, challenges the universality of the Western scientific method, and creates a discursive space for reconstructing the dualisms embedded in the modern worldview. It suggests that an understanding of knowledge systems other than the modern one can aid us in constructing epistemologies that result in less dominating ways of producing knowledge.

The language of development economics reads like a chapter in the Enlightenment dream, a dream that promised an orderly progress from poverty and ignorance to prosperity and modernity. It is a discourse infused with the Enlightenment ideal of innocent knowledge, an ideal that masks the instrumental role that development has played in maintaining global structures of neocolonialism and dependency. Instead of progress and prosperity, much of the world has experienced profound poverty, growing income inequality, high debt burdens, and environmental degradation. By the 1980s, even the proponents of development had agreed that their policies had been largely unsuccessful. Policy interventions designed to foster economic growth and alleviate poverty were abandoned in favor of neoliberal orthodoxies (Escobar 1995, 73-94). Privatization, trade liberalization, and fiscal austerity were the new strategies that would enable free-market capitalism to work its magic. Missing from this analysis, however, was any awareness of the role that development rhetoric and policies played in producing underdevelopment, exploitation, and oppression.[1]

Women in the South have been especially affected by the development process. They make up a disproportionate share of the world's poor and bear the double burden of unpaid household work and low-wage market work.

Moreover, sex and gender biases in mainstream development policies increase women's unpaid work and worsen already oppressive and exploitative conditions. Scholars and activists initially responded to these circumstances by theorizing the role of women in development and working for practical solutions to empower women and improve their economic and social status (Boserup 1970, Tinker 1976). This early work created Women in Development (WID) as a legitimate field of inquiry in development economics. It focused on changing the priorities and practices of development agencies such as the World Bank. It did not question the values and goals of the development process or the paradigm of liberal economic theory that underpinned economic development rhetoric and practice (Tinker 1990, 45). Contained within the material constraints of the development bureaucracy and the theoretical constraints of liberal economic theory, this early work participated in a discursive construction of Third World women as a passive, kindred, and oppressed group—the resources for the economic interests of corporate capitalism and the intellectual interests of development experts.

Other scholars brought to the fore an explicitly feminist analysis of the connections between patriarchy, capitalism, and women's oppression. For example, Lourdes Benería and Gita Sen (1981) developed a Marxist-feminist analysis of the relationship between the process of capital accumulation and the sexual division of labor. Sen and Caren Grown (1987) examined the links between gender subordination and other forms of oppression and argued that the empowerment of women was necessary for the economic development of the Third World. This scholarship demonstrated the role of gender in the sexual division of labor and illustrated the crucial importance of reproductive labor to economic well-being. It continues to be an important contribution to our understanding of the lives of women in the South. It is, however, firmly grounded in Enlightenment thought, and does not question the notions of linearity, modernization, and progress embodied in development discourse.

This essay reviews a body of recent literature on feminism, sustainable development, and knowledge construction that addresses questions about women, development, and modernization within explicit critiques of the Enlightenment project. This literature challenges the hegemony of the Western scientific method, and it uncouples the development equals modernization paradigm that naturalizes the institutions and processes of industrial capitalism and justifies environmental degradation. The literature reviewed here is postmodern in the sense that the authors consciously seek to contest the seeming universality of Enlightenment conceptions of human nature, reason, and truth and challenge the mind-body, nature-culture, and superstition-knowledge dualisms that provide the foundation for modern conceptions of rationality and science. Moreover, this literature rejects essentialist and universalizing constructions of women in favor of accounts that produce a richer and deeper understanding of how women construct their identities within material and discursive boundaries that are both particular and contingent.[2]

Locating these discussions in the context of the debates over the relationship between women and sustainable development highlights the importance of both the material and the symbolic, and draws into focus the notion that social constructivism is not a form of idealism. Similarly, the emphasis on context, embodiment, and identity formation illustrates why rejecting an Enlightenment conception of truth is not a form of relativism. Relativism is not possible for a situated and embodied subject. The debate over whether postmodern feminism negates the possibility of building coalitions for effective political actions is also addressed. The motif that emerges from these readings is that although there may be no essential quality—biological, social, or cultural—that women share, one that binds them together in common cause, this realization does not preclude the establishment of historical, contingent, and variable connections. Moreover, the rejection of fixed, essential qualities is necessary in order to theorize adequately the multiplicity of relations of oppression.

I begin with an examination of *Women, the Environment and Sustainable Development: Towards a Theoretical Synthesis* (Braidotti et al. 1994) because its exploration of the interconnections between women, the environment, and sustainable development can frame many important themes in these works. The authors arrive at a theoretical synthesis by examining several bodies of literature—feminist critiques of science, feminism, alternative development, deep ecology, social ecology, and ecofeminism—through the lens of postmodern materialism. The chapter written by Rosi Braidotti, outlining the significant moments and debates in feminist critiques of science and feminist epistemologies, provides the theoretical foundation for the author's conception of postmodern materialism. She argues that what is really at stake in these debates is whether feminists should remain faithful to the humanist tradition of the Enlightenment and seek to enlarge the scope of scientific rationality, or should they adopt a radical form of epistemology that denies access to the real world independent of discourse. For Braidotti, an examination of the underside of the historical legacy of the Enlightenment—genocides, colonialism, slavery, and environmental degradation—provides the answer: a postmodernist position is the only ethically and politically defensible one.

Braidotti draws on the work of Sandra Harding (1991) and Donna Haraway (1991) to flesh out some of the important contours of a radical epistemology that would be consonant with a postmodern-materialist approach. In a theme that recurs throughout the literature reviewed here, Braidotti argues that such an approach is necessary because the internal logic of domination cannot be remedied by simply reversing the balance of power: such a reversal leaves the dialectical opposition intact. Dissolving or rethinking the gender dualisms intrinsic to the Enlightenment project requires disentangling difference from a hierarchy of values and reassembling a vision of female subjectivity that will recognize multiple axes of identity, as well as the variously situated, variously embodied nature of the female subject.

Emphasizing the embodied nature of the feminist subject does not entail essentialism, because bodily experience cannot be reduced to either the purely biological or the purely social. The body is the site of intersection of the natural with the cultural, and cannot be wholly explained by either. This emphasis suggests another recurrent motif in this literature: the mind-body dualism characteristic of Cartesian rationality is a culturally specific construction. It is an integral part of a scientific worldview that regards the body and the natural world as machines, devoid of cognition and creativity, rather than as living organisms.

Women, The Environment and Sustainable Development goes on to trace the development of the women, environment, and development (WED) discourse. WED encompasses several schools of thought—feminism, environmentalism, and women and development—as well as grassroots social movements. It mounts a critique of the entire development process and the hegemony of Western scientific discourse, and offers a perspective that emphasizes the interrelationships between people, their communities, and their life support systems. WED discourse is heavily influenced by the work of ecofeminists Vandana Shiva (1989) and Maria Mies (1988). Shiva and Mies both theorize from a position that valorizes the essential connection between women and nature, and advocate a wholesale return to subsistence agriculture as a necessary part of any solution to the problems of poverty and environmental degradation. While the work of Mies and Shiva has been foundational in pointing out the violent and exploitative consequences of Western-style development, Braidotti et al. are uncomfortable with its essentialism, its emphasis on women's closer ties to nature, and its idealization of traditional agriculture. They argue instead for an approach like the one proposed by Bina Agarwal (1991), who argues that the important issue is to deconstruct the power structure that fosters a patriarchal ideology, conflates women and nature, and creates a specific sexual division of labor. The theoretical synthesis offered by these authors works toward this end.

Feminist Perspectives on Sustainable Development (Harcourt 1994b) begins with Wendy Harcourt's essay (Harcourt 1994a) framing the issues in terms of a contemporary critique of development that challenges the language and power relations implicit in development discourse. Writers in this tradition (Escobar 1992, Sachs 1992) reject the commodification of people and the environment and stress the importance of creating a discursive space for subjugated people and their knowledge. This analysis considers women as voices of resistance and repositories of knowledge and creativity. Harcourt points out the hidden dualism in their arguments: while they call attention to dualistic divisions in development discourse, they seem to reverse the categories and evoke notions of the "good, premodern, traditional world and the honorable, resisting Third World, and the bad, modern, industrialized world and the thoughtless, greedy Westerner" (Harcourt 1994a, 17). Harcourt argues that nature and tradition can no longer be opposed to culture and modernity, because all people are now part of a highly technical, computerized world. Therefore it is necessary to reconstruct the dualism in a way that affirms both the parts and reconceptualizes their relationship in non-hierarchical ways. Harcourt maintains that modernity, with all its attendant ills, can still be a liberating discourse in certain circumstances.

The possibility of moving outside binary oppositions by understanding encounters between modernity and traditional nonmodern forms of cognition is perhaps the leitmotif of this volume. The essay by Frédérique Apffel-Marglin and Suzanne Simon (1994) is an excellent example. They trace the historical continuity between the perception of Third World women in the WID discourse and the perception of the colonized woman by Victorian feminists. Colonial narratives portrayed colonized women as victims of the backwardness and savagery of their own cultures. The treatment of women was considered the measuring rod of civilization, and the standard of British Victorian womanhood was the standard against which all others were measured. Freeing women from the oppression of their own cultures was a large part of the moral rationale for the colonial enterprise.

Apffel-Marglin and Simon argue that the feminism that informs the WID discourse descends directly from Victorian colonial feminism. Tradition and social constraints are identified as barriers to women's access to the market. Women's emancipation will come through modernization and integration into industrial capitalism. This discourse posits an essentialized universal subordination of women and promotes development as the vehicle for eradicating sexism. Thus, as in the colonial literature, it is the oppression of women that justifies the need for development intervention and the transformation of entire ways of life in the South. In the development rhetoric, poverty shares the same status as suttee, the veil, or genital mutilation—symbols of oppression and patriarchy that must be eradicated if women are to be liberated. The Third World woman is again judged in reference to the emancipated First World woman: an autonomous and economically independent woman free of traditional constraints and obligations.

According to Apffel-Marglin and Simon, modern Westerners' perception of non-white women is flawed because it is founded on a valorization of a type of personhood specific to industrial capitalism. The modern individual is a person separate from and in competition with other similar persons, owning its own labor and able to sell it on the market, and pitted against an inert environment from which resources must be extracted. The body is a part of nature, a machine powered by the energy of the passions, which are controlled by Cartesian rationality. The language of modern liberal humanism—rights, equality, and autonomy—is based on this concept of the commodified individual.

Historically, the reproductive capacity of women's bodies presented some particular problems for this construction. For women, to control their reproductive labor would have entailed its commodification and alienability through wages. This created a contradiction because men insisted on their rights as the co-owners of the products of women's reproductive labor. Thus reproduction was considered part of the natural-biological sphere, inaccessible to women's minds. Reproduction became an activity devoid of consciousness and rationality. This modernist understanding implies a fundamental split between women's natural (or biological) processes and their cultural (or symbolic) capacities. It is here that the modernist dualism between nature and culture is located, and this dualism results in an estrangement between the human and the non-human worlds. As long as generative capacity is seen as a purely biological concern, the rift between the human and non-human worlds cannot be repaired. Nature and women's bodies are both resources to be acted on instrumentally.

Apffel-Marglin and Simon argue that if we listen to the voices of non-Western people, we can learn of nonmodernist ways of being in the world, that is, ways of being where the rift between nature and culture is unknown and where women's generative activities are not separate from their cultural activities. In this worldview the self is not bounded by the skin but is embedded in relationships to others and to the non-human world. Similarly, the body is not a machine but rather a place where spirits and deities dwell, and is made of the same elements as the non-human world. This is a way of being that does not privilege nature over culture, but rather describes a way of being without a radical division between the human and non-human world, between human welfare and the welfare of the environment.

Marja-Lüsa Swantz (1994) explores the effects of development planning on matrilineal communities in southern Tanzania, communities that are traditional, or nonmodern, in the sense described by Apffel-Marglin and Simon. Swantz argues that development creates often unresolvable contradictions in people's lives. Although the Tanzanians desire to participate in modern life, they fear losing the capacity to regenerate their communities. For them, the regenerative project is both symbolic and physical, and their participation in modern life threatens regeneration and the continuity of life. Swantz frames this issue in terms of women's bodily experiences, using as an example the attempts to retrain traditional midwives in modern medical practices. The philosophy behind this program is to promote self-reliance and to interfere as little as possible in traditional practices. Birth typically occurs at home; traditionally, families supplied the tools and compensated the midwife with beer and gifts. The retrained women, however, are neither paid by the government nor compensated by the families nor even supplied with instruments. In the eyes of the community, Western medical training, however minimal, removes the midwives from the sphere of regeneration and transfers them to the modern sphere of reproduction, thus separating them from communal relationships and shared responsibility.

Swantz's analysis uses this and other case studies to illustrate encounters between traditional and modern knowledge systems. Her argument is that the integration of knowledge systems takes time. Unless the dominating system of knowledge changes, traditional systems are in danger of disappearing before they have time to become an integral part of the change. For traditional societies, this loss threatens the very meaning of life, and "it must be realized that continuity of life itself is threatened if regenerative forces are not given precedence over productive and market forces" (Swantz 1994, 105). Development cannot succeed if it is understood solely in terms of marketed and consumed production, because that sort of limited understanding fosters policies that threaten people's existential base and their ability to live meaningful lives.

The essays in *Feminism/Postmodernism/Development* (Marchand and Parpart 1995) address the ways postmodern feminist thinking can contribute to the construction of an empowering and transformative development discourse. They call into question the role of the development expert, examine the connections between control over discourse and assertions of power, and recover and valorize women's knowledge and voices. This recovery is a complex project that entails an analysis of how women construct their identities within the material and discursive constraints of their lives. The essays problematize the notion of the "Third World Woman" and adopt an approach that avoids essentialism and recognizes the multiple identities and axes—race, class, age, culture—that shape women's lives. They also address the issue of how to build effective coalitions to work for material change when identities are fragmented and knowledge is partial and situated.

Mitu Hirshman's (1995) essay illustrates how postmodern feminism can illuminate the universalism and essentialism that may be unwittingly embedded in feminist standpoint epistemology. Hirshman presents a critical discussion of Sen and Grown's acclaimed monograph, *Development, Crises, and Alternative Visions* (Sen and Grown 1987).[3] Sen and Grown argue that while women constitute the majority of the poor and are the most economically and socially disadvantaged, it is their work that provides the human link in the availability of food, water, and energy sources for many parts of the world. Therefore development planning should be begin from the standpoint of poor women. Hirshman acknowledges that the project that Sen and Grown are engaged in is a noble one; it is the ultimate goal of the humanist enterprise, the improvement of the human condition. The thorny question for international feminists working toward this goal is how to effect a reconciliation between the presumed universal nature of gender oppression and individual women's concrete experiences. These experiences are embedded in their memberships in diverse social and political groups, as well as their participation in diverse cultural practices and symbolic forms. The answer for Sen and Grown, as well as for many feminist theorists and activists, is to build on the common opposition to gender oppression and hierarchy. For these theorists, the sexual division of labor provides the basis for understanding this oppression.

Hirshman argues that positing the sexual division of labor as a universal category that constructs the category of women commits a type of essentialism. It is an essentialism based on sociological and anthropological universals that constitute the sexual division of labor. This strategy is mistaken, because it fails to acknowledge that the concepts of labor and production are themselves rooted in the culture of capitalism and modernity, and are thus inadequate to the tasks of describing nonmodern societies. Moreover, implicit in these categories is a productivist ideology that sees human beings as laborers, seeking their purpose in the conquest of nature. This ideology leads to an implicit belief that material needs constitute the sole determinant of human existence, a belief that relegates the cultural and the symbolic to second-class status.

Several of the essays in this volume speak to the importance of the cultural and the symbolic in understanding both the material and discursive strategies used by non-European women in a postindustrial, postcolonial world. For example, Catherine Raissiguier's (1995) essay analyzes the process of identity formation among working-class girls of Algerian descent in a French school. This provocative essay attempts to frame a nonessentialist analysis of the construction of subjectivity that both allows for agency for these young women and recognizes the existence of the material and discursive boundaries within which they constitute their identities. These girls are positioned at the crossroads of several contradictory discourses. This particular placement creates the potential for a rebellious consciousness while at the same time anchoring the girls to some of the traditional values of their communities. Raissiguier's analysis shows that close empirical attention to the process of identity formation can enable us to explore beyond the limiting dualities of resistance-accommodation and freedom-determinism, and to understand how particular material and discursive boundaries frame the struggle to re-invent identities, among both Northern and Southern women.

The essays in *Decolonizing Knowledge: From Development to Dialogue* (Apffel-Marglin and Marglin 1996) challenge Cartesian rationality claims to universality by illuminating the specific historical context of this type of cognition, contrasting it with other modes of cognition rooted in different cultural contexts, and creating a discursive space for theorizing modern knowledge as a particular form of local knowledge. One common theme in these essays is the notion that the ontological divide between mind and the world and body, central to Cartesian rationality, is a particular cultural and historical construct rather than a universal truth. Another is the *episteme/techne* distinction made by Stephen Marglin. *Episteme* refers to abstract, analytical knowledge that is based on logical deduction from first-principles. *Techne*, in contrast, is concrete knowledge, specialized in nature and closely tied to time and place. The epistemological test for *techne* is practical efficacy rather than right method.

Stephen Marglin's (1996) essay illustrates the interactions between science, the ideology of science, and political economy in the development and global diffusion of high tech agriculture, and the genesis of the Green Revolution. The Green Revolution resulted in an enormous increase in food production, but at substantial environmental and social costs. It seriously narrowed the genetic base, increased dependency on water, chemical fertilizer, and pesticides, and transformed agrarian economic relationships. Marglin shows that although there were alternative methods of increasing yields and reputable critics of high tech agriculture, both were ignored. Alternative methods involved paying attention to local practices and ecologies; however, these practices were part of traditional peasant cultures, and the policymakers were too enamored of science and technology to take them seriously. Moreover, the hybrid seeds central to high tech agriculture must be produced anew in each generation, creating a new role for seed companies and new opportunities for profit from the commodification of knowledge and the commercialization of agriculture.

Marglin frames his account in terms of the interplay between the expert's *episteme* and the farmer's *techne*. Marglin argues that all knowledge and action are a combination of both *episteme* and *techne*. The imperialistic and hegemonic qualities of Western science arise when *episteme* refuses to be subordinate to a cosmology and assumes itself to be a cosmology, a theory of reality. As such it leaves no room for other systems of knowledge and no place for local and particular *techne*. It is *episteme* as a cosmology that prevents peaceful coexistence between Western science and other knowledge systems.

In "Rationality, the Body, and the World: From Production to Regeneration" (1996), Apffel-Marglin introduces the reader to the contemporary nonmodern lives and experiences of the Oriya villagers in India. As a prolegomenon to her presentation, she presents a historical summary of the emergence of Cartesian rationality in order to make visible the culturally and historically specific nature of categories such as "biology" and "ritual." In Western thought the biological, or the natural, is opposed to the cultural or the symbolic, and as such is a category bereft of cognition. Similarly, ritual is a category bereft of effective rational action. Apffel-Marglin argues that these categories are specific to Cartesian rationality, and that to use them as though they were neutral and universal does invisible violence to different realities and robs them of their potential to be perceived as alternatives to modernity. The relationship between the emergence of Cartesian rationality, the commodification of the self, and industrial capitalism has been explored by a variety of scholars. What makes Apffel-Marglin's exposition unique is her analysis of the contradictions that this process created for women and the specific role of the body in creating those contradictions.

She argues that when anthropologists encounter cultures that do not separate a natural and cultural domain, this is generally seen as a lesser form of primitive local knowledge. This attitude is rooted in the mistaken notion that the mind-body dualism in Cartesian rationality is a universal rather than a cultural construction. Other nonmodern cultures show that when biology is infused with mind, the boundary between minds and bodies is fluid and the dualism disappears; nature is something that is touched and transformed by the human mind. Apffel-Marglin theorizes the festival of the menses (Raja Parba) among the Oriya villagers as an example of cognition in a culture with a noncommodified conception of the self and a non-Cartesian mode of cognition.

The festival celebrates the annual menstruation of the goddess Haracandi. The practices of the festival are reproduced in the women's monthly cycles. Following these rules and practices ensures the continuity of life because for the Oriya villagers, the identity between women, the earth, and Goddess is substantive rather than symbolic. This is not just a matter of belief; it is what Apffel-Marglin calls "enactive cognition." Enactive cognition is embodied and arises from human activity interacting with others and the world. Both menstruation and observing the rules of menstruation articulate the human order with the order of the seasons and ensure order and the continuity of life. (It is also important to note that men have a role in these practices.) Rather than being an objective given, nature or the environment emerges out of the interactions between humans, both male and female, and the world. Enactive cognition, then, is an epistemology that transcends or dissolves the mind-body, culture-nature, reason-passion, symbolic-material dualisms embedded in Cartesian rationality.

The message that I take away from the literature discussed in this essay is not that we should replace Cartesian rationality with enactive cognition and *episteme* with *techne*, but that a genuine and sympathetic reading of nonmodern ways of being can help us construct radical epistemologies that result in nondominating ways of producing knowledge. Such new epistemologies and methodologies are necessary if women and men from different class, ethnic, and cultural positions are to engage in collective emancipatory projects without reproducing patterns of hierarchy and domination. Third World poverty and debt, profound environmental degradation, and unequal North-South relations are integral parts of the Enlightenment legacy. Solutions to these problems need to come from feminist positions that deconstruct that legacy and valorize local knowledge systems without romanticizing them.

NOTES

1. For further reading see Escobar (1995). His monograph, *Encountering Development*, provides a critical examination of development discourse and practice. He examines development in terms of the forms of knowledge that define it, the systems of power that regulate its practice, and the forms of subjectivity fostered by its discursive practices.

2. See Chandra Mohanty (1991, 1995) for an eloquent analysis of the discursive construction of the "Third World woman" in Western feminist texts.

3. The Sen and Grown (1987) monograph was commissioned by DAWN, Development Alternatives with Women for a New Era, a group of activists, researchers, and policymakers. The group was formed to define development issues from women's perspectives, and the monograph was commissioned in preparation for the 1985 U.N. End of the Decade Conference in Nairobi.

REFERENCES

Agarwal, Bina. 1991. Engendering the environmental debate: Lesson learnt from the Indian subcontinent. *CASID Distinguished speakers series*. Monograph No. 8. East Lansing: Michigan State University.

Apffel-Marglin, Frédérique. 1996. Rationality, the body, and the world: From production to regeneration. In *Decolonizing knowledge: From development to dialogue*. See Apffel-Marglin and Marglin 1996.

Apffel-Marglin, Frédérique, and Stephen A. Marglin, eds. 1996. *Decolonizing knowledge: From development to dialogue*. Oxford: Clarendon Press.

Apffel-Marglin, Frédérique, and Suzanne L. Simon. 1994. Feminist orientalism and development. In *Feminist perspectives on sustainable development*. See Harcourt 1994b.

Benería, Lourdes, and Gita Sen. 1981. Accumulation, reproduction, and women's role in economic development: Boserup revisited. *Signs* 7(21): 279-98.

Boserup, Ester. 1970. *Women's role in economic development*. New York: St. Martin's Press.

Braidotti, Rosi, Ewa Charkiewicz, Sabine Häusler, and Saskia Wieringa. 1994. *Women, the environment and sustainable development: Towards a theoretical synthesis*. London: Zed Books.

Escobar, Arturo. 1992. Reflections on "development": Grassroots approaches and alternative politics in the Third World. *Futures* (June): 411-36.

———. 1995. *Encountering development: The making and unmaking of the Third World*. Princeton: Princeton University Press.

Haraway, Donna J. 1991. *Simians, cyborgs and women: The reinvention of nature*. New York: Routledge.

Harcourt, Wendy. 1994a. Negotiating positions in the sustainable development debate: Situating the feminist perspective. In *Feminist perspectives on sustainable development*. See Harcourt 1994b.

———. ed. 1994b. *Feminist perspectives on sustainable development*. London: Zed Books.

Harding, Sandra. 1991. *Whose science? Whose knowledge? Thinking from women's lives*. Ithaca: Cornell University Press.

Hirshman, Mitu. 1995. Women and development: A critique. In *Feminism/postmodernism/development*. See Marchand and Parpart 1995.

Marglin, Stephen. 1996. Farmers, seedsmen, and scientists: Systems of agriculture and systems of knowledge. In *Decolonizing knowledge: From development to dialogue*. See Apffel-Marglin and Marglin 1996.

Marchand, Marianne H., and Jane L. Parpart, eds. 1995. *Feminism/postmodernism/development*. London: Routledge.

Mies, Maria, with Claudia von Werlhof and Veronika Bennholdt-Thomsen. 1988. *Women: The last colony*. London: Zed Books.

Mohanty, Chandra Talpade. 1991. Under Western eyes: Feminist scholarship and colonial discourse. In *Third World women and the politics of feminism*, ed. Chandra Mohanty, Ann Russo, and Lourdes Torres. Bloomington: Indiana University Press.

———. 1995. Feminist encounters: Locating the politics of experience. In *Social postmodernism: Beyond identity politics*, ed. Linda Nicholson and Steven Seldman. Cambridge: Cambridge University Press.

Raissiguier, Catherine. 1995. The construction of marginal identities. In *Feminism/postmodernism/development*. See Marchand and Parpart 1995.

Sachs, Wolfgang, ed. 1992. *The development dictionary*. London: Zed Books.

Sen, Gita, and Caren Grown. 1987. *Development, crises, and alternative visions: Third World women's perspectives*. New York: Monthly Review Press.

Shiva, Vandana. 1989. *Staying alive: Women, ecology and development*. Delhi/London: Kali for Women/Zed Books.

Swantz, Marja-Lüsa. 1994. Women/body/knowledge: From production to regeneration. In *Feminist perspectives on sustainable development*. See Harcourt 1994.

Tinker, Irene. 1976. The adverse impact of development on women. In *Women and world development*, ed. Tinker and Michelle Bo Bramsen. New York: Praeger.

———. 1990. The making of field: Advocates, practitioners, and scholars. In *Persistent inequalities: Women and world development*, ed. Irene Tinker. New York: Oxford University Press.

11

Resisting the Veil of Privilege: Building Bridge Identities as an Ethico-Politics of Global Feminisms

ANN FERGUSON

Northern researchers and service providers espousing modernist theories of development in order to understand and aid countries and peoples of the South ignore their own non-universal starting points of knowledge and their own vested interests. Universal ethics are rejected in favor of situated ethics, while a modified empowerment development model for aiding women in the South based on poststructuralism requires building a bridge identity politics to promote participatory democracy and challenge Northern power knowledges.

THE NEED FOR BRIDGE IDENTITIES

A number of feminist researchers interested in issues of global development (cf. among others, Calás and Smircich 1996; Harding 1998) have maintained that those who provide Northern funded social services and general researchers who attempt to intervene in the situation of people in the countries of the South face a serious ethical danger.[1] Many of these people, whether they are indigenous to Southern countries or inhabit countries in the North, are funded by governments, foundations, corporations, or funds based in, or receiving the preponderance of their money from, sources in Europe and North America. Funding from such sources tends to derive from people who are privileged and tends to be aimed at those who are less privileged. Therefore it evokes the danger of colluding in knowledge production that valorizes status quo economic, gender, racial, and cultural inequalities.

As most social research projects are set up, researchers take part in a process that authorizes them to be a part of an expert group of "subjects of knowledge" who are investigating other humans as "objects of knowledge." Even when funding comes from nongovernmental organizations (NGOs), such as church groups or progressive organizations, the pay that researchers receive and the articles and books they write often create and maintain an economic class difference between themselves and those they are studying. Furthermore, most researchers and social service providers from the North, even when they are anti-imperialists and advocates of social justice, have a horizon of ignorance around their own "othering" practices and privileges that distorts their investigative and service-offering practices.

In an earlier paper (Ferguson 1996) I argued that we need to connect the ethical and political critiques of feminist identity politics based on modernist presuppositions with a poststructuralist critique of investigators, including ourselves, who are engaged in the production of academic or policy research which creates "power/knowledges." There I outlined an ethico-politics of what I call "building bridge identities," a process of self-interrogation and a political practice of rejecting and reconstituting our given social identities in the context of the production of new knowledges. Such an ethico-politics requires an understanding of international feminist politics as a process of interconnecting and producing multiple knowledges based on both local contextual understandings and actions and on some shared generalized analytical categories or starting points.

In this paper I summarize the feminist critiques and alternatives to modernist developmental models and their ethical presuppositions given in that earlier paper. I go on to elaborate more fully what is involved in bridge identity politics and how it is grounded in a more situated ethic that resists modernist code ethics.

THE ETHICS OF MODERNISM AND ITS IMPACT ON DEVELOPMENT

Generally shared among researchers from the North, as well as those schooled in or influenced by Northern ideas, is the set of ethical, political, and metaphysical presuppositions derived from the European Enlightenment that has been called "modernism." These modernist assumptions have been shared not only by mainstream thinkers who otherwise disagree strongly about economic and social policy, but also by most feminist researchers. These assumptions have supported an ethics of progress that underlies much of the legitimization of the funding practices not only of hegemonic institutions like the International Monetary Fund and the World Bank, but also many Northern-based NGOs that fund development projects in the South.

The modernist worldview is based on the following beliefs: that human nature is rational and self-interested; that each individual human has inherent human rights regardless of his or her culture of origin; that capitalist economic development is good because it leads to progress; that such development will benefit all humans in the long run; and that human ethics and knowledge are capable of being developed from a universal, impartial standpoint. Of course, the right to be represented fairly in a constitutional government and the right of access to investments in the capitalist market have never applied to all people. In different historical periods, indigenous peoples, slaves and their descendants, women, the working classes, and immigrants have all been denied full citizenship, and therefore full title to human rights, on the grounds that they were not fully human. Nevertheless, classical liberalism's claim to provide a basis for a universal ethic of justice has been used by many social justice movements, such as abolitionism, the women's movement, the civil rights movement, and the labor movement, to demand the expansion of human rights to all humans. Thus the theory has provided a way to challenge the biased practice of those ruling groups who deny such rights to those they subordinate.

While a positive aspect of these presuppositions is that they are connected to a belief in fundamental human equality, a negative aspect has been the implication that countries that are more economically developed (in the sense of capitalist markets) are, for that very reason, farther along the path to the rational human ideal of progress and equality than other countries. This suggests that a paternalistic relationship between Northern and Southern countries is ethically justified, for as John Stuart Mill put it, the full right to human liberty is not present in human subjects "in their nonage," or infancy, which he thought was true of those living in pre-industrial societies (Mill [1859] 1975).

Various commentators have challenged modernist researchers from the North for ignoring their own very partial interests in knowledge production of the "development discourse" (Escobar 1995; Harding 1998; Mohanty, Russo, and Torres 1991). Likewise, I argue here that modernist ethical presuppositions have blinded such researchers, including Western feminists, from understanding our ethical complicity in the perpetuation of neocolonial domination relations between North and South.

Within the modernist paradigm there are two basic ethical justifications to legitimate any strategy: either a Kantian approach based on human rights and general principles, or a Utilitarian approach based on claims to maximize the general happiness of all or most involved as compared to other alternatives.[2] Both of these justificatory strategies start from what Michel Foucault calls a "code ethics" approach, since they assume that we can develop a universalist ethics based on a code of following general principles that should apply in any context or general rules of thumb that in turn are assumed to promote the general happiness in this sort of context (Foucault 1985).[3]

Northern cultures and Northern-influenced religions and educational establishments socialize their inhabitants to universalized code ethics, which then help form the horizon of ignorance of researchers influenced by them.

This allows researchers and providers from such contexts to ignore their often suspect contextual relationship to the human objects of their research and recipients of their services. Feminist researchers must develop a more contextual ethics based on local understanding rather than universal code knowledge (Walker 1989), dialogical rather than solipsistic reflection (Jaggar, 1997) as well as "practices of liberty"; that is, practices of the self that reconstitute one's self-understanding and ethical relations to others (Foucault 1985, 1989).

In contrast to modernist beliefs about human nature, a feminist historical materialist and radical communitarian approach would argue that human nature is inherently social rather than inherently self-interested (compare Ferguson 1995). Like classical Marxism, the claim is that human nature is socially and historically constructed. Thus "rational self-interest" as opposed to "my neighbor's interest" or "collective good" are concepts that developed only under Western capitalism; they are not universal. Challenging economic arguments based on human nature undercuts claims about the superiority of capitalist markets as well as justifications of governments based on Kantian social contract theory or Utilitarianism.

Even though a feminist materialist ethics rejects a universalist and fixed approach to ethical values based on some unchanging "authentic" human nature, it does not follow that ethical values are entirely subjective or relative. Every historical period and mode of social organization develops its version of a potentially universalizable ethics, although in practice it does not achieve the values it claims to promote. Therefore, we can critique the developing capitalist global economy for failing to achieve the historically developed values that its own defenders claim legitimate it, in particular the ideal of democracy and self-determination for all. In effect, what the capitalist modernization process yields is lip service to formal democracy for all at the expense of substantial democracy for the majority of those who do not control surplus value-creating property. One key aspect of substantial democracy is the ability of the majority collectively to determine social policy decisions that affect their lives, not merely through representative democracy, but through participatory democracy. Thus the modernization process hides a trade-off in values in which a formal democracy (to maintain civil rights against the state, to vote for a representative government) is substituted for a participatory democracy, or the ability to have real influence over economic and other policy decisions. Global feminist interconnected organizing around issues of concern to women at the local level is coming increasingly to recognize the significance of the demand for a participatory democratic process of decisionmaking which empowers women as a key demand around which we can unite.[4]

VALUES AND STRATEGIES IN DIFFERENT DEVELOPMENT MODELS

Modernization, Gender, and Feminist Modifications

Modernization theory assumes that policies that allow an economy to become industrialized will benefit the entire population. But the effort to expand capitalist markets puts an emphasis on expanding wage labor. Such an emphasis usually ignores women's unequal participation in new wage labor because of their unpaid subsistence labor, which is central to meeting people's material needs, particularly in rural production economies (Boserup 1970). Thus industrialization often makes women's position more economically and socially unequal to men's, because it provides men with wage labor or cash crops while women provide the bulk of production for the entire family's use. When women are drawn into wage labor, they face double-day problems; that is, doing twice as much work as before, both waged and unwaged labor.

The Women in Development (WID) paradigm, developed by liberal feminists and adopted by The U.S. Agency for International Development and the World Bank, responds to the invisibility of women's work in the classic modernist by an additive approach; that is, instead of critiquing the sexual division of labor or the public/private split of work, they simply create compensatory programs for women. According to this model, gender fairness requires population control projects to reduce the costs of excess childcare to women and to recruit women into entrepreneurial projects or wage labor (Tinker 1982a, 1982b). In this way, it is thought women's exceptional positions or unfair starting points in the race for capital and status can be eliminated. What such policies ignore is that reproductive decisions depend not merely on women's assessments of their individual interests, but on collective rational interests which in situations of rural poverty may support large families as a goal, as people depend on their children as a labor force and as care providers in old age. Furthermore, many cultures value children simply for themselves. Hierarchical population projects imposed by the North as a paternalistic gesture ignore the importance of participatory democracy in balancing such culture values with other concerns. Even well-meaning distinctions, such as between women's "strategic" and "practical" gender interests, made by Maxine Molyneux in her case study of Nicaraguan women and the Sandinista revolution (Molyneux 1985), assume that there is some Archimedean point from which researchers can determine women's deeper interests as a gender, regardless of their actual beliefs.[5; 6]

Southern women's NGOs such as DAWN (Development and Women for a New Era) (see Antrobus 1996) have been developing an alternative paradigm for international development, often called the "empowerment approach." The problems seen with the WID/equity approach are partly that development projects intended to benefit women in the South have been designed almost exclusively by women in the North. Thus, they are subject to paternalism (or more appropriately, "maternalism"), by being aid projects designed to benefit women seen as Other, as objects of relief rather than as subjects who could take part in the planning process themselves. Furthermore, WID/Equity feminists tend to assume, like liberal feminists, that the goal of developmental projects promoting gender fairness is women's equality with men. The goal of equality with men ignores class, racial, sexual, and other power and status differences between women. It also allows a group of educated, middle-class women, either from the recipient country or the North, to become the leaders, or even the whole staff, of the funded NGO. Such women have a vested interest in obscuring class differences which give them more power than working-class and poor women in determining what development projects will be funded.

The empowerment approach sets as a goal of development the empowerment of individual women by stressing participatory democracy as a process value, both in the initial planning and the content—which must include consciousness-raising workshops for recipients as a central component. Such projects must emphasize a contextual and intersectional, rather than additive, analysis of understanding gender, race, class, sexual, and national domination (Spelman, 1988). In this way, the women involved can personally situate themselves in all analyses of social domination. Thus, rather than accept a choice between two forms of code ethics (Kantian or Utilitarian), those developing the Empowerment model below have suggested a contextual, process ethics based on an "integrative strategy"; that is, on making the means indistinguishable from the ends, and not allowing for value separations between the personal and the political (see Miles 1996).

Planning and consciousness-raising workshops framed in an Empowerment paradigm often engage in popular education using the analytical concepts of gender, race, class, sexuality, and imperialism. Each of these concepts, however, is capable of being understood as a structural, symbolic or contextual identity concept (cf. Ferguson 1997b). Since these yield different analyses, it is important to distinguish them. By "structural gender" is meant gendered divisions of labor in waged and unwaged work, while "symbolic gender" refers to the exclusive speaking positions and social norms associated with masculinity and femininity, both in dominant and subordinate symbolic systems. Contextual gender identity, however, as it is also constrained by classed, raced, sexual, and national domination relations, is not reducible to either structural or symbolic gender. The analyses of structural and symbolic features of each of these domination relations may be facilitated and guided by trained educators and paid staff. However, the emphasis on the value of participatory democracy and non-hierarchical process goals, and the refusal to separate the value of means from the value of ends, yield a model of the ideal workshop: an equal mix of experiential feedback, emphasizing the diverse contexts from which the participants come (that is, the diversity of their concrete gender identities based on different racial, ethnic, class, and other contexts), and participatory decisionmaking moments, evaluations, and planning for future workshops and projects.[7]

In contrast to the modernization paradigm assumed by the WID/Equity feminists, empowerment paradigm feminists tend to assume that the contemporary world order involves societies in internal and external social conflicts or contradictions. Therefore, transforming society involves radical change; evolutionary change will not lead to social justice goals. Rather than assuming that everyone is equal in the capitalist market place, empowerment analysis looks for social structures—for example, the continued unequal distribution of property and capital—in which power is unevenly concentrated. Social change is thought possible in spite of such unequal power relations because of structural conflicts and contradictions that keep the powerful from really being able to control such conflicts. An example is business cycles, which make the capitalist global economy unstable. Finally, given this analysis, social justice requires challenging structural inequalities, such as the unequal division of power and property in society or the sexual division of labor (Paulston 1976; Moser 1993; Cohen 1995).

Deconstructive and Poststructuralist Critiques

Although empowerment paradigm feminists sets themselves up as radical critics of modernization theory, and of WID/Equity feminists in particular, both paradigms have been challenged by postmodern and poststructuralist feminists who object to the universalization implicit in any general paradigm as a starting point for theory (Fraser and Nicholson 1990; Miles 1996). They argue that general paradigms involve discourses for categorizing the world, which, connected with political power—in this case the financial power of funding agencies—constitute what Foucault calls "power/knowledges" (Foucault 1977, 1980). These paradigms are seen as discourses which not only create the objects of their discourse but also legitimize experts in the use of the discourse to determine what truths can be attributed to the objects of discourse. What such experts conveniently ignore in constituting a new "science" of development is the value-laden nature of their own starting points and their power to ignore their own horizons of ignorance. Thus, project funders and staffers can ignore their own privileged positions, both in formulating the concepts and projects and in controlling the funded practices.

Although this may be more obvious in the case of the WID/equity approach, which ignores process values, it is also a problem for the empowerment approach. As Arturo Escobar brings out (Escobar 1995), even when non-hierarchical process and participatory democracy is stressed, the empowerment approach staff facilitators are still the ones who produce the knowledge that comes to and from the workshops. Because they are paid for their work, they get benefits, status, and training from their role in the project. Only the ongoing destabilization of such power and privileges of the staff and researchers by social movements which rearticulate their own political analyses and ethical and political priorities can avoid the reification of such status distinctions.

Escobar is a good example of a poststructuralist critic of all notions of progress based on a modernization model of political economy. Much in the same vein as Laclau and Mouffe (1985), he argues that we must create multiple centers of discourse to challenge such hegemonic control of the notion of development by capitalist economists, or, for that matter, by economists at all. Rather, we must challenge Western policy makers and academics' claim to universal expertise by juxtaposing voices of dissent based on hybrid cultures— those with one foot in traditional knowledges and beliefs and the other in modern science.

Although the Foucauldian idea of "opening up spaces for subjugated knowledges to speak" is appealing, it does not acknowledge that no deconstructive approach can provide a positive answer to how the world ought to be developed: that is, what principles of justice to use to redress unequal distribution of property and resources. For example, traditional cultures often vest communal or individual property rights in men, so that if women are divorced, they are left with no access to land. Is this just? We would hear disagreement about the best principle of fair distribution to use in agrarian land reform if we were to listen both to traditional voices and to a modernist feminist Kantian principle of justice based on the universal rights of all persons regardless of gender.

Poststructuralist and deconstructive critiques demonstrate what Angela Miles (1996) calls a reductionist tendency which does not acknowledge the necessity of what Gayatri Spivak calls "strategic essentialism" even in historically situated discourse (Spivak 1993; Fuss 1989). Jacqui Alexander and Chandra Mohanty (1997) argue that relativist postmodern practice can lead to the denial of the category "race" and its privileges, given that none of us chooses the discourses that mark us, and whiteness is just as socially constructed as other racial categories.

Furthermore, postmodernists tend to ignore their own essentialist moments, or starting points. For example, Foucault never acknowledges that his own concept of power as disciplinary, connected to discursive practices, and productive of the very objects the discourse claims to discover, study and control, is itself a foundational starting point that he, as a twentieth-century Western academic theorist, has a vested interest in promoting. And although Arturo Escobar critiques modernist development discourse, his own poststructuralist critique comes perilously close to continuing the tradition of presenting nonacademic women, like peasants, as victims of this power/knowledge, and therefore as objects of knowledge, rather than subjects of resistance. Finally, as

Linda Alcoff and Nancy Hartsock have argued, feminism as an engaged standpoint cannot be satisfied with mere deconstructive or genealogical critiques but must develop positive visions and ethico-political strategies to challenge social domination (Alcoff 1990; Hartsock 1990).

Indeed, multicentered feminist discourses on global development are developing that are simultaneously self-critical of their own power/knowledge starting points, historically and contextually grounded, and yet unapologetically integrative and positive about the need to provide directions for the future based on the present actual and potential networks of oppression and solidarity between women in the North and South, or between the First and "Two-Thirds" World (Deschamps 1997; Harcourt 1994; Mies 1986; Shiva 1989).[8]

The Modified Empowerment Strategy

The modified empowerment paradigm now used by various feminist Third World organizations such as DAWN in the West Indies is an alternative to more universalized, therefore more modernist, theories of women's liberation through development, including WID, early empowerment approaches, and traditional Marxism. It emphasizes field-based inquiry and development programs that can be situated in particular women's realities rather than universalized claims. Unlike the totally contextual ethics of Northern postmodern feminists, however (Walker 1989; Flax 1998), the ethico-politics of such an approach insists on developing universal visions of social justice (for example, that women's rights are human rights), but doing so not by abstracting away from local contexts. Instead, the starting point is that the clients of development projects must be involved in a knowledge production process in which they help to decide what count as women's and human rights in their contexts and in language accessible to them, and what their local priorities are for trying to implement these rights.

The modified empowerment paradigm emphasizes the following: inquiry strategies that start with women's current position and their goals for research; methods that represent locally understood ways of articulating concepts, ideas and values for all women participants; and respect for alternative ways of representing knowledge that are situated in women's experiences. This methodology can be thought of as similar to participatory action research methodology, with the additional feature that it insists on a process of self-interrogation by funded researchers and an acknowledgment of their power position in the construction of the knowledge being researched. The aim is that participatory practices can attempt to counterbalance researchers' power by insisting on a group process of self-reflection to correct results that reflect this inherent power. Research projects are consciously organized so that researchers and project coordinators develop a practice of self-interrogation that continues to destabilize their given identities and to uncover their horizons of ignorance. Finally, modified empowerment theorists who suspect the power/knowledge aspect of modernist research paradigms resist the attempt at epistemological reconciliation between mainstream modernization theory and sustainable development that many Green Economics advocates propose. The latter ignore both feminist issues and postmodernist critiques of development discourse (Antrobus 1996; Cohen 1995; Sachs 1992; Mies and Shiva 1993).

The notion of a "bridge identity" politics is a strategy for pursing the modified empowerment approach for Northern feminist researchers. Such a politics would allow the development of a situated yet nonrelativist knowledge base, informed by poststructuralism but going beyond the latter's merely critical position. Researchers who tie their theoretical claims more concretely to political practice in alliance with particular women in situated communities can justify their theoretical and empirical knowledge claims as joint products of thought from Northern researchers and from consciousness-raising and consensus-producing indigenous movements. This is particularly true if researchers work in contexts that allow them to project the growth of a consensus in their research agendas. This will allow research based on the process value of participatory democracy.

Resisting the Veil of Privilege: Building Bridge Identities

What self-interrogation practices do feminist researchers and project coordinators need to destabilize given identities and uncover horizons of ignorance? We require an alternative ethico-political strategy that resists the simplifications of an additive, ahistorical identity politics, blind to positional differences between participants. As we have seen, WID/Equity feminists tend to assume a nonproblematic sisterhood based on identity politics, which masks their own paternalistic stand. Their reliance on universalist code ethics allows them to abstract from their own privileged position as constructors of knowledge and funders of projects. On the other hand, we must also reject the relativism of poststructuralist critics who would leave us with a participatory democratic politics so pluralistic and contextualized that it lacks any generalizable base for solidarity politics.

There is a third option: still a kind of identity politics, but one very different from the essentialized versions. Positive identity politics, as I call such essentialized versions, assume general authentic traits that go with certain social groups, but ignores crosscutting social differences and contexts which undercut such generalizations. Such positive identity politics cannot take into account powers and privileges that some in an identity group have over others: for example, positive feminist gender identity politics downplays class, racial, national/ethnic and sexual differences between women. Finally, as poststructuralist critics have emphasized, positive identity politics tends to reinstitute the same dualisms as those in socially dominant positions do, for

example, between man and woman, white and black (or "of color"), heterosexual and homosexual. This marginalizes those who do not fit comfortably
into such categories, such as hermaphrodites, transsexuals, and people of
mixed race. Can a politics of liberation that polices the borders of its own
membership (see Butler 1993) really succeed?

Multiple systems of social domination are responsible for these differences
in social power. Identity politics based on a commitment to multiple social
liberations from all forms of domination therefore must conceive of a historical
process of reconstituting identities. This process will involve two separate
aspects depending on one's social position. The first will be an affirmative
identity building for those in groups oppressed in relation to other groups
(what we can call "target group identity politics"). The second is a "negative
identity" or identity-dismantling process for those in dominant groups (what
we can call "ally identity politics"). The overall process is confusing, in that
most people will be in both oppressed and dominant positions in relation to
some other groups at the same time. Therefore they will have to undergo both
an affirmative and a negative identity politics in relation to different groups of
people, often simultaneously. However, both forms of identity building must
be interpreted differently than they have been under essentialist forms of
identity politics.

I call this type of project building bridge identities (cf. Ferguson, 1996). It
assumes that we need to reconstitute our identities rather than reaffirming or
revalorizing the authentic underlying identity, as essentialist identity politics
supposes. This is not a one-step goal, but involves a process with several stages
and aspects. The difference in the process for target identities and for ally
identities is that the former involves a different first step. Step 1 for target
identities (those in subordinate or oppressive relations with another social
group) involves an affirmative identity politics, the simple affirmation of
potential value in oneself as a member of a social group. Unlike positive
identity politics, such an affirmative identity politics can avoid being essentialist by refusing to reverse the dualist discourse used to oppress the group (for
example, where white was once good, black bad, now black is affirmed as good,
white bad). Instead, it can challenge one's negative valorization as a member
of the target social group by reinterpreting the group's history and imputed
characteristics: in other words, making a re-valuation occur (hooks 1990;
Hoagland 1988). In contrast, the first step for those in dominant positions who
wish to be allies against the oppression of target groups is to make a critique of
the hitherto negative aspects of one's social identity; that is, a devaluation of
one's assumed moral superiority.

The approaches of both target and of dominant groups in this sort of
devaluation and demand for revaluation can be seen as a type of negative
identity politics, as opposed to the type of positive identity politics that aims
to uncover a specific superior moral content to an identity that has been

"alienated" or denied its "authentic" expression under social domination. What exactly is involved in a negative identity politics? As Michel Foucault once said in an interview, we must "refuse who we are" rather than try to affirm who we are (Foucault 1989; Halperin 1995; Rajchman 1991). For women committed to reconstituting ourselves as feminists, this means that rather than first trying to revalue the feminine, we should resist the symbolic tyranny of the feminine over us by becoming "gender traitors" (Heldke 1998). This involves challenging traditional gender norms, rather than gender supporters who simply accept gender dualism but try to revalorize the femininity we have been taught. We can also reinterpret or rearticulate a radical femininity that could be reconstituted under different relations of gender and class, such as one that might help to challenge social domination; caring not just for our families but for strangers and those "othered" from us by social class, race, or national divides (Ferguson 1995).

Second, we must acknowledge the nonadditive embeddedness of our particular gender identities. I am not just a woman, but a white, Euro-American, middle-class, academic woman, and reconstituting that contextual identity requires a traitorous relation not merely to the cultural norms of womanhood but also to the assumption of white, U.S. class and academic privilege. Thus, although I may be subject to mainstream symbolic gender norms in common with other American women, my class, race, and academic positioning may make me more likely to achieve "good woman" status than many of those automatically positioned as "bad women." Furthermore, I may be bound by norms specific to my contextual situation as a white, Euro-American, Protestant, middle-class woman that undermine my self-esteem in ways not applicable to those women not in this category (such as African American or Jewish women). On the other hand, I may be subject to some of the same material gender constraints across such differences, such as being a single mother (Ferguson 1997a).

A negative identity politics may take one of several tacks, either of which challenge the strategy of a more universalizing identity politics. Whereas this latter aims to revalue femininity by revealing hidden strengths in women's unique moral voice (Gilligan 1982), women's incorporative rather than oppositional gender personalities (Chodorow 1978), or the values of women's maternal thinking (Ruddick 1989), the former resists automatically accepting any given personality traits as given strengths around which women can bond (Hoagland 1991). Either one adopts a positional identity politics (Alcoff 1988; De Lauretis 1987; Riley 1990; hooks 1990) or one advocates queer politics, thereby rejecting even any fixed positional starting point for one's politics (Butler 1993; Warner 1993). As Alcoff, De Lauretis, Riley, and hooks explain the notion of positional identity, it is an identity we find ourselves assigned to by social definition, usually by opposition to another social category, such as "woman"= "not-man," "white"="not-black," and "middle-class"= "not-upper-class and not-working-class or poor." We can develop an identity politics based on this social positionality that resists constituting a new essence of femininity, blackness, multicultural whiteness, upwardly mobile working-class-ness. Instead, we can constitute our politics by agreeing with others defined by a similar positionality to fight for certain social justice demands, such as abortion rights, freedom from male violence, affordable childcare, or adequate research on women's health issues.

A somewhat different negative identity politics would resist organizing around given positionalities, on the grounds that they still exclude people from the group many perceive as "natural" allies. For example, many "natural born" lesbians will not ally with gay drag queens or transsexual male-to-female lesbians. To resist this exclusion, queer politics is an attempt to make alliances across given social dualisms based on a felt sense of deviance or solidarity with those defined as deviant who act as gender traitors (Heldke 1998; Ferguson 1995) and undermine normalizing gender performances (Butler 1990, 1993; Warner 1993). An analogous strategy to challenge racism is proposed by Linda Alcoff and Naomi Zack (Alcoff 1995; Zack, 1993). It would create or valorize a third identity, a mixed-race or "mestizo" identity. In this way, the normative definition of "white" as "pure" or unmarked is challenged, particularly if those who are white in the sense of having no ancestors of color begin to define themselves as multiracial because of their friendships or chosen kin or family connections.

The first stage of the negative identity politics process, of rejecting who we have been socially constituted to be, though necessary to challenge social domination, is not sufficient. This is particularly true for those whose complex contextual identity involves one or more socially dominant categories—white, Euro-American, middle or upper class, heterosexual, academic, and what is particularly relevant to our discussion, citizen of the North in relation to citizens of the South. Social dominants must refuse who we are by uncovering our horizons of ignorance around the material structures and ideologies, as well as the individual habits of behavior that perpetuate our social privilege. This involves regular organizational and individual networking with our counter-parts in socially subordinate positions in practices that cede them epistemic privilege to challenge our unacknowledged racism, sexism, and other traits. We must also commit ourselves to altering our segregated friendships, economic networks, loving and living patterns that keep our privileges hidden from us. This means establishing affinity networks with friends and co-workers engaged in similar pro-justice sorts of bridge identity building (Haraway 1985). All of these ongoing practices are what Foucault would call "practices of liberty" or "practices of care of the self" (Foucault 1985, 1989) for one who wishes to reconstitute one's subjectivity in resistance to categorizations and ethical norms embedded in one's socially given identities.

An example of recent efforts to challenge the epistemic privilege of white-ness has involved theory and histories showing that the notion and identity of whiteness is not an inherent human racial sorting device based on skin color and other recognizable biological characteristics. Instead, it is a legal and economic category which has been historically developed in the U.S. racial formation by the imperialist practices of European invaders in connection with indigenous peoples, the economic practices of racial slavery using black people imported from Africa, and the legal practices of denying citizenship rights, racial intermarriage, and legal immigration to target populations "of color." Who counts as "populations of color" has varied at different periods of racial nation building, and has included not only black Africans and yellow and brown Asians but also mixed-race and "white" Hispanics, Irish, Italians, Jews, and Arabs (Allen 1991; Roediger 1991; Frankenberg 1993; Omi and Winant 1994).

What Foucault calls "practices of liberty" (1989) to reconstitute either a bridge "white" or a Northern identity must involve not only re-learning the social history of one's identity groups but also different bodily practices of bonding across tabooed class, race, and national divides. They would involve new emotional activities that would create new habits of identifying one's communities of interests, so that one identifies more with oppositional communities that challenge one's privileged position as a researcher "in the know," or "normal" American, or more "advanced" feminist (Ferguson 1995). Some of these activities could involve organizations, such as economic and consumer cooperatives, which build forms of participatory democracy into their decisionmaking and do not allow wealth or expertise to have more final say in the outcome than members without such privileges. It could also involve NGO practices with ongoing decisionmaking and attempts to build in participatory democratic structures rather than merely representational democracy. Most important, the participatory democratic process would have to facilitate a new way for aid recipients in the South to develop their own voices, theoretical understandings, and value priorities, in order for Northern hegemony not to spring up again through the general influence of Northern "power/knowledges" (see Foucault 1977b).

CONCLUSION

Bridge identity politics is a necessary antidote to the neo-imperialist relations that exist between countries, funders, researchers, and project workers from the North and citizens to be studied and aided in the South. The affinity networks and practices proposed as a way to counter Northern or class-based "power/knowledges" can empower those who have been historically oppressed and transfigure those who constitute themselves as allies from social dominator positions. In this sense, they can achieve a prefigurative ethico-political goal of validating egalitarian relations that do not aim to separate the means from the ends of social transformation. The modified empowerment paradigm that connects with bridge identity politics tends toward a politics of inclusive rather than exclusive agendas. The inclusive or integrative feminism that it supports defines global feminism as a solidarity between women that must be struggled for rather than automatically received (hooks 1984; Miles 1996), a solidarity that fosters alliances to fight any other social domination relations of key importance to those in one's affinity networks (such as national liberation and environmental movements, liberation theology struggles, trade union rights, and rights to subsistence resources, such as water and land). This feminist ethics of international development is neither an abstract universalist code of human rights nor a utilitarian defense of free markets as a means to freedom, democracy or general happiness. It is a situated ethic emphasizing the world-wide, historically salient process goals of participatory democracy and egalitarianism as a part of a reconstitutive struggle of bridge identity building.

NOTES

1. Since the fall of the Soviet Union and China's entrance into the global capitalist marketplace, the distinctions between First World industrial capitalist countries in Europe and North America, Second World socialist countries (the USSR, China, and their satellites), and Third World rural countries, most of which are former First World colonies, has become confusing. In this paper, I will follow the usage that defines industrial and postindustrial capitalist countries of Europe, along with the United States, as countries of the North, and all other countries as countries of the South. The increasing concentration of world capital and resources in the hands of Northern states marks an increasingly racialized economic inequality between North and South.

2. Utilitarian theorizing based on the assumption that the development of capitalist markets will benefit countries has been used in question-begging ways. For example, structural adjustment requirements for loans to poor countries from the World Bank and the IMF are defended a priori on the grounds that economies with more space for capitalist markets and less government social spending will promote the greatest happiness or utility for the greatest number in the long run. Marta Calás and Linda Smircich have pointed out (Calás and Smircich 1997) that the academic practice of mainstream business ethics, dominated by analytic philosophers and status quo managerial corporate apologists, has also used Kantian and Utilitarian presuppositions in question-begging ways. For example, it assumes that corporations are moral, not just legal persons, from a Kantian perspective, and therefore have moral rights to property, or it gives implausible, Utilitarian-style arguments that minimize the negative social consequences of capitalist bottom-line business practices—pollution, unemployment, and dispossession of peasants.

3. I do not mean to imply that only Western liberal ethics are code ethics. Surely Islam, and perhaps some Eastern religions, can be said to involve code ethics. But these religions have not been used historically by colonizers to justify or withhold foreign aid

to colonized countries from a code ethics point of view; so the question of the ethical presuppositions of researchers and funders involved in such aid projects has not become an issue.

4. Compare also Iris Young's argument (1990) that justice is a process value involving weighted participatory democratic structures.

5. I am grateful to Neta Crawford for pointing out that an earlier version of this paper, which involved a critique of Maxine Molyneux's distinction between women's strategic and practical gender interests as it applies to Nicaraguan women (Molyneux 1985), actually conflicted with the turn toward a bridge identity politics I espouse here. I plan to develop a different way of critiquing Molyneux's distinction in a later paper.

6. Mary Hawkesworth suggests that there is a general danger to be avoided when employing general categories like gender. Theorists should avoid constructing narratives that universalize an underlying cause for particular social functions performed by gender. Such explanations shift gender from an analytic, heuristic place marker that needs to be historically specified to an unprovable ontological status, as when gender is claimed to operate in the interests of ensuring reproduction of the species or promoting male domination (Hawkesworth 1997). Similarly, the claim that women's strategic gender interests involve interests in controlling reproduction in specific contexts, even when the women in those contexts do not agree with this value-laden claim, seems neither verifiable nor falsifiable, and thus loses its political utility. Only when women begin to develop a vision of a different sort of life, involving different relations to men, children, the family, and other women, can they see the goal of having fewer children as an advantage, and therefore in their interest.

7. Angela Miles gives a very similar characterization of the ethics of what she calls "integrative feminism" and argues that there have been First and Third World feminists (that is, feminists from the North and South) in all the more standard tendencies of feminism—liberal, Marxist, radical, socialist, postmodernist—and that these have been integrative, as opposed to what she calls "reductionistic," feminists (Miles 1996).

8. Miles (1996) uses this phrase to refer to people in the South of the world, as opposed to the Northern postindustrial countries.

REFERENCES

Alcoff, Linda. 1988. Cultural feminism vs. poststructuralism: The identity crisis in feminist theory. *Signs* 13(3): 405-36.

———. 1990. Feminist politics and Foucault: The limits to a collaboration. In *Crises in continental philosophy*, ed. Arleen B. Dallery and Charles E. Scott. Albany: State University of New York Press.

———. 1995. *Mestizo* identity. In *American mixed race: The culture of microdiversity*. See Zack 1995.

Allen, Theodore W. 1991. *The invention of the white race, vol.1: Racial oppression and social control*. London: Verso

Alexander, Jacqui, and Chandra Talpade Mohanty. 1997. *Feminist genealogies, colonial legacies, democratic futures*. New York: Routledge.

Antrobus, Peggy. 1996. "United Nations" conferences: A framework for feminist research and action. *Caribbean Studies* 28(1): 21-30.

Bar On, Bat Ami and Ann Ferguson. 1998. *Daring to be good: Essays in feminist ethico-politics*. New York: Routledge.

Boserup, Ester. 1970. *Women's role in economic development*. New York: St. Martin's Press.

Butler, Judith. 1990. *Gender trouble, feminism and the subversion of identity*. New York: Routledge.

———. 1993. *Bodies that matter: On the discursive limits of "sex."* New York: Routledge.

Butler, Judith and Joan Scott, eds. 1992. *Feminists theorize the political*. New York: Routledge.

Calás, Marta, and Linda Smircich. 1996. From the "woman's" point of view: Feminist approaches to organization studies. In *Handbook of organization studies*, ed. S. Clegg, C. Hardy, and W. Nord. London: Sage.

———. 1997. *Predicando la moral en calzoncillos*: Feminist inquiries into business ethics. In *Women's studies and business ethics*, ed. Andrea Larson and R. Edward Freeman. New York: Oxford University Press.

Chodorow, Nancy. 1978. *The reproduction of mothering*. Berkeley: University of California Press.

Cohen, Joanie. 1995. Women and development: Issues and trends. Manuscript, Center for International Education, Uuniversity of Massachusetts, Amherst.

De Lauretis, Teresa. 1987. *Technologies of gender*. Bloomington: University of Indiana Press.

Deschamps, Alexandrina. 1997. Feminization of development: Alternative futures for women, a context-centered approach. Manuscript. Women's Studies, University of Massachusetts, Amherst.

Escobar, Arturo. 1995. *Encountering development*. Princeton: Princeton University Press.

Ferguson, Ann. 1991. *Sexual democracy: Women, oppression, and revolution*. Boulder, CO: Westview Press.

———. 1995. Feminist communities and moral revolution. In *Feminism and Community*, ed. Penny A. Weiss and Marilyn Friedman. Philadelphia: Temple University Press.

———. 1996. Bridge identity politics: An integrative feminist ethics of international development. *Organization* 3(4): 571-87.

———. 1997a. Gender and race: Structures, ideologies and performances. Manuscript, Women's Studies, University of Massachusetts, Amherst.

———. 1997b. Moral responsibility and social change: A new theory of self. *Hypatia* 12(3): 116-40.

Flax, Jane. 1998. Displacing woman: Towards an ethics of multiplicity. In *Daring to be good: Essays in feminist ethico-politics*. See Bar On and Ferguson 1998.

Foucault, Michel. 1977. *Discipline and punish: The birth of the prison*. New York: Pantheon.

———. 1980. *Power/knowledge: Selected interviews and essays*. Ed. Colin Gordon. New York: Pantheon.

———. 1985. *The use of pleasure: History of sexuality, vol. 2*. New York: Pantheon.

———. 1989. The ethics of the concern of the self as a practice of freedom. In *Foucault live: Interviews 1961-1984*, ed. Sylvere Lotringer. Trans. Lysa Hockroth and John Johnston. New York: Semiotext(e).

Frankenberg, Ruth. 1993. *The social construction of whiteness: White women, race matters*. Minneapolis: University of Minnesota Press.

Fraser, Nancy and Linda Nicholson. 1990. Social criticism without philosophy: An encounter between feminism and postmodernism. In *Feminism/postmodernism*. See Nicholson 1990.

Fuss, Diana. 1989. *Essentially speaking: Feminism, nature and difference*. New York: Routledge.

Gilligan, Carol. 1982. *In a different voice: Psychological theory and women's development*. Cambridge: Harvard University Press.

Halperin, David. 1995. *Saint=Foucault: Toward a gay hagiography*. New York: Oxford University Press.

Haraway, Donna. 1985. A manifesto for cyborgs: Science, technology, and socialist-feminism in the 1980s. *Socialist Review* 15(2): 65-107.

Harcourt, Wendy, ed. 1994. *Feminist perspectives on sustainable development*. London: Zed Books.

Harding, Sandra. 1998. *Is science multicultural? Postcolonialisms, feminisms and epistemologies*. Bloomington: Indiana University Press.

Hartsock, Nancy. 1990. Foucault on power: A theory for women? In *Feminism/postmodernism*. See Nicholson 1990.

Hawkesworth, Mary. 1997. Confounding gender. *Signs* 22(3): 649-86.

Heldke, Lisa. 1998. On being a responsible traitor: A primer. In *Daring to be good: Essays in feminist ethico-politics*. See Bar On and Ferguson 1998.

Hoagland, Sarah. 1988. *Lesbian ethics: Toward new value*. Palo Alto, CA: Institute of Lesbian Studies.

———. 1991. Some thoughts about "caring." In *Feminist ethics*, ed. Claudia Card. Lawrence: University of Kansas Press.

hooks, bell. 1984. *Feminist theory from margin to center*. Boston: South End Press.

———. 1990. *Yearning: race, gender, and cultural politics*. Boston: South End Press.

Jaggar, Alison. 1997. Telling right from wrong: Toward a feminist conception of practical reason. Manuscript. Women's Studies, University of Colorado, Boulder.

Laclau, Ernesto and Chantal Mouffe. 1985. *Hegemony and socialist strategy: Towards a radical democratic perspective*. London: Verso.

Mies, Maria. 1986. *Patriarchy and accumulation on a world scale*. London: Zed Books.

Mies, Maria and Vandana Shiva. 1993. *Eco-feminism*. London: Zed.

Miles, Angela. 1996. *Integrative feminism*. New York: Routledge.

Mill, John Stuart. [1859] 1975. *On liberty*. Ed. David Spitz. New York: W.W. Norton.

Mohanty, Chandra Talpade, Ann Russo and Lourdes Torres, eds. 1991. *Third World women and the politics of feminism*. Bloomington: Indiana University Press.

Molyneux, Maxine. 1985. Mobilization without emancipation? Women's interests, state, and revolution in Nicaragua. *Feminist Studies* 11(2): 46-51.

Montenegro, Sofia. 1995. *Primer seminario nacional de mujer y politico*. Pamphlet produced by Sofia Montenegro of the Malinche Feminist Collective for the Organizing Commission of the First National Seminar on Women and Politics. Managua, October 1995.

Moser, Caroline. 1993. *Gender planning and development*. New York: Routledge.

Nicholson, Linda, ed. 1990. *Feminism/postmodernism*. New York: Routledge.

Omi, Michael and Howard Winant. 1994. *Racial formation in the United States*, 2d edition. New York: Routledge.

Paulston, Rolland. 1976. *Conflicting theories of social change and educational change: A typology review*. London: University Center for International Studies.

Rajchman, John. 1991. *Truth and eros: Foucault, Lacan and the question of ethics.* New York: Routledge.

Riley, Denise. 1990. *"Am I that name?" Feminism and the category of "women" in history.* Minneapolis: University of Minnesota Press.

Roediger, David R. 1991. *The wages of whiteness: Race and the making of the American working class.* London: Verso.

Ruddick, Sarah. 1989. *Maternal thinking: Toward a politics of peace.* Boston: Beacon Press.

Sachs, Wolfgang, ed. 1992. *The development dictionary: A guide to knowledge as power.* London: Zed Books.

Shiva, Vandana. 1989. *Staying alive: Women, ecology and development.* London: Zed Books.

Spelman, E. V. 1988. *Inessential woman.* Boston: Beacon Press.

Spivak, Gayatri Chakroavorty. 1993. *Outside in the teaching machine.* New York: Routledge.

Tinker, Irene. 1982a. *Feminist values: Ethnocentric or universal?* Washington, DC: Equity Policy Center.

———. 1982b. *Gender equity in development: A policy perspective.* Washington, DC: Equity Policy Center.

Walker, Margaret Urban. 1989. Moral understandings: Alternative "epistemology" for a feminist ethics. *Hypatia* 4(2): 15-28.

Warner, Michael, ed. 1993. *Fear of a queer planet: Queer politics and social theory.* Minneapolis: University of Minnesota Press.

Young, Iris. 1990. *Justice and the politics of difference.* Princeton: Princeton University Press.

Zack, Naomi. 1993. *Race/mixed race.* Philadelphia: Temple University Press.

———. 1995. *American mixed race: The culture of microdiversity.* Lantham, MD: Rowman and Littlefield.

12

Maquiladora Mestizas and a Feminist Border Politics: Revisiting Anzaldúa

MELISSA WRIGHT

This essay argues that a new, politicized mestiza is emerging within the cultural borderlands of the Mexico-U.S. divide. She works in the upper ranks of the multinational maquiladoras and raises many challenges for a feminist theorization of a new border politics. Through a presentation of research in one maquiladora, the essay demonstrates how understanding the dynamic between metaphorical and material space is vital for imagining a feminist politics in the cultural borderlands.

IMAGINING THE BORDER

Along stretches of the Mexico-U.S. border, a new *mestiza* is emerging. Her language is Spanish, English, and "Spanglish," and her job is in the *maquiladoras*.[1] Sometimes she has a college degree, but often she has simply worked her way through the corporate ranks, moving up from hourly wage positions and into jobs with prestige, power, and significantly more pay. She comes from both sides of the political border. Her nationality is Mexican or American, but she calls herself "*mexicana*," among the other place-based identifiers, such as Mexican American, *fronteriza*, *norteña*, American, and Chicana.[2] A number of these *mexicanas* hold prestigious posts in community and business associations on both sides of the border. They have defied expectations limiting their role to the low-wage and unskilled positions (see Frobel 1979). And they raise some sticky issues for a feminist approach to the politics of race, gender, class, ethnicity, and nationality along a border where such identifiers compromise the distance between the politics of Left and Right.

I refer to these *mexicanas* as "*mestizas*" in order to engage with Gloria Anzaldúa's discussion of a "new *mestiza*" (Anzaldúa 1987). The *mestizas* I discuss are new political subjects in the Mexico-U.S. borderlands who, by reinforcing the symbol of the border as a permanent division cut across the social terrain, have made gains as self-identified *mexicanas* in the *maquiladoras*. They raise challenges for Anzaldùa's argument, which contends that only through resistance to the discourse of a border as dividing line can a *mexicana* community gain political ground in the cultural borderlands. And they challenge feminist theory, more generally, to examine how a politics of geographic difference intersects with assertions of identity and the conceptualization of communities in which women hold power and prestige and instigate change.

Anzaldúa's image of the new *mestiza* is as a cultural subject who forges political unity by dissolving the international divide from both the social imagination and political practice. "The U.S.-Mexican border *es una herida abierta* [an open wound]," she writes, "where the Third World grates against the first and bleeds." Along this border flows "the lifeblood of two worlds merging to form a third—a border culture" (Anzaldúa 1987, 3). She argues that in the divided border geography of the post-colonial period, the *mexicana* is devalued and her cultural integrity defiled. Writing as a new *mestiza*, Anzaldúa calls for "an exoneration, a seeing through the fictions of white supremacy, a seeing of ourselves in our true guises and not as the false racial personality that has been given us and that we have given ourselves. I seek our woman's face, our true features" (1987, 87). Her prophetic vision is a battle cry for *mexicanas* to seek unity where the state, along with heterosexist, misogynist, imperialist, and racist ideologies, has segregated *mexicana* from *mexicana* throughout the borderlands. At the heart of this journey for cultural reunification is a political subversion of the meaning of the border in both discourse and practice. Through reimagining the border not as the place of division but as the unified seam, where different manifestations of an essentially unified culture meet, she foresees an emerging geography that will ground a reinvigorated cultural and feminist politics.

Anzaldúa offers an imaginative elixir for a practical problem that plagues *mexicanas* who are involved in political community groups who attempt to organize cross-border events.[3] Today, on the U.S. side, a dramatic militarization (Dunn 1996), a rekindled enthusiasm for walls that physically delineate the political line (see Fox 1995-96), and widespread condemnation of Mexican immigrants as parasites in "American" society have strained social networks and antagonized historical tensions on both sides (see also Anaya and Lomelí 1989). Imagining a unified border subject is no easier on the Mexican side, where the divisions between Mexicans and Americans, of Mexican descent or otherwise, are steadfastly reinforced by nationalist ideologies that separate "real" Mexicans from emigrants and their descendants in the United States (see Córdoba and Socorro 1995-96).

While these stubborn assertions of geographic division stand at odds with Anzaldúa's vision of geopolitical unity, they do not necessarily represent insurmountable obstacles for the conceptualization of a cross-border politics.

Instead, they illustrate the need for understanding how discourses of geographic difference work into the materialization of political subjects and their communities.

Against the background of Anzaldúa's work, I present some of my ethnographic research on how *mexicanas* navigate the shifting social terrain of the Mexico-U.S. borderlands in their attempts to scale the corporate ladder in the multinational *maquiladoras*. These *mexicanas* represent a new *mestiza* in the sense that they have subverted historical discourses of who they are as women of Mexican descent and where they consequently belong in the multinational firm.[4] I call them "*maquiladora mestizas*" because they express a cultural identity based on their deft navigation of the multinational *maquiladora* workplace and the politics of difference that characterize the Mexico-U.S. borderlands.

Through a focus on the *maquiladora mestiza*, I hope to demonstrate that a feminist politics should, following Iris Young's (1990) argument, consider how expressions of difference actually consolidate communal borders. Crucial to this endeavor is a critical inquiry into the relationship between the border as a metaphor for myriad social divisions and the border as a material space, that is policed, enforced and physically crossed (see Katz and Smith 1993).

In seeking to understand how metaphoric spaces materialize into places characterized by particular sorts of residents, I draw from Judith Butler's (1993) work on the interplay of discourse with matter in the formation of intelligible social subjects. Butler argues that discourse performs on matter such that the discursive markers of identity, as in race, sex, ethnicity, and so on, come into view as the materials that constitute the *real* corporeality of the body. Consequently, what is perceived to be materially grounded is actually discursively constituted, and is therefore in flux, despite its location in seemingly immutable matter. With this argument, Butler carves out a political space between discourse and matter, in which she demonstrates that political action can include efforts to disturb the codes for constructing subjects from the materials identified to be located in their bodies (see also Butler 1997). She refers to such disturbances as "resignifications," or "radical rearticulation(s) . . . of the symbolic horizon in which bodies come to matter at all" (Butler 1993, 23).

This notion of resignification is important for my own interpretation of the *maquiladora mestiza* as a new subject who has subverted the historical meanings of her language, body, sexuality, opinions, and labor in the *maquiladora* corporate community. Her move up the corporate ladder and her recent prominence in probusiness cultural groups such as LULAC (The League of United Latin American Citizens) involves rethinking a vision of the unified mexicana who has a foothold in a unified border geography. While the *maquiladora mestiza*, who can claim a significant measure of status and material wealth, challenges representations of *mexicanas* as the unskilled and docile labor force of international renown, she simultaneously reinforces practices for exploiting *mexicana* labor, at the average price of fifty cents per hour, and for excluding the majority of mexicanas from the benefits of the international mobility that multinational capital and its managers enjoy. The *maquiladora mestiza* demonstrates that her social strength rests on an interpretation of a bifurcated border geography and of a differentiated *mexicana* subject. Therefore, with the concept of resignification, I hope to show how a class politics is inextricable from both the politics of place (see Harvey 1996) and from the negotiations of identities articulated as part and parcel of the production of places. Further, I aim to demonstrate that a feminist politics of the Mexico-U.S. border, one that takes into account how women on both sides conceptualize their communities and alliances, must understand that class neither forms a discrete category nor is isolated from the social politics of identity in the cultural borderlands.

What follows is an interpretation of ethnographic research I conducted within a *maquiladora*, which I shall refer to as Mexico on the Water (MOTW), an offshore facility of a U.S.-based multinational firm that is located in Ciudad Juárez, Chihuahua, across the border from El Paso, Texas.[5] This case is taken from a year long ethnographic inquiry in the *maquiladoras* (Wright 1996). The experiences of the *mexicanas* in MOTW that I present here reveal how a metaphor of the Mexico-U.S. border operates as a cultural, ethnic, classed, raced, and sexed divide that materializes through the production of space and subjects representative of border residents.[6]

MEXICO ON THE WATER

The day starts at MOTW in Ciudad Juárez when the American managers and engineers drive across the international bridge and park at the factory. Several hundred Mexican operators, technicians, and administrative assistants stream out of buses that have carried them from Ciudad Juárez's scattered reaches. This international meeting occurs each morning, moments before the production lines start pumping out the sundry parts of motorboats—ignition switches, carburetors, electrical harnesses, gauges—that MOTW has produced for more than a decade. When I arrived at MOTW in September 1993, all managers and engineers were American and the wage-laborers Mexican. I was invited by the plant manager to conduct my study on the organization of multinational firms, and I was allowed to park my car in the American area of the parking lot; this reflected my welcome into the American domain of MOTW administration, where I was provided with my own office.

I began my research in MOTW within a month of the highly publicized "Border Blockade," later renamed "Hold the Line," an operation undertaken by the U.S. Border Patrol in September 1993.[7] Justifications for this militarization of an officially peaceful border frequently invoked the crisis represented by the immigrant *mexicana*, her pregnancies, her poor children, and their consumption of U.S. social services. As I sought to understand how space and work were organized at MOTW, I came to see how the divide between the American administrative and the Mexican production areas was policed to ensure the exclusion of the *mexicana*. Over time, I heard discourses within MOTW, which echoed those heard throughout the United States, arguing that Mexican women must be prohibited from taking advantage of tax-funded social services in U.S. territory. Similarly, in MOTW, representations of the *mexicana* centered on her reproductive drive and her sexuality, which precipitated waste of U.S. resources (see also Fernández-Kelly 1983).

The policing of the *mexicana* social mobility in MOTW focused on where she appeared in the workplace. The verbal descriptions of the factory itself incorporated references to a nationalized "border" that separated the Mexican from the American areas. Doors, language surveillance, and uniforms marked this imaginary divide and brought the border to life in the internal spaces of MOTW. A *mexicana* presence was tolerated in the managerial domain only if it was accompanied by strict surveillance.

On my initial tour of MOTW, the plant manager, Steve, an "Anglo" male most recently from Georgia, explained that the physical plant was divided along a national line. "In here," he narrated as we walked through the shop floor, "is where we put our Mexican employees. We've got about five hundred now, about half female. That's a lot less than other *maquiladoras* because we started off as a machine shop, but now we've got more of the electrical work that the girls do." We walked past the almost totally male-staffed carburetor tooling and assembly operation, and he proceeded to describe his plans to promote some Mexican employees because he believed that "Mexico can produce good quality engineers and I think we should support that."

However, as we continued our journey through the expansive operation and reached the predominantly female populated areas of electrical assembly and wire cutting, I realized that his optimism for Mexico's technical ability did not extend to *mexicanas*. "I don't think we'll have many promotions from here," he replied in answer to my question as to whether he intended to promote employees from the electrical assembly operations. "Mexican women just don't have the cultural upbringing for industrial careers. They're here to find a mate and raise some kids. Sounds harsh, but that's the reality here." When we had completed our rounds of the production operations, we stopped at a metal door with an opaque window. "Now our administration," he said while holding open the door. "This is where the Americans have their offices. We have two assistant plant managers, and managers for the other departments— engineering, the warehouse."

When passing through this door, I could not deny the palpable sensation of crossing from a consciously designed Mexican domain into an American one. I noticed that several of the posters on the wall advertised the thrilling experience of operating MOTW motorboats. Some encouraged teamwork for quality production; all were in English. The audible language was also English in the administrative area, an expansive space segmented into several offices along the side and filled with cubicles in the middle. These visual and audible markers contrasted with the Mexican area, where a sound system broadcast popular tunes from a local Ciudad Juàrez radio station and notices in Spanish outlined corporate policies regarding safety and general comportment. These markers revealed a concerted effort to reproduce in the firm's social and spatial arrangement the hierarchy of Mexicans to Americans articulated in larger border discourses.

The international divide in the factory also represented a divide in the labor code, pay structure, and tax system.[8] Mexican employees worked under the guidelines imposed by the Mexican labor laws, and while Americans had to respect these laws in their treatment of Mexican workers, the general understanding of the law was that Americans were bound by the U.S. code in their treatment of each other. Under no circumstances, Steve explained, was a Mexican to hold authority over or earn more money than an American. "That goes against the grain of an American company," he said.

However, unlike the immigration authorities who policed the international line only a few miles away, passage across the international border inside MOTW did not depend on a birth certificate. One's citizenship was not under scrutiny; rather, it was the performance of identity that was subject to examination. Any performance by a woman that might be interpreted to signify the presence of a *mexicana* in the American domain of administration was considered dangerous.

For example, even though Steve described the area as the preserve of American management, the vast majority of the people working in that room were Mexican administrative staff, all women. Many had migrated from various parts of northern Mexico to find work in the *maquilas*, and they now facilitated the MOTW paperwork for a poverty-level, minimum wage. Everything about their job performance, from how fast they typed to what they wore, how they spoke, and how they presented themselves was carefully scripted, all in the effort to demonstrate a U.S. managerial control over the out-of-control *mexicana*. I noticed that the fifteen or so secretaries and clerks wore the same outfit—a drab gray pinstripe dress suit with a red blouse and matching pumps. "Are they wearing uniforms?" I asked. Steve explained that there were uniform regulations for the Mexican women in administration because "you should have seen what they used to wear. It looked like one of those cantinas down on Juárez avenue [the red light district]. It made some of the guys uncomfortable."

Reference to prostitution when discussing women employees came up on more than one occasion in my research at MOTW. For example, when I asked one of the production managers, Roger, to describe the labor force, he said, "Some of these girls have second jobs. You know, I've even heard that some work the bars." The message that you cannot tell the difference between a prostitute and a female *maquiladora* worker was common in my interviews. "We don't know what these girls do at night," Burt, another production manager said, "but we don't want them to bring it in here." Steve, the general manager, further explained in a later conversation, "It's important for our clients to feel like they're in an American office when they're in here. Also, it just makes the secretaries seem more professional, not just some girl walking in from the street."

This managerial narrative of the female Mexican employee at MOTW was an effort to help me see her as they did and to bring her to life as the embodiment of that sexually chaotic third world woman so common, according to corporate gurus, to other industrial worksites around the globe (cf. Ong 1987). This version of the female *maquiladora mexicana* is not particular to MOTW (see also Salzinger 1997; Wright 1997), and she was not a static figure, found only in people born on one side of the border or the other. Rather, she traveled with the discourses that sought her out and recreated her in the gestures, clothing, language, hair styles, and attitudes of the female labor force. All women employees at MOTW had to stake her position as non-*mexicana* or risk being interpreted as another instance of her dangerous corporeal configuration. And to be seen with such an embodiment would threaten any woman's career into the decidedly American domain of MOTW management.

I encountered this very threat when two self-described *mexicanas* attempted to change jobs and ascend the MOTW corporate ladder. Each of these women described herself to me as *mexicana*, and each faced the challenge of having to navigate the discourse of the *mexicana* in order to legitimate her claim to residency in the American domain of administration, where she could earn a higher salary and exercise more authority. In these two cases, being an American or a Mexican, masculine or feminine, Anglo or *mexicana* hinged on a performance of the subject position as it is understood in the symbolic realm of representation. We shall see how a woman who was born and raised in Mexico transforms herself into an American, while a woman born and raised in the United States slides down the corporate scale as she is seen to embody the *mexicana* image. Each encountered a discourse that recreated a historical representation of *mexicanas*, in general, as vulnerable to their sexual drives and dangerous for corporate capitalism as their bodies, language, and mannerisms were screened for evidence of the *mexicana* who might lurk within her. And each struggled to resignify herself within the dominant discourse of who *mexicanas* are and what they provoke inside and outside of the MOTW walls.

ROSALÍA

When I met Rosalía, she was the personnel director for Mexican employees. She had been working in the *maquilas* for twelve years, having started out as an operator, then having moved from clerk to secretary, and finally to the assistant personnel director position at her previous *maquila* employer. She was raising her two children single-handedly and had just received her college degree in business administration after years of night school. She was the only career woman in her immediate family, and she expressed pride in her accomplishments. "A lot of people say that women can't have a career. You hear that about Mexican women especially, but it's not true. You have to want it, but you can do it," she told me when I asked her to describe her career history.

At the time of that conversation, Rosalía's office was in one of the cubicles designated for Mexican administrative staff in the production area. In the history of MOTW, no Mexican woman had ever moved above that position; however, within two months of my research, Rosalía not only would make a bid for a promotion, she would be the first *mexicana* to occupy an office in the American administrative area, and she would hold authority over American employees. A month after this promotion, I asked Rosalía to describe the events surrounding her move. "It was obvious that Steve needed some help with the American personnel. I was already doing the insurance work . . . I told him I could do the job. I showed him my books on the U.S. labor code . . . He knows that I'm professional. I'm not just any *mexicana*."

Steve explained his decision to me this way: "I knew it was a big deal to move Rosalía into this office, but I also knew that she was the best for the job. They look at her and see just another Mexican woman, but I know Rosalía. And I know she's tough as nails and ambitious. She'll end up showing us all that she's not just some Mexican woman who's in over her head. She'll fit in with the Americans."

Still, when he announced Rosalía's promotion, four of the five managers stormed out of the meeting in protest.

"This is an invasion of my privacy," one production manager, Roger, growled as he marched out of the office. "What's wrong?" I asked Burt, the other production manager, as he exited the staff meeting room. "Roger is pissed about Rosalía. I am, too. I don't see why she should have an office here. She was fine where she was," he replied as he walked toward his office, located across the hall from hers. Outside I asked Roger what irritated him so about Rosalía's promotion, "I don't want to sound like a bigot, cause I don't have anything against Mexican people. But she's very Mexican and a woman in that culture doesn't know what it's really like to play hardball."

"What does this have to do with privacy?" I continued.

"Look, she's just not qualified to oversee our affairs. For Christ's sake, she's just a secretary. They're probably having a goddamned affair," Roger barked. Burt jumped in, "She's supposed to handle our insurance claims or worker's comp?" He added sarcastically, "She doesn't even know what that means."

Inside, the grumblings from other American employees were more subtle but still audible. I approached Cynthia, one of the quality engineers, who said,

"What does a Mexican woman know about sexual harassment? She's *mexicana mexicana*." *Mexicana mexicana*, as I was assumed to understand, meant that Rosalía was a particularly Mexican *mexicana*, who would then fit within the lower ranks of MOTW's political and economic hierarchy.

On this issue, Cynthia was quite vocal: "Do you realize that she is now my boss? And she makes more money than I do. That's an insult." Part of the protest was directed at Steve, who had disrupted the social code by allowing Rosalía to move physically into American social space. They feared a sullying of the American domain by the presence of a *mexicana*. Burt and Roger summed up this sentiment when each complained, "What do you think our bosses in Illinois are going to think when they come into our offices and see her?" Cynthia was also concerned about the image: "Rosalía won't know how to act around corporate people. She looks out of place, and that's no accident."

Rosalía knew of these misgivings. She immediately enrolled in an intensive English course, bought some new suits at Dillard's in El Paso, and filled out the paperwork for a green card. She would be moving to El Paso. Within one month, she had checked out the El Paso schools for her children and chosen the neighborhood where she would like to live. I asked her why she was making the move, and she responded, "Well, the job is an American job. That means I have to get a green card."

In order to qualify for the human resources position as it was structured in the corporation, Rosalía had to become an American resident with a green card. The human resource manager's position was a structurally "American" one. It was paid in U.S. dollars; it forfeited taxes to the U.S. government; and it fell under the U.S. labor code. No less significantly, it was ranked above several American positions in terms of pay, status, and corporate power. Rosalía was demonstrating that this human resource manager was not going to be a Mexican but rather an American employee.

She put it this way: "In the *maquilas*, you have to understand the difference between being Mexican and being American. They say right to my face that a *mexicana* can't do this job. That I don't understand sexual harassment or can't stop a strike. You watch. I am *mexicana* but I have American business sense, and that means I know both sides." In showing that she could reside in the U.S., Rosalía played off the metaphor of the international border outside the firm in order to renegotiate her position vis-á-vis the border inside it. She was leaving her *mexicanismo* behind. She was Americanizing and, no less significant, she was proving that unlike the overwhelming majority of *mexicanas*, she was not culturally bound to sexual chaos.

Steve told me one day over lunch, "She really surprised a lot of people when she announced that. I think they thought she wouldn't be able to leave Mexico. But you know I think she's got her sights set on an international posting. She's serious. She wants to be treated like an American and have a real career. . . . I think she can do it."

However, Rosalía's own description of this movement reveals that she considers herself to be a new kind of *mexicana*, one who understands how the border as a metaphor interacts with the material organization of power, capital, and prestige in the political borderlands. When I asked her if she would miss living in Ciudad Juárez, she said, "I will always be *mexicana*, but I also need to understand American issues. Here I am American. I represent American employees to the corporation. I translate policy. So I need to know what it means to cross the bridge every day, to have your kids in an American school and try to keep up with what they want. I am *mexicana* but I'm not the traditional version."

And she did transform herself in front of everyone's eyes into what was broadly construed as the prototype of an American manager. Her dress suits changed to darker hues; her hems grew longer and her heels shorter.[9] Within a few weeks of her language class, she rarely spoke Spanish. She also handled a delicate insurance problem regarding offshore American employees and impressed her skeptical colleagues with her acumen in a U.S. corporate bureaucracy. I asked Steve how he found her job performance. "You know, she really has changed. I think they don't even know she's Mexican up in headquarters."

Rosalía's apparent abilities to dispel labor disruptions further impressed the other managers. In February 1995, following a seventy percent peso devaluation (against the U.S. dollar), thousands of workers walked off their jobs in the *maquiladoras*. Rumors spread that someone was trying to organize unions throughout the industry as factory managers came under pressure to raise wages both to compensate for the immediate cheapening of their labor force (in dollar terms) and to stem the decline of the workers' buying power. Two of the factories neighboring MOTW were paralyzed by a walk-out, and the almost five thousand striking workers at the nearby RCA television manufacturer forced a shut down in the firm's Illinois operation (see Kern and Dunn 1995). Yet at MOTW, work continued as usual. Steve was bursting with praise for Rosalía when I asked him how MOTW stayed in operation. "She really knew what to do. She had informants spread out all over the place. . . . In the doctor's office. Everyone talks to their doctor, and on the lines. She's tough, tougher than anyone thought she could be. She's shown that she's not your average Mexican woman. In fact, I think she's as American now as I am."

Rosalía was also making her presence known beyond the MOTW walls. One year after her promotion, she was appointed to a prominent position in the *maquiladora* trade association in Ciudad Juárez, and she expressed the hope of opening the door for other *mexicana* managers to participate in the group.

As Rosalía crossed some Mexico-U.S. divides, she resignified herself in MOTW. She became a professionally savvy *mexicana* by rearticulating what it

meant to have her knowledge as a *mexicana*, her language, and her own
political vision. She manipulated the border as a metaphor for division in order
to carve her place as a particular type of *mexicana* with mobility across the
international divide. And she assumed a politics of geographic difference. Her
movement into American space meant putting some distance between herself
and the majority of *mexicanas* employed at the firm. Yet she still identified
herself as a *mexicana*, one with the ability to make links across the border, to
forge political connections and to strengthen her position through her own
awareness of herself as a political agent. She is not the kind of new *mestiza*
Anzaldùa envisions, but she is the type that is becoming more prominent in
the contemporary place that is the Mexico-U.S. borderland.

Alongside Rosalía's efforts for promotion there was another attempt by one
of her American colleagues, Cynthia, also to gain ground in management.
Rosalía was the corporation's point person for managing this affair, and her
handling of it reveals her view that the failure to recognize the politics of
geographic difference in the *maquiladoras* is disastrous for a *mexicana* who
aspires to improve her own material standing.

CYNTHIA

When I first met Cynthia in September 1993, she worked as a quality
engineer overseeing the production of the fuel systems. The job description for
this position involves more managing than engineering, and her role was as
the managerial liaison to the manufacturing engineers, all Mexican men, on
the shop floor. With a college degree in engineering and chemistry, Cynthia
had the most years of education in her family, and she was taking night classes
at the University of Texas in El Paso to complete the requirements for a
master's degree in industrial engineering. Although her parents were first-gen-
eration immigrants from Mexico, she said she learned to speak Spanish well in
high school. She had started working at MOTW two years earlier when she
decided that even though she was from Ohio, her roots were along the border.
"You know," she told me, "my family was all migrant workers. Picking toma-
toes. My mom told my dad one day that she just couldn't stand the sight of
another tomato, and they went to Ohio and opened up a *panaderia* (Mexican
bread store). That's where I worked as a kid."

Cynthia described herself as ambitious. She spoke of her participation in the
probusiness group LULAC (League of Unified Latin American Citizens) and
in El Paso political circles. She told me of her aspirations to move into
management from our first interview. "I'm a good manager and I'm the best
writer they've got around here. I write all of the reports even for the other guys.
I'm working on something for Steve right now." Steve agreed, "Cynthia writes
well. She's talented, but she's always in some controversy. I can't tell you how
much time we spend trying to figure out the 'Cynthia problem.' "

This was evident after just a few days at MOTW. During one of the weekly managers' meetings, soon after Rosalía's promotion, Cynthia's name came up when Roger stated, in a commanding tone, "Somebody has got to talk with Cynthia."

The next morning, Cynthia came into my office and closed the door. "Do you know what they said to me? Those fuckers. . . . My bows. They say I can't wear my hair bows." She took a sparkling purple bow from her hair and showed it to me. "My mom gave these to me for my birthday. . . . And it's Rosalía telling me this. . . . First it was my hair, 'tone it down.' Steve calls me in his office and says he wants me to look more like an American engineer. He said I had gone too Mexican. Who the hell does he think he's talking to?"

Over a series of conversations, Steve explained to me that Cynthia simply did not look professional, given her position. "I don't know if she's here to discover her roots or what. I don't care. I just want my engineers to act like engineers. I can't have my boss coming down here and bumping into glitz and bows when he wants to talk about the fuel system. . . . This might sound bad, but that's just how it is in this world. If she wants to be a manager, she had better tone down the Mexican stuff."

Cynthia was not bending to the pressure. One day she came in wearing a violet blue dress suit with rhinestone buttons and a bow to match. "I dare them to say anything," she told me in the hallway. When I asked Cynthia if she was tempted to yield in an effort to mitigate tensions, she expressed anger and said, "Look, I'm not a white girl like you. And I'm not ashamed of who I am. I show it. I'm a woman, I show it. I'm *mexicana*, I show it. Outside, I wear blue jeans but here I'm professional and that's what I show. If they don't like it, fuck 'em."

Meanwhile, she had received written memos not detailing the nature of her clothing but stating in vague terms that she was not fulfilling her professional duties. One of the evaluations gave her low marks on professional conduct, and Cynthia understood this to be in preparation for her legal dismissal. Rosalía explained the conflict in these terms: "Here you have to be one thing or the other. You are either Mexican or American. There is no place for a Mexican American here."

Paradoxically, while hours of staff time were dedicated to the controversy over Cynthia's appearance, her performance as a quality engineer, measured in terms of product defects and reliability, won the highest award in the company, worldwide. The corporation flew her and her parents to Miami so that she could attend the award ceremony. However, this award did not prevent her forced resignation a short while later.

In the days just preceding her resignation, Steve made an announcement that he had promoted a Mexican man into the engineering manager job that Cynthia had coveted. "I don't think the *maquilas* are ready for a Cynthia yet," he told me in explanation of this decision. "This guy acts like an engineer. I know where he's coming from." By this I understood that he was impressed with a strictly masculine presentation, the wearing of ties and an unambivalent understanding of the difference between the Mexican and the U.S. domains in MOTW.

I asked Rosalía to explain why Cynthia's self-presentation was such a problem and worth so much attention when her work was clearly helping the company. She justified the concern over Cynthia's appearance by discussing how the international border operates. "Well, it might seem irrelevant, but how people look and act is really important for keeping everything running. It's like the border, you have to show your papers. It doesn't matter who you are. If you don't act right, then they won't let you in. They have their rules. So do we. Cynthia doesn't want to accept them. She doesn't seem professional and it bothers everyone. She really doesn't know who she is here. That's her biggest problem."

What Cynthia presented was an incongruous image at MOTW. She asserted herself as a "Mexican American" woman, a particular version of *mexicana*, in a context where a clear-cut division was the norm. By refusing to acknowledge the border as a metaphor for division, she threatened a social order built around an international segregation within the division of labor. And she directly challenged the predominant discourse of the *mexicana* as unprofessional. This was an effort at resignification not simply of her individual self, but also of the symbolic interpretation of the *mexicana* in general. Unlike Rosalía, she was not adjusting her own presentation to fit the dominant symbolic framework of space and subjects. Instead, she tackled the representation and perceived place of the *mexicana* and met forceful opposition. In some ways, she, like Anzaldúa, imagined a possible unification of the Mexican with the American side. She attempted to negotiate a social ambiguity, inserting the Mexican with the American, and the feminine with authority, in a context where such discursive and material alignments were cast as impossibilities.

However, Cynthia's expressions of social unity across a rejoined geography did not challenge the class divides inherent in the division of labor that separate professional *mexicanas* from day-laboring *mexicanas* across a nationalized border. "These girls," she explained in reference to the female operators under her charge, "are lucky to have this job and they don't even know it. Mexican culture really doesn't teach them how to respect their jobs. My family is Mexican but when it comes to work, we've got the American work ethic." Cynthia may have threatened a social order crafted around the exclusion of a particular manifestation of *mexicanas* in American administration, but she expressed steadfast dedication to the nationalized and sexualized bordering of class divisions that preserved the capitalist integrity of the operation. For example, when she heard that I had attended a labor meeting in Ciudad Juárez, she called me at home. "Are you one of those bleeding heart labor people?" she asked. When I replied that I didn't know what she meant, she informed me that she could not take any risks and would not talk to me again. I then received a call from Steve, who asked if I was a "labor spy."

Despite her problems at MOTW, Cynthia did not leave in a weak position. She sought support and advice from an extensive legal community both in El Paso and in Ciudad Juárez. Fearing a lawsuit, Steve authorized a bonus and provided strong recommendations to another company, where she began working. Shortly afterwards, she was named in a widely circulated industry trade magazine as one of the top women employees and as a highly regarded engineer in the *maquiladora* industry. She attributed much of her success to her experience as a woman knowledgeable of both the American and the Mexican cultures located in the border environment.

As she said to me before her resignation, "You know I think these white guys are in for a big surprise. . . . There's a lot of us, and we know what we're doing. This is one of the few places where a *mexicana* can really do something in industry and be recognized. We know both sides down here and that scares them."

FEMINIST POLITICS AND THE *MAQUILADORA MESTIZA*

Speaking of the new *mestiza* and *mestizaje* almost ten years after the publication of *Borderlands/La Frontera*, Anzaldúa says, "The new *mestiza* is sensitive to and aware of her ethnic and cultural *mestizaje*. She is politically aware of what goes on in these different communities and worlds and therefore brings a different perspective to what is going on. She is no longer just a Chicana. That is not all that she is. She is the feminist in the academy, the dyke in the queer community, and the person working in straight America" (Anzaldúa and Hernández 1995-96, 9). And at MOTW, she is the *mexicana* working in American administration. To borrow (and thereby distort Anzaldúa's image) she is the *maquiladora mexicana* resignified to be the new *maquiladora mestiza*.

Rosalía and Cynthia raise the following question for Butler's version of resignification as it applies to this new *mestizaje*. Can we think of resignification as a partial subversion or, more to the point, even as a radical rearticulation with status quo conditions and subjections? The *maquiladora mestiza* is resignified to the extent that she was never predicted to emerge and is still a surprise when she does. But her resignification as a new border subject is simultaneous with the reinforcement of the corporate script for crafting employee identities around the markers of sex, nationality, and culture into the spaces and positions of the corporate workplace. While each woman expresses a cultural hybridity that resonates with Anzaldúa's vision for *mestizaje*, each actively works toward maintaining the border of a class division on which the *maquiladora* industry thrives. As Rosalía Americanizes and Cynthia makes a name for herself throughout the industry, the majority of *mexicanas* in the *maquiladoras* continue to work for poverty wages. Many live in economically strained conditions, and fewer than a fraction will ever rise in the corporate ranks. Their success begs the question, is a political articulation possible between Anzaldúa's version of a radical *mestiza* and the probusiness, *maquiladora mestiza* in a feminist border politics?

Rosalía and Cynthia raise this question as they disrupt some codes for interpreting their subject positions while holding steadfast to others. Their new *mestizaje* is evident in their hybridity and in their proclamation of themselves as women who know both sides of the border and the subjects who inhabit those places. Yet excluded from their *mestizaje* is a mixing with non-professional *mexicanas*, and even with each other in a social sense, except that each of them supports *maquiladora* trade associations and is active in politically conservative business groups. Moreover, each brings diversity to the firm and provides corporate managers with evidence of the firm's commitment to moving women and minorities through the ranks. In seeking how they might articulate with Anzaldúa's vision of a new *mestiza*, it is useful to address how these women appear different from each other and to what extent their negotiations of difference beget joint effects.

Rosalía shows that *mexicanas* can "do American"—she changes her language, her dress, her social circles, her national residency, and her children's schools. She crosses the border outside the firm and reflects the one she crossed within it. In so doing, she breaks down the concept of the *mexicana* who is tradition-bound, who is culturally destined for a nonprofessional future and who is eternally socially subordinate.[10] Yet to demonstrate this change, she disavows her status as a *mexicana* in the firm. She subverts the expectations for who that *mexicana* is by demonstrating her distance from that category. In other words, the continuity of the category, *mexicana*, allows Rosalía, through her disavowal of it, to rise above the possibilities it allows. She therefore desires that the *mexicana* exist as a viable subject, for without it she could not stand in its contrast (cf. Butler 1997), and she will not allow Cynthia, or anyone else, to subvert the meaning of this subject which is so valuable for her and for the firm. Meanwhile, as Rosalía proves that "once a *mexicana*, not always a traditional *mexicana*," the majority of those who bring the *mexicana* subject to life in the *maquiladora* industry continue to work for low wages and enjoy few prospects of professional advancement as they create those many products coveted in the U.S. market.

Cynthia, on the other hand, refuses to "do American" according to the MOTW corporate narrative. She is not, like Rosalía, a recent immigrant to U.S. territory, but expresses her identity as an "American" with a long Mexican heritage who is entitled to residency there. She consequently struggles in MOTW because she challenges the corporate version of *mexicana* as a homogenous subject who represents the unprofessional employee. She attempts to "smuggle" her type of *mexicana* into the American domain, where the *mexicana* is expressly barred, and she is soon forced to evacuate this place. But her story is hardly a tragedy. After experiencing blatant sexual and racial harassment at MOTW, she finds employment in another firm and continues to occupy a prominent place—as a *mexicana*—in the Mexican *maquiladora* industry.

Even though Rosalía and Cynthia express contempt for each other at some level, they both effectively pull the image of the *mexicana* from the shadows of *maquiladora* offices and production floors and place her front and center with respect to the positions of power in those firms. They are new *mestizas*, therefore, in the sense detailed by Anzaldúa, insofar as they have reinvented themselves as women of power whose base emanates from their cultural heritage and knowledge of the worlds defined by the border and borderlands. Yet clearly they are not the sort of new *mestizas* Anzaldúa had in mind, for the joint effects of their self-inventions, or resignifications, also work to exclude other *mexicanas* from the material and social benefits accruing to *maquiladora* managers.

Rosalía and Cynthia illustrate what is at stake in the formation of border subjects around a geography of difference and what, therefore, must be challenged by a feminist politics located in the borderlands. In their efforts we see how a geography of difference integrates class into the formation of border subjects and the political divide, and we see how the border as a symbol of division resonates throughout daily activities. A feminist politics that seeks to join forces across this geography will have to address how perceptions of difference are incorporated in the daily activities that bring the borderlands, border activities, and border residents, such as the *maquiladora mestiza*, to life.

NOTES

1. *Maquiladoras* are export-processing facilities located in Mexico.

2. I use the term American in reference to its common deployment in Ciudad Juárez and El Paso and in the *maquiladoras* to refer to U.S. citizens, although the term is misleading.

3. Sporadic and small-scale efforts are made to form binational links and organizations, but beyond corporate organizations and some ecumenical activities, such efforts continue to be piecemeal, underfunded, and stretched for human resources.

4. For a fuller discussion of the cultural context of the multinational firm see Schoenberger (1997) and Martin (1994).

5. I use pseudonyms for all references to individuals and corporations, as agreed with my informants.

6. I offer this account as my interpretation of events, conversations, and responses to questions. Like many ethnographers, I believe that a representation of myself does not have to be front and center for my role as an interpreter to be understood (see Strathern 1991; Geertz 1988).

7. This operation involved the positioning of U.S. Border Patrol agents every 200 yards of a twenty mile stretch of the border in the Ciudad Juárez-El Paso area to create a physical blockade that would deter illegal immigration. This operation is still in effect.

8. At the time I conducted this study, the majority of MOTW workers were operators who, like those throughout the *maquiladoras*, earned the minimum wage which was just less than U.S. $1.00 per hour. After a series of peso devaluations since 1994, the minimum wage is now worth about U.S. $0.50 per hour. Jobs above operator earn slightly more. The supervisor is the lowest ranking salaried employee. U.S. supervisors earned salaries ranging in the mid-twenties per year, while the Mexican supervisors earned from $8,000-$13,000 per year. Engineers earned above that amount, again with the discrepancy between U.S. and Mexican employees. The U.S. managers earn considerably more at a range between $40,000 and $130,000 per year.

9. Throughout the *maquilas*, attention to women's dress styles is continually artic-ulated as an American or Mexican affect, and often in reference to a cultural represen-tation rather than to a national divide. The difference is generally discussed as one of length; fit, in terms of degree of snugness; color (bright or subdued); shoe style; make-up applications and hairstyle. However, there is a continual negotiation of this difference that cannot be explored within the confines of the essay (cf. Garber 1992; Bourdieu 1984).

10. For discussions of how this discourse of women in Third World regions is representative of the tradition-bound and socially subordinate subject, see Mohanty (1991). For evidence of how this discourse is put into practice in political and economic analyses of Third World regions, including Mexico, see Frobel (1979).

REFERENCES

Anaya, Rodolfo and Francisco Lomelí, eds. 1989. *Aztlán: Essays on the Chicano Home-land*. Albuquerque: University of New Mexico Press.

Anzaldúa, Gloria. 1987. *Borderlands/La Frontera: The New Mestiza*. San Francisco: Spinsters/Aunt Lute Press.

Anzaldúa Gloria and E. Hernández. 1995-96. Re-Thinking Margins and Borders: An Interview. *Discourse*, 18 (1-2): 7-15.

Bourdieu, Pierre. 1984. *Distinctions: A Social Critique of the Judgement of Taste*. New York: Routledge.

Butler, Judith. 1993. *Bodies That Matter: On the Discursive Limits of "Sex"*. New York: Routledge.

———. 1997. *The Psychic Life of Power: Theories on Subjection*. Stanford: Stanford University Press.

Dunn, Tim. 1996. *The Militarization of the U.S.-Mexico Border*. Austin: The University of Texas Press.

Fernandez-Kelly, María P. 1983. *For We Are Sold, I and My People: Women and Industry in Mexico's Frontier*. New York: State University of New York Press.

Fox, Claire F. 1995-96. The Fence and the River: Representations of the US-Mexico Border in Art and Video. *Discourse*, 18(1-2): 54-83.

Frobel, Frobel. 1979. *The New International Division of Labor*. New York: Cambridge University Press.

Garber, Marjorie. 1992. *Vested Interests: Cross-Dressing and Cultural Anxiety*. New York: Routledge.

Geertz, Clifford. 1988. *Works and Lives: The Anthropologist as Author*. Stanford: Stanford University Press.

Harvey, David. 1996. *Justice, Nature and the Geography of Difference*. Oxford: Basil Blackwell.

Katz, Cindi and Neil Smith. 1993. Grounding Metaphor: Towards a Spatialized Politics. In *Place and the Politics of Identity*, ed. M. Keith and S. Pile. London: Routledge.

Kern Suzan and Tim Dunn. 1995. Mexico's Economic Crisis Spawns Wildcat Strike in a *Maquiladora* Plant. *Labor Notes* 194: 16.

Martin, Emily. 1994. *Flexible Bodies: Tracking Immunity in Amerian Culture from the Day of Polio to the Age of AIDS*. Boston: Beacon Press.

Mohanty, Chandra T. 1991. Under Western Eyes: Feminist Scholarship and Colonial Discourses. In *Third World Women and the politics of feminism*, ed. Chandra T. Mohanty, Ann Russo, and Lourdes Torres. Bloomington: Indiana University Press.

Ong, Aihwa. 1987. *Spirits of Resistance and Capitalist Discipline: Factory Women in Malaysia*. Albany: State University of New York Press.

Salzinger, Leslie. 1997. From High Heels to Swathed Bodies: Gendered Meanings Under Production in Mexico Export-Processing Industry. *Feminist Studies* 23(3): 549-574.

Schoenberger, Erica. 1997. *The Cultural Crisis of the Firm*. Oxford: Basil Blackwell.

Strathern, Marilyn. 1991. *Partial Connections*. Savage: Rowman & Littlefield.

Tabuenca Córdoba, María Socorro. 1995-96. Viewing the Border: Perspectives from the 'Open Wound.' *Discourse*, 18(1-2): 146-195.

Wright, Melissa W. 1997. Crossing the Factory Frontier: Gender, Place and Power in a Mexican *Maquiladora*. *Antipode* 29(3): 278-296.

———. 1996. Third World Women and the Geography of Skill. Ph.D. diss. The Johns Hopkins University.

Young, Iris. 1990. *Justice and the Politics of Difference*. Princeton: Princeton University Press.

13

Burnt Offerings to Rationality: A Feminist Reading of the Construction of Indigenous Peoples in Enrique Dussel's Theory of Modernity

LYNDA LANGE

The philosopher Enrique Dussel offers a critical analysis of European construction of indigenous peoples which he calls "transmodern." His theory is especially relevant to feminist and other concerns about the potential disabling effects of postmodern approaches for political action and the development of theory. Dussel divides modernity into two concurrent paradigms. Reflection on them suggests that modernism and postmodernism should not be too strongly distinguished. In conclusion, his approach is compared with that of Mohanty.

In his book *The Invention of the Americas*, the philosopher Enrique Dussel (1995) makes an important and interesting contribution to the critical analysis of European modernity and colonization that includes an approach to the critique of modern philosophy. From his location in South America, he is responding particularly to the history of the Spanish conquest of South and Central America, a conquest Tsvetan Todorov terms the worst genocide the world has ever seen (Todorov 1984, 5). Dussel aligns his postcolonial theory with feminism, noting the intersection of colonization and patriarchy that makes women a special part of the spoils of conquest for European men, although he does not elaborate on questions concerning women or refer to feminist texts. However, reading Dussel from the perspective of a democratic feminist critic, there are many similarities to be noted between his approach to postcolonial criticism and that of some feminist criticism, similarities that encourage us to make use of his work for the task of "postcolonial feminism."

His position with regard to the ongoing confrontation between "modernism" and "postmodernism" is of interest to feminist critics who are convinced of the cultural and gender bias in many modernist concepts and values but also concerned about the negative implications for political action that seem to flow from certain types of postmodernism. More would be in moral agreement with efforts to respect non-European cultures and avoid a Eurocentric approach to the history of modernity, than would agree to such postmodern views as that truth and value cannot be communicated across cultures, or across such differences in life forms as gender or sexual orientation. There are broad similarities between the variety of politicized critiques of "philosophy" extant right now, such as feminist critique, anti-racist critique, queer critique, and post/colonial critique. They all seek to expose the biases of philosophical concepts, and especially to show how philosophical concepts presented as universal may be implicitly particular to the degree that they are shaped by the socioeconomic and cultural locations of their inventors. They all seek to show, to use Nancy Tuana's (1992) useful critical concept, who is "located in the text," that is, who is taking to whom, about whom.

However, I believe that there are noteworthy differences among these critiques, which make their implications for both philosophy and political practice different as well. I am not referring to differences between feminist, anti-racist, and other approaches, which are also important, but to philosophical and epistemological differences that may be found in any of these approaches. Dussel's work makes an interesting case study for illustrating this point. In addition, because Dussel's work is much less well known in North America than the work of Europeans in the same areas, I am also concerned simply to present his ideas and to discuss how we can best understand what he is doing and what it may imply for us.

Dussel shares the radical, politically positive edge of postmodernism, which is to affirm the dignity and validity of "the other." In fact, he used to call himself a postmodernist. However, he now presents a theory of modernity (which he terms "transmodern"), which affirms "that rationality can establish a dialogue with the reason of the Other, as an alterative reason" (Dussel 1995, 132). At the same time, it seems to me that he deepens our appreciation of the difficulty of overcoming a Eurocentric perspective in a manner that is as relevant to "white European feminism" as it is to masculinist Eurocentrism. He could be thought of as saying, "Yes, it is in principle possible to overcome Eurocentrism by rational and imaginative means, but it is harder than you may think."

According to Dussel, not only proponents or defenders of the ethos of European modernity but also many of its postmodern or postcolonial critics remain Eurocentric insofar as they presuppose, whether positively or negatively, that there is an inner dynamic of European modernity that has caused it to have superior power or effectiveness over non-European peoples. So, for example, a classical affirmation of European superiority considered as beneficial is that of Max Weber, that only on "Western soil" have there been cultural phenomena that have produced signs of "evolutionary advance and universal validity" (*Sociologie, Westgeschichtliche Analyzen, Politik,* quoted in Dussel 1995, 10). This may be contrasted with a postcolonial view that also presupposes a purely inner dynamic of European modernity; for example, that of the African humanist Aimé Césaire, that "Europe is indefensible," and that at the end of all the mere "boastfulness," as he terms it, colonization is a poison "instilled into the veins of Europe and, slowly but surely, the continent proceeds toward *savagery* (1972, 13). Although writing from Africa, Césaire had in mind, among other things, the holocaust of the midtwentieth century which occurred within Europe's own boundaries. According to Dussel, however, the power of modernity (which he does not mean to deny) is the *result*, and not the *cause*, of the centrality of Europe in a world or global system. The success of violent conquest and colonization of the Americas and Africa gave western Europe a formidable advantage over the non-Christian East. European modernity therefore originates, and is constituted by, a dialectical relationship with nonEurope. Although this view of the constitution of European modernity has been propounded in other disciplines, Dussel suggests it can be applied specifically to the nature of modern European philosophy, as such.

Dussel holds the view (contrary to many postmoderns) that it is not modern philosophical or scientific rationality that has been an instrument of terror, but a distinctively modern Eurocentric irrational myth that has resulted in the terror of what he calls "sacrificial violence." Dussel therefore distinguishes two concurrent paradigms of modernity. One is the rational, emancipatory conceptual content of modernity. The other is the negative and irrational myth, in which Dussel traces the justification of colonial violence to a "developmental fallacy." This fallacy rests on the view that Europe is the endpoint of a universal developmental process, toward which all other peoples must and will go. It is especially relevant for philosophers (feminist and otherwise) that he finds this "irrational myth" exemplified by philosophy itself. It should not be viewed, therefore, as "cultural myth," with reference to which modern philosophy has stood as a critic on the basis of reason. Dussel's positioning of the "irrational myth of modernity" is contrary to modern philosophy's positioning of itself as distinct from and opposed to "myth." This is intriguing as a criticism from one who now distances himself from postmodernism.

Dussel maintains that the developmental fallacy is still present in much philosophy. However, in my view, even the bare bones of his theory, as presented so far, imply an intention to recuperate philosophic reason. In this light, postcolonial critique cannot be leveled in a general way at modern philosophy as such; it can be aimed only at particular texts. Dussel's work suggests that it is not the case that philosophy *cannot* stand as a critic of culture on the basis of reason, but that for the most part it *does not*. He therefore avoids what I call a "pan-critical" effect of postmodernism which disables the very notion of philosophy. Avoiding this makes it possible to consider postcolonial, feminist, and other politicized critiques of "philosophy" to be themselves "philosophy" (or so I maintain).

How can a postcolonial critique of texts be effected? First, it may be shown that Europeans saw non-Europeans in terms of their own categories, in itself hardly a surprise. However, without a presumption of European supremacy, a possible result of this observation is the identification of European categories of thought as historically particular, by means of comparisons with other cultural paradigms with noncorresponding categories. If we take this line of thought seriously, it implies that from different perspectives, the world is quite literally *perceived* and not just *interpreted*, as cut up in different ways.[2] This view can amount to a claim that a European category posited as "universal" is actually "particular" to European intellectual culture. Dussel argues that Europeans saw non-Europeans exclusively in terms of their own categories of thought, especially in the early stages of contact in the sixteenth century. The Spanish perception of the indigenous peoples of the Americas was entirely self-referential: they literally did not perceive the "other" as "other," but rather as deficient examples of "the same." According to Dussel, the Spanish could not, therefore, be said to have "discovered" them. Instead, they "invented" them, first as Asians, and then as undeveloped inferior peoples who would benefit from the arrival of the Europeans. In the first century of encounter, Spanish selfreferentiality was so strong that even the dazzling evidence of urban development among the Aztecs and Incans that was *superior* to what the Spanish would have known in Europe failed to suggest to them that these peoples might be best thought of as simply different from them, rather than inferior to them. Then again, while the label "Indians" for the peoples of the Americas can be explained as an initial mistake, what depth of self-referentiality explains why the name stuck for five hundred years?

South and Central America were therefore "invented" as undeveloped, regardless of the actual levels of development of different peoples, which the evidence indicates varied greatly. This invention was then given a brutal epistemological guarantee, as major cities were reduced to rubble, the people forced into slave labor, and the population decimated to a small fraction of its previous size.[3]

Another strategy for a postcolonial critique is to show the action in texts of relations of domination and subordination. Nancy Tuana's concept of "location in the text," developed for feminist criticism, may be used to analyze to whom a text is speaking and about whom it speaks. Those spoken about but not directly addressed are subordinated in the text to those for whom the text is intended. Thus theory about indigenous peoples of the Americas and Africa was developed by Europeans for other Europeans, and never in discursive communication with indigenous peoples themselves. Dussel may also be thought of as identifying what is called in cultural studies "the gaze," although he does not use that term himself. "The gaze" exemplifies the fundamental asymmetry between those who look, stare boldly, and identify, and those who are stared at and labeled. It's a bit like putting something on a board with a pin—there is no question of interaction between subjectivities. In the case of people, this asymmetry, which may be identified in both texts and social practices, is a type of profound inequality very familiar to feminist critics. Nothing the indigenous peoples could do counted as evidence of a high stage of development or political sophistication or true morality, because in European eyes they lacked these things by definition.

There are other strategies that may illuminate a critical postcolonial understanding in one way or another. Dussel employs those (such as the ones described above) that lend themselves to political understanding and political action. A more ready affinity with political action is a feature of his work that sets him apart from some more clearly postmodern approaches.

A subtlety of Dussel's approach is that he does not deny that there were (and are) different levels of development, which may be considered as different levels of value; for example, in the technology of production, or in the complexity or sophistication of social governance. He avoids the extreme of the postmodern impulse that will brook no comparison but that of "difference." Nevertheless, he denies that the European model of development is the only one. A particular limitation of the developmental fallacy is that it presupposes that humans are inferior at less complex stages of development, and even that the peoples of less developed cultures are *to blame* for their condition. Dussel quotes Kant from 1784: "Enlightenment is the exit of humanity . . . from a state of culpable immaturity. . . . Laziness and cowardliness are the causes which bind the great part of humanity in the frivolous state of immaturity" ("Answering the Question: What is Enlightenment?," quoted in Dussel 1995, 19-20). Although he is a critic of Enlightenment thinking, Dussel is a humanist in his affirmation that human development (by which I think he means simply whatever it is that makes us different from other beings) was pretty much fully achieved in its present form in neolithic cultures. In my own view, while cultures may vary in type and complexity, it is a fallacy of composition to presume that individuals in a less complex culture, are less fully human or less capable of development, than *individuals* in more complex cultures.

Regarding the action in texts of relations of domination and subordination, Dussel points particularly to the inadequacy of "communicative ethics," (mentioning Habermas and Apel), which does not take into account the profound asymmetry in the *effectiveness* of speech and argument created by domination. This critique is similar to one that has been raised from a feminist perspective by Alison Jaggar regarding the speech of women. Dussel usefully identifies what are termed the "conditions of entry" into a discursive community, calling attention to the very harsh and thorough exclusion of indigenous peoples from dominant European discursive communities, an exclusion that was not significantly breached until after the mid-twentieth century. The significance of conditions of entry in Dussel's thought will be revisited on closer examination of the developmental fallacy, in which it is the "conditions of entry" to discursive community that can be seen as key points of inconsistency with the imagined ideals of European discursive communities. Dussel maintains a modernist (or at least "nonpostmodernist") distinction between rationally held belief (which can be mistaken) and irrational myth. However, part of the power of his work for me is the way he shows that the point at which "rational belief" slips over into "irrational myth" can be difficult to discern.

Arguing a Myth

To look more closely at the claim of irrationality regarding European beliefs about development, the argumentative stages of the myth of modernity need to be examined. The case of Juan Ginés de Sepulveda, a Spanish philosopher and theologian of the sixteenth century, illustrates how the irrationality might be spelled out in a particular thinker's ideas.

According to Dussel, in its secondary and mythic content, modernity justifies an irrational praxis of violence, despite its ideal of discursive community in which coercion is unacceptable. First and foremost, Europe understands itself as more developed, its civilization superior to others. It lacks awareness of its own historical specificity. This self-image can be accounted for by Europe's practical centrality in a world system *in conjunction with* its own highly developed notions of "universality," "impartiality" and "objectivity."

In light of that fundamental first stage, a second argumentative step is that a culture's abandonment of its "barbarous" differences spells "progress, development, well-being, and emancipation for that culture" (Dussel 1995, 66). Thus, one may defend Europe's domination over other cultures as, in Dussel's words, "a necessary pedagogic violence," which may take the form of a "just war." The other culture's anguish is justified as the necessary price of civilization and modernization, as well as expiation for its culpable immaturity. Since barbarians always resist this civilizing process, modern praxis is compelled, quite rightly, to exercise violence as a last resort in order to overcome obstacles to modernization. However, the barbarian is at fault for opposing the civilizing process. Civilizing heroes may then justify the treatment of their victims as "a sacrifice," "a quasi-ritual act" for the salvation of the victims. Dussel terms them "holocausts of a salvific sacrifice." He is using the term "holocaust" in its ancient general meaning of "a sacrificial offering the whole of which is consumed by fire; hence, a complete or thorough sacrifice or destruction" (Webster's New International Dictionary). Finally, the suffering and sacrifice of backward and immature peoples is regarded as the inevitable cost of modernization. As Dussel puts it, "the myth of modernity declares the Other the

culpable cause of its own victimization and absolves the modern subject of any
guilt for the victimizing act" (Dussel 1995, 64).

Considering philosophy, in the case of Hegel, for example, Dussel's main
point is not, as might be expected, that Hegel's philosophy helped to inspire
and justify colonialism. (This is certainly part of what he seeks to show, and is
in itself hard to take issue with.) Dussel's more original argument, however, is
that Hegel's philosophy should be understood as a *result* of Europe's successful
colonization of non-European peoples, and not as a basic ideological source of
certain attitudes. The conquest of Mexico was the beginning of a process that
made a philosopher like Hegel possible, because Europe's de facto domination
made possible a seemingly reasonable and common-sense belief that Europe
was the center of the world, and the point of reference for everything else.
Consider the following quotations from Hegel:

> Universal history goes from East to West. Europe is absolutely
> the *end of universal history*.

> Regarding America, especially Mexico or Peru, and its degree
> of civilization, our information indicates that its culture expires
> the moment the Spirit draws near. . . . The inferiority of these
> individuals in every respect is entirely evident.

> Africa . . . does not properly have a history. For this reason, we
> abandon Africa, we will mention it no more. (in Dussel 1995,
> 20-22)

What if an intellectual from West Africa, or the middle of South America,
wrote the same things with reference to those cultures, and their relation to
other cultures and locations? Far from attracting widespread study of a difficult
text, it would be taken as the ravings of a lunatic, would it not? Whatever we
may think of Dussel's work, should we not, indeed, be asking: What are the
conditions that enable someone to think this way and be taken seriously?

Apart from philosophy, and apart from consideration of the especially
rapacious activity of the early Spanish occupation, there is ample evidence
that the majority of European missionaries and colonial administrators
throughout the Americas and Africa believed it necessary to destroy indigenous cultures, even at the cost of great suffering, before the people could be
"civilized," educated, and prepared to adopt a saving Christianity. Dussel
maintains that the modern belief that within the discursive community only
argumentation is appropriate was already undisputed in principle in fifteenth
century Spain. He emphasizes that the justification of violent recruitment into
"Europe" (as an ethos) must therefore be about *how one enters* the discursive
community, and not about how one behaves within it.

The Spanish *conquistadores* of the sixteenth century thought of themselves
as evangelists and liberators; or at least, this was a self-image that was culturally

available to them should they feel the need of self-justification. Given the most cursory knowledge of what they did to the indigenous peoples, this self-image is now, on the face of it, almost incomprehensible. Yet there is not only a plausible historical account of it, but in light of Dussel's analysis, there is even an account to be offered of links between this attitude and modern humanism and individualism, showing how some of their fundamental philosophical principles can be implicated in the irrational myth of modernity.

How can violent conquerors be evangelists and liberators? In the early eighth century, a movement began for the Christian Spanish "reconquest" of what is now Spain from the powerful Muslim Moors. This process took a full seven hundred years, several centuries longer than the period of modernity now under discussion! According to Dussel, over the centuries a Spanish judicial-military culture developed of *conquista* (conquest), with a highly positive identity for *conquistadores* (those who conquer). The reconquest was completed in 1492, and the *conquistadores* were liberators of the Spanish people and proponents of Christianity against powerful unbelievers. The Spaniards at once expelled all the Jews from Spain, along with the Moors, in the same year as the storied "discovery" of America. Nothing intervened in the transfer of *conquistador* values to their dealings with peoples initially perceived as "Eastern," like the Moors, and without question unrepentant unbelievers.

Dussel finds a "definitive and classical" expression of the irrational myth of modernity in the thought of the theologian Juan Ginés de Sepulveda. Dussel considers him a modern humanist, because he simultaneously expresses the irrational myth of modernity and the rational and positive content of modernity as Dussel sees it. Sepulveda engaged in a famous controversy with Bartolomé de las Casas. Although las Casas embraced the value of Christian evangelization of the indigenous peoples in America, he was nevertheless an advocate for them against the forces of violent conquest and exploitation. In 1550 Sepulveda published a defense of "the just cause of war against the Indians."[4]

Sepulveda's approach is a mixture of Aristotelianism, humanism, and even modern liberal individualism (a not uncommon mix in early and late modern philosophy). According to the historian Anthony Pagden (1987), there were other voices in this controversy besides Sepulveda and las Casas. Important theologians rejected Aristotle's concept of "natural slavery," on which Sepulveda relies. However, Dussel's focus on Sepulveda's thought is sadly justified, because it was Sepulveda's point of view that carried the day. Moreover, it is sobering to note that Sepulveda was the most "modern and enlightened" theologian in the debate, not least because of his use of ancient philosophy. His colleagues criticized him for his more historical and philosophical approach, and it was the more traditional theologians who argued for the inherent rights of the Indians of the Americas in virtue of their humanity.

Sepulveda's appropriation of Aristotle enables him to argue that the Indians are "natural servants," and that therefore it is good and right for them to be governed by those who are rational, more perfectly developed as human beings, and better. The potential affinity between the resistance of women and the resistance of other oppressed groups may be seen in Sepulveda's smooth Aristotelian amalgamation of a great range of forms of domination in the single figure of the elite European male.

> This war and conquest are just first of all because these barbaric, uneducated, and inhuman [Indians] are by nature servants. Naturally, they refuse the governance which more prudent, powerful, and perfect human beings offer and which would result in their great benefit. By natural right and for the good of all, the material ought to obey the form, the body the soul, the appetite the reason, the brutes the human being, the woman her husband, the imperfect the perfect, and the worse the better. (Dussel 1995, 63)

While this may not sound very humanistic, much less liberal, in the late twentieth century, central values of modern liberal moral and political philosophy, for example, that all individuals are of equal moral worth and equally entitled to autonomy in virtue of their intrinsic rationality have virtually always been held as hypothetical. These values have been limited by stipulation of the nature of rationality (that is, if an individual is of a certain type, then . . .) and virtually all modern philosophers have believed that some groups of humans failed to meet the criteria. These groups have encompassed women, people without property, non-Christians, and people of color. All these exclusions still continue to require contestation.

Sepulveda is quite clear that even considering the splendid cities of the Aztecs and Incas, their irrationality is evident in the fact that they are not entitled to own property and bequeath it to their biological heirs, and in their failure to resist the authority of the rulers who have so much power over them. In other words, according to Dussel, they have failed to embrace modernity's supreme characteristics—subjective liberty and autonomous resistance to the arbitrariness of rulers (Dussel 1995, 65). Critique of arbitrary forms of power is rightly identified as a central modern and humanist idea. In addition, even the most severe postmodern critics seem to take it for granted. This makes it all the more disconcerting to see what Sepulveda does with this same modern principle.

Sepulveda justifies violence as a means of bringing indigenous peoples into the modern European discursive community, even though rational autonomy and subjective liberty are core ideals of that community, and most especially the philosophical community. How? It is a modern ideal of equality that power over others, to be legitimate and morally acceptable, should be not just rationally justified by elite philosophers, but in principle justifiable to all members of a society in terms of some version of the "rational self-interest" of each. In modern secular philosophy, equality is premised on the innate rational ability of each person to determine his or her own self-interest, rather than have it imposed by someone else, no matter how well intentioned. Power should not be mere successful coercion, or custom and tradition that have not been evaluated and found acceptable. The consent of those who live under power is supposed to follow from power's justification in terms of their own good, as those who are rational consent to what is rational, by definition. However, as mentioned above, modernist ideals of equality have from the beginning been qualified by stipulations of what rationality is, and there have always been some types of people presumed to be exceptions to this "universal" ideal. What of them? The ideal of consent may continue to be given lip service. However, their consent or lack of consent ceases to be a primary consideration. It becomes rather *a goal*; how can "we" who are rational get "them" to see the light and consent?

Sepulveda has linked the rational justification of power to particular substantive claims about rationality that are recognizably modern and individualistic, wedding these claims to Aristotelian claims of inherent inequality of rational capacity. In his view, if those marked for appropriate power are not actually in positions of power, they are justified in using force to bring about arrangements that will enable them to govern, much as a parent fences in a child and supervises its activities "for its own the good."

From our perspective, the most striking error in this argument regarding the indigenous peoples is the Aristotelian concept that there can be such a thing as "natural human slaves or servants." In my view, however, Dussel's critical analysis works even if this Aristotelian element is eliminated, because the developmental fallacy does not actually require the notion of inherent inferiority. There was controversy in sixteenth century Spain over whether the Indians were inherently (and therefore permanently) inferior to Europeans, or whether they simply lacked the education and culture that would enable them to become as "civilized" as Europeans. If the view were taken, as it was by many, that the Indians belonged to such a benighted culture and belief system that they would never *willingly* embrace European values (even though in principle they were capable of doing so), then initial coercion in setting them along that path could still be justified. As a justification for coercive interference in indigenous cultures, the argument then becomes recognizable as the attitude, for example, of governments in the United States and Canada in subsequent centuries

In my view, it could even be said that these attitudes come too close to well-intentioned late twentieth century beliefs about the mission of liberal political ethos to be easily dismissed as a self-evidently wrong product of a colonial age.[6] Contemporary movements for self-government by indigenous peoples in North America have been criticized by their most sympathetic supporters for failing to be as crucially concerned about subjective liberty or individual rights as Western liberals are. So, the argument runs, should they be "allowed" self-government before they agree, for example, to European feminist standards of gender equality, or accept as primary principles of liberal individualist rights and freedoms? These standards may well cut across the cultural distinctiveness that is the basis of their desire for self-government. There is a fine line between support (moral or practical) for the aspirations of women or other oppressed groups in societies simultaneously struggling for self-determination, and the denial of self-determination to the group as a whole. The latter means keeping control, with the unacknowledged implication that the society in question is somehow less able to resolve its inner conflicts than "we Europeans" are to solve our own inner conflicts, and that the society actually benefits from our continuing control. There is no reason (except a very naive notion of "progress") to suppose that the colonizers and missionaries of modern Europe were, on the whole, less consciously well intentioned than we are now.

For Sepulveda, the nonarbitrariness of power is justified by the rational nature of those holding power. They are those with the capacity, or *power*, to promote the highest forms of human development, and therefore uplift those in whom this capacity or power is not present. There is, therefore, an equivocation on the term "power." It may refer to an inherent quality or a de facto social position. Because indigenous leaders clearly held power as a matter of fact, it cannot be power alone that justifies itself from a modernist point of view. As a result, it is the very concept of rationality embraced by Sepulveda that seems to justify the assumption of power by whatever means are necessary, on the part of those with the "rational" and "right" view of society.

In the relations to Europeans in which they were placed, indigenous peoples could thus only attempt to demonstrate their rationality, and therefore their right to subjective liberty and consent, by the contradictory means of voluntarily accepting the domination of the Spaniards! In the light of overarching principles, they are to be "forced to be free." Yet this notion is itself contradicted. Given the terms of their entry, they will actually be inducted into European forms of subordination (or as Dussel would put it, "internalized," "covered over"), analogously to working or propertyless people, women, some internal ethnic and religious minorities, and so on. To a very large extent, this has actually been the fate of the indigenous peoples of the Americas, a self-fulfilling prophecy of an irrational notion of development that has oppressively constrained them in a "no-win" situation in relation to those of European origin.

Dussel's analysis suggests that irrationality and self-contradiction can be recognized in the developmental fallacy of modernity even when viewed "from inside"; that is, by the standards of the rational, emancipatory paradigm of modernity. He does not want to step away from problems of justification in the spirit of postmodernism wherein one "discourse" may be set beside another but there can be no overarching standards or values by which to compare them. However, looking closely at how someone like Sepulveda justified violent domination of whole peoples—someone who held the modern value that only argumentation is appropriate in discursive community—raises some doubts in my mind about Dussel's neat separation of the rational, emancipatory, conceptual content of modernity and the negative and irrational myth of development. These two paradigms of modernity seem to be more entangled than Dussel wants to admit.

Dussel abjures the term "postmodern," presumably because it carries some unwanted epistemological and political associations. However, it seems that his analysis of modernity would be supported by a characteristically postmodern observation: that the belief that one possesses of "universal truth" of any sort may function as a powerful background support to any impulse to enforce a particular view of rationality, tending to silence those who do not embrace it. Although he does not want the term, his nuanced conclusions could still be called "postmodern," inasmuch as they provide an alternative to the features of modernism that have abetted colonization and modern patriarchy by crowning them with self-affirming philosophies. However, Dussel wants to retrieve the possibility of cross-cultural "truth," so as to be able to say that the destruction of colonization was wrong and to offer a positive vision for the future.

> This book serves only as a historico-philosophical introduction to an intercultural dialogue that will encompass diverse political, economic, theological, and epistemological standpoints. Such a dialogue endeavors to construct not an abstract universality, but an analogic and concrete world in which all cultures, philosophies, and theologies will make their contribution toward a future, pluralist humanity. (Dussel 1995, 132)

At this stage in my thinking, Dussel's analysis suggests to me that it is unproductive to counterpose "modernism" and "postmodernism" too strongly. Dussel seems to hold out the belief that the critical detachment of philosophy is at least possible, but his analysis also conveys an important cautionary observation. Authentic recognition of those "other" to our own culture is more difficult than we may imagine, and the obstacles to it may include what we hold as best among our values, rather than what we more readily recognize as our cultural potential for bias.

Included in what we hold as best may be our feminist convictions, even when they are applied (we may assume with good intentions) to groups of women much less privileged than Western middle-class women. For example, Dussel's analysis is consistent with, and further illuminates, the argument of

Chandra Mohanty (1991) regarding the treatment by feminists of "third world women." Mohanty argues that an initial positioning of "women" as a homogeneous category, which has been characteristic of both liberal and radical feminism in the West, leads to the creation of another homogeneous category: "third world women." The implicit self-presentation of Western feminist women as secular, rational, and knowledgeable about the "real" issues, by comparison with "third world women" thought to be more oppressed by religion, family, and tradition, betrays a modernist assumption of superior subjectivity. Mohanty points out that the discursive self-presentation of Western feminists as "liberated" and "having control over their own lives" would be problematic without the foil of "third world women," because it does not correspond to the reality of "first world" women. I would also note that the discursive strategy of positioning oneself as the more conscious component of a basically homogeneous oppressed group stands in the way of material and political analysis of the extent to which "first world" women benefit from imperialism themselves.

Mohanty also stresses that there is great diversity among women of the "third world," not just by culture, but also by class and other forms of social power. As a result, her critique includes the more privileged women of the "third world" who write about lower-class, poor, or rural women using the same Western-influenced discursive formations. She differentiates among women not by "identity" but by material circumstances, cultural context, and politics. Like Dussel, therefore, her analysis does not tend to posit "cultural differences" which we can hope to do no more than "appreciate," but rather suggests the possibility, at least, of general critical analysis that helps motivate political action.

Reading Dussel from the perspective of democratic feminism, the enormity of the holocaust of the indigenous peoples of the Americas once again reminds us that it is impossible to conceive of any meaningful polarity between "women" and "men" as such. Paying attention to differences of class, race, and colonization inevitably shows that, even from within their own relative oppression, in these supposedly postcolonial times, middle- and upper-class women of European origin still have vastly more privilege and power than many groups of women and men combined.

NOTES

This paper was originally prepared for "Globalization From Below," a conference of the Radical Philosophy Association, Nov. 14-17, 1996. Thanks are due to the anonymous referees for *Hypatia*, whose thoughtful remarks have made the paper better.

1. "In satisfying a frequently sadistic voluptuousness, Spaniards vented their purely masculine libido through the erotic subjugation of the Other as Indian women" (1995, 46).

2. Although this type of claim may be freighted with political significance, it will not be news to anyone who has studied W. V. O. Quine, the early Richard Rorty, or Paul Churchland in the fields of epistemology and philosophy of science in the last several decades.

3. The point regarding the epistemological guarantee was made in a graduate seminar of mine by Anandi Hattiangadi.

4. Ginés de Sepulveda's *De la justa causa de la guerra contra los indios* was published in Rome in 1550. Dussel's references are to the Spanish edition published in Mexico by Fondo de Cultura Económica, 1987.

5. In Canada in the twentieth century, the forcible removal of native children from their homes and communities to residential schools was driven by this logic. Taking them away from the "backward" influence of their own culture and compelling them to learn European language and culture is a good example of the operation of "necessary pedagogical violence" meant to induct them into "Europe."

6. Dussel himself saw this attitude in operation in the United States during the Gulf War (Dussel 1995, 64). It appeared that extreme violence—indeed, a self-proclaimed "storm" of violence—was the just exercise of those whose ostensible principle was subjective freedom.

REFERENCES

Césaire, Aimé. 1972. *Discourse on colonialism*. New York: Monthly Review Press.
Dussel, Enrique. 1995. *The invention of the Americas: Eclipse of "the other" and the myth of modernity*. Trans. Michael D. Barber. New York: Continuum.
Mohanty, Chandra Talpade. 1991. Under Western eyes: Feminist scholarship and colonial discourses. In *Third world women and the politics of feminism*, ed. Chandra Mohanty, Ann Russo, and Lourdes Torres. Bloomington: Indiana University Press.
Pagden, Anthony. 1987. Dispossessing the Barbarian: the language of Spanish Thomism and the debate over the property rights of the American Indians. In *The languages of political theory in Early-Modern Europe*, ed. Anthony Pagden. Cambridge: Cambridge University Press.
Todorov, Tsvetan. 1984. *The conquest of America: The question of the other*. New York: Harper and Row.
Tuana, Nancy. 1992. *Women and Western philosophy*. New York: Paragon House.

14

Gender, Development, and Post-Enlightenment Philosophies of Science

SANDRA HARDING

Recent "gender, environment, and sustainable development" accounts raise pointed questions about the complicity of Enlightenment philosophies of science with failures of Third World development policies and the current environmental crisis. The strengths of these analyses come from distinctive ways they link androcentric, economistic, and nature-blind aspects of development thinking to "the Enlightenment dream." In doing so they share perspectives with and provide resources for other influential schools of science studies.

A VIEW FROM THE EXTREMITIES OF THE ENLIGHTENMENT

Since World War II, Northern agencies have tried to modernize the so-called underdeveloped societies of the South so that their standards of living would catch up to those in the North. Yet there is now general agreement that standards of living have deteriorated during the development decades for the majority of those living in the underdeveloped societies—namely, those already most economically and politically vulnerable. Reevaluations of modern science and its philosophy figure in these assessments because development was conceptualized as transferring to the South sciences, technologies, and their philosophies that were presumed to be responsible for the industrial development of Europe and North America in the nineteenth and early twentieth centuries. Modern science is also at issue because of the terrifying escalation of environmental destruction in the South, as well as globally. Northern philosophies of nature seem to be implicated in that debacle.

The gender, environment, and sustainable development (GED) analyses enter these issues about the global development and environment crisis, as it is called, from the standpoint of the majority of women's lives in the South.

These accounts have their origins in the early "women in development" attempts to get governmental and nongovernmental development agencies to assess the impact of development policies on women and, usually, to "add women" as recipients of Third World development benefits (as they were then understood). In the three decades since, these feminist analyses have come to challenge most of the terms in which the original issues were posed, as have other critical development analyses with which this branch of feminist thinking has interacted.

In seeking to determine just how development policies should be changed, this literature also offers resources to philosophy that are otherwise undervalued or unavailable. It emerges from locations in global politics that enable the identification of otherwise hard-to-detect assumptions in the philosophies of science that have guided development thinking and that mark these philosophies as considerably less than universally valid. Moreover, these analyses are responding to urgent practical concerns to develop more reliable patterns of knowledge, and processes of legitimating it, for projects important to the world's economically and politically most vulnerable citizens in non-Western cultures—and, indeed, to many of the rest of us. Thus they must forfeit the luxurious "handmaid" role favored in mainstream philosophy of science and much of northern science studies: these Owls of Minerva must work a second shift in daylight. Such engaged philosophy sharpens the ability to detect how philosophic assumptions function in daily life. Finally, such concerns have led the GED movement to an expanded set of coalitions with other progressive science groups. These coalitions contribute innovative critical perspectives to the project of figuring out how to extract ourselves from the now problematic elements of Enlightenment scientific rationality.[1]

The Enlightenment philosophies defined the growth of scientific knowledge and the social progress this was supposed to bring in ways that devalued women, nature, and "backward cultures." The new philosophies of knowledge and power emerging from the gender, environment, and sustainable development discussions and the analyses on which they draw represent the return of the Enlightenment's others—the return of women, nature, and "backward cultures" from positions of more than instrumental value (at best) in modernity's thinking. Knowledge is power, as the familiar saying goes; and it is from the extremities of knowledge-power networks that we can best perceive the limitations of how knowledge and power create and nourish each other at the centers.

The project of this paper is, first, to show how the GED debates link criticisms of androcentric, economistic, and nature-blind aspects of development thinking to challenge the epistemology and philosophy of science of "the Enlightenment dream."[2] Sections 3 and 4 show how GED analyses can be supported with and, in turn, support arguments produced in post-Kuhnian and postcolonial science studies. Thus there are three influential post-World War

II schools of science studies, in addition to northern feminism, that arrive, from somewhat different starting points, at common assessments of Enlightenment philosophies of science. The concluding section summarizes how philosophic positions in this collection of analyses differ from those that were centered in the Enlightenment philosophy. Obviously, this essay can only map in very broad outlines a philosophic terrain that deserves more detailed attention (some of which, of course, it has already received in the literature indicated).

GED CRITICISMS OF ENLIGHTENMENT ASSUMPTIONS

The focus below will be on three issues.[3] These are how Enlightenment philosophies appear complicitous with the androcentrism, economism, and devaluing of nature in Third World development policies and practices.[4]

Is Development Gendered?

Four issues link the GED and other feminist analyses: women's work, gender as an analytic category, the androcentrism of science and technology thinking, and the standpoints of women of color. First, a main theme in early feminist criticisms of development was that women were being left out of development, as literacy and job-training programs were designed for men only, and men were given favored access to income-generating work. Often the only attention women officially received from development planners occurred under the heading of controlling women's reproduction. Moreover, as men were drawn into urban manufacturing, mining, or plantation agriculture, women were left to become a higher proportion of rural populations, with increased responsibility for the care of the young, old, and disabled and with fewer social and environmental resources to sustain life, environment, and community. Development policies bypassed women, the argument went.

Or were women actually left outside such modernization planning? A second round of analyses showed that these very processes of "leaving women out" actually provided necessary new resources for modernizing national economies. Achieving economic growth required increasing women's unpaid domestic labor, enticing or forcing women into the lowest-paid manufacturing and agricultural labor, and appropriating their inherited land rights. Their land rights tended to shift to men when only men were taught to farm in modern, scientific ways. At other times, these rights were directly appropriated, so the land could be used for export production by denying women access to community-owned common agricultural, forest, or grazing areas. Peasants as a class, both women and men, also suffered from some of these forms of appropriation (Mies 1986, Shiva 1989).

Thus the dedevelopment of women and peasants was a necessary condition for development in the South. "Progress for humanity" meant regress for women (and peasants), as Northern feminist historians had put a similar point.[5] Did the scientific and technological rationality being transferred from North to South include directions or, at least, permission for such banditry (as it could reasonably be called)? At any rate, the language of development, modernization, and scientific progress was being used to obscure the actual mechanism responsible for much development success. Structural adjustment policies intended to resolve the debt crisis of the 1980s followed the same pattern, further undermining the conditions of women in the developing countries. Here the International Monetary Fund and the World Bank ordered the indebted Southern governments to cut their social services in order to repay development loans to the Northern investing classes. Thereby women's unpaid labor was to be substituted for their formerly paid labor in state-provided educational, health, child care, and other social services so as to maintain the wealth of the most advantaged classes in the North (Sparr 1994).

Some of the feminists concerned with these labor issues also began to identify problems with the economism, the production model, of both neoclassical and neo-Marxian economists' attempts to address women's issues, and with the deteriorating environments that development policies created for women's subsistence and wage labor. These concerns lead to coalitions with relevant other groups.

A second important resource for the GED analyses was the more complex and comprehensive understanding of gender that they used. It was gender relations, not just women (as in the early "women in development" accounts), that were the object of GED concern. Gender was conceptualized not primarily as a property of individuals, but as an analytic category like race and class, through which one could understand the structure of societies and their symbolic systems. In order to understand women's situations and the meanings of the womanly or feminine in development policies and practices, one had to look also at men's situations and the meanings of the manly or masculine.

Gender, like class and race, is fundamentally a relationship. Thus GED accounts, like other feminist ones, argued that the problem with Enlightenment philosophies was not only that women had been excluded from articulating them and overtly maligned in them, but that Enlightenment standards of the human, the good, progress, social welfare, and economic growth, as well as of objectivity, rationality, good method, and what counted as important scientific problems, were all defined in terms of masculine and bourgeois interests and meanings. They were part of historically varying but nonetheless persistent androcentric and class discourses. Among its other benefits, understanding gender as structural and symbolic facilitated the integration of GED analyses with other groups' criticisms of structural and representational aspects of Enlightenment assumptions.[6]

This brings us to a third issue. Central themes in northern feminist science and technology accounts independently emerged or were transformed in the GED analyses. The GED discussion was created mainly in regional and international agencies rather than in the university and laboratory contexts in which northern feminist science and technology discussions were shaped.[7] The androcentric structures and meanings of modern scientific and technological worlds shaped also international, national, and local development agencies and their thinking. The obscuring and often misogynous dualisms identifed by northern feminists, postcolonial studies, and the environmental movement operated through development rhetoric to shape policies that systematically discriminated against the economically and politically most vulnerable populations (Barker 1998). And the questions, the problems, that development addressed were never ones defined by women or from the standpoint of women's lives. Development was gendered, as even one document from the United Nations Commission on Science and Technology for Development put the point by the mid-1990s (Kettel 1995). Feminist concerns with the androcentric standards for objectivity, rationality, evidence, good method, and what counts as science were centered in GED analyses also.

Finally, GED discussions paralleled analyses in the writings of African American and other feminists of color in the metropolitan centers, which made possible additional coalitions. These discourses, both in the North and in the GED accounts, helped to redefine subjects of knowledge as having multiple and often conflicting identities because of their race, class, gender, ethnicity, sexuality, and other histories. They revealed the multiplicity of conflicting knowledge systems that different cultural histories will produce. They insisted on the importance of empowering marginalized racial and ethnic groups as a condition of democratic dialogue and coalition; difference, as well as affinity, must be recognized and respected. In both the South and the North, these writings have produced a powerful critique of positivism and neopositivisms, and have developed illuminating forms of feminist standpoint epistemology. (In the north, for example, Anzaldúa 1987; Collins 1991)[8]

These feminist origins of Enlightenment reevaluations were strengthened and expanded in the GED accounts through their links to criticisms of development economism and ignorance about nature's limits.[9]

Is Enlightenment Philosophy Economistic?

Does the Enlightenment scientific ethos depend on a bourgeois economic model of human progress? Of course, in many respects, Enlightenment philosophies of science can usefully be read as radically democratic with respect to class, race, and other social markers, considering that it is the effective use of scientific methods (or some other property of scientific processes) that is to ensure the reliabilty of knowledge claims, rather than the social status of the knower, inherited or not. The modern liberal state is supposed to be neutral toward the often diverse conceptions of "the good" of its subgroups and their members, whether such conceptions are biological, religious, ethnic, racial, class, or gender based. Any differences in treatment must be rationally justified. And modern states' information-producing institutions must be similarly value-neutral to enable the state to achieve policies unbiased toward conceptions of "the good." Through rigorous research methods, the goal of value neutrality has been "operationalized" for the sciences.

Of course, hardly anyone thinks it defensible any more to assume that the natural sciences are really neutral to the values and interests of their cultures. Even post-Kuhnian studies—the least overtly politically radical of the science studies movements that have emerged since World War II—have been busy showing the integrity of modern sciences with their historical eras, to paraphrase Thomas Kuhn himself (1970, 1). That is, scientific projects and their results always bear the fingerprints of the historic eras in which they emerged and that continue to find them valuable. I cannot discuss here the value-, interest-, discourse-, and method-ladenness of modern science in general (See Harding 1992; 1996; Proctor 1991). The issue instead is whether economistic values and interests permeate it.

Development was initially conceptualized as economic growth. Thus human progress was thought of in terms of increased production and consumption. In the first place, this approach failed to perceive women's work in the household as real work, or, therefore, as activity that contained elements of a history of human progress. This conception was as prevalent in the Marxian as in the liberal analyses. Thus the need for childcare and household labor was perceived by development thinkers as a drain on maximum economic growth by peasant and working classes in the South, and as an opportunity to recruit middle- and upper-class women North and South into the "consumption-work" that was required to keep production profitable. Poor women were to be drawn into productive agricultural or manufacturing labor and left to get childcare and domestic work done as best they could, while women in the economically advantaged classes were to devote increased time and energy to childcare and domestic tasks, regardless of the purportedly labor-saving devices and services they could use, so as to consume at higher and higher levels. Thus to feminists, conceptualizing development and human progress only in economistic production terms left women and the life of the household intensely vulnerable to exploitation.

In the second place, modernization theory routinely conceptualized population growth in developing countries as a major obstacle to raising standards of living. Population growth causes poverty, this theory insisted. From this perspective, women's bodies were a major obstacle to social progress, and coercive population control policies appeared justifiable. Finally, in the 1990s, even the United Nations Population Conference officially recognized what feminists and progressive economists had been arguing for years: it is poverty that causes population growth, not the reverse. Only many children can provide poor households with the economic and social supports that the state and the economy provide to middle-class households. Conventional Western scientific wisdom had the causal direction backwards.

A third problem with the economic growth conception of development was that nature itself limits economic growth, as feminists, environmentalists, and critics of neoclassical and Marxian economics argued. The world does not have enough resources to support today's global population even at the consumption levels of moderately well off Third World middle classes. And achieving that standard of living for today's most politically and economically vulnerable populations would require a lowering of consumption levels among the more advantaged half of the world's population that is virtually unimaginable. What political process could bring this about?

Finally, conceptualizing development in terms of greater economic produc-tivity and consumption ignores and devalues all other "goods" that women and their cultures prioritize, such as ethical, political, aesthetic, and spiritual values.

Such considerations lead to the suspicion that rational man, who seeks information always in order to maximize his own benefits, ensures the destruc-tion of the very conditions necessary for his survival when those benefits are conceptualized solely as economic. (This is a point about the values and standards of development and other modern institutions concerned with human progress, not those of individual scientists or institutional actors, of course.) Neither nature nor social life can be sustained when such a rationality is the dominant institutional rationality of states and transnational corpora-tions (TNCs) and is held accountable to no other social values.

The question arises as to what extent this self-destructive rationality is an inherent feature of Enlightenment rationality. Modern sciences emerged as part of European postmedieval economic, political, and social formations. One issue is that the modern scientific ideal of value neutrality and the autonomy of knowledge seeking from social accountability makes modern sciences and technologies a "fast gun for hire." Ethics committees in scientific work sites are better than nothing, but they have no power over TNCs, which at present appear accountable to no civic groups at all. Must the sciences internalize democratic ethical and political principles in order to avoid the "fast gun" status? Another issue is whether the increased access to nature's resources that is one of modern sciences' central goals encodes or legitimates using up and degrading environments in order to benefit the groups that modern sciences serve. Nature limits economic growth and any form of human progress that requires such growth. But where is this recognized in Enlightenment philosophies of science?

An Enlightenment Philosophy of Environmental Destruction?

It would take unimaginable sacrifices by middle and upperclasses in the North and South to bring underdeveloped populations up even to standards of living of lower middle classes in these societies. What governance practices could bring that about? Furthermore, the growth models of development consistently sacrifice sustainable environments to short-term consumption goals. Natural resources are disappearing not only through consumption, but also through the effects of military activities, agricultural, urban, and other kinds of toxic pollution of air, water, and other nutrients that human and nonhuman life require.

Women suffer in distinctive ways from the limits that nature places on economic growth, and their disadvantage is passed on to children and others dependent on their energies and resources. They are frequently last in line for economic resources in their households, and disproportionately among the last within their societies. To them is assigned responsibility for doing or managing daily sustenance and the health and welfare of dependents, household, kin, the elderly, the sick, as well as their communities and environments. Moreover, manufacturing and rural wage labor expose them as well as men to toxic dangers in addition to the toxic threats endemic in poor people's household life, such as vermin, gasses from open hearths, and the like. Life- and health-threatening conditions in mining, construction, manufacturing, and agriculture make for nasty, short and brutish lives for the men as well as the women who constitute the politically and economically most vulnerable classes.

Wherever labor and interactions with nature are sex-segregated, environments are usefully conceptualized as gendered. The point here is not that environmental preoccupations with men's issues should be replaced by a preoccupation with women's issues, but that addressing men's problems does not automatically address women's issues in this case or any other.

Critics argue that the Enlightenment entrenches a faulty philosophy of nature. Nature is not a cornucopia, available to satisfy limitless desires, as in the infant's dream of mother. Moreover, sciences and philosophies of nature and of science, like all other human creations, are importantly *in* nature, not autonomous from it. Sciences, their philosophies, and their relations with the societies that use them should all be explained together. Yet modern philosophies' attempted isolation and immunization of natural sciences from social explanation, and their devaluation of local knowledge, have worked against such comprehensive understandings. Even the language in scientific philosophies about nature—whose principles exist outside of all human cultures and whose unique order can be identified and explained only by a universally valid science—though it has many appealing features, nevertheless obscures what happens in human environments. Yet such environments are by definition the only parts of nature with which humans interact, whether this nature is located en route to Mars, out past Jupiter, in the factory, or in the kitchen. We need philosophies of environments and of human interactions with them to replace Enlightenment philosophies of nature and science.

In drawing together resources from feminism, political economy, and environmental studies, GED theory shows the importance of intellectual and political coalitions between analyses that often have been at odds with each other. Moreover, Enlightenment philosophies are our worldview—modernity's world view—and their assumptions permeate institutions and practices far removed from the studies, libraries, classrooms, and conferences where we are used to doing philosophy. Transforming Enlightenment philosophies of science requires insights from all the centers and peripheries where such beliefs have come to structure social relations and their meanings.

For those of us working in the North to refocus Enlightenment philosophies in directions more useful for guiding the production of the knowledge we need for democratic politics, the resources of two additional science studies movements will also be important. The insights of both the postcolonial and the post-Kuhnian science and technology studies support and extend the GED synthesis of Enlightenment critiques in directions valuable to northern post-Enlightenment projects.[10]

ANOTHER PERSPECTIVE ON MODERN SCIENCE'S SUCCESS STORY: POSTCOLONIAL SCIENCE AND TECHNOLOGY STUDIES

Postcolonial science and technology studies criticize Enlightenment philosophies and their effects in development policies from the perspective of anti-Eurocentric histories of modern sciences, and also the related studies of non-Western cultures' own science and technology traditions. In these accounts, development policies are understood as a continuation of the European expansion that began in 1492. European expansion, moreover, has played a far greater role than previously acknowledged in the growth of modern science in Europe and its achievement of a unique epistemological status as capable of providing the only true account of nature's order. That is, the plausibility of the epistemology of modern sciences has depended on the success of European expansion, not just the self-regulating powers of rationality. Modern sciences need the power of national or international state institutions to legitimate and conduct scientific work. Expansionist state power makes it possible to forage in other cultures' knowledge traditions, to test hypotheses in non-European environments around the globe, and to destroy, intentionally or unintentionally, those other traditions that could have created competition for modern scientific claims and practices. This school of thought can trace roots back to the 1940s, but it began to flourish with conferences and publications in English only in the 1980s.[11] Two of its focuses are especially relevant here: comparative ethnosciences and "science-and-empires."

A new kind of comparative ethnoscience emerged in anthropology and history from the older, Eurocentric colonial frameworks. The latter had represented other cultures' knowledge traditions as the products of "savage minds," superstitions, magic, or mere speculation, inextricably mired in religious and other cultural beliefs, or as mere technological knowhow. Other cultures had local knowledge systems, but only modern science produced claims that were universally valid, according to the Eurocentric view.

The anti-Eurocentric comparative ethnoscience movement began to reevaluate the sophistication of other cultures' scientific and technological achievements and the contributions these had made to the development of modern sciences in Europe that have gone unmentioned in the conventional histories of science. It also began to use the tools of ethnography and social history to reexamine modern Western sciences as local knowledge systems, integrated into their particular cultures. For example, historian Joseph Needham shows the distinctively Christian meanings of the notion of laws of nature as it directed scientific method until the twentieth century (Needham 1969). To take another case, European expansionist thinking and its representations of the Edenic Americas, the declining cultures of Asia, the destiny of Christian Europe, and so forth, pointed toward the need for knowledge about particular parts of nature's order that greatly advanced the development in Europe of oceanography, climatology, geology, cartography, diverse engineering projects, tropical medicine, pharmacology, agricultural sciences, evolutionary biology, and many other modern sciences (see, for example, Brockway 1979, Goonatilake 1984, Kochhar 1992-93, McClellan 1992). Culturally local discourses have positive effects on the growth of science, not just the negative effects on which conventional philosophies focus.

In a second and related project, the "science-and-empires" approach, the postcolonial histories of science and technology emerged as part of the new anti-Eurocentric global histories. Here they look at how European and non-European cultures have been interacting for perhaps as long as a millennium, and certainly actively in the five centuries since 1492. In such encounters, cultures exchanged beads, manufactured goods, cattle, women, and scientific and technological ideas. Thus the Voyages of Discovery and the subsequent colonial era, on the one hand, and the development of modern sciences in Europe, on the other, were conditions for each other's success (see, for example, Brockway 1979, Goonatilake 1984, McClellan 1992, Petitjean et al. 1992, Sardar 1988). They continue to nourish each other through development policies, described in this literature as the continuation of colonialism by other means. That is, development policies and their scientific and technological questions primarily continue to advance European expansion and not the societies that are the policies' overtly intended beneficiaries.

What does the postcolonial literature mean by calling both modern sciences and the knowledge traditions of other cultures "local knowledge systems"? This notion has moved to center stage in all the other science movements discussed here (see Harding 1998a, 1998b; Watson-Verran and Turnbull 1995). One way to conceptualize the point is that cultures have distinctive locations in heterogeneous nature and distinctive interests in those surroundings. People living in deserts or beside oceans will tend to produce different patterns of knowledge (and ignorance). Their hypotheses (usefully) always extend considerably beyond the available evidence, which is one reason why these patterns of knowledge cannot fit together like the pieces of a jigsaw puzzle. Even in the same environment—along the Atlantic, say—different cultures will have distinctive interests in the ocean and produce different patterns of knowledge and ignorance depending on whether they are interested in fishing it, desalinizing drinking water from it, dumping garbage in it, mining minerals under its floor, or using it as a trade route or military highway.

Two more features provide local resources for cultures' knowledge projects. Different cultures have access to different discursive resources: Christian models of nature's order; organicist, mechanistic, or biblical models of nature; or environmental notions of lifeboat Earth or spaceship Earth. Each such discourse directs scientific attention to different aspects of nature's regularities and orders them in different causal configurations. Finally, there is no one scientific method or, more generally, one way of organizing the production of knowledge that can claim credit for the various kinds of knowledge of nature's order that different cultures have produced—or even that modern sciences have produced. Fruitful inquiry methods are as varied as human styles of thought and social organization.

Of course, not all local knowledge systems are equally powerful for all projects. Modern biomedicine is valuable for many purposes; but acupuncture, chiropractic, and vitamin and exercise therapies may be more valuable for some health purposes that modern biomedicine has neglected or misunderstood. Modern philosophy of science's claims to unique and universal validity obstruct our ability to think our way through such issues. The universality claims are scientifically and politically dysfunctional.

Thus these postcolonial studies replace the Enlightenment histories and epistemologies of modern sciences with more objective ones, stimulated initially by questions from the standpoint of those who have benefitted least from the development of modern sciences in Europe. Such questions propose that the sciences that were best for the West are not necessarily best for the rest of the world, and that the "Western" sciences we have today are also not good for the West. Those sciences produce systematic ignorance that endangers the human species, destroys nature and other valuable knowledge traditions, and produces antidemocratic social relations. Moreover, this literature is full of specific reevaluations of Enlightenment philosophies of science. These have focused especially on the philosophies' unearned presumptions to model unique ideals of objectivity, rationality, and good method, and on their ontologies that conceptualize nature as isolated bits of dead matter in motion. The reevaluations have criticized the idealized claims of scientific experts who are often ignorant of local conditions and alternative knowledge systems, and the rejection of internal moral and political constraints on the accountability of scientific rationality. The postcolonial studies perceive the epistemology of modern science in effect as predatory, as legitimating sciences' foraging in, while also destroying, all other knowledge systems. The unique status of modern sciences is primarily a result of that epistemology and the successes of European expansion.

Issues about women and gender have been largely absent from the grand narratives of these postcolonial accounts, except as GED writers have occasionally participated in them—for example, Vandana Shiva (1989). Yet their questions about Enlightenment philosophies converge with those in the GED discussions.

AFTER "AUTONOMOUS SCIENCE": POST-KUHNIAN HISTORY, PHILOSOPHY AND SOCIAL STUDIES OF SCIENCE

It is useful to save for last a review of the challenges to Enlightenment thought produced by post-Kuhnian Northern philosophies and social studies of science and technology. Many would regard this school as the most conservative of the movements of interest here, and yet its analyses have often followed much the same lines as the most radical tendencies in the others, even though these Northern accounts emerge from the older historical and geographical map. One could start by pointing out that all the other literatures set out to show how modern sciences and technologies are integrated with different aspects of their historical eras—with gender structures and meanings, with local and global economic projects, with historically distinct environmental attitudes and conditions, with European expansionist and colonial projects, and with attitudes toward and conditions of women's lives under development policies. On this point alone, the post-Kuhnian science and technology studies join these other movements in challenging the conventional idea that the philosophically relevant histories of modern sciences are only intellectual ones.

Let us consider briefly two focuses of this kind of Northern Enlightenment critique that offer opportunities to expand and strengthen coalitions between the post-Kuhnian, postcolonial, and feminist projects. First, did a European Scientific Revolution appear, as part of the "European Miracle," out of the

Dark Ages? All five terms of such a claim—European, scientific, revolution, miracle, and Dark Ages—now appear problematic. Historical studies of medieval Europe and its sophisticated scientific and technological activities show that thinking of the period as the Dark Ages tells more about the speaker than about medieval Europe. There was no European miracle or scientific revolution, but only a slow process that began as far back as the eleventh century. In that process, the components of what were eventually dubbed modern science came together as part of equally gradual political, economic, and social changes. Moreover, given the immense presence in medieval and early modern Europe of Islamic culture, the borrowings in early modern sciences of Egyptian mystical thought and other non-European elements, and the political fragmentation, until at least the late Renaissance, of what we now call Europe, it is misleading to speak of modern sciences as European. Nor do early modern sciences look much like what counts as science today, with their empirical claims shaped by alchemy, sun worship, astrology, and other mystical beliefs and investigatory practices—not to mention overtly Christian metaphysics and epistemology, as Needham and others point out (1954, 1969; Blaut 1993; Yates 1969).

This kind of reconceptualizing of the origins of modern science links post-Kuhnian accounts with postcolonial studies and with the interests in local knowledge systems found throughout the GED literatures. Through such analyses,—even of late Twentieth Century physics—Northern science studies have shown that no element of science is immune from cultural shaping, and every element of science has epistemological consequences (Forman 1987; Pickering 1992).

For a second focus, consider recent arguments against the unity of science thesis—the form in which Enlightenment assumptions about the universality of modern scientific claims coalesced in the late nineteenth and early twentieth centuries and remain powerful today (see Galison and Stump 1996; Harding 1998a). The unity of science thesis held that there was one world, one truth about it, and one and only one science capable of capturing that truth. Obscured in the scientists' and philosophers' formulations of the argument was a fourth assumption: that there was one "class" or group of humans capable of articulating that science and thus recognizing that truth—scientific experts.[12] Leaving aside questions about the usefulness of the "one world" hypothesis (but see Dupre 1993), the other three assumptions have been firmly undermined by post-Kuhnian science studies. This is not to say that these positions are uncontroversial, but rather that many historians, sociologists, ethnographers and philosophers of science agree that the unity assumptions have outlived their usefulness, at least in their stronger initial formulations and in the ways they are articulated today. The "one truth" hypothesis requires various forms of reductionism that are unrealistic; even as an ideal, this claim blocks knowledge. The "one science" hypothesis is meaningless even in modern sciences, in light of the valuable proliferation there of specialized research fields, their distinct methods, and distinct representational resources. Modern sciences are themselves many local knowledge systems linked in pragmatic but not necessarily perfectly coherent ways, from this perspective.

The challenge then becomes not how to reduce this multiplicity to one unity through some kind of fancy discursive footwork, but rather to understand how such local knowledges do travel from one culture to another, and how elements from different contexts of production are linked and reconstructed in ways that help to produce new knowledge. How can practitioners from fields with conflicting definitions of key terms come to work together effectively?[13] What is gained and what lost when knowledge is detached from one cultural system and inserted into another at a distant time or place, as has occurred recently, for example, in the case of acupuncture's move into modern biomedicine? How is information that must be passed on over generations standardized in cultures of only oral literacy (Watson-Verran and Turnbull 1995)?

The universality ideal also appears scientifically and epistemologically dysfunctional, for many reasons. It legitimates appeal to monolithic science to support otherwise inadequately supported individual scientific claims, and it legitimates resistance to valuable criticisms that are inconsistent with prevailing views. It inappropriately devalues cognitive diversity. It obscures the inevitable limitations of any one science. It also promotes systematic ignorance in the social sciences and other fields that model themselves on philosophies of the natural sciences. Moreover, the universality ideal is politically costly in three ways. It devalues and destroys knowledge traditions that are crucial to the survival of other cultures. It elevates a model of the admirably human that is defined in terms of its opposition to and distance from the womanly, non-European, and economically vulnerable. And it elevates cognitive authoritarianism and problematic "religious" ideals to the status of the highest human ideals; it does this through its monovocality and xenophobia; its hierarchical social structures with their elite group of experts who have the status of "chosen people," and its formal and informal ways of protecting from public scrutiny the complete processes of sorting belief.[14]

Finally, this school of science studies, too, shows that the standards of modern science have historically changed over time and are always rhetorically constituted and deployed. What counts as good method, as a proof in mathematics, as objectivity and rationality, not to mention as "real" or material, varies from era to era and often from field to field within the sciences. Epistemological and ontological standards of the sciences, too, have an integrity with their historical era (Proctor 1991; Schuster and Yeo 1986; Shapin 1994; Shapin and Schaffer 1985).

Thus post-Kuhnian histories and philosophies of modern science are thematically linked to the others in their critiques of Enlightenment philosophies of science, and provide valuable possibilities for the coalition work necessary to stabilize post-Enlightenment philosophies of science. What will such philosophies look like?

POST-ENLIGHTENMENT PHILOSOPHIES OF SCIENCES: NEW QUESTIONS

We are now in a position to summarize some of the new philosophical themes emerging from GED analyses that appear also in postcolonial and post-Kuhnian studies.

After the Universality ideal: Local Knowledge Systems

The Enlightenment philosophies were preoccupied with eliminating the local in scientific processes so as to obtain transcultural, universally valid knowledge claims. Elements of many bodies of systematic scientific knowledge (and of systematic scientific ignorance) find homes in later knowledge configurations, though the models of the universe in which they lodge, and the relations they claim between observed phenomena can differ vastly in successive systems. The new philosophies ask how and what kind of local knowledge "travels," and—because cultures are tool boxes as well as prison houses for the growth of knowledge—what is lost and what is gained when it does. They are interested in globalizing processes, but not in achieving universality.

Smart Knowers and Imperfect Knowledge Systems

Such conditions of actual and ideal knowledge production require a model (or rather many such) of knowers and knowledge systems that is different from the familiar one of dumb knowers who must struggle to learn the one correct knowledge system. These philosophies explore other possible models. One, drawn from the realities of both everyday life and contemporary scientific practice, posits smart knowers and imperfect knowledge systems. Here, knowers—scientists or citizens—always have only imperfect knowledge systems with which they must make daily decisions as well as life-or-death ones, though most knowers these days always have more than one such system available.

Consider, for example, the daily health maintenance practices of middle classes in the metropoles. Here individuals commonly use several conflicting knowledge systems. In the United States we use revised vitamin, acupuncture, chiropractic, dietary, exercise, and meditation therapies, not to mention Grandma's home remedies—which modern biomedicine, until the last few years, claimed were of little or no value. But we also use modern biomedicine. Another version of this situation occurs for people in non-Western cultures who have access both to modern biomedicine and other modern Northern sciences and to indigenous health and other knowledge systems (see, for example Bass 1990). All of us have to be very clever about which knowledge system we use and when; this can be a life-or-death matter. The point is that cognitive diversity is an important scientific value.[15]

Resisting Relativism and Idealism

In almost all the writings in these diverse literatures, the rejection of Enlightenment absolutism and excessive materialism is specifically not permitted to be a reason to adopt cognitive relativism or idealism. Different cultures actually do have different scientific and epistemological standards, and this is merely an obvious historical or sociological claim—it is historically or sociologically relative. But not all knowledge systems are equally powerful at grasping the diverse aspects of nature's heterogeneous order. Many people lead short and unhappy lives by following the recommendations of local knowledge systems—including those of our own "local knowledge system," modern science.

Consider our own system's toleration, until recently, of smoking and inadequate vitamins, not to mention industrially-caused environmental toxins. Some sciences are better if you want to get to the moon; others if you want to maintain sustainable environments. So instead of pursuing issues about the virtues of absolutism or realism, these accounts are interested in how to articulate such practical standards of belief sorting. And rejecting the idea that our glassy minds can perfectly mirror a reality that is "out there" in the nonsocial universe similarly never forces these accounts to an idealism, in which only human ideas and the social are real. Instead, the dichotomy between material and ideal, like absolute versus relative cognitive judgments, has itself become the object of historical scrutiny: what social and intellectual conditions made such problematic conceptual frameworks look reasonable?

Nature: Social and Emergent

For the Enlightenment philosophies, nature was, in principle, readable by science, and the questions were about how to accomplish such perfect readings. In the literatures examined here, there is no possibility of one perfect scientific reading of nature's order. In part, this is because of the sometimes fruitful, sometimes knowledge-obstructing ways that humans work nature into an object of observation through cultural interests, discourses, and ways of organizing the production of knowledge. This nature that scientists observe is, in such respects, always also social. (Not "nothing but" social; only always also social.) Here the questions shift to how what counts as nature and what counts as the social are coconstituted in societies that favor such a dichotomy, and more generally, how human material and symbolic practices change nature's order. How should sciences and their philosophies, sciences' order and philosophies' order be conceptualized as also "in nature," requiring explanation alongside the accounts they provide of sciences' and nature's order? What resources from philosophies of social sciences could be useful in such explanations?

Another cause of nature's unreadability is its emergent character. Nature is constantly producing new phenomena, such as ozone holes, and new categories of diseases that are unpredictable. How should this aspect of nature be characterized in the new philosophies?

Internalized Democratic Ethics and Politics in Sciences

With a multiplicity of culturally local sciences, presumably a multiplicity of culturally local ethics and political philosophies will be integrated into these sciences. Enlightenment notions of rationality locate ethics and politics outside the borders of rationality. In recent years, feminist theorists, among others, have developed post-Enlightenment theories of rationality, in which moral decisions and the emotions also have their rationality. The postcolonial and GED analyses clearly are exploring appropriate ways to internalize democratic ethical and political ideals within scientific rationality, because such a rationality bereft of such accountability is incapable of adequate self-regulation. What "democratic" will mean, how such a standard will function in particular contexts—these are difficult but important questions the GED and postcolonial accounts address. One possible democratic ethos to internalize in science—one that emerges from several of the kinds of accounts here—would be that those who bear the consequences of scientific and technological decisions should have a proportionate share in making them. In different historical and cultural contexts, different kinds of institutions and practices would best facilitate such an ethos: small, face-to-face communities and large bureaucratic ones need different kinds of democratic institutions and practices.

Whose Philosophies of Science?

And what of philosophies of science, such as those with common themes that are emerging from so many diverse post-World War II science and technology studies? We have noted that they, too, can usefully be conceptualized as "part of nature" and subjected to analyses alongside the other social and natural elements of our surroundings. We can also see that they must remain permanently unfinished and continually regenerated through collective processes achieved through fruitful coalitions and respectful dialogues.

NOTES

Comments by Ann Garry and Uma Narayan helped to improve this essay.

1. "Enlightenment science" or "Enlightenment scientific rationality" is not the way such fields are characterized by their adherents. But it is the way they are referred to in the GED debates, as well as in postcolonial and some Northern feminist science studies. The target here is much broader than positivism or logical positivism, including much of Marxian and post-Marxian philosophies of science and other science movements. Other terminology taken from the literatures discussed will also appear odd to some readers; for example, "North" and "South" to refer to the West and "the rest"; "science" to refer to any culture's systematic knowledge about the natural surround; "postcolonial science studies," and "local knowledge systems." I shall try to make clear to what such terms refer to as they appear. See Harding (1998a) for further discussion of these issues and of the postcolonial science and technology studies that inform this paper.

2. Drucilla Barker (1998) has usefully summarized important aspects of this dream (her phrase). "Economism" is explained below.

3. I draw here on writings by a number of participants in the GED debates (as indicated), but especially on the work of Rosi Braidotti, Ewa Charkiewicz, Sabine Hausler, and Saskia Wieringa in *Women, the Environment and Sustainable Development: Towards a Theoretical Synthesis* (Braidotti et al. 1994). Braidotti and her colleagues have pulled together the most comprehensive theoretical analysis in and of the GED discussions to date, focusing both on how institutional priorities have shaped these discussions and on the philosophical issues, problems, and possibilities that these accounts raise.

4. Brief outlines of the history of the GED analyses can be found in this issue in Barker 1998 and Ferguson 1998. See also Braidotti et al. 1994, especially chapter 5, and the introduction to Harcourt 1994. Central arguments in this history are developed in Agarwal 1993; Boserup 1970; Dankelman and Davidson 1988; Mies 1986; Sen and Grown 1987; Shiva 1989; and Sparr 1994.

5. Modernization ("development") in Europe took exactly this pattern with enclosure of commons, which forced migration from rural to industrializing areas, creation of a proletariat, new marriage and inheritance laws favoring men, and so on. See, e.g., Kelly-Gadol 1976.

6. Yet the term *gender* has its own problems. It has no home in many European languages, where "sexual difference" is used to do much of the work that "gender" does in English. (See Braidotti et al. 1994, 36-43, for a useful discussion of the history of problems with the term; and Harding 1986, 52-56, for an early attempt to insist on the importance of symbolic and structural forms of gender.) Moreover, this term has developed in other problematic ways; see, e.g., the account of one U.S.-trained Nigerian sociologist, Oyewumi (1997).

7. Braidotti et al. give a good sense of how this development agency context shaped the GED discussions (in 1994, chaps. 5, 7).

8. Donna Haraway's work (1989, 1991, 1997) has been especially important to the GED synthesis precisely for the way she has linked, through poststructuralist and materialist discourses, concerns with Enlightenment conceptions of nature, science, gender, race, and imperialism.

9. A few other feminist accounts (in addition to Haraway's) have also drawn on the combined resources of political economy and environment studies for their science studies projects (e.g., Seager 1993; Plumwood 1993). These both overlap and diverge from the GED concerns.

10. The work of these two schools of post-World War II science studies is, of course, familiar to some of the GED writers.

11. For an overview of this literature see Harding 1998a, Chapters 2 and 3. See also Adas 1989; Blaut 1993; Brockway 1979; Crosby 1987; Goonatilake 1984, 1997; Headrick 1981; Hess 1995; Kochhar 1992-93; Kumar 1991; Lach 1977; McClellan 1992; Nandy 1990; Needham 1954ff, 1969; Petitjean et al. 1992; Reingold and Rothenberg 1987; Rodney 1982; Sardar 1988; Watson-Verran and Turnbull 1995; Weatherford 1988. This movement is internally diverse with many ongoing debates; its representatives come from Northern as well as Southern cultures as the above list indicates. Many Third World scientists, like their colleagues in the North, are untroubled devotees of Eurocentric accounts of modern sciences, and thus have no interest in these discussions. Entering modern science is for them, as for cultures of Europe and its diasporas, a way of gaining local social status, entering international society, and engaging in projects that do in many respects offer resources against oppressive traditional thinking and practices. Contrary to the impression given in some of the postcolonial literature, it is not modern science, the Enlightenment, or modernity per se that GED (or this author) sees as problematic, but only certain aspects in distinctive contexts.

12. Val Plumwood pointed this out in conversation.

13. See, e.g., Peter Galison's introduction to his and David J. Stump's collection (1996), in which he discusses how such agreement about how to conceptualize randomness was reached in the 1940s and 1950s between atomic bomb designers, logicians, statisticians, and aeronautical engineers as they tackled the problem of how to construct computer-simulated realities.

14. See the essays by David Stump and Ian Hacking in Galison and Stump 1996; and Harding 1998a.

15. I explored some such models as they appeared in the postcolonial science literature in the concluding section of Harding 1994.

REFERENCES

Adas, Michael. 1989. *Machines as the measure of man.* Ithaca: Cornell University Press.
Agarwal, Bina. 1993. The gender and environment debate: lessons from India. *Feminist Studies* 18(1).
Anzaldúa, Gloria. 1987. *Borderlands/La Frontera.* San Francisco: Spinsters/Aunt Lute.
Barker, Drucilla. 1998. Dualisms, discourse, and development. *Hypatia* 13(3)xxxx.
Bass, Thomas A. 1990. *Camping with the prince, and other tales of science in Africa.* Boston: Houghton Mifflin.
Blaut, J. M. 1993. *The colonizer's model of the World: Geographical diffusionism and Eurocentric history.* New York: Guilford Press.

Boserup, Ester. 1970. *Women's role in economic development.* New York: St. Martin's Press.

Braidotti, Rosi, Ewa Charkiewicz, Sabine Hausler, and Saskia Wieringa. 1994. *Women, the environment, and sustainable development: Towards a theoretical synthesis.* London: Zed Books/ INSTRAW.

Brockway, Lucille H. 1979. *Science and colonial expansion: The of the British Royal Botanical Gardens.* New York: Academic Press.

Collins, Patricia Hill. 1991. *Black feminist thought: Knowledge, consciousness, and the politics of empowerment.* New York: Routledge.

Crosby, Alfred. 1987. *Ecological imperialism: The biological expansion of Europe.* Cambridge: Cambridge University Press.

Dankelman, Irene, and Joan Davidson. 1988. *Women and environment in the Third World.* London: Earthscan Publications Ltd.

Dupre, John. 1993. *The disorder of things: Metaphysical foundations for the disunity of science.* Cambridge: Harvard University Press.

Ferguson, Ann. 1998. Resisting the veil of privilege: Building bridge identities as an ethico-politics of global feminisms. *Hypatia* 13(3)xxxx.

Forman, Paul. 1987. Beyond quantum electronics: National security as a basis for physical research in the U.S., 1940-1960. *Historical Studies in Physical and Biological Sciences 18.*

Galison, Peter, and David J. Stump, eds. 1996. *The disunity of science.* Stanford: Stanford University Press.

Goonatilake, Susantha. 1984. *Aborted discovery: Science and creativity in the Third World.* London: Zed Books.

———. 1997. *Mining civilizational knowledge.* Bloomington: Indiana University Press.

Haraway, Donna. 1989. *Primate visions: Gender, race and nature in the world of modern science.* New York: Routledge.

———. 1991. *Simians, cyborgs, and women: The reinvention of nature.* New York: Routledge.

———. 1997. *Modest witness@Second_millennium.FemaleMan meets_onco-mouse: Feminism and technoscience.* New York: Routledge.

Harcourt, Wendy, ed. 1994. *Feminist perspectives on sustainable development.* London: Zed Books.

Harding, Sandra. 1986. *The science question in feminism.* Ithaca: Cornell University Press.

———. 1991. *Whose science? Whose knowledge? Thinking from women's lives.* Ithaca: Cornell University Press.

———. 1992. After the neutrality ideal: Science, politics and "strong objectivity." *Social Research* 59: 567-87; reprinted in *The politics of Western science, 1640-1990,* ed. Margaret C. Jacobs. Atlantic Highlands: Humanities Press, 1993.

———, ed. 1993. *The "racial" economy of science: Toward a democratic future.* Bloomington: Indiana University Press.

———. 1994. Is science multicultural? Challenges, resources, opportunities, uncertainties. *Configurations* 2(2) and in *Multiculturalism: A reader,* ed. David Theo Goldberg. London: Blackwell's, 1994.

———. 1995. "Strong Objectivity": A response to the new objectivity question. *Synthese* 104(3): 1-19.

———. 1996. Multicultural and global feminist philosophies of science: Resources and challenges. *Feminism, sciences, and the philosophy of science,* ed. Lynn Hankinson Nelson and Jack Nelson. Dordrecht: Kluwer.

———. 1997. Women's standpoints on nature: What makes them possible? *Osiris* 12. Special issue on Women, Gender, and Science, ed. Helen Longino and Sally Gregory Kohlstedt.

———. 1998a. *Is science multicultural? Postcolonialisms, feminisms, and epistemologies.* Bloomington: Indiana University Press.

———. 1998b. Is modern science an ethnoscience? *Sociology of the sciences yearbook: Science and technology in a developing world*, eds. Terry. Shinn, Jack Spaapen, and Raoul Waast. Dordrecht: Kluwer.

Headrick, Daniel R., ed. 1981. *The tools of empire: Technology and European imperialism in the nineteenth century.* New York: Oxford University Press.

Hess, David J. 1995. *Science and technology in a multicultural world.* New York: Columbia University Press.

Kelly-Gadol, Joan. 1976. The social relations of the sexes: Methodological implications of women's history. *Signs* 1(4): 809-824.

Kettel, Bonnie. 1995. Key paths for science and technology. *Missing links: Gender equity in science and technology for development*, ed. Gender Working Group, U.N. Commission on Science and Technology for Development. Ottawa: International Development Research Centre.

Kochhar, R. K. 1992-93. Science in British India. *Current Science* (Delhi, India). Part I, 63(11): 689-94; Part II, 64(1): 55-62.

Kuhn, Thomas S. 1970 [1962]. *The structure of scientific revolutions*, 2d ed. Chicago: University of Chicago Press.

Kumar, Deepak. 1991. *Science and empire: Essays in Indian context (1700-1947).* Delhi: Anamika Prakashan/National Institute of Science, Technology and Development.

Lach, Donald F. 1977. *Asia in the making of Europe*, Vol. 2. Chicago: University of Chicago Press.

McClellan, James E. 1992. *Colonialism and science: Saint Domingue in the Old Regime.* Baltimore: Johns Hopkins University Press.

Mies, Maria. 1986. *Patriarchy and accumulation on a world scale: Women in the international division of labor.* Atlantic Highlands, NJ: Zed Press.

Nandy, Ashis, ed. 1990. *Science, hegemony and violence: A requiem for modernity.* Delhi: Oxford University Press.

Needham, Joseph. 1954ff. *Science and civilisation in China* (7 vols.). Cambridge: Cambridge University Press.

———. 1969. *The grand titration: Science and society in East and West.* Toronto: University of Toronto Press.

Oyewumi, Oyeronke. 1997. *The invention of women: Making an African sense of Western gender discourses.* Minneapolis: University of Minnesota Press.

Petitjean, Patrick, Jami Moulton, et al., eds. 1992. *Science and empires: Historical studies about scientific development and European expansion.* Dordrecht: Kluwer.

Pickering, Andrew, ed. 1992. *Science as practice and culture.* Chicago: University of Chicago Press.

Plumwood, Val. 1993. *Feminism and the mastery of nature.* New York: Routledge.

Proctor, Robert. 1991. *Value-free science? Purity and power in modern knowledge.* Cambridge: Harvard University Press.

Reingold, Nathan and Marc Rothenberg, eds. 1987. *Scientific colonialism: Cross-cultural comparisons.* Washington, DC: Smithsonian Institution Press.

Rodney, Walter. 1982. *How Europe underdeveloped Africa.* Washington DC: Howard University Press.

Sardar, Ziauddin, ed. 1988. *The revenge of Athena: Science, exploitation and the Third World*. London: Mansell.

Schuster, John A., and Richard R. Yeo, eds. 1986. *The politics and rhetoric of scientific method: Historical studies*. Dordrecht: D. Reidel.

Seager, Joni. 1993. *Earth follies: Coming to feminist terms with the global environmental crisis*. New York: Routledge.

Sen, Gita and Caren Grown. 1987. *Development crises and alternative visions: Third World women's perspectives*. New York: Monthly Review Press.

Shapin, Steven. 1994. *A social history of truth*. Chicago: University of Chicago Press.

———and Simon Schaffer. 1985. *Leviathan and the air pump*. Princeton: Princeton University Press.

Shiva, Vandana. 1989. *Staying alive: Women, ecology and development*. London: Zed Books.

Sparr, Pamela, ed. 1994. *Mortgaging women's lives: Feminist critiques of structural adjustment*. London: Zed Books.

Watson-Verran, Helen, and David Turnbull. 1995. Science and other indigenous knowledge systems. In *Handbook of science and technology studies*, ed. Sheila Jasanoff, George Markle, Trevor Pinch, and James Petersen. Thousand Oaks, CA: Sage. p. 115-139.

Weatherford, Jack. 1988. *Indian givers: What the Native Americans gave to the world*. New York: Crown.

Yates, Frances. 1969. *Giordano Bruno and the hermetic tradition*. New York: Vintage.

15

What Should White People Do?

LINDA MARTÍN ALCOFF

In this paper I explore white attempts to move toward a proactive position against racism that will amount to more than self-criticism in the following three ways: by assessing the debate within feminism over white women's relation to whiteness; by exploring "white awareness training" methods developed by Judith Katz and the "race traitor" politics developed by Ignatiev and Garvey, and; a case study of white revisionism being currently attempted at the University of Mississippi.

In the movie *Dances with Wolves* (1991), Kevin Costner plays a white Union soldier stationed on the Indian frontier who undergoes a political transformation. He comes to realize that the native peoples his militia intends to kill are not the uncivilized heathens they were portrayed to be, and in fact have a rich civilization in many ways superior to his. Thus, he realizes that he is fighting on the wrong side. The remainder of the movie chronicles his struggle to figure out what this realization means *for him*.

I believe that this narrative represents a collective, semiconscious undercurrent of psychic and political struggle occurring now in the United States among significant numbers of white Anglos. Throughout U.S. history, some white people have joined in common cause with people of color to fight slavery, racism, and imperialism, from the New York Conspiracy of 1741 to the John Brown uprising to white supporters of civil rights and white protesters against the racism of the Vietnam War (Ignatiev and Garvey 1996, 131). Today, the scope of this disallegiance has expanded, as many whites have begun to doubt not only specific racist institutions or aggressions but also the racialized legitimation narratives of "Western civilization" and the purported superiority of all things European.

Dances with Wolves, though politically flawed, nonetheless revealed the significance of this awakened white consciousness by winning the academy award for Best Picture of 1991.[1] White support for antiracism is often similarly flawed: riven with supremacist pretentions and an extension at times of the colonizer's privilege to decide the true, the just, and the culturally valuable. However, it is unwarranted to argue that these deep layers of persistent racism represent the core of all apparent white antiracism. Although it is important— and often easy—to expose the persistent racism in avowedly antiracist efforts, we need also to affirm that *some* of the time, in *some* respects even when not in *all*, whites empathize and identify with nonwhites, abhor how white supremacy has distorted their social interactions, and are willing to make significant sacrifices toward the eradication of white privilege.

For white North Americans, nevertheless, coming to terms with white privilege exacts a price. For Costner's Captain Dunbar, the effort costs him a good beating and nearly his life, but for contemporary whites, the price is more often psychological. As James Baldwin said years ago, "It is not really a 'negro revolution' that is upsetting the country. What is upsetting the country is a sense of its own identity" (Baldwin 1988, 8). And as one white student put it, "I mean now I really have to think about it. Like now I feel white. I feel white" (Gallagher 1994, 165). This "feeling white," when coupled with a repudiation of white privilege, can disable a positive self-image as well as a felt connection to community and history, and generally can disorient identity formation.

Chauvinist legitimation narratives that portrayed European-based societies as the progressive vanguard of the human race produced an almost invisible support structure for the collective self-esteem of all those who could claim such a European identity. In the first half of the twentieth century, the plausibility of these narratives was undermined by the profit-motivated violence of World War I and the technologically orchestrated genocides of World War II. As a response to that disillusionment, new narratives were developed, based on a thorough repudiation of "old world" ethnic hatreds and blind political obedience. The "new" or "modern world" legitimation narratives proclaimed that European-based societies led the world in maximizing individualism, civil liberties, and economic prosperity, which were assumed to be the highest human goods. Of course, many nonwhites are able to participate in these narratives and to see themselves to some extent as a part of the liberatory vanguard. But because it was the cultural traditions and economic methods of Europe and the United States that inspired and guided this progress, naturally whites were at the center and the forefront, with nonwhite allies alongside but to the back.

In the second half of this century, internal disillusionment with these white-vanguard narratives has grown strong once again, primarily because of the civil rights movement and the Vietnam War, but also in light of events in South Africa, Ireland, and now in Central Europe, which have engendered doubt about whether the white race is less violent, less "uncivilized," or more democratic than any other. As a result, the cultural mechanisms supporting white self-esteem are breaking down and a growing white backlash has developed in response to this psychic threat.

Backlash, however, is not the only contemporary white response to the declining plausibility of white supremacist narratives. This paper explores other kinds of white responses, all of which, in one way or another, seek to transcend white vanguardism and move toward a proactive position against racism that will amount to more than mere self-criticism.

The issue I want to put center stage, however, is white identity. Many race theorists have argued that antiracist struggles require whites' acknowledgment that they are *white*; that is, that their experience, perceptions, and economic position have been profoundly affected by being constituted as white (Frankenberg 1993). Race may be a social construction without biological validity, yet it is real and powerful enough to alter the fundamental shape of all our lives (Gooding-Williams 1995; Taylor 1996; Alcoff 1996). Part of white privilege has been precisely whites' ability to ignore the ways white racial identity has benefitted them.

But what is it to acknowledge one's whiteness? Is it to acknowledge that one is inherently tied to structures of domination and oppression, that one is irrevocably on the wrong side? In other words, can the acknowledgment of whiteness produce only self-criticism, even shame and self-loathing? Is it possible to feel okay about being white?

Every individual, I would argue, needs to feel a connection to community, to a history, and to a human project larger than his or her own life. Without this connection, we are bereft of a concern for the future or an investment in the fate of our community. Nihilism is the result; and we see abundant signs of it all around, from the unchecked frenzy of consumption that ignores its likely long-term effects to the anarcholibertarianism that is rife in the corporate United States at all levels and that values only immediate individual desires.

If this analysis is correct, and everyone does need some felt connection to a community with both past and future, what are North American whites to do? Should they assimilate, like Captain John Dunbar in *Dances with Wolves*, as far as possible into non-European cultures, as some New Age advocates argue? Should they become, as Noel Ignatiev and John Garvey argue, race traitors who disavow all claims or ties to whiteness? Can a liberal repudiation of racial identity and an avowal of "color-blindness" produce the consciousness of white privilege that antiracism requires? Can a deracialized individualism provide the sense of historical continuity that moral action seems to require?

Feminism has usefully problematized the notion of a monolithic white identity by raising issues of gender and sometimes class. In the next section I will analyze white feminists' assessment of whiteness. Then, in the following three sections, I will explore three further "answers" to the white question: the early, influential antiracist "white awareness training" methods as developed by Judith Katz and others, the "race traitor" politics developed by Ignatiev and

Garvey, and finally, a kind of case study of white revisionism being attempted at the University of Mississippi. Each of these is an example of a response developed by whites for whites.

Before I go any further, I need to tell something about my own identity, which, like an increasing number of others in this country, is racially complex. In some places in the United States, I am perceived to look "white" and am assumed to be white. This means that, in those contexts, in one sense I am white, and therefore I know something about white privilege from the inside. Moreover, though born in Panamá, I was raised in the southern United States (Florida), where conditions of Jim Crow segregation reigned either officially or unofficially for most of my childhood. My mother and stepfather are white southerners, with all that that can imply. However, my father was Latino with mixed Spanish, Indian, and African heritage. His family, and thus that part of my family, never left Panamá, and his own sojourn here was mainly as a college student. Growing up in Florida, my sister and I were generally introduced to newcomers as my mother's "Latin daughters." So I have also known something about white chauvinism, mostly of the cultural sort (for example, "You must be so thankful to be in this country" and other assorted baseless assumptions).

I once heard the legal theorist Gerald Torres joke that Latinos have a tendency toward arrogance about racial matters; because Latinos are usually racially mixed, they often assume that they know what it is to be Indian, to be white, *and* to be black! Latinos also sometimes assume ourselves incapable of anti-black or anti-Indian racism because most of us have some black and indigenous forbears.[2] I do not want to make these assumptions, and my skin color certainly compels against them. But I have tried to use my intersectional location as a resource for considering the multiple "lived experiences" of racialized identity in the United States.[3]

WHITE WOMEN AND WHITE IDENTITY

Whiteness is both homogeneous and fractured. Unlike Latino identity, which is understood to be mixed, and unlike African American identity under the strictures of the one-drop rule, whiteness is accorded only to those who are (supposedly) "pure" white. In the recent historical past this was not so clear-cut, as Jews, Irish, Italians, and other southern Europeans were sometimes excluded from whiteness and at other times enjoyed a halfway status as almost white, but not quite (unlike those with partial African heritage, no matter how light). But today, in mainstream white bread America, the borders around whiteness are assumed to be clear.

In another sense, whiteness has always been fractured by class, gender, sex, ethnicity, age, and able-bodiedness. The privileges whiteness bestowed were differentially distributed and were also simply different (for example, the privilege to get the job for a man, the privilege not to work for women, and so on). In much feminist literature the normative, dominant subject position is described in detail as a white, heterosexual, middle-class, able-bodied male. This normative figure carries the weight as well in the cultural narrative of reconfiguring black-white relations; there have been far more "buddy" movies about white men and black men than films exploring women's relationships.[4] In *Dances with Wolves*, the revision of the Manifest Destiny narrative centers on a white, normative male to carry the story; this seems to assume that if whiteness is to be recast, it must be recast from the center out. Anything else—any revision that centered on a woman, for example—would not have the cultural force, the felt *significance*, of a white man relearning his place. This situation must raise the question, what is white women's relation to whiteness?

Feminist theory has given various answers to this question, and much of the debate has centered on the question of whether white women benefit on the whole from whiteness, or whether whiteness is a ruse to divide women and to keep white women from understanding their true interests. Some feminists have argued that sexism is more fundamental than racism, in the sense that sexual identity is more important in determining social status than racial identity. For example, Shulamith Firestone (1970) argues that the racism that exists among white women is a form of inauthenticity or false consciousness that does not represent their true interests. Mary Daly (1978) similarly argues that charges of racism against feminists serve patriarchal ends by promoting divisiveness among women. According to Daly, feminists should disengage from male-created identifications with race, nation, or ethnicity.

Other feminists have criticized this view. Margaret A. Simons (1979) argues that the claim that sexism is primary trivializes racist oppression and implausibly assumes that sexism alone can provide an adequate explanation for genocide and war (for example, that white men "feminized" nonwhite or Jewish men). The existence of some form of sexist oppression in every society does not justify a conception of patriarchy that generalizes the relations between all men and all women in one undifferentiated analysis. According to Simons, white women's identity must be understood both as white and as female. Gloria Joseph (1981) also argues that white women are both tools and benefactors of racism, and that feminists must recognize and address white women's social position as both oppressors and oppressed. In fact, Joseph contends that given the extensive privileges of whiteness, white women's immediate self-interest is to maintain racism. She suggests that we need to explore the concept of "white female supremacy" as well as white male supremacy.

Adrienne Rich's "Disloyal to Civilization: Feminism, Racism, Gynephobia" (1979), a paper that has been very widely used in women's studies courses, takes up these issues in a way that mainly addresses a white feminist audience. In this paper, Rich develops the concept of "white solipsism" to describe a perceptual practice that implicitly takes a white perspective as universal. She argues that "colorblindness," or the ideal of ignoring racial identities, falls into white solipsism because a racist society has no truly accessible colorblind perspective. The claim to a colorblind perspective by whites works just to conceal the partiality of their perceptions.

Rich provides a very perceptive critique of colorblindness and, unlike other radical feminists, she acknowledges the significance of white women's racism. However, Rich continues to put sexism at the center of all women's lives and to portray white women as primarily victims of racism rather than agents who help to sustain it. Rich claims that white women did not create racism but have been forced to serve racist institutions, and that those who think they benefit from racism are deluded. In her view, white women's racism is actually a misdirected outlet for their rage over their own powerlessness, a view that only slightly revises Firestone's. In Rich's account, slavery is more accurately described as an institution of patriarchy than one of white supremacy; to blame white women is to impede the process of forging political and emotional connections between white and nonwhite women. The apparent protection some white women receive from patriarchy degrades them by enforcing child-ishness and helplessness. Therefore, white women's true interests lie in making alliances with other women, not with men. This analysis suggests that the "whiteness" of white women is not in any sense the same as the "whiteness" of white men.

In contrast, Marilyn Frye (1983, 1992) has suggested that despite the severity of sexism, white women do not escape race privilege. It is a feature of this race privilege that white women have a choice to hear or not to hear—and to respond or not to respond—to the demands and criticisms of women of color. Racism differentially distributes general epistemic authority to make judgments and determinations, such that, for example, whites often assume the right to decide the true or accurate racial identity of everyone. When white feminists proclaim that white women are primarily *women*, this is an extension of an essentially white privilege.

In Frye's view, white feminists should be disloyal to whiteness. Because white women understandably want to be treated as human beings, their feminism often takes the form of pursuit of the full entitlements of "whiteli-ness," which Frye defines as a socially constructed status that confers entitle-ments and authority. For example, the demand for equality has implicitly and practically meant the demand for equality with white men (a demand for equality with, say, *puertorriqueños* would hardly mean liberation). But the demand to be equal to white men is necessarily a demand to achieve "whiteli-ness," a status that depends on racist structures of social relations for its power and autonomy. Like Rich and Firestone, Frye argues that solidarity with white men is not in white women's ultimate interest. Racism has motivated white men to oppress and constrain white women's sexuality and reproductive powers in order to secure the regeneration of a "pure" white population. Thus, we must become disloyal to whiteness and unlearn our "whiteliness" assumptions of entitlement and authority.

What does "becoming disloyal" mean in practice? For Frye and Rich, it clearly cannot mean upholding some form of colorblindness or individualism, which would only conceal white privilege and implicit white perspectives. So how can whites be disloyal to whiteness while acknowledging the significance of their own racial identity?

ANTI-RACISM TRAINING

A liberal approach to answering this question is developed in Judith Katz's now-classic *White Awareness: Handbook for Anti-Racism Training* (Katz 1978). This book is representative of the popularized psychological approach to antiracism, an approach often generated in, and aiming to be suited for, the kinds of in-house workshops and encounter groups that have developed from corporate America since the 1960s, though Katz's own context was closer to universities. Many corporations have discovered that racism (sometimes) impedes productivity, and therefore they have been hiring consultants to retrain and "sensitize" white management personnel. This is, of course, only part of the audience for "antiracism training"; some universities and movement organizations have also tried this approach. But the specific social location and source of economic funding needs to be kept in mind when analyzing the reeducation approaches used in antiracism workshops.

White Awareness attributes widespread responsibility for racism to whites. However, Katz is highly critical of white guilt fixations, because these are self-indulgent. She explains that such criticisms led her to move from black-white group encounters to all-white groups. She also avoided using people of color to reeducate whites, she says, because she found that this led whites to focus on getting acceptance and forgiveness from their nonwhite trainers.

Facing the enormity and depth of racism is painful and demoralizing, as one loses one's sense of self-trust and even self-love; but Katz nonetheless holds out the hope that whites can become antiracist and that "we may ultimately find comfort in our move to liberation" (1978, vii). Racism causes whites to suffer; it cripples their intellectual and psychological development and locks them "in a psychological prison that victimizes and oppresses them every day of their lives" (14). Such claims do not, of course, entail that whites' victimization by racism is worse than or equal to that of other groups, but Katz's wording is striking. Throughout the book, racism is portrayed as a kind of macro-agent with its own agenda, operating separately from white people.

This problem takes on added significance given that antiracism and sensitivity training is a growth industry in corporate America today, the same corporate culture that continues to use racism and cultural chauvinism as an excuse to pay people of color far lower wages by undervaluing what is actually comparable or more difficult work. Katz makes no reference to exploitation or the need for a redistribution of resources, and instead treats racism as a psychological pathology that can be solved through behavior modification. Although racism no doubt is debilitating for whites in a number of ways, unless we analyze who benefits from and promotes racism, we cannot see clearly what needs to be done to counter it.

However, *White Awareness* usefully develops processes that can permit collective exploration of and critical reflection on white racial consciousness. It builds on whites' own tacit knowledge of racism to promote reflection, thereby enhancing whites' confidence in their own agency and counteracting fatalism. And it helpfully acknowledges the likelihood of white emotional responses like anger, guilt, and resistance, without seeing these as indicative of an insurmountable racism. Instead, it develops group processes and supportive environments in which such emotional responses can be aired, worked through, and transcended. I have at least anecdotal reports that the book has been used productively in contexts of political organizing to initiate an exploration and reflection by whites about the many subtle layers of racism and supremacist assumptions embedded in their interactions.

A notable weakness of *White Awareness* is that it does not offer a transformative, substantive white identity. Katz argues against replacing whiteness with ethnic identities on the grounds that this obscures the racialized organization of white supremacy, and thus she maintains the need to self-identify as white. But whiteness figures in *White Awareness* only as an identity of unfair privilege based on white supremacy; unlike ethnic identities, it has no other substantive cultural content. Stage Five of the training process is called "Individual Racism: The Meaning of Whiteness," and the first goal listed is to help participants "explore their White culture and develop a sense of positive identification with their whiteness" (135). However, the workshops in this stage discuss only the luxuries and privileges associated with whiteness. Among the directions to the facilitator is the following:

> You should also help the group identify positive aspects of being White. It is important for them to feel good about themselves as White people. All too often Whites deny their whiteness because they feel that being White is negative. (Katz 1979, 145)

However, the book provides no help in determining what these positive aspects might be, and given its context, readers must find it difficult to guess how Katz would substantively define whiteness except in terms of racism and unfair privilege.

In 1992, on the quincentenary of Columbus' invasion, I participated in a public debate in Syracuse with the local Italian American booster club over the political meanings of Columbus Day. They argued that Italian Americans suffered intense and ongoing discrimination in this country and that the celebration of Columbus Day was very important for raising community pride and instilling recognition of the important contributions Italians have made. I agreed with their depiction of the situation and the need for positive cultural symbols but asked why Leonardo da Vinci, Michelangelo, and even Mario Cuomo could not be used instead of a man responsible for transcontinental genocide and enslavement of Native Americans. The Italians have a par-ticular wealth of admirable cultural leaders, and this club's continued insistence on Columbus suggested to me that more than achieving group equality was at stake.

If white identity is to be transformed, it does need more of a substantive reconstruction, including a revision of historical narratives and cultural focuses. The following two sections explore more recent attempts to transform whiteness, both of which take some issue with the liberal approach.

TRAITORS TO WHITENESS

One of the most radical positions on white antiracism that has emerged in recent years can be found in the journal *Race Traitor: A Journal of the New Abolitionism*. The journal has created a space where radical whites can share and spread ideas, get feedback and criticism from people of color, and help to educate themselves and their readers on the "true" history of the Civil War and the neglected legacy of white resistance to racism. They can also develop their critical analyses of current social phenomena, such as multiculturalism and the increasing cultural crossovers of white youth.

Journal editors Noel Ignatiev and John Garvey are anticapitalist, and they believe that we must be willing to take up arms. Their politics are probably best classified as libertarian anarchist, and it is other anarchist journals and 'zines that seem most often to reprint or refer to *Race Traitor*. The editors strive for a strong working-class political perspective, and they have managed to develop class inclusiveness among the journal's writers, a characteristic too rarely found in leftist journals of any type. In an interesting way, they have put less effort into making allies among feminists or gay activists, perhaps because they do not view these issues as centrally connected to white supremacy. This follows from an analysis found regularly in the journal that "white supremacy" has largely been an ideology used by the wealthy and powerful to fool the white poor into being more race-loyal than class-loyal, blinding them to their own interests. As we have seen, however, a similar case could be made for white women and also for white gays.

The most interesting aspect of this approach is its declared focus on whites. Unlike other leftist publications that have tried to develop multiracial groups, *Race Traitor* seems to believe that a political network of white traitors is needed to focus on retrieving white antiracist history, deepening the analysis of whiteness and racism, and encouraging the small but growing tendency among white youth to rebel against racist cultural hierarchies and enforced segregation. Consider the editors' report of the following news item:

> According to press reports and our own correspondents, the white race is showing signs of fracture in the rural midwest. Several female students at North Newton Junior-Senior High School near Morocco, Indiana, who call themselves the "Free to Be Me" group, recently started braiding their hair in dreadlocks and wearing baggy jeans and combat boots, a style identified with Hip-Hop culture. Morocco is a small farming community seventy miles south of Chicago; of the 850 students at the school, two are black. Whites in the town accuse the group of "acting black," and male students have reacted by calling them names, spitting at them, punching and pushing them into lockers, and threatening them with further violence. Since mid-November there have been death threats, a bomb scare, and a Ku Klux Klan rally at the school. "This is a white community," said one sixteen-year-old male student. "If they don't want to be white, they should leave." (Ignatiev and Garvey 1996, flyleaf)

Not only have the students encountered violent opposition, but school officials have suspended them with the excuse of "dress code violations." This example, which received wide publicity on the *Montel Williams Show*, is clearly the kind of spontaneous, "in your face" rebellion that *Race Traitor* hopes to encourage. The editors comment, "This incident reveals . . . the tremendous power of crossover culture to undermine both white solidarity and male authority."

It is important to understand why *this* sort of event is what *Race Traitor* finds so hopeful, rather than the more common and certainly more tame occurrences of white antiracist organizing on college campuses and white support for such political efforts as the Free Mumia Abu-Jamal campaign, union campaigns, and Martin Luther King Day rallies. What happened in Morocco, Indiana, differs from those events in that it was a spontaneous (every anarchist's dream) rebellion that involved a *repudiation of white identity*.

The cornerstone of the *Race Traitor* position is, "nothing less than the abolition of the white race will lay the foundation for a new departure" (1996, 2). The journal's main slogan is "treason to whiteness is loyalty to humanity" (10). Whites need to challenge the "normal operation" of "the institutions that reproduce race as a social category" (3). Sounding like Foucault at times, the editors argue that whiteness is made real through social practices that occur in a multitude of daily social interactions, and that this process works only because it assumes that people designated white will play by the rules. "But if enough of those who looked white broke the rules of the club" such that, for example, the police would "come to doubt their ability to recognize a white person," this could disrupt the whole mechanism, and whiteness might be abolished (13). How many such white dissidents would it take? "One John Brown—against the background of slave resistance—was enough for Virginia" (13). His deeds "were part of a chain of events that involved mutual actions and reactions on a scale beyond anything they could have anticipated—until a war began" (13). Thus, given the persistence of rebellions by people of color, white acts of treason might be just what is needed to ignite a civil war, one that perhaps this time could truly be a revolutionary war as well.

Such strategic thinking obviously resonates with the postmodern sensibilities of radical youth today, which accounts in part, I believe, for the increased interest in anarchist theories of social change. That is, both postmodernism and anarchism offer a theoretical justification for the current belief that old-fashioned, barricade-style "wars of position" are hopeless in a shifting terrain of capitalist power, with resources that are not themselves centralized or geographically stable in any way. In a situation in which political power cannot be mapped, economic power exists on no fixed grid, and the causal relations between politics, economics, and culture have no stability, it is possible to hope that enough incidents like the Morocco case might be just the catalyst needed.

But what other sorts of white treason can one engage in today? In the civil rights movement white individuals refused white solidarity over Jim Crow and sat in at lunch counters with African Americans, rode in the backs of buses, and marched in open opposition to their communities. These were public acts of social treason without a doubt, and they incited violent reactions sometimes as brutal as black people themselves suffered. In the absence of such a political movement, there are other actions whites can take that are less dramatic but that can send similar messages, such as the clothing styles chosen by the "Free To Be Me" group in Morroco, or the choice of schools and neighborhoods, realtors and other services or businesses. However, outside the context of a widely publicized political movement, the meanings of such acts are less predictable, and they may even have harmful unintended effects, as when the choice of a minority neighborhood by whites actually aids gentrification. In the Morocco case, one of the two black students also was threatened and harassed, and his mother was attacked and beaten by two white men while she was shopping in town. Thus the most violence was suffered by the black families in the school, families that were not consulted and probably unprepared for the attack. Given that we lack total control over the meanings and the effects of our actions, and given the absence of a widely publicized political movement of "white treason" that could confer meaning, the real effects of individual actions is uncertain.

The major problem with *Race Traitor*'s proposal, however, is that, in one important sense, whites cannot disavow whiteness. One's appearance of being white will still operate to confer privilege in numerous and significant ways, and to avow treason does not render whites ineligible for these privileges, even if they work hard to avoid them. In one essay for the journal, Edward H. Peeples recounts a small incident that happened to him at a Richmond newsstand in 1976. When he went to purchase an African American newspaper, the white cashier looked at him and explained "You don't want this newspaper; its the colored newspaper." Peeples responded, loudly enough for others in the shop to hear, "You must think I'm white." He explains what happened next.

> [The cashier] was startled. But within seconds she came to realize that these simple words represented a profound act of racial sedition. I had betrayed her precious "white race". . . . The cashier became furious. But she was clearly at a loss of what to do with this Judas. (Quoted in Ignatiev and Garvey 1996, 82)

I do not doubt that such an act in the South *is* a profound sedition. But such a practice could not completely eliminate the operation of white privilege, for the reasons already stated. And some "treasonous" whites, with white privilege still largely in place, might then feel entitled to disengage with whiteness without feeling any link of responsibility for white racist atrocities of the past; or they might consider a declaration that they are "not white" as a sufficient solution to racism without the trouble of organizing or collective action. This position would then end up uncomfortably similar to the "colorblindness" attitude that pretends ignorance about one's own white identity and refuses responsibility.

These worries relate to another feature I found in *Race Traitor*, the tendency to emphasize that most whites have not committed racist violence (see, for example, 16-17). The authors have developed a rhetorical strategy intended to promote a disassociation or disidentification between whites (especially the working class) and racist institutions; to say, in effect, "this is not really *your* history, so why defend it?" On the one hand, this strategy is based on a more accurate telling of Southern history than I myself received in grade school: I was never told that there were a significant number of white deserters and dissenters during the Civil War. Among whites in the South, it was commonly said during the civil rights movement that the only whites who crossed lines of racial solidarity and supported the "rabble-rousers" like Dr. Martin Luther King were Northerners (Yankees!), and Jewish to boot. An accurate revision of white history would be enlightening and encouraging to whites with anti-racist tendencies.

Yet there is a danger in the strategy of disassociating white workers from past racist violence: some white workers *did* participate in such violence. It is notoriously difficult to tell how many, given the secretive nature of Ku Klux Klan activity. Judging from the documented public announcements and celebrations of lynching, as when W. E. B. DuBois sorrowfully describes passing a severed black finger displayed for the public while he was on his way to work in Atlanta, we have to conclude that, like the German population during the Nazi regime, white working-class people in the South and elsewhere largely knew about the atrocities and largely approved of them.

Shortly before he died, I discovered that my own grandfather had participated in Klan violence in his youth. He was a semiliterate sharecropper who lived poor and died poor, sneered at by the rich folks he worked for; but I also believe that his sense of white superiority must have helped to produce the self-confidence it took for him to go back to school as an adult and learn to read, write, and do enough arithmetic to improve his job skills. Therefore, although I believe, like Ignatiev and Garvey, that an argument can be constructed that it is actually not in poor whites' overall economic interest to maintain racism (certainly, taking more than one generation into account), I think these authors sidestep the issue of moral culpability and its relation to social identity. Ignatiev writes "It is our faith . . . that the majority of so-called whites in this country are neither deeply nor consciously committed to white supremacy; like most human beings in most times and places, they would do the right thing if it were convenient" (12). But white supremacy may be deeply held *because* it is not conscious. If the collective structures of identity formation that are necessary to create a positive sense of self—a self that is capable of being loved—require racism, then only the creation of new structures of identity formation can redress this balance. Racism appears to be deeply sedimented into white psyches in a process that is newly reenforced each day.

Thus, the issue of convenience unfortunately misses the point. In regard to clearly identified racist acts of commission that require conscious intent, Ignatiev may be right. But this notion can coexist with the idea that white people's sense of who they are in the world, especially in this country, depends deeply on white supremacy. And this dependence may often operate precisely because they are themselves oppressed; that is, because their immigrant relations were a humble lot without other cultural resources from which to draw a sense of entitlement. White supremacy may be all that poor whites have to hold on to in order to maintain a sense of self-love. The very genealogy of whiteness was entwined from the beginning with a racial hierarchy, which can be found in every major cultural narrative from Christopher Columbus to Manifest Destiny to the Space Race and the Computer Revolution. Staying in the vanguard is quite often inconvenient; it requires war and great sacrifice to remain "ahead." But it is pursued evertheless, precisely because it is necessary for the possibility of self-love. So here is the predicament: we *must* tell the full story of white racism in all its complexity, and this complexity cannot be fully resolved through a class analysis that sequesters the guilty as only among the rich. Yet facing the reality of whites' moral culpability threatens their very ability to be moral today, because it threatens their ability to imagine them-selves as having a socially coherent relation to a past and a future toward which anyone could feel an attachment.

Race Traitor's attention to crossover culture may be motivated by this concern, in the hope that a "mixed" cultural identity could replace whiteness and thereby avoid its moral legacy. Paradoxically, although its contributors criticize all variants of multiculturalism because, among other reasons, it tends to talk about oppression without naming any oppressors, *Race Traitor* is very optimistic about white crossover. The editors recognize that "the willingness to borrow from black culture does not equal race treason" (3). Yet they interpret the increase in white crossover as signaling the fracturing of white supremacy. Phil Rubio even claims that "white cultural assimilation . . . is already a form of political awareness" (in Ignatiev and Garvey 1996, 161).

This position has elicited skepticism from some readers of color, whose critiques the journal has printed. Salim Washington and Paul Garon both have expressed concern that examples of race traitors are being romanticized. Washington points out that black artists continue to "suffer through dimin-ished access to and control of the means of cultural production" (Ignatiev and Garvey 1996, 166). Merely to appreciate and acknowledge black influences in dominant culture does nothing to remedy this. Garon similarly stresses that the usual economic effects of crossover are that white performers are enriched and black performers have even less chance to make a living. Garon also challenges the view (not necessarily held by Rubio) that no essential musical integrity is lost when white performers play the blues. Context affects the meaning imparted, and in Garon's view, race is a salient feature of musical context.

This issue illuminates the difficulties of white transformation. When does the transcendence of cultural chauvinism merge into cultural appropriation? Especially in a consumer society, the core of white privilege is the ability to consume anything, anyone, anywhere. The desire to crossover itself is coter-minous with a colonizing desire of appropriation, even to the trappings of social identity.

Contemporary music does model, at times, an exemplary globalism, in which borrowings are so rapid and multidirectional that the concepts of "origin" and "identity," as well as "private property," are quickly losing their intelligibility. This does not mean that the culture industry transcends the racial hierarchies of existing political economies; hybridity in cultural forms does not entail a corresponding distribution of economic success. However, in trying to overcome unfair distributions of financial resources or access to cultural production, it is unrealistic to propose a voluntary self-segregation or, for example, that whites stick to white music. Hybridity, and therefore cross-over, is an unstoppable force. Racism has not, on the whole, slowed cultural hybridization. This means that cultural hybridization is not a sufficient cause or even a necessary indicator of antiracism.

To analyze the political implications of crossover culture, it might be helpful to use Sartre's analysis of the Look and its role in social relations. According to Sartre, in the Look of the Other we perceive the Other's subjective con-sciousness—that is, the Other's interior life similar to our own. We also perceive our being-for-others, or the value and meaning we have in the eyes of the Other. As Lewis Gordon has recently argued in his interesting book *Bad Faith and Antiblack Racism*, white racism is generally predicated on the need and desire of whites to deflect the Look of the Black Other, a Look that will reveal guilt, accusation, and moral deficiency (Gordon 1995, especially chapter 14). If racism is the attempt to deflect a Black Look, then what is crossover?

Sartre, who was famously pessimistic about the egalitarian potential of human relations, presented two options that can be taken toward the Other. The first involves an attempt to transcend the Other's transcendence, or negate the Other's own freedom, especially the freedom to judge and value. This mode is characteristic of hate and sadism. The other mode involves the attempt to incorporate the transcendence of the Other; that is, to have the Other's love, but freely of the Other's own choosing. This is the paradox of love: we want the Other to love us in a way that is absolute, unchanging, and reliable, but we want this love to be freely given without coercion. Thus we want the love to be simultaneously noncontingent and contingent. Sartre characterizes this as the desire to incorporate the Other's freedom *within me*, such that my needs and desires are still at the center and the Other exists only as a portion of my arranged world without real autonomy.

White attempts to appropriate black culture may fall into this category, as a strategy that does not seek to deflect the Black Look or repress it into blank submission but instead seeks to incorporate the Black Look within oneself. In other words, attempts by whites to assimilate wholly to blackness may be motivated by the desire to make the Black Look—or Black subjectivity, which is what the Look signifies—safely internal and thus nonthreatening to the self. The recognition of an irreducible difference, a difference that crossover tries to overcome, would maintain the Other's own point of departure, the Other's own space of autonomous judgment, and thus the possibility for a truly reciprocal recognition of full subjectivity.

Such an analysis does not require a wholesale rejection of crossover, but counsels a careful scrutiny of crossover postures that would seek to erase difference. An example of such a posture would be one that Garon criticizes, the view that the blues are a transracial, universally accessible cultural form. It may be that the denial of the black specificity of blues, with the argument that suffering is available across race is motivated by unease about what expressions of *black* suffering especially signify for white listeners. Universal suffering is nonaccusatory; black suffering is implicitly accusatory, just by making reference to black history. Thus, to incorporate the blues as a cultural form that is proper to American experience without a racial specificity helpfully deflects the potential meaning for whites of a blues identified as black. This does not entail that white antiracists should never sing the blues, or that they cannot develop new forms of the blues, but that the blackness of the blues, or at least of its cultural genesis, should not be dismissed as irrelevant.

NEW TRADITIONS IN MISSISSIPPI

If the main problem with Katz's *White Awareness* is a lack of social and historical context or class analysis, *Race Traitor* provides class analysis without sufficient attention to cultural processes of identity formation. The final white antiracist example I will discuss is more consciously situated in a particular context and aimed at transforming white self-understanding.

The conclusions of Ruth Frankenburg's ethnographic study of white women suggest that whiteness is an invisible racial identity to whites (Frankenberg 1993). Katz similarly argues that the first task of antiracism is for whites to come to understand that they are white. But where I grew up, whiteness was a substantive racial identity whose political privileges were well known and mostly considered justified. The cultural substance of whiteness consisted in such elements as putting peanuts in your R.C. Cola and souping up your car engine. There was a recognizably white way to dance, get drunk, and sing in church. Ethnic differences among whites were subordinated to the all-important racial identification that secured one's place in a segregated society. Because Southern whiteness has had a high degree of racial self-consciousness, then, it should be an instructive location at which to observe attempts at antiracist transformation.

About ten years ago, the University of Mississippi decided to go proactive against racism, as well as sexism, by instituting a mandatory course for all freshmen. Michael L. Harrington, chair of the Philosophy Department, was asked to design a suitable course. Harrington called the course University Studies 101, taught it himself for a number of years, and developed a textbook that continues to be used. Harrington is a white Southerner who both knows the mindset of white Mississippians very well and has fought racism in the South and at the University of Mississippi since the 1960s. Being asked to design this course was just the sort of chance he had been waiting for.

The University of Mississippi, or "Ole Miss," as it is affectionately called, is one of the most racist institutions in the South. It has played key roles in defending the Confederacy, fighting Reconstruction, and maintaining segregation. In 1963, it took more than thirty thousand federal troops to enforce the admission of Ole Miss's first African American student, James Meredith. White residents of Oxford, the town that Bob Dylan memorialized, came to campus armed and organized when the court order was issued to admit Meredith, and several journalists and soldiers were killed before the rioting was over. Even after this, the university administration continued actively to oppose integration. It took another ten years before faculty could speak up in favor of integration without losing their jobs. Still, to this day, Ole Miss keeps its reputation across the South as a school where whites can go and be openly racist, as I remember vividly from a conversation I had with the Homecoming Queen in my high school in Florida who decided to attend college there. At Ole Miss, rebel flags wave at sports events and hang from dormitory windows; the university band plays "Dixie" as a fight song.[6] For obvious reasons, then, in a state in which African Americans make up nearly half the population, the black student body at Ole Miss is still under 10 per cent. In this environment, to teach against racism in a mandatory course was surely to engage the struggle in the belly of the beast.

Harrington's strategy was to envelop an antiracist and antisexist message in a course ostensibly organized around the topic of university life, what a university is, and what an intellectual community needs in order to flourish. In this way, the message could be framed as a series of do's rather than don'ts. For example, maintaining a university with high standards is in every student's interest; to protect and develop such a university, students need to value and respect cultural diversity and gender equality. The university traditions of intellectual diversity and academic freedom require sufficient tolerance of diversity so that critical debate can develop. The textbook for the course, *Traditions and Changes: The University of Mississippi in Principle and in Practice*, thus presents three full chapters before the subject of racism is broached. Both the textbook and the course, then, are as strategically thought out and organized as the workshops in *White Awareness* and as carefully directed in their goal of producing lasting changes in the thinking and behavior of whites.

Harrington did not shy away from providing an accurate history of racism at Ole Miss, although the text acknowledges the pain these accounts invoke. He gives and assesses the entire history of the institution, so that students have the historical facts concerning the university's legacy of support for white supremacy. Harrington provides a revised narrative of U.S. history and Southern history as well, but here he adopts a two-sided approach. U.S. cultural and political traditions are argued to have a dual character, on the one hand institutionalizing inequality and on the other hand valuing and slowly extending equality. The overall argument is that there *is* something positive from the past to draw from, but it is a potential not yet fully realized. White Mississippians will benefit overall from developing a cooperative spirit with black Mississippians in order to advance common goals, but this can come about only through fully acknowledging and overcoming racism. Harrington hopefully declares that from the "disaster of the human spirit in Mississippi" arises "the opportunity for a phoenix redemption" (Harrington 1996, 141). The significant diversity of the state can be a rich resource from which to build a stronger society that is a "shining symbol to a nation and to a world battling the same demons we can exorcize" (141).

Traditions and Changes has significant limitations. It offers no class analysis, nor does it explore any issues of reparation or redistribution of economic resources. The projection of a shared interest glosses over real class disparities that are likely to continue to be disproportionately distributed between whites and blacks, even though many whites are also poor in the state. This is, however, a course for freshmen at the University of Mississippi and its task is to move students from an initial starting position that is comparatively low.

It is interesting to note the different strategies offered here and in *Race Traitor*. The latter makes its appeal to whites by arguing that racist practices really served only the interests of the rich, and thus that poor whites were used as dupes to support racism. Although this strategy supplies a needed class analysis of the history of racism, it does not help whites think about how to overcome their own connection to a racist past. It simply says, "you are not really connected to that racist past." But in the South, white culture has been more widely supportive of racist practices like segregation and discrimination and racist symbols, such as the Rebel flag and "Dixie." Whites gain other benefits besides economic ones from racism, such as a collective sense of superiority and entitlement. Reductive arguments that portray these as merely bourgeois scams cannot make sense of the complicated realities.

In relation to this issue, it is interesting that both *Race Traitor* and *Traditions and Changes* reject multiculturalism. Harrington defines multiculturalism as the premise that "all cultural differences are equal in value," contrasting it with cultural diversity which promotes "tolerance for cultural differences, leaving open the question of which are desirable or superior" (1996, 38). In Mississippi, an antiracist cannot argue for the equal rights of diverse cultural traditions without undercutting the ability to argue against continued veneration of the Rebel flag.

Thus, despite its limitations, I found *Traditions and Changes* to provide a helpful model for acknowledging white complicity in racism and the need to repudiate key aspects of white identity within an overall project that seeks to develop a collective transformation toward a nonracist white identity. Utilizing the positive traditions of critical, open, and democratic reflection, University Studies 101 and its textbook aim to create a series of open-ended discussions that will get white students to contribute in transforming their university, their community, and in the process, themselves.

WHITE DOUBLE CONSCIOUSNESS

I have wanted to suggest that there is an ongoing but rarely named struggle among whites as a result of liberation movements and the declining plausibility of white supremacist narratives. Antiracist theorists need to acknowledge that the struggle occurs not only in relation to conscious choices and objectively determinable economic interests but in relation to psychic processes of identity formation, which means that rational arguments against racism will not be sufficient to make a progressive move. As whites lose their psychic social status, and as processes of positive identity construction are derailed, intense anxiety, hysteria, and depression can result. The most likely solution to this will be, of course, for new processes to develop that simply shift targets to create new categories of the abject through which to inflate collective self-esteem, and this is already happening in revivals of nativism, the vilification of illegal immigrants, a state-sponsored homophobia, and so on.

Such developments may prompt the question: why maintain white identity at all, given that any group identity will be based on exclusion and an implicit superiority? Should we not move beyond race categories? I doubt that this can be done anytime soon. The weight of too much history is sedimented in these marked bodies with inscriptions that are very deep. Rather than attempting to erase these inscriptions as a first step, we need a period of reinscription to redescribe and reunderstand what we see when we see race. Paul Gilroy's study *The Black Atlantic: Modernity and Double Consciousness* traces outlines of an identity configuration of a multinational black culture that does not seem to rely on an objectification (or abjectification) process involving repudiation of the Other (Gilroy 1993). His characterization of black Atlantic identity portrays it as working more through an invocation of a shared past and shared present cultural forms than through a shared discrete set of substantive or essential Afrocentric elements that require contrasting, excluded alternatives. Daniel and Jonathan Boyarin have done similar work in relation to Jewish identity, invoking a "diaspora identity" that is not based on exclusion or identity borders (Boyarin and Boyarin 1995). However, both the Boyarins and Gilroy understand such identities as relying heavily on a shared history, which is precisely what is problematic for whites. The attempt to emphasize the genuinely positive moments of that past and to see only those moments as representative of the true core of whiteness is too obviously implausible, as well as susceptible to becoming part of a rewriting of the supremacist or vanguard narrative once again.

Perhaps white identity needs to develop its own version of "double consciousness"; indeed, to name as such that two-sided sense of the past and the future that can be found in aspects of the works discussed in this essay. White double consciousness is not the move between white and black subjectivities or black and American perspectives, as DuBois developed the notion. Instead, for whites, double consciousness requires an everpresent acknowledgment of the historical legacy of white identity constructions in the persistent structures of inequality and exploitation, as well as a newly awakened memory of the many white traitors to white privilege who have struggled to contribute to the building of an inclusive human community. The Michelangelos stand beside the Christopher Columbuses, and Noam Chomskys next to the Pat Buchanans. The legacy of European-based cultures is a complicated one. It is better approached through a two-sided analysis than an argument that obscures either its positive or negative aspects. White representations within multiculturalism must then be similarly dialectical, retrieving from obscurity the history of white antiracism even while providing a detailed account of colonialism and its many cultural effects. This, then, is the challenge: to transform the basis of collective self-respect from global, racial vanguardism to a dedicated commitment to end racism.

NOTES

1. For balanced critiques of the movie, see Bird 1996. The movie champions one group of Indians by demonizing another group in traditional one-dimensional fashion. It replays a "going native" transformative narrative in which Europeans shed their enculturated deformities to return to an original nobility, in which native peoples are mere instruments toward this end.

2. For an excellent antidote to this, see Ramos 1995.

3. For more on my own identity, see Alcoff 1995.

4. For a critique of the way racism survives in these movies, see Wiegman 1995, esp. chap. 4.

5. For a recently published case, see D'Orso 1996. This tells the story of the town massacre also chronicled in John Singleton's film *Rosewood* 1997. See also Jordan 1968; Gossett 1965; Hudson 1972; Acuna 1988; and Mills 1997.

6. As this essay goes to press, the playing of Dixie at sports events is being challenged and may soon end at the University of Mississippi.

REFERENCES

Acuna, Rodolfo. 1988. *Occupied America: A history of Chicanos.* 3rd ed. New York: HarperCollins.

Alcoff, Linda. 1995. *Mestizo* identity. In *American mixed race: The culture of microdiversity,* ed. Naomi Zack. Lanham, MD: Rowman and Littlefield.

Alcoff, Linda Martín. 1996. Philosophy and racial identity. *Radical Philosophy* 75 (January-February): 5-14.

Baldwin, James. 1988. A talk to teachers. In *The Graywolf annual 5: Multi-cultural literacy,* ed. Rick Simonson and Scott Walker. Saint Paul, MN: Graywolf Press.

Bird, Elizabeth S., ed. 1996. *Dressing in feathers: The construction of the Indian in American popular culture.* Boulder, CO: Westview Press.

Boyarin, Daniel, and Jonathan Boyarin. 1995. Diaspora: Generation and the ground of Jewish identity. In *Identities,* ed. Kwame Anthony Appiah and Henry Louis Gates. Chicago: University of Chicago Press.

Daly, Mary. 1978. *Gyn/Ecology: The metaethics of radical feminism.* Boston: Beacon Press.

D'Orso, Michael. 1996. *Like judgment day: The ruin and redemption of a town called Rosewood.* New York: Berkley Publishing Co.

Firestone, Shulamith. 1970. *The dialectic of sex.* New York: William Morrow.

Frankenberg, Ruth. 1993. *White women, race matters: The social construction of whiteness.* Minneapolis: University of Minnesota Press.

Frye, Marilyn. 1983. *The politics of reality: Essays in feminist theory.* Trumansburg, NY: Crossing Press.

———. 1992. *Willful virgin: Essays in feminism.* Freedom, CA: Crossing Press.

Gallagher, Charles. 1994. White reconstruction in the university. *Socialist Review* 94(1 and 2): 165-88.

Gilroy, Paul. 1993. *The black Atlantic: Modernity and double consciousness.* Cambridge: Harvard University Press.

Gooding-Williams, Robert. 1995. Comments on Anthony Appiah's *In my father's house.* Paper presented at the American Philosophical Association Central Division Meetings, Chicago, April.

Gordon, Lewis. 1995. *Bad faith and antiblack racism.* Atlantic Highlands, NJ: Humanities Press.

Gossett, Thomas F. 1965. *Race: The history of an idea in America.* New York: Schocken.

Harrington, Michael L. 1996. *Traditions and changes: The University of Mississippi in principle and in practice.* 2d ed. New York: McGraw-Hill.

Hudson, Hosea. 1972. *Black worker in the deep South: A personal record.* New York: International Publishers.

Ignatiev, Noel and John Garvey. 1996. *Race traitor.* New York: Routledge.

Jordan, Winthrop. 1968. *White over black: American attitudes toward the Negro 1550-1812.* Baltimore: Penguin Books.

Joseph, Gloria. 1981. The incompatible menage à trois: Marxism, feminism, and racism. In *Women and revolution,* ed. Lydia Sargent. Boston: South End Press.

Katz, Judith. 1978. *White awareness: Handbook for anti-racism training.* Norman: University of Oklahoma Press.

Mills, Charles. 1997. *The racial contract.* Ithaca: Cornell University Press.

Ramos, Juanita. 1995. Latin American lesbians speak on black identity—Violeta Garro, Minerva Rosa Pérez, Digna, Magdalena C., Juanita. In *Moving beyond boundaries, Volume 2: Black women's diasporas,* ed. Carole Boyce Davies. New York: New York University Press.

Rich, Adrienne. 1979. Disloyal to civilization: Feminism, racism, gynephobia. In *On lies, secrets, and silence.* New York: W. W. Norton.

Simons, Margaret A. 1979. Racism and feminism: A schism in the sisterhood. *Feminist Studies* 5(2)(Summer): 384-401.

Taylor, Paul. 1996. A new Negro: Pragmatism and black identity. Unpublished ms.

Wiegman, Robyn. 1995. *American anatomies: Theorizing race and gender.* Durham: Duke University Press.

16

Locating Traitorous Identities:
Toward a View of Privilege-Cognizant
White Character

ALISON BAILEY

I address the problem of how to locate "traitorous" subjects, or those who belong to dominant groups yet resist the usual assumptions and practices of those groups. I argue that Sandra Harding's description of traitors as insiders, who "become marginal" is misleading. Crafting a distinction between "privilege-cognizant" and "privilege-evasive" white scripts, I offer an alternative account of race traitors as privilege-cognizant whites who refuse to animate expected whitely scripts, and who are unfaithful to worldviews whites are expected to hold.

I had begun to feel pretty irregularly white. Klan folks had a word for it: *race traitor*. Driving in and out of counties with heavy Klan activity, I kept my eye on the rear-view mirror, and any time a truck with a confederate flag passed me, the hair on the back of my neck would rise. . . . I was in daily, intimate exposure to the cruel, killing effects of racism, which my Black friends spoke of in the same way that they commented on the weather, an equally constant factor in their lives. . . . I began to feel more uneasy around other whites and more at ease around people of color. . . . Maybe whiteness was more about consciousness than color? That scared me, too, the possibility of being caught between the worlds of race, white people kicking me out, people of color not letting me in.
(Mab Segrest, *Memoir of a Race Traitor*, 1994, 80)

Recent scholarship in multicultural, postcolonial, and global feminisms has motivated a reanalysis of both feminist and mainstream philosophical texts, methodologies, concepts, and frameworks. One project springing from these new approaches is a literature critical of white identities. At present, white identity is constituted by and benefits from injustice. Transformative work demands that whites explore how to rearticulate our identities in ways that do not depend on the subordination of people of color.

This paper addresses a simple but troublesome puzzle: the problem of how to describe and understand the location of those who belong to dominant groups yet resist the usual assumptions and orientations of those groups. The discussion begins against the background of three archetypes of knowers: the disembodied spectator, the outsider within, and the traitor. It sets out Sandra Harding's (1991) account of traitorous identities. Then, it takes issue with her portrayal of traitors as insiders, who as a result of a shift in the way they understand the world, "become marginal." I argue that Harding's description is misleading and that it fails to capture her intended meaning. The paper offers an alternative characterization of traitors that is less prone to misinterpretation. Crafting a distinction between "privilege-cognizant" and "privilege-evasive" white scripts, I characterize race traitors as privilege-cognizant whites who refuse to animate the scripts whites are expected to perform, and who are unfaithful to worldviews whites are expected to hold. Finally, the paper develops the notion of traitorous scripts and explains how animating them helps to cultivate a traitorous character. Using Aristotle's view of character formation (1980) and María Lugones's (1987) concept of "world" traveling, I briefly sketch what it might mean to have a traitorous character.

Disembodied Spectators, Outsiders Within, and Traitors

Feminist epistemologists have long been attentive to the relationship between knowing subjects' locations and their understandings of the world. Dissatisfaction with Enlightenment accounts of knowing subjects as faceless, disembodied spectators who hover over the Cartesian landscape has led feminist theorists to consider knowers as embodied subjects situated in politically identifiable social locations or contexts. Attention to knowers as socially situated creates a new angle of vision that allows us to consider the alternative epistemic resources these situated subjects offer. Patricia Hill Collins (1990) and Sandra Harding (1991), whose writings represent the variety of feminist standpoint theory I have in mind here, prefer this approach because it is attentive to the social and political structures, symbolic systems, and discourse that grant privilege to some groups at the expense of others.

If the archetypal knower in Cartesian epistemic dramas is the disembodied spectator, then the starring role in feminist standpoint theory is played by the outsider within. Collins's description of Black female domestics offers a clear illustration of this second archetype (Collins 1986, s14-s15; also 1990, 11-13). As outsiders within, Black women working as domestics have an unclouded view of the contradictions between the actions and ideologies of white families. This unique angle of vision is rooted in the contradictory location of the domestic, who is at once a worker, "privy to the most intimate secrets of white society," and a Black woman exploited by and excluded from privileges granted by white patriarchal rule. Her "Blackness makes her a perpetual outsider," but her work of caring for white women "allows her an insider's view of some of the contradictions between white women thinking that they are running their lives and the actual source of power in white patriarchal households" (Collins 1990, 11-12).

Outsiders within are thought to have an advantageous epistemic viewpoint that offers a more complete account of the world than insider or outsider perspectives alone. Their contradictory location gives rise to what W. E. B. DuBois refers to as a "double-consciousness," a sense of being able to see themselves through their own eyes and through the eyes of others (DuBois 1994, 2). Extending Collins's analysis, Harding argues that women scientists, African American women sociologists, or lesbian literary critics doing intellectual work in the predominantly white, heterosexual male academy also have "identities [that] appear to defy logic, for 'who we are' is in at least two places at once: outside and within, margin and center" (Harding 1991, 275). As strangers to the social order of the academy, they bring a unique combination of nearness and remoteness to their subject matter that helps to maximize objectivity (Harding 1991, 124).

Because insiders have few incentives or opportunities to cultivate a bifurcated consciousness, their identities are understood as obstacles to producing reliable accounts of the world. For example, class privilege makes it a challenge for those with money to understand why moving out of poverty is so difficult; the privilege afforded to white people by racism makes it hard for whites to grasp its pervasiveness. Similarly, heterosexuals are rarely in a position to analyze either heterosexual privilege or institutional and personal homophobia.[1]

For all of the social benefits afforded to insiders, some members of these dominant groups resist the assumptions most of their fellow insiders take for granted. Feminist standpoint theory has been less attentive to such subject positions than to disembodied spectators and outsiders within. However, in the final chapters of *Whose Science? Whose Knowledge?* (1991), Harding makes a compelling case for expanding the insights of standpoint theory to consider how traitorous identities might serve as sites for liberatory knowledge. Reaching deeper into the logic of standpoint theory she explains:

> One can begin to detect other identities for knowers . . . standing in the shadows behind the ones [identities] on which feminist and other liberatory thought has focused, identities that are struggling to emerge as respected and legitimate pro-

ducers of illuminating analyses. From the perspective of the
fiercely fought struggles to claim legitimacy for the
marginalized identities, these identities appear to be monstrous:
male feminists; whites against racism . . . heterosexuals against
heterosexism; economically overadvantaged people against
class exploitation. (Harding 1991, 274)

Harding's discovery suggests that insiders are not, by virtue of their social
location, immune to understanding the viewpoints and experiences of
marginalized groups. Anti-racist whites do criticize white privilege, and feminist men do resist gender roles that reinforce women's oppression. So, "People
who do not have marginalized identities can nevertheless learn from and learn
to use the knowledge generated from the perspective of outsiders within"
(Harding 1991, 277). Those who do are said to have "traitorous identities" and
to occupy "traitorous social locations" (Harding 1991, 288-96).

Harding observes a significant epistemic difference between how insiders
who are "critically reflective" of their privilege, and insiders who are oblivious
to privilege, understand the world. Traitors do not experience the world in the
same way outsiders within experience it, but outsider-within political analyses
do inform their politics. Outsider-within standpoints provide tools for members of dominant groups who may be unable to articulate or clarify the
occluded nature of their privilege and its relation to the oppression experienced by outsiders. By learning about lives on the margins, members of
dominant groups come to discover the nature of oppression, the extent of their
privileges, and the relations between them. Making visible the nature of
privilege, enables members of dominant groups to generate liberatory knowledge. Being white, male, wealthy, or heterosexual presents a challenge in
generating this knowledge, but is not an insurmountable obstacle.

Knowledge emerging from outsider-within locations, then, is valuable on
two counts. First, it calls attention to the experiences of marginalized groups
overlooked by earlier epistemological projects. Second, those who occupy the
center can learn from and learn to use the knowledge generated by the analyses
of outsiders within to understand their relationships with marginalized persons
from the standpoint of those persons' lives (Collins 1986, s29; Harding 1991,
277). Harding describes insiders who adopt a critically reflective stance toward
privilege as "becoming marginal." But I think this phrase leads to a misunder-
standing about what it means to be a traitor.

IN WHAT SENSE DO TRAITORS "BECOME MARGINAL"?

Describing subject identities in spatial terms initially offers a useful way of
seeing social structures and imagining the power relations between knowers.
In the margin-center cartography of feminist standpoint theory, traitors are

described as people who "choose to become marginalized" (Harding 1991, 289, 295). But this description is misleading for several reasons. The problem with describing traitors as becoming marginal is more clearly understood if we keep an historical example in mind.

In 1954, Anne and Carl Braden purchased a home in a white section of Louisville, Kentucky, for the purpose of deeding it to Charlotte and Andrew Wade, a Black couple. Andrew Wade, a politically conscious member of the Progressive Party and a World War II veteran, was furious that, even with his service record, he could not purchase the home he wanted. The Bradens, a progressive couple who opposed segregation, agreed to buy the house and deed it to the Wades. Their choice to break with the unspoken practice that middle-class whites sell their homes only to other whites ostracized (marginalized?) them in a way that other white families, who followed expected house-selling practices, were not. After the transaction, Louisville's segregationists publicly denounced the Bradens as "traitors to [the] race." They argued that the Bradens ought to have known better than to transgress the unspoken rule that the races ought to live in separate communities (Braden 1958, 82). Within hours of the title transfer, the Bradens received threatening phone calls and bomb threats. Months later they were charged with attempting to overthrow the government of the Commonwealth of Kentucky. In what sense then, could the Bradens be said to have chosen to become marginal? In her memoir, Anne Braden explains how, in the events that followed the house purchase, "some of the protections that go with white skin in our society fell from Carl and me. To an extent, at least, we were thrown into the world of abuse where Negroes always live" (Braden 1958, 7).

Braden's choice of words here suggests that the couple's subject position changed in some sense, but it also presents two problems. First, at a glance, to describe the Bradens as having become marginal makes it sound as if the Bradens actually came to occupy outsider-within subject positions like those occupied by the Wades. Deeding the house to the Wades did cause the Bradens to lose privilege in their community, so it might be said that they became marginal in the sense that they were ostracized from the white community because of their actions. But being cast out does not amount to the same thing as being situated as an outsider within. Given the wrath of segregationist whites, the Bradens' subject position might be said to have shifted in relation to white citizens who saw them as race traitors. However, because they were white in the eyes of those who did not know them, they did not completely lose their privilege. In spite of their actions, the Bradens continued to bear a socially privileged racial identity; the Wades never had this privilege. Whites who engage in traitorous challenges to segregation may undergo some shift in their subject position in the sense that they may be ostracized from certain communities, but they do not exchange their status as insiders for outsider-within status.

Harding anticipates this confusion and clarifies her position using the example of privilege-cognizant heterosexuals.

> Some people whose sexual identity was not "marginal" (in the sense that they were heterosexual) have "become marginal"— not by giving up their heterosexuality but by giving up the spontaneous consciousness created by their heterosexual experience in a heterosexist world. These people do not think "as lesbians," for they are not lesbian. But they do think as heterosexual persons who have learned from lesbian analyses. (Harding 1991, 289)

Although the Bradens did not live as Black families in segregated Louisville lived, they could understand, even if incompletely, what it might be like to live in Louisville as the Wades lived in it. It is precisely this understanding that Harding thinks the narratives and analyses generated by persons of color can foster.

Thus, Harding's intended meaning here is that it is possible for people like the Bradens to learn about the world of segregated Louisville as the Wades experienced it without actually coming to inhabit that world as do those who are marginal. Describing the Bradens as "becoming marginal" best describes a shift in their way of seeing, understanding, and moving through the world. Part of the reason for this confusion is that the words "margin" and "center" are usually used in standpoint theory to describe subject locations, and here they are being used to describe an epistemic shift. "Becoming marginal" refers to the shift from a perspective to a standpoint. The first is the product of an unreflective account of one's subject location; the second, as the word "anti-racist" indicates, is a political position achieved through collective struggle (Harding 1991, 123-27; Jaggar 1983, 317).

Harding's intended meaning of "becoming marginal" should now be clearer. However, even if we understand "becoming marginal" to refer to an epistemic shift, I would argue that this phrase does not really capture the meaning of the traitorous standpoint Harding finds so compelling. Describing traitors as "becoming marginal" encourages a blurring or conflating of the location of the outsiders within and the location of traitors. The description makes it sound as if traitors have a foot in each world and are caught equally between them, and this picture does not foreground white privilege. If, for the moment, we retain the language of standpoint theory, it is more accurate to describe the Bradens' actions as destabilizing the center. Race traitors are subjects who occupy the center but whose way of seeing (at least by insider standards) is *off-center*. That is, traitors destabilize their insider status by challenging and resisting the usual assumptions held by most white people (such as the belief that white privilege is earned, inevitable, or natural). Descriptions of traitors as decentering, subverting, or destabilizing the center arguably work better than "becoming marginal" because they do not encourage this conflation of the outsider within and the traitor. Decentering the center makes it clear that traitors and outsiders within have a common political interest in challenging white privilege, but that they do so from different social locations. Understanding traitors as destabilizers tidies up earlier misunderstandings, but I still think standpoint theory's margin-center cartography tends to restrict Harding's description of these subjects. If this language encourages misperceptions about traitors, then we need to consider alternative descriptions of these disloyal subjects.

PRIVILEGE-COGNIZANT AND PRIVILEGE-EVASIVE WHITE SCRIPTS

Perhaps a clearer, more descriptive picture of traitors, one that focuses on their decentering projects, will emerge if we think of traitors as privileged subjects who animate privilege-cognizant white scripts. The distinction Harding observes between insiders who are critical of their position and insiders who are not is more accurately expressed as a distinction between "privilege-cognizant" and "privilege-evasive" white scripts (Frankenberg 1993, 137-91). Understanding traitors along these lines requires spelling out what is meant by a racial script and how privilege-cognizant and privilege-evasive white scripts differ.

Like sexism, racism is a social-political system of domination that comes with expected performances, attitudes, and behaviors, which reinforce and reinscribe unjust hierarchies. Feminists have long paid attention to the ways gender roles encourage habits and nurture systems that value men's ideas, activities, and achievements over those of women. The existence of sexism and racism as systems requires everyone's daily collaboration.

To understand the nature of this collaboration, it is helpful to think of the attitudes and behaviors expected of one's particular racial group as performances that follow historically preestablished scripts. Scripts differ with a subject's location within systems of domination. What it means to be a man or a woman is not exclusively defined by one's physical characteristics. Similarly, what it means to be Black, white, Comanche, Korean, or Latina is defined not only by a person's physical appearance (so-called "racial" markers such as skin color, hair, facial features, body shape), but also by that person's performance— by the script that individual animates. When the concept of racial scripts is applied locally, what it means to be a white woman in Louisville, or an African American man in Chicago includes a person's gestures, language, attitudes, concept of personal space, gut reactions to certain phenomena, and body awareness. Attention to race as performative, or scripted, reveals the less visible, structural regulatory function of racial scripts that exclusive attention to appearance overlooks.

Marilyn Frye's (1992) discussion of "whitely" behavior and "whiteliness" offers a conceptual distinction that is instrumental in understanding the performative dimensions of race and the distinction between privilege-evasive and privilege-cognizant scripts. Frye recognizes the need for a terminology that captures the contingency between phenotype (racial appearance) and the value of whiteness. Paralleling the distinction feminists make between *maleness*, something persons are born with by virtue of their biological sex, and *masculinity*, something socially connected to maleness but largely the result of social training, Frye argues for an analogous pair of terms in racial discourse and coins "whitely" and "whiteliness" as the racial equivalents of maleness and masculinity, respectively. As Frye explains: "Being white skinned (like being male) is a matter of physical traits presumed to be physically determined: being whitely (like being masculine) I conceive as a deeply ingrained way of being in the world" (Frye 1992, 150-51). The connection between "acting white" and "looking white" is contingent, so it is possible for persons who are not classified as white to perform in whitely ways and for persons who are white not to perform in whitely ways. Racial scripts are internalized at an early age to the point where they are embedded almost to invisibility in our language, bodily reactions, feelings, behaviors, and judgments. Whitely scripts are, no doubt, mediated by a person's economic class, ethnicity, sexuality, gender, religion, and geographical location, but privilege is granted on the basis of whitely performances nevertheless (Davion 1995, 135-39). A few examples can highlight some facets of whitely, or privilege-evasive scripts.

Lillian Smith, a white woman growing up in Jim Crow Georgia, offers one illustration of a whitely script. She was taught to "[act] out a special private production of a little script that is written on the lives of most Southern children before they know words" (1949, 21).

> I do not remember how or when, but. . . . I knew that I was better than a Negro, that all black folks have their place and must be kept in it, that sex has its place and must be kept in it, that a terrifying disaster would befall the South if ever I treated a Negro as my social equal and as terrifying a disaster would befall my family if ever I were to have a baby outside of marriage. . . . I had learned that white southerners are hospitable, courteous, tactful people who treat those of their own group with consideration and who carefully segregate from all the richness of life "for their own good and welfare" thirteen million people whose skin is colored a little differently from my own. (Smith 1949, 18)

Smith describes this script as a "dance that cripples the human spirit." It was a dance she repeated until the movements "were made for the rest of [her] life without thinking" (Smith 1949, 91). What I find remarkable about Smith's "little script" is the clarity with which she connects racial segregation and the control of white women's sexuality.

Anne Braden recounts a similar script growing up in Alabama and Mississippi in the 1930s. Braden's description is especially attentive to the spatial dimensions of racial scripts.

> Most of these things, it is true, were never said in words. They were impressed on the mind of the white child of the South's privileged class. . . .
>
> It was a chant of . . . we sit in the downstairs of the theater, Negroes sit upstairs in the balcony—you drink from this fountain, Negroes use that fountain—we eat in the dining room, Negroes eat in the kitchen—colored town, our streets—white schools, colored schools—be careful of Negro men on the streets—watch out—be careful—don't go near colored town after dark—you sit on the front of the bus, they sit in the back—your place, their place—your world, their world. (Braden 1958, 21)

Braden also acknowledges an interesting linguistic facet of whitely scripts.

> Sometimes the commandments became quite explicit. For example, I could not have been more than four or five years old when one day I happened to say something to my mother about a "colored lady." "You never call colored people ladies [her mother replied]. . . . You say colored woman and white lady— never a colored lady." (Braden 1958, 21)

Attentiveness to maintaining the boundaries of one's racial location, then, is a strong dimension of all racial scripts.

Racial scripts are not regulated only by attitudes and an awareness of people's appropriate place; scripts also have a strong corporeal element that emerges in gestures and reactions to persons who we think of as being unlike ourselves. We are all, on some level, attentive to the race of persons with whom we interact, and this shapes our encounters. Even privilege-cognizant whites who are consciously committed to combating racism may react with aversion and avoidance toward people of color. African Americans receiving these avoidance behaviors feel noticed—marked. In his essay "A Black Man Ponders His Power to Alter Public Space," Brent Staples (1986) offers the following account of a white women who passes him on the street at night.

> I often witness the "hunch posture," from women after dark on the warrenlike streets of Brooklyn, where I live. They seem to set their faces on neutral and, with their purse straps strung across their chests bandoleer style, they forge ahead as though

> bracing themselves against being tackled. I understand, of
> course, that. . . . women are particularly vulnerable to street
> violence, and young black males are drastically over-
> represented among the perpetrators of violence. Yet these
> truths are no solace against the kind of alienation that comes
> of being ever the suspect, against being set apart, a fearsome
> entity with whom pedestrians avoid making eye contact.
> (Staples 1986, 54)

The majority of whitely scripts include being nervous around people of color, avoiding eye contact with them, or adopting closed, uncomfortable postures in their presence. The repeated animation of these scripts, however, reinscribes a racial order in which white lives, culture, and experiences are valued at the expense of the lives of persons of color, whose bodies are fearsome to whites and are who are cast as deviant, dirty, criminal, ugly, or degenerate.

These accounts of privilege-evasive scripts provide a contrast to my account of privilege-cognizant scripts; they also help to explain why privilege-cognizant scripts count as traitorous. What all racial scripts have in common is that in a white-centered culture, everyone is more or less expected to follow scripts that sustain white privilege. The whitely scripts described by Smith, Staples, and Braden are privilege-evasive: they do not challenge whites to think about privilege, and their reenactment reproduces white privilege. If scripts sustaining white privilege are required by members of all racial groups, then members of both privileged and oppressed groups can refuse to cooperate. What holds racism in place, metaphorically speaking, is not only that African Americans have sat in the back of the bus for so long, but also that whites have avoided the task of critically examining and giving up their seats in front. By refusing to examine privilege, whites uncritically resign themselves to whitely scripts— to having their identities shaped in ways they may not have chosen (Harding 1991, 294).

Recognizing that whites can use the analyses of outsiders within to forge traitorous scripts means we can learn to think and act not out of the "spontaneous consciousness" of the socially scripted locations that history has written for us, but out of the traitorous (privilege-cognizant) scripts we choose with the assistance of critical social theories generated by emancipatory movements (Harding 1991, 295). A key feature of privilege-cognizant standpoints is the choice to develop a critically reflective consciousness. As one participant in Ruth Frankenberg's study of white women observes "coming from the white privileged class . . . means you don't have to look at anything else. You are never forced to until you choose to, because your life is so unaffected by anything like racism" (Frankenberg 1993, 161). Traitors *choose* to try to understand the price at which privileges are gained; they are critical of the unearned privileges granted to them by white patriarchal cultures, and they take responsibility for them.

Choosing to take responsibility for my interactions requires that I take responsibility for my "racial social location, by learning how I am connected to other whites and persons of color; by learning what the consequences of my beliefs and behaviors as a European American woman will be" (Harding 1991, 283). An integral moment in understanding my relation to people differently situated from me comes in learning to see how I am seen by outsiders. It requires a variation on DuBois's double consciousness.

Unlike whites who unreflectively animate whitely scripts, the traitor's task is to find ways to develop alternative scripts capable of disrupting the constant reinscription of whitely scripts. Privilege-cognizant whites actively examine their "seats in front" and find ways to be disloyal to systems that assign these seats. Some obvious examples include choosing to stop racist jokes, paying attention to body language and conversation patterns, and cultivating an awareness of how stereotypes shape perceptions of people of color. Telling, and permitting others to tell, racist jokes reinscribes images that are harmful. The traitor knows when it is appropriate to stop this reinscription. Similarly, the white woman who clutches her bags or steers her children away from African American youth, or the white man who acts uncomfortable or nervous in the presence of people of color, sends signals to those around him that members of these groups are to be feared. Whites who interrupt, ostracize, or dismiss the contributions of students of color in the classroom reproduce their invisibility by sending the message that these students' contributions are unimportant. If traitors can rearticulate white scripts in ways that do not reinscribe these subordinating gestures, then we can begin to imagine ways of being, as Adrienne Rich (1979) says, "disloyal to civilization."

The language of racial scripts presents an account of traitors that avoids the misunderstandings generated by standpoint theory's margin-center cartography. It also offers a dynamic account of traitors that is consistent with the epistemic framework of standpoint theory. This distinction between privilege-cognizant and privilege-evasive scripts is another way of articulating the distinction standpoint theorists make between a standpoint and a perspective. Privilege-evasive white scripts might be said to have unreflective perspectives on race. For example, most liberal discourse on racism illustrates a form of linguistic privilege-evasiveness characteristic of the whitely scripts. Phrases such as "I don't see color, I just see people," or "We all belong to the same race—the human race" erase color, which also amounts to a failure to recognize whiteness (Frankenberg 1993, 149). Privilege-cognizant scripts rely on anti-racist standpoints because they come about through collective resistance to naturalized patterns of behavior and social actions that reproduce white privilege. Animating a privilege-cognizant script requires more than occasionally interrupting racist jokes, listening to people of color, or selling Black families real estate in white neighborhoods. An occasional traitorous act does not a traitor make. Truly animating a privilege-cognizant white script requires that traitors cultivate a character from which traitorous practices will flow.

CULTIVATING A TRAITOROUS CHARACTER

When traitors refuse to act out of the spontaneous whitely consciousness that history has bestowed on them, they shift more than just their way of seeing and understanding the world. To be a race traitor is to have a particular kind of character that predisposes a person to animate privilege-cognizant scripts. The shift from privilege-evasive to privilege-cognizant white scripts, then, can be understood as a shift in character. It is this change in character that causes whites to move "off-center," to reposition themselves with regard to privilege. This final section briefly explores what it might mean to cultivate a traitorous character and demonstrates why developing a traitorous character must include being a "world traveler."

The idea that animating privilege-cognizant scripts helps to cultivate a traitorous character, and that traitorous characters are more likely to animate these scripts is, at root, Aristotelian: becoming traitorous is a process similar to the acquisition of moral virtue (Aristotle 1980). For Aristotle, virtues arise through habit, not nature. Virtue is a disposition to choose according to a rule; namely, the rule by which a truly virtuous person possessed of moral insight would choose. All things that come to us by nature we first acquire potentially; it is only later that we exhibit the activity. We become virtuous by doing virtuous deeds. Although states of character arise from activity, Aristotle makes a distinction between two sorts of activities and their ends. There are activities such as shipbuilding, in which the product of one's activity (the ship) is an end distinct from the process of shipbuilding; and, there are activities such as getting in shape where the product (a healthy and fit body) is part of the activity of working out and not a distinct end. The activity of virtue resembles the workout example. Just as a person does not become fit by doing a series of situps and then declaring, "There, I am fit!" so a person does not become virtuous by doing a series of good deeds and then declaring, "Finally, I am virtuous!" Virtue and fitness arise in the process of continually working out or doing good deeds. We become virtuous when we have the practical wisdom, for example, to act courageously to the right degree, for the right reasons, and under the right circumstances.

When Harding describes standpoints as achievements, I think she means "achievement" in the sense in which having a virtuous character is an achievement (Harding 1991, 127). Achieving a traitorous standpoint, like cultivating virtue, is a process. When a person has the practical wisdom to know which lines in whitely scripts to change, when to change them, and when to leave them alone, then they can be said to possess the practical wisdom necessary for a traitorous character.[2] Having a traitorous character is not the same thing as possessing a particular trait. Just as there is no recipe for attaining a virtuous character, there is no one formula for becoming a race traitor. It is a mistake to think that becoming traitorous is tantamount to completely overcoming racism. There will be times when our traitorous practical wisdom will be a bit off and we will fall back into privilege-evasive scripts, often without being aware that we are doing so. An account of traitorous character recognizes this instability. Developing a traitorous character requires a political strategy. It is not enough, as Harding says, to repeat what African American thinkers say, and never to take responsibility for my own analyses of the world that I, a European American, can see through the lens of their insights. A "functioning anti-racist—one who can pass the 'competency test' as an anti-racist—must be an actively thinking anti-racist, not just a white robot programmed to repeat what Blacks say" (Harding 1991, 290-91).

Developing a traitorous character requires lots of legwork. Learning about the lives of those on the margins means understanding the material conditions that give rise to outsider-within analyses; and to gain such an understanding, traitors must be "world travelers." In her now-classic essay, "Playfulness, 'World'-Traveling, and Loving Perception" (1987), María Lugones offers an account of identity in which subjects are shifting and multiplicitous. Recognizing identities as plural takes place through a process she calls "world" traveling.[3] Lugones believes that women's failure to love one another stems from a failure to identify with women who inhabit worlds they do not share; it is a failure to see oneself in other women who are different. Lugones's work addresses this failure, which she attributes to seeing others, who occupy worlds outside the ones in which we feel comfortable, with "arrogant eyes." When white women perceive Asian women with "arrogant eyes," or when African American women view Jewish women with arrogant perception, they fail to interact and identify with one another lovingly. Because arrogance blocks coalition building, world traveling must be done with loving perception.

The notions of "world," "world-traveling," and "loving perception" help Lugones to explain why she is perceived as serious in Anglo, or white, worlds where she is not at ease, and as "playful" in Latina worlds where she is at home. The failure of white women to love women of color is implicit in whitely scripts in which Anglo women "ignore us, ostracize us, render us invisible, stereotype us, leave us completely alone, interpret us as crazy. All of this *while we are in their midst*" (Lugones 1987, 7).

The privilege-evasive scripts animated by white women are easily explained in the logic of world travel. The failure of whites to see race privilege is, in part, a function of a failure to world travel. In the United States, people of color world travel out of necessity, but white privilege ensures that most whites need to world travel only voluntarily. When Anglo women refuse to travel to worlds where they are ill at ease, they are animating privilege-evasive scripts. Most whites are at ease in white worlds where we are fluent speakers, where we know and can safely animate whitely scripts, where people of color are out of our line of vision, and where our racial identity is not at risk. When I restrict my movement to worlds in which I am comfortable, privilege is difficult to see, and whitely scripts are never challenged. Loving perception requires that white women world travel as a way of becoming aware of the privilege-evasive scripts we have learned.

World travel, then, is an indispensable strategy for cultivating a traitorous character. Traitors must get out of those locations and texts in which they feel at home. World travel forces us to put our privileged identities at risk by traveling to worlds where we often feel ill at ease or off-center. Like virtuousness, traitorousness requires developing new habits; and one crucial habit might be to resist the temptation to retreat back to those worlds where we feel at ease—whole. In the process of traveling, our identities fall apart, our privilege-evasive scripts no longer work, and the luxury of retreating to a safe space is temporarily removed. Travel makes privilege-evasive scripts visible and we get a glimpse of how we are seen through the eyes of those whom we have been taught to perceive arrogantly.

Mab Segrest's story is a moving illustration of how world travel is integral to coalition building across boundaries of race, gender, class, and sexual orientation. As a white lesbian doing civil rights work in North Carolina, Segrest explains how "with Reverend Lee and Christina in my first months at Statesville, I crossed and recrossed more racial boundaries than I had ever managed in the eighteen years I had lived in my similar Alabama hometown. With them, I had access to the Black community, and I saw white people through their eyes" (Segrest 1994, 17). Learning to see ourselves as others see us is a necessary starting point for learning to undo privilege-evasive scripts. Whites like Segrest, who, with "loving perception," travel to the worlds inhabited by African American civil rights activists in the South, put their identities at risk and, in so doing, realize the difficulties surrounding the process of unlearning privilege-evasive scripts.

The approach I have outlined here is not a radical break from Harding's original insight. What I have tried to do is to rearticulate her insights in a language that avoids some of the confusion I think the margin-center cartography of feminist standpoint theory encourages. I have also tried to explore what it might be like to cultivate a traitorous character in a way that focuses on traitorous performances, rather than on traitorous identities and locations. The idea that traitorousness requires developing a traitorous character that makes one more likely to animate a privilege-cognizant script is very much in the spirit of Harding's work. Although Harding's descriptions of traitors as "becoming marginal" through a process of "reinventing oneself as other" limits her descriptions of traitors, I think what she is after is an active account of traitorousness as more than just a political identity. Recall that "reinventing ourselves as other" refers to a shift in one's way of seeing, and Lugones's sense of world travel certainly does this. Harding hints at this when she says "intellectual and political *activity* are required in using another's insights to generate one's own analyses" (Harding 1991, 290). Harding's description of traitorousness as political activity is closer to the performative notion I have in mind, and I think it is one with which she would agree.

NOTES

This paper is the product of many conversations I had during a National Endowment for the Humanities summer seminar on feminist epistemologies, June-July 1996, Eugene, Oregon. I would like to thank Drue Barker, Lisa Heldke, Sarah Hoagland, Amber Katherine, Shelly Park, and Nancy Tuana for their thoughts on this topic during our time together. I would also like to thank the editors of this volume for their comments on earlier drafts of this essay.

1. As standpoint theory focuses on institutional systems, practices, and discourses that unequally distribute power, the word privilege is used to refer to systematically conferred advantages individuals enjoy by virtue of their membership in dominant groups with access to resources and institutional power that are beyond the common advantages of marginalized citizens (Bailey 1998).

2. Traitorous acts committed just for the sake of traitorousness can be dangerous. History and literature are filled with cases of well-meaning whites whose good intentions put the lives, jobs, or achievements of friends and acquaintances of color in jeopardy. See, e.g., the fictional case of Bigger Thomas in Richard Wright's novel *Native Son* (Wright 1940).

3. For those unfamiliar with Lugones's work, "worlds" are neither utopias nor constructions of whole societies. They may be small parts of a society (e.g., a barrio in Chicago, Chinatown, a lesbian bar, a women's studies class, or a farmworkers community). The shift from having one attribute, say playfulness, in a world where one is at ease, to having another attribute, say seriousness, in another world Lugones calls "travel" (Lugones 1987).

REFERENCES

Aristotle. 1980. *Nichomachean ethics.* Translated by W. D. Ross. New York: Oxford University Press.

Bailey, Alison. N.d. Privilege: Expanding on Marilyn Frye's "oppression." *Journal of Social Philosophy.*

Braden, Anne. 1958. *The wall between.* New York: Monthly Review Press.

Collins, Patricia Hill. 1986. Learning from the outsider within: The sociological significance of black feminist thought. *Social problems* 33(6): s14-s32.

———. 1990. *Black feminist thought: Knowledge consciousness and the politics of empowerment.* New York: Routledge.

Davion, Victoria. 1995. Reflections on the meaning of white. In *Overcoming racism and sexism*, ed. Linda Bell and David Blumenfeld. Lanham, MD: Roman and Littlefield.

DuBois, W. E. B. 1994 [1903]. *The souls of black folk*. Mineloa, NY: Dover.

Frankenburg, Ruth. 1993. *White women, race matters: The social construction of whiteness*. Minneapolis: University of Minnesota Press.

Frye, Marilyn. 1992. White woman feminist. In *Willful virgin: Essays in feminist theory*. Freedom, CA: Crossing Press.

Harding, Sandra. 1991. *Whose science? whose knowledge?: Thinking from women's lives*. Ithaca: Cornell University Press.

Jaggar, Alison. 1983. *Feminist politics and human nature*. Totowa, NJ: Rowman and Allanheld.

Lugones, María. 1987. Playfulness, "world"-traveling, and loving perception. *Hypatia* 2(2): 3-21.

Rich, Adrienne. 1979. Disloyal to civilization: Feminism, racism, and gynophobia. In *On lies, secrets, and silences*. New York: W. W. Norton.

Segrest, Mab. 1994. *Memoir of a race traitor*. Boston: South End Press.

Smith, Lillian. 1949. *Killers of the dream*. New York: W. W. Norton.

Staples, Brent. 1986. Just walk on by: A black man ponders his power to alter public space. *Ms.* 15(3): 54, 86.

Wright, Richard. 1940. *Native son*. New York: Harper and Brothers.

17

Multiculturalism as a Cognitive Virtue of Scientific Practice

ANN E. CUDD

I argue that science will be better, by its own criteria, if it pursues multiculturalism, by which I mean an ethnic- and gender-diverse set of scientists. I argue that minority and women scientists will be more likely to recognize false, prejudiced assumptions about race and gender that infect theories. And the kinds of changes that society will undergo in pursuing multiculturalism will help reveal these faulty assumptions to scientists of all races and genders.

Despite nearly two decades of pathbreaking feminist epistemological research and writing and almost as many years of work on postcolonial and racial critiques of science, the mainstream of philosophical literature has yet to absorb the lessons of this work. I find this especially disappointing because of the inroads made by the social epistemology movement, which now seems to have entered the mainstream of philosophy of science and epistemology. Mainstream philosophers require not merely good arguments but good reasons, stated in their terms, and using their traditions. And being the mainstream, they are able to demand that. In this paper, I shall argue for the lessons of the feminists and marginalized others in the language of the mainstream, making the arguments from the traditions of analytic philosophy. In particular, the lesson I intend to impart is that the dominance of white male Westerners in science impoverishes science on its own terms, and that the inclusion of excluded others will improve the content and the very objectivity of science. In short, multiculturalism is a cognitive virtue (not to mention a requirement of justice) for science.

FOUNDATIONS DENIED

Foundationalism in the theory of knowledge is the idea that there are some first principles that can be established to be beyond doubt, and that on them we can justify whatever we are able to call knowledge. Foundationalists oppose skepticism about our knowledge of the external world, but different foundationalists disagree about the source of that ultimate knowledge. However, many agree that our foundational knowledge must come to us as lone thinkers and perceivers; we cannot look to society for justification of the knowledge, even if it is in society that we first learn or discover what we come to know. Rene Descartes, in the first of his *Meditations on First Philosophy*, writes that after becoming aware of all the false opinions he had held from his youth, "I realized that for once I had to raze everything in my life, down to the very bottom, so as to begin again from the first foundations, if I wanted to establish anything firm and lasting in the sciences. . . . I have secured for myself some leisurely and carefree time, I withdraw in solitude. I will, in short apply myself earnestly and openly to the general destruction of my former opinions" (Descartes 1980, 57). For Descartes, this project of finding the first foundations of science must be done in solitude because it requires clear thought, unbiased by the ideas or beliefs of others. He needs to wipe his mind clean of the traditional beliefs of his society; what can be known can be discovered by the lone thinker without prejudice from social influence.

Foundationalism of one sort or another has had a long run in epistemology. It is fair to say that it was the going view in much of Western philosophy for nearly three hundred years after Descartes. There is good reason for this: if we can have a firm foundation for our knowledge, then we can justify our beliefs one by one, knowing that justification entails that those beliefs are true, where "truth" is absolute, independent of all observers, for all time. But in the last forty years the foundations have crumbled, and antifoundationalist theories have taken their place in contemporary epistemology. Some of these theories suggest that what we really ought to be doing in epistemology is cognitive psychology: we need to get clear on how our brains gather and sort information, create theories, and decide on evidence.[1] This approach is naturalized epistemology. Other antifoundationalist theories suggest that epistemology ought to study how persons transmit knowledge within and across cultures, how experts in knowledge production are created, why some forms of systematic information do not count as knowledge, and what standards of objectivity, rationality, and good method are still useful. This approach is sometimes called social constructivism. Finally, a third group of antifoundationalist theories suggests that what we call epistemology is really ideology, that there is no such thing as objective knowledge, and that the word "knowledge" is simply an honorific for the pronouncements of those in power. This is postmodernism. In this paper I shall argue for a conservative version of social constructivism, and shall show that it is a consequence of the social constructivist position that multiculturalism does indeed have something to offer to science on science's own cognitive terms.

To begin, we need to survey the rise and fall of foundationalism in the twentieth century. The most important foundationalist theory in epistemology and the philosophy of science in the first half of this century was logical empiricism, or logical positivism. The logical empiricists held that the foundation of our knowledge is to be found in perceptual experience, and that our perceptual experience can be rigorously analyzed so as to clear away any dubitable or biased elements. Because the method simply requires attention to observation and adherence to a rigorous, logical method of analysis, it can be employed by a lone thinker. And because the methods of analysis are logical, and hence universal, they are untouched by social, cultural, or moral values. The empiricist theory of perceptual knowledge is phenomenalism; that is, the idea that physical objects are mental (logical) constructions out of sense data. C. I. Lewis held that perceptual experience has two elements: the given and the concept. The given is the noninferential, experiential element of knowledge—the raw data. The concept consists of the judgments we make from this raw data.

To illustrate the difference, imagine a tennis ball. The given element is that part of perception that forces itself on us, that is there for the perceiver who has never experienced tennis or tennis balls, as well as for you and me. The "given" must exist, Lewis claimed, or our perceptual experience would be "contentless and arbitrary" (Lewis 1929, 39). The concept is the judgment "there is a tennis ball." It is also the judgment "there is something solid, spherical, fuzzy, and yellow-green." The concept is equally important, for, Lewis writes, "if there be no interpretation or construction which the mind itself imposes, then thought is rendered superfluous, the possibility of error becomes inexplicable, and the distinction of true and false is in danger of becoming meaningless" (Lewis 1929, 39). While the concept can vary among different perceivers, the given, because it is given by the objects themselves, cannot vary, though we can fail to be attentive to it in all its detail.

A. J. Ayer, in his 1940 book *Foundations of Empirical Knowledge*, also held a phenomenalist view of perception but, unlike Lewis, was reluctant to try to separate the given from the concept. To talk of the given, he argued, leads us to conflate the perceived and the perceiving; that is, the material thing and the sense-datum. Instead, he proposed to keep these distinct by means of a specialized language. This "sense-datum language" is the language of appearances, which describes the perception as it appears to the observer. Looking at the tennis ball, you might say, in sense-datum-ese, "I am having a sensation of a round, yellow-green, fuzzy patch in my visual field." Sense-datum language does not posit the existence of things that correspond to our perceptions, but refers only to that experience that the observer is actually having. Thus "in the domain of sense-data whatever appears is real" (Ayer 1971 [1940], 123). For Ayer, the issue of how to interpret perceptual experience is a matter of language, not a matter of fact.

Rudolf Carnap, in his 1928 book *The Logical Construction of the World* (hereafter LCW), attempted to present a method for logically grounding scientific theories in perceptual data. He contended that legitimate scientific talk can be reduced to talk about experiences and logical constructions out of experiences, and that each of us can do it for ourselves, provided we have a detailed enough description of the logical interconnections given by the scientific theory. The fundamental unit of confirmation of scientific theories is the "protocol sentence," which is a phenomenalistic description of the observer's experience. Carnap proposed a way of reducing scientific theories to their confirming protocol sentences. To test a theory, a scientist was to deduce from the theory a set of observations that would appear to an observer given a certain set of initial conditions. If the observer could affirm the protocol sentences, then the theory was confirmed to some degree. Thus the truth of a theory could be determined, at least to some degree, by its empirical adequacy. Later Carnap replaced the phenomenalistic language with physical descriptions of definite, quantitative, space-time points. He considered this language better because it provided a unique description for all the senses and all observers. But it is important to see that these physical descriptions are just as *given* as the phenomenalistic descriptions they replaced; only the form of the description has changed.

These foundational theories were constructed to interpret and rationally reconstruct scientific theories. They draw a distinction between the context of discovery, the processes by which individual scientists happen upon their hypotheses, and the context of justification, the empirical and logical method of confirming or disconfirming theories. Justification, but not discovery, is philosophically fathomable. With this distinction these foundationalists claim that science can and should be value-free; that moral and social values are not to play a role in the justification of scientific theories.

The foundational theories of science and perceptual knowledge met serious difficulties around midcentury with the work of Wilfrid Sellars and W. V. O. Quine. Sellars, in his 1956 paper "Empiricism and the Philosophy of Mind," showed that the idea of the given element in experience was a myth. The problem he recognized with givenness can be explained by the following argument. First, it is clear that one thing cannot be at once inferential and noninferential knowledge, by the law of the excluded middle. The set of noninferential "raw data," which is what we are supposed to receive without conceptualizing, cannot itself give rise to inferences, because it is not yet categorized and therefore not linguistic.[2] The inferential element in perception is the part of the sense-data that is laden with judgment. While we can draw inferences from it, it already is theorized information, not pure data. Thus either the given is noninferential, in which case it cannot give rise to *justified* knowledge; or it is inferential, in which case it cannot be pure, indubitable, *foundational* knowledge. Either way, this argument shows that phenomenalism cannot lead us to foundations in empirical knowledge. Furthermore, it suggests that there can be no pure sense-data that are untainted by our own prejudgments; and hence that those prejudgments become interesting subjects of epistemological inquiry in themselves. Appeal to "looks talk" (as in, "this tie looks green") or sense-datum language is of no help here, according to Sellars, because to say that an object looks green, one first has to master the claim that the object is green under some set of standard viewing conditions, and to know how to withhold endorsement of that claim when one is not certain whether the conditions are standard. That is, one has first to assume that the gap between sense-data and objects themselves is, in principle, a bridgeable gap, which is just what Sellars's argument denies.

Quine, in his 1953 paper "Two Dogmas of Empiricism," presents another catastrophic argument for empirical foundationalism. The two dogmas to which the title refers are, first, the idea that there is a sharp, and non-theory dependent distinction to be drawn between analytic and synthetic statements; that is, that there are two different kinds of sentences, one that is made true or false by the meanings of the words alone (what Ayer called a matter of language), and the other whose truth conditions depend on empirical facts (Ayer's matter of fact). The second dogma is reductionism, the idea that physical theories can be reduced to observation sentences and analytically connected bridge principles that connect the observation reports to theoretical entities and laws. This is just Carnap's project in LCW.

It seems reasonable to suppose that there is a component of language and a component of fact involved in determining the truth of sentences, and that therefore there should be a continuum of the amount of each in different sentences and thus some sentences in which the factual component is null. Quine, however, showed that there is no neat, nonquestion-begging way of drawing the distinction. He showed this by considering exhaustively the possibilities for defining analyticity and related notions, ultimately showing that they are all defined in relation to each other, and that in order to define any one of them we have to assume an understanding of at least some of the others. Thus he concluded that the analytic-synthetic distinction is a metaphysical article of faith.

The kind of reductionism at issue for Quine is the view that every statement can be translated into a statement about immediate experience. By the time Quine was writing, Carnap had given up phenomenalism in favor of physicalism, using as his basic protocol sentences sentences of the form "Quality q is at x,y,z;t," where x;y;z;t defined a point in space-time. Quine then showed that the reductionist program of Carnap and others requires an undefined element that cannot be eliminated. In the example, the phrase *is at* had to be the undefined primitive that indicated the givenness of the location. Quine argued that the ultimate problem with reductionism is that it assumes that each sentence in isolation can be confirmed or disconfirmed. In contrast, Quine proposed a holistic view of confirmation of science that has come to be known as the Duhem-Quine thesis: "Our statements about the external world face the tribunal of sense experience not individually but only as a corporate body" (Quine 1980, [1953] 41).

The two dogmas are closely connected. Quine even claims that they are "at root identical," because they both depend on the idea that the truth of a statement is completely analyzable into a factual and a linguistic component. (As we have noted, Ayer traded on this analysis.) Reductionism concerns the truth conditions of the factual component; analyticity the linguistic component. In both cases, the mistake stems from the idea that the unit of empirical significance is the statement or the term, when actually it is the whole of experience. Thus, when we confront an experience that contradicts our beliefs or our theories, we have many possible options: we can reject the belief or theory, or we may readjust some of our other beliefs to account for the anomalous experience. Once we accept holism, however, we come to see that the truth of theories is not uniquely determined by their empirical adequacy. Sense data come to us already informed by our theories and not as raw data, and we reinterpret experience in light of our whole belief system. Therefore, no one experience by itself counts against or for a theory without all sorts of other background assumptions. Given enough readjustments in our belief system, we can retain any theory in light of any experience. This means that our theories are underdetermined by the empirical evidence we have for them. We need to bring other values to bear in judging our scientific theories, values such as internal consistency, simplicity, and coherence with other beliefs and values.

Thus the history of epistemology in the first half of the twentieth century was marked by a great optimism for empirical foundationalism grounded in a logical analysis of language and theories, and by a subsequent rejection of that foundationalism. The resulting holism or pragmatism left epistemologists to search for new criteria of adequacy for theories or knowledge claims. Unless one can hold that the data reveal the hypotheses themselves, there is an epistemological gap between the evidence from the data and the hypotheses. This gap is filled by background assumptions, including values, some of which, like the theoretical values of simplicity and coherence, are more or less consciously held by scientists, and some of which lie hidden from them.

EPISTEMOLOGY WITHOUT FOUNDATIONS: SOCIAL CONSTRUCTIVISM

The demise of empirical foundationalism leaves philosophers with the task of formulating new approaches to belief formation and justification. But the distinctions between the process of belief formation, the context of discovery, and the context of justification now blur. Justification cannot be viewed as a logical pursuit, free from the context of the scientists, for their culturally shaped background assumptions help determine how they gather and interpret evidence and assess theories. That is to say, justification comes to be much like belief formation, and therefore subject to the same contingent and value-laden motivations and background assumptions as the context of discovery.

Postpositivist philosophy of science has therefore focused much more on the process of discovery and the practices of theory testing and analysis, trying to locate in these practices some identifying feature of the activity. Postfoundationalist epistemology tries to justify confidence in that activity as a source of knowledge. One important postfoundationalist epistemology that I shall defend is social constructivism. This is the thesis that knowledge is essentially a social construction; that knowledge production is governed by a set of social norms that are justified within a community of knowers but that cannot be justified outside of all social norms or communities. Knowledge, then, is relativized to the society in which it is produced and sanctioned. But social constructivism does not give up the idea that knowledge production can be objective. Helen Longino, in her book *Science as Social Knowledge* (1990), presents a version of a philosophy of science that would correspond to a conservative reading of social constructivism with what she calls *contextualist empiricism*.

Contextual empiricists hold that the relation between theory and evidence contains a logical gap. Evidence for a theory does not come with a label that explains what the data are or what they show; to believe otherwise is to fall prey to the myth of the given. To interpret data as evidence for or against a particular theory requires some background assumptions. For example, I come home around five o'clock, put my bicycle in the barn, and see three other bikes there. From this I reason that my partner must be home. Three bikes in a barn does not naturally mean he is home; I infer this because I have a particular set of background beliefs: that he goes places with his bike, that he does not have the habit of going for a walk alone in the evening before I get home, that if he were doing something unusual this evening he would have told me about it, and so forth. Now if I had slightly different beliefs, I might have inferred some other hypothesis; for example that he had not ridden his bike to work that day. The logical gap between data and evidence and between evidence and theory is filled by such background assumptions. In addition, our interests guide us toward certain questions and issues. I might have inferred from the three bikes in the barn something about the number three, about the absence of bike thieves in the neighborhood, or about the amount of space left in the barn for other outdoor equipment. But I was not interested in these things; I was interested at the time only in whom I might find in my house. These background assumptions and interests which determine how data are relevant for us, are not, even in principle, specifiable in complete detail.[3]

What sorts of things count as background assumptions? The psychological answer is that anything goes—political values, moral values, prejudices, causal beliefs, warranted and unwarranted assumptions of all sorts. There is no limit. The kinds of things that the positivists thought were influences only in the context of discovery turn out to play a role in the crucial justificatory practices of finding evidence and testing theories. Epistemologists are not usually primarily interested in the psychological answer, though. They want to know what the legitimate influences are.

The background beliefs that come into play cannot all be transparent to the investigator or her peers. This is because not all of our beliefs are transparent to us, and any of them can play a role. It is difficult to give examples of current scientific theories that contain such hidden beliefs, because if I can name them they are not very hidden anymore. But we have many historical examples. Take chemists in the seventeenth century. One of their background beliefs (of which they were not aware) was that anything we could see had to be a substance. Flames had to be substances; and so they posited phlogiston. Because of the unavoidable influences of background beliefs that are invisible to the scientist, scientific knowledge is relative to the beliefs of the scientific community, which are in turn influenced by the larger community.

This is a problem if we think that the goal of science is to ascertain the truth in a correspondence theory sense of truth. The contextualist empiricist takes the internal goal of science as to extend its explanatory theories to wider arrays of phenomena, and to be coherent with what the community takes to be the known facts. Science is characterized by an attempt to interpret empirical phenomena through experimental testing or similar confrontations with data. While truth may not be ascertainable, it can become clear when personal preferences or social biases lead to false, incoherent theories. So science must also aim to clear out personal preferences and pernicious prejudices that hinder its pursuit of coherent, fruitful, empirical explanation.

Science, in the contextualist view, is an essentially social activity in at least three senses.[4] First, it is the product of many people working together, and of different groups of people repeating, criticizing, and amending each other's theories. John Hardwig has pointed out that many experiments in physics now require dozens of collaborating scientists, no one of whom can understand entirely the details of the experiments or the conclusions reached from them (Hardwig 1991). They are essentially group projects, as is their acceptance and understanding by scientists. Second, scientists undergo a common educational process. They are trained in the same canon of examples and solutions; they share the same literature, beliefs, and epistemic values. Furthermore, they are typically socialized into the same or similar culture, and so share a set of background cultural interests and values. Third, in an obvious and political sense science is social because it depends on the support of the larger society for funding. This is much truer today than it was in previous centuries, since it has become so much more technology dependent and therefore expensive. Science is supported by government, industry, and to a lesser extent, private philanthropy. Large groups of people spend significant amounts of time deciding what are useful proposals for investigation, and so what questions will be asked, what experiments will be run, what field observations will be made, what techniques will be perfected, and when a research program has run its course. Both the background assumptions and the interests of scientists are socially generated, and socially expressed through funding decisions.

Given these social features of scientific enterprise, plus the general agreement that science funding is a public good and that science plays such a critical role in the development of society, justice clearly requires that as a society we offer equal opportunity to persons of all races and genders to create and influence the direction of science. My project here, though, is to show that multiculturalism has cognitive benefits for science. I argue that science will be better off, by its own internal goals, if society pursues a policy of multiculturalism within science and a policy of race and gender equality in the society as a whole. While positivists could agree that justice requires society to pursue policies that diversify the population of scientists, they would disagree that this has anything to do with the epistemic goals of science. To see how the contextual empiricist justifies the claim that it does, we now need to examine further the character of science.

The empirical foundationalists believed that objectivity was guaranteed by adhering to strict standards of rigorous hypothesis testing by evidence. If a theory were a false description of reality, an anomalous experiment sooner or later would reveal that. All the scientist had to do was to design experiments that would expose the truth would and to be open to interpreting the data correctly. In the contextual empiricists view, there is no such neat relationship between theory and evidence; instead, the social character of science can make it objective. Because they concede that knowledge is relative sociologically or historically, contextual empiricists do not therefore concede that scientific knowledge is subjective, or that anyone's beliefs are as good as anyone else's. To see this, we need to focus on knowledge formation processes, or the practices of scientific investigation.

By practices, I mean everything from the education of graduate students to the laboratory and field procedures of peer scientists, to the funding decisions of peer reviewers. The first thing to notice is that the social character of science makes it public knowledge in two senses. First, its theoretical assumptions, methods, and even background assumptions are available to anyone who undertakes the same training and immersion in science. Second, its evidence and explanations may be subjected to review and criticism by all who have this training and background. The same things cannot be said of mystical or emotional experiences, which are clearly subjective experiences. Science is self-critical; it proceeds by critical review of hypotheses and of the relevance of evidence to the hypotheses. In the latter way, especially, background assumptions are revealed and questioned and sometimes modified.

Longino uses a poignant example from the history of physics to illustrate this questioning of background assumptions and the consequent progress of science. Before Einstein's relativity theory took hold, physicists believed that light was propagated through a medium called the "ether." (They believed that all waves had to be propagated in some medium.) The Michelson-Morley experiment was supposed to measure the relative motion of the earth in the ether by the difference in the speed of light beams sent out at 90 degrees from each other. That difference could be inferred from the shifts in the interference fringe the beams produced on an interferometer. However, no significant displacement of the interference fringe took place. Some physicists interpreted this null result as a confirmation of the Lorentz-Fitzgerald contraction hypothesis. By criticizing the background assumption of the existence of the ether, however, relativity theorists were able to abandon that assumption and make a significant advance in physical theory. Science often progresses in this way by challenging the background assumptions that an experiment was not originally intended to test (Longino 1990, chaps. 3-4). These challenges come often not from the scientist who develops the experiment but from others, who can see the underlying background assumptions but do not share them. The point is that the objective character of science comes from its practice of public, intersubjective, critical review. But how can scientists critically assess their collective assumptions to root out personal preference and pernicious prejudices that hinder progress in the sciences when these preferences and prejudices are themselves socially influenced and maintained?

PERSPECTIVES OF THE OPPRESSED

Longino explains well how background assumptions sometimes need to be rejected to move forward toward a better, more coherent, more fruitful explanatory theory. In her book, she argues that culturally based prejudices against women have led scientists to make assumptions, for example, of universal male dominance, which not only turn out to be false on direct examination but also to cause to misinterpretation of data and the construction of bad theories. Still, this does not tell us how generally we can influence science to discover its hidden assumptions that are based on social prejudice.

Sandra Harding's notion of strong objectivity helps here. She claims that the main problem with the positivist notion of objectivity, which she terms "objectivism," is that it fails to recognize that when science or other knowledge-producing institutions are practiced by only a privileged section of society, they will overlook the same observations and problems with the theories that the practitioners would tend not to notice. The result is not only bad science, but also further oppression and mystification of what knowledge is and how it is produced. The solution, Harding argues, is to begin with those observations that are invisible to the privileged elite, in order to formulate new research programs and possibly new methodologies. In *Whose Science? Whose Knowledge?* she writes that in "a society structured by gender hierarchy, 'starting thought from women's lives' increases the objectivity of the results of research by bringing scientific observation and the perception of the need for explanation to bear on assumptions and practices that appear natural or unremarkable from the perspective of the lives of men in the dominant groups" (Harding 1991, 150). The scientist should begin from the lives of the oppressed to gain a better understanding of phenomena, and the epistemologist also should do so for a better understanding of knowledge formation processes.

One might object that this leads to a vicious regress of victimology, in which the most oppressed have the purest possible epistemic position. One need only consider the implication that the elderly atheist lesbian woman of color with AIDS would have to be the best physicist to see how absurd such a position would be. But Harding does not fall prey to this objection, because she recognizes that not just any observations of the lives of the oppressed will be helpful. Harding argues that the epistemologist or scientist who "begins from the lives of the oppressed," by which she means someone who recognizes the social nature of the oppression, has a less distorted picture of reality than the rest of us. According to Harding, "women's experiences in themselves" do not necessarily provide reliable grounds for knowledge claims. Thus her distinction between beginning from "women's lives" and taking "women's experiences" for granted.

Starting from women's lives does not mean taking for granted what women say about them. Instead, we examine women's situation from a theoretical, critical understanding of patriarchy, racism, and imperialism; that is, from a feminist and multiculturalist standpoint. As an example, Harding mentions our understanding of rape within marriage, which, before the feminist movement, could not have come from women who thought rape in marriage a conceptual impossibility even while they suffered from it. It was only when we could see women as oppressed through marriage, and as having human rights despite being in that institution, that we could see marital rape as a conceptual possibility. If we take seriously the notion that all observations are theory laden, and we accept that some oppressed persons have mistaken or underdeveloped theories about their lives, we recognize that there are better and worse ways of understanding the experiences of the oppressed. Equally, however, we notice the experiences of the oppressed only when we observe the lives of the oppressed with a sensitivity to their oppression. That requires us to observe from the perspectives of the oppressed. It is quite plausible that the members of oppressed groups themselves would be more successful than the rest of us in making science take the perspectives of the oppressed into account. Therefore it is a plausible consequence of Harding's arguments that science benefits from oppressed persons' actually entering science. Harding's concept of strong objectivity builds in contextualism, requiring that the perspectives of the oppressed be mediated through theory. In this way she avoids committing the multicultural version of the myth of the given by taking the data of the oppressed to have immediate, natural significance.

Instead of the lone thinker seated before the fire, the metaphors that best fit the social constructivist epistemologist are Neurath's metaphor of the boat that one must constantly rebuild while one is afloat in it, and Rawls's reflective equilibrium between theory and practical application. Social constructivists must take the perspective of the oppressed but reconstitute that data using critical social theory. In the face of enough contradicting evidence, they must also alter their theory to be consistent with their observations of the oppressed. They rebuild their boat, trying to maintain an equilibrium between scientific theory and personal observations of the oppressed, and this makes their view of the world less distorted, less partial, than others'. To reformulate Descartes' passage in light of these epistemological lessons, we realize that we cannot *raze* everything in our lives, *down to the very bottom*, so as to begin again from the first foundations. If we want to establish anything firm and lasting in the sciences, we should come together in all our diversity critically to assess our collective background assumptions. We should, in short, apply ourselves earnestly and openly to generally destroying our former opinions when they turn on assumptions that, we now can see, lead to incoherent theories.

There are two in in which multiculturalism has something to offer science, if this view of objectivity is correct. First, when science pursues social policies that will bring people of color and women, false assumptions based on prejudice against these groups will become noticeable and subject to critical inquiry. Thus multiculturalism as a social project of ensuring diversity and equality will itself lead to better science. Because strong objectivity does not require one actually to be a member of an oppressed group in order to begin from the standpoint of the oppressed, nearly all scientists are likely to gain a better understanding of the ideological motivations of their theories under the influence of multiculturalism. Second, those scientists who are members of oppressed classes will be most likely to question and critically assess background assumptions that degrade, defame, or otherwise harm their members. Thus multiculturalism, considered as a broader representation of the human experience in science, will lead to better science.

An important question at this point is where will multiculturalism make a difference. Will it make a difference in physics, biochemistry, the foundations of economic theory? Or will it only make a difference in those theories that directly deal with race, sex, or gender? Scientists and philosophers have only just begun the difficult work of showing where beginning from the lives of the oppressed is useful and where it is not. I have little hope for a general solution to this question; it seems likely that it will turn out to be an empirical question in every case.[5] If it does, then we need to look at work that attempts to build new theories from the perspectives of the oppressed. There have been some significant results in all of the social and biological sciences and in the philosophy of science, if the general line of argument of this paper is correct. The effects have been far wider ranging than simply theories about race or about sex or gender, though I hasten to add that given the right interests, these theories alone can be a significant portion of the social and biological sciences. Two examples from the science most familiar to me, economics, show how bringing in a multicultural presence and sensitivity has changed theory.

FEMINIST ECONOMICS OF THE FAMILY

Even though "economics" comes from the Greek *oikonomikos*, referring to household management, economic theory has often neglected the family in the past. Today we still see textbooks in which lists of important social institutions overlook the family (Ferber and Nelson 1993, 5). In the history of the discipline, we can see three models of the family: the father-as-dictator model, the aggregated household model, and recently, under the influence of feminist economics and the women's movement generally, the competing-but-unequal-agent model. The first of these can be traced at least to Hobbes, but perhaps is best summarized by James Mill:

> One thing is pretty clear, that all those individuals whose interests are indisputably included in those of other individuals may be struck off without inconvenience. In this light may be viewed all children, up to a certain age, whose interests are involved in those of their parents. In this light also, women may be regarded, the interests of almost all of whom is involved either in that of their fathers or in that of their husbands. (Quoted in Folbre and Hartmann 1988, 188)

This model assumes that women need protection by sovereign men, and that men will provide this protection without undue selfishness. This makes attention to the family unnecessary theoretically; economic theory can assume that individuals are male and that whether they have wife and family is irrelevant.

In the 1960s economic theory began to look at households with what is called the "new home economics." The 1992 Nobel Prize in Economics was awarded to the founder of the new home economics, Gary Becker of the University of Chicago. Becker's motivation was to try to apply economic theory to all sorts of behavior that mainstream economics had overlooked: crime, animal behavior, and drug use, among others. Becker argues that the family is guided by altruism, and that it acts to maximize total household utility. He first endows each member of the family with an individual utility function that she or he tries to maximize. Then he shows, in the Rotten Kid Theorem, that if there is an altruistic family member—by which he means a member whose utility function has other family member's utilities as arguments—then it is rational for the selfish family members to maximize total family utility as well (Becker 1981). Thus he derives the patriarchal family as an invisible-hand-result of each person pursuing her own good.

Well, there is no arguing with mathematics. But how shall we interpret this theory of the family? Somewhat concealed by the mathematics are three other critical assumptions. First, wealth or control of income is unequally distributed, so the altruist is able to redistribute income to maximize his utility function (I use "his" here because Becker quite explicitly assumes that the altruist is the father). Second, it assumes that the egoists in the family (including the altruist's wife) have no better option than the one the altruist gives them. Third, the use of the positively ethically loaded term "altruist" presumes that his utility function ought to be maximized. Becker thus confirms the older economic view of the family as a unit, a single individual, represented by an altruistic "head." He thereby shows that there is no theoretical need to look inside those families. In such a situation, there is no need for the intrusion of law; what Rawls calls the "circumstances of justice" do not arise because ultimately there is no competition for resources. The father's paternalistic wishes must be fulfilled. Equality is not an issue.

Becker believes that marriage evolved as a deal to protect women, and his model of the family seems to confirm that view. Women can be seen as making a kind of Hobbesian deal: trading the promise of security for subjugation to sovereign power. However, as feminists have been pointing out, the claim that marriage protects women does not square with the empirical evidence that it exploits and oppresses them, for instance, by longstanding, socially sanctioned spousal abuse. Married women were, until relatively recently, prohibited from owning property, subject to unequal divorce laws, and affected by countless other laws and norms that constitute the double standard for married men and women.

If his work is so faulty, how do we explain Becker's Nobel Prize? His theory is just what the dominant strain of economists (in terms of theoretical as well as political commitments) love: it extends the neoclassical economic approach to a new area, the family, yet appears to vindicate the longstanding tradition of overlooking intrafamily economic issues, while justifying the political status quo concerning gender relations. Thus, the comfortable, sexist, gendered, political ideology for economists lends the theory cognitive authority that it did not warrant scientifically.

Since the 1980s a growing number of feminist economists have uncovered these hidden assumptions and interests behind economic theories of the family.[6] By paying attention to the inequalities in marriage and the consequent harm to women, they have been able to develop theories that can help guide social policy to address those harms. The models these economists have developed are versions of what Amartya Sen calls the cooperative conflict model. In this model, each person maximizes her or his expected utility, recognizing the gains to be won from some cooperation and, at the same time, the conflict of interests among the agents. Each spouse tries to maximize her or his own utility, there is a pool of goods to allocate, and each must agree to the allocation, on pain of the breakdown of the relationship. Some readers may object that this model views families as the site of conflict rather than cooperation. But that objection misses the point that all cooperation is ultimately motivated and justified by the interest of each party in the cooperation. If there were no such interest for any member of the cooperative group, then that member would be acting against her interests; that is, she must be exploited or coerced. This model reveals the degree to which each person's interests are satisfied, and thereby allows comparisons between spouses. With the addition of general, gender-related features of the economy, this kind of model reveals institutionalized gender inequality in the society.

The point of this example is to illustrate how hidden background assumptions about gender and economists' interests lead to different theories. In the earlier models, the economists assumed that men would head households, the best arrangement for all concerned. This allowed economists to overlook injustices in families and even to assume that families were uninteresting economic institutions. Feminist economists and the women's movement, which raised society's sensitivity to issues of gender inequality, revealed the falsity of those assumptions. Furthermore, women economists have a direct interest in revealing gender injustice. The result is a more nuanced theory of the family that fits much more of the data about gender and that can guide social policy regarding the family.

THE POLITICAL ECONOMY OF FAMINES
AND THE CAREER OF AMARTYA SEN

Until the groundbreaking work of the Indian economist and philosopher Amartya Sen, beginning in the 1970s, famine had not been a major concern of economic science since the eighteenth century. Until Sen's work, it was dogma among economists that famines were caused by food shortages or overpopulation and that free-market mechanisms would, if left unhindered by government interventions, solve the problem by supplying food in the region and at the localities where demand was greatest. Sen, who as a child had witnessed the Great Bengal Famine of 1943, showed, through statistical research, that famines often happen when there is no shortage of food in the region where people are starving, and that famines happen in times of economic boom (the Great Bengal Famine was an example) as well as economic decline(Sen 1981). Sen was able to show theoretically how market mechanisms can thwart relief efforts. Indeed, during many famines food can be seen being *exported* from the affected region. This happens because the people who need the food cannot "demand" it in the economic sense; that is, they have no legal entitlement to it because they cannot pay for it (Sen 1981, 161). Sen's theory of famines is that they are failures of entitlements, not food shortages.

As a result of his work on famines, as well as his more general concern with microeconomic theory, Sen has developed a theory of capabilities that rivals the expected utility theory on which current, neoclassical economics is founded (Sen 1987; Nussbaum and Sen 1993). While utilities are essentially expressions of subjective preference, capabilities measure individuals' objective abilities to attain goods.

Sen's career as an economist has been nothing short of stellar. He has made original and important contributions to fields as diverse as social choice theory, welfare economics, development economics, economics of the family, and microeconomic theory.[7] His work is as broad as Gary Becker's, and in many ways deeper. In addition, Sen is surely the subtlest and most important philosopher among the economists. He is celebrated widely as both. Yet as of the writing of this article, he has never won the Nobel Prize for Economics. There are, I think, two main reasons for this. First, he has a multicultural outlook, expressed through his choice of problem areas and his selection of collaborators. Second, his keen philosophical mind leads him to question basic assumptions of economic theory. In particular, his criticism of utility theory, especially the revealed preference form of it, alienates many economists. Much of his work is seen as leading in mathematically intractable directions, and this diverges from the current passion for mathematics in economics. Although these reasons are not directly connected to his being non-white (the Nobel Prize in Economics has had one previous non-white winner, Sir Arthur Lewis, 1979), I think there is an indirect connection in the sense that his work is not seen as mainstream. Instead, with the exception of his work on social choice theory, it diverges a bit from the main interests of economics; one is tempted to say that it is too ethnic. I find it somewhat ironic that famine and hunger could fail to be a central concern of economics.

Sen's work on famines and on capabilities illustrates how a multicultural outlook and experience can lead to productive new fields of research and to new theories in old territory. Of course, it might be argued that Sen is simply a genius, and that genius, from any cultural background or either gender, will bring about novel and productive work. While this may be true, it is also undoubtedly the case that Sen's direct experiences with colonialism and famine led him to his analysis of famines as caused by political and legal structures rather than by shortages of food.

OBJECTIONS

There are two kinds of objections that I want to address in conclusion. The first is what I call the "Barbarians at the Gate" objection. Social constructivism degenerates into a subjective relativism, which holds that all knowledge is partial to some person or group of persons, and that there is no real hope for objectivity. The best we can achieve is recognition of the partiality of our own theories. "Knowledge" is a term that those in power use to "privilege" their beliefs and desires, and hence to justify their continued power over others. "Science," likewise, simply names the practices they use to reap a greater share of social goods than others, and to develop technology that serves the interests of the powerful. However, I have argued that it is possible to hold on to contextual empiricism and not have to give up the claim that science proceeds objectively, though it is not the unique form of inquiry to do so. The relativist suggests that what needs to be done is to support all claims to knowledge, to find the least partial truth by combining the most sources of data. But it makes all the epistemic difference what we do with our data in this regard: what counts as data, how much weight each piece of data gets, how we reconcile apparently inconsistent data. Answers to these questions are difficult theoretical issues, I grant, and the questions have been answered in the past in ways that further oppress certain groups. But they must be answered to get anywhere at all. Contextualist empiricism's form of social constructivism offers this answer: the scientists themselves decide in open debate about the simplicity, empirical adequacy, and coherence of the resulting theories, and questions about cultural, class, or gender bias are not ruled out of court.

The second objection is what I call the "So What?" objection. It is the claim that my view of what multiculturalism has to offer science is merely a practical point about doing science, not an epistemic point. I have two responses here. First, to call it "merely" a practical point is a mistake. Science is largely constituted by its practices. To say that its practices need to be changed because that will make a difference in terms of the theories we will accept seems to me a major point. So I would challenge the dichotomy of epistemic and practical values that lurks in this objection. Second, this objection does not properly recognize the epistemological gains. The argument I have made is that social and cultural values and group-related interests play a role in the direction of research and in what counts as fact. This latter point especially deserves emphasis. If what counts as a fact, as a relevant phenomenon to be explained by a theory, is determined partly by the social groups who are allowed to be scientists, then what counts as a good, confirmed theory will depend also on who the scientists are. I just fail to see how this could not be an epistemological point.

Multiculturalism will lead to better science, by science's own criteria, than we have had with a race- and gender-exclusive community of scientists. I have argued that this is true for two reasons. First, the minority and women scientists themselves will be more likely to recognize the false, prejudiced assumptions about race and gender that have lurked in the background, guiding scientists as they interpret evidence and build theories. Second, the kinds of changes that society will undergo in pursuing multiculturalism will help reveal these faulty assumptions and change the interests of scientists of all races and genders. The interests of truth and justice come together in the demand for diversity in science.

NOTES

Earlier versions of this paper were presented to audiences at Wichita State University and Occidental College. I thank the Philosophy Departments of those institutions for the opportunities to present my work, and the audiences there for helpful discussions. I am also grateful for the thoughtful comments of Sandra Harding and three anonymous reviewers for *Hypatia*.

1. The *locus classicus* of this approach is Quine 1969. See also Kornblith 1985; Antony 1993.

2. This point was understood by Locke and by Berkeley, as well, as their blind man who suddenly regains sight. See Locke 1975, 52; Berkeley (1979) "First Dialogue."

3. This claim comes from a thesis in cognitive science known as the "frame problem," which says that there is no principled way of delineating every possible relevant fact for making inferences from data.

4. I owe the original description of these three senses to Longino (1990, chap. 4).

5. See Anderson (1995) for several illustrative examples of the mistakes that feminist scientists have uncovered.

6. See McCrate 1987; Sen 1984; McElroy and Horney 1981; Manser and Brown 1980.

7. In social choice theory, Sen is responsible for the theorem stating the "impossibility of a paretian liberal" and for various criticisms of the Pareto Principle; in welfare economics, he is best known for his analysis of measurements of welfare outcomes; in development economics, his theory of famines is his best-known achievement; in microeconomic theory he is best known for his criticism of revealed preference theory and his theory of capabilities. Articles containing many of these contributions are collected in Sen 1982.

REFERENCES

Anderson, Elizabeth. 1995. Feminist epistemology: An interpretation and a defense. *Hypatia* 10(3): 50-84.

Antony, Louise. 1993. Quine as feminist: The radical import of naturalized epistemology. In *A mind of one's own*, ed. Antony and Charlotte Witt. Boulder: Westview Press.

Ayer, A. J. 1971 [1940]. *The foundations of empirical knowledge*. London: Macmillan.

Becker, Gary. 1981. *A treatise on the family*. Cambridge: Harvard University Press.

Berkeley, George. 1979. *Three dialogues between Hylas and Philonous*. Indianapolis: Hackett.

Carnap, Rudolph. 1967 [1928]. *The logical construction of the world*. Trans. Rolf A. George. Berkeley: University of California Press.

Descartes, Rene. 1980 [1641]. *Meditations on first philosophy.* Trans. Donald A. Cress. Indianapolis: Hackett.

Ferber, Marianne A., and Julie A. Nelson. 1993. *Beyond economic man: Feminist theory and economics.* Chicago: University of Chicago Press.

Folbre, Nancy, and Heidi Hartmann. 1988. The rhetoric of self-interest: Ideology and gender in economic theory. In *The consequences of economic rhetoric,* ed. Arjo Klamer, Donald N. McCloskey, and Robert M. Solow. New York: Cambridge University Press.

Harding, Sandra. 1991. *Whose science, whose knowledge?: Thinking from women's lives.* Ithaca: Cornell University Press.

Hardwig, John. 1991. The role of trust in knowledge. *Journal of Philosophy* 37(12): 693-708.

Kornblith, Hilary. 1985. *Naturalizing epistemology.* Cambridge: MIT Press.

Lewis, C. I. 1929. *Mind and the world order.* New York: Scribner's.

Locke, John. 1975 [1689]. *An essay concerning human understanding.* Oxford: Clarendon Press.

Longino, Helen. 1990. *Science as social knowledge: Values and objectivity in scientific inquiry.* Princeton: Princeton University Press.

Manser, Marilyn, and Murray Brown. 1980. Marriage and household decision-making: A bargaining analysis. *International Economic Review* 21(1): 31-44.

McCrate, Elaine. 1987. Trade, merger and employment: Economic theory on marriage. *Review of Radical Political Economics* 19(1): 73-89.

McElroy, Marjorie B., and Mary Jean Horney. 1981. Nash-bargained household decisions: toward a generalization of the theory of demand. *International Economic Review* 22(3): 333-49.

Nussbaum, Martha, and Amartya Sen. 1993. *The quality of life.* Oxford: Oxford University Press.

Quine, W. V. O. 1969. Epistemology naturalized. In *Ontological relativity and other essays.* New York: Columbia University Press.

———. 1980. Two dogmas of empiricism. In *From a logical point of view.* Cambridge: Harvard University Press.

Sellars, Wilfrid. 1963. Empiricism and the philosophy of mind. In *Science, perception, and reality.* London: Routledge and Kegan Paul.

Sen, Amartya. 1981. *Poverty and famines.* Oxford: Clarendon Press.

———. 1982. *Choice, welfare and measurement.* Oxford: Basil Blackwell.

———. 1984. Economics and the family. In *Resources, values, and development.* Oxford: Basil Blackwell.

———. 1987. *The standard of living.* Cambridge: Cambridge University Press.

Notes on Contributors

LINDA MARTÍN ALCOFF is Professor of Philosophy at Syracuse University. She works primarily in continental philosophy, epistemology, feminist theory, and philosophy of race. She has co-edited *Feminist Epistemologies* (Routledge, 1993) and written *Real Knowing: New Versions of the Coherence Theory* (Cornell, 1996), and edited *Epistemology: The Big Questions* (Blackwell, 1998). She has written over twenty articles on topics concerning Foucault, sexual violence, the politics of knowledge, and gender and race identity, and is at work on a new book entitled *Visible Identities*.

ALISON BAILEY is Associate Professor at Illinois State University, where she teaches philosophy and women's studies. She is the author of *Posterity and Strategic Policy: A Moral Assessment of Nuclear Policy Options* (University Press of America, 1989), and a number of articles on feminist peace politics, privilege, and white identity. Her current research addresses questions related to the construction of privileged identities, moral responsibility, and possibilities for resistance.

DRUCILLA K. BARKER received her B.A. in Philosophy from Sonoma State University and her Ph.D. in Economics from the University of Illinois. She has been on the faculty at Hollins University since 1985 where she is Associate Professor of Economics and Director of Women's Studies. Her interests include radical political economy, feminist epistemologies, and philosophy of economics. She is a founding member of the International Association for Feminist Economics. (e-mail: dbarker@hollins.edu)

LORRAINE CODE is Distinguished Research Professor in the department of philosophy at York University in Toronto, where she also teaches in the Graduate Programs in Social and Political Thought, and Women's Studies. She is the author of *Epistemic Responsibility* (Brown University, 1987), *What Can She Know? Feminist Theory and the Construction of Knowledge* (Cornell, 1991), and *Rhetorical Spaces: Essays on Gendered Locations* (Routledge, 1995).

PATRICIA HILL COLLINS is currently the Charles Phelps Taft Professor of Sociology and Chair of the department of African-American Studies at the University of Cincinnati. Her first book, *Black Feminist Thought: Knowledge, Consciousness, and the Politics of Empowerment* (Routledge, 1990), has won many awards. Her second book, *Race, Class, and Gender: An Anthology* (edited with Margaret Andersen [Wadsworth, 1998]), currently in its third edition, is widely used in undergraduate classrooms throughout the United States.

Fighting Words: Black Women and the Search for Justice was published by the University of Minnesota Press in 1998.

ANN E. CUDD is Associate Professor of Philosophy at the University of Kansas. Her research and teaching interests are in decision theory, feminism, social and political philosophy, and philosophy of economics. She is currently writing a book on the material and psychological causes of oppression. (e-mail: acudd@ukans.edu)

ANN FERGUSON is a socialist-feminist philosopher who is Director of Women's Studies and Professor of Philosophy at the University of Massachusetts at Amherst. She has written two books in feminist theory: *Blood at the Root: Motherhood, Sexuality and Male Dominance* (Pandora/Unwin Hyman, 1989) and *Sexual Democracy: Women, Oppression, and Revolution* (Westview, 1991). Her interests include feminist and lesbian theory, social and political philosophy, philosophy of sexuality, ethics, race, class, and gender, and international development, particularly in Latin America and in China. (e-mail: ferguson@philos.umass.edu)

SANDRA HARDING is Professor of Education at the University of California–Los Angeles. She is the editor of *The "Racial" Economy of Science Toward a Democratic Future* (netLibrary, 1997), and the co-author of a chapter in UNESCO's *World Science Report 1996* entitled "Science and Technology: The Gender Dimension." Her most recent book is *Is Science Multicultural?: Postcolonialisms, Feminisms, and Epistemologies* (Indiana University, 1998). (e-mail: sharding@csw.ucla.edu)

AÍDA HURTADO is Professor of Psychology at the University of California–Santa Cruz. Professor Hurtado's research focuses on the effects of subordination on social identity, educational achievement, and language. Her most recent publications include *Strategic Interventions in Education: Expanding the Latina/Latino Pipeline*, co-edited with R. Figueroa and E. García (University of California, 1996), and *The Color of Privilege: Three Blasphemies on Race and Feminism* (University of Michigan, 1996).

ALISON M. JAGGAR is Professor of Philosophy and Women's Studies at the University of Colorado at Boulder. Currently, she is working on a book tentatively entitled *Sex, Truth and Power: A Feminist Theory of Moral Reason.* "Globalizing Feminist Ethics" draws on that work-in-progress.

LYNDA LANGE is in the philosophy department of the University of Toronto. She has published *The Sexism of Social and Political Theory: Women and Reproduction from Plato to Nietzsche* (University of Toronto, 1979), and numerous essays on Jean-Jacques Rousseau. She is currently working on a book titled *Claiming Democratic Feminism*, forthcoming from Routledge, editing *Feminist Interpretations of Rousseau*, forthcoming from Penn State Press, and pursuing work on aboriginal rights and postcolonial critiques of philosophy. (e-mail: lange@scar.utoronto.ca)

UMA NARAYAN is Associate Professor of Philosophy at Vassar College. Her areas of interest are social and political philosophy, philosophy of law, applied ethics, and feminist philosophy. She is the author of *Dislocating Cultures: Identities, Traditions, and Third World Feminism* (Routledge, 1997) and co-editor, with Mary Lyndon Shanley, of *Reconstructing Political Theory: Feminist Perspectives* (Pennsylvania State University, 1997). (e-mail: narayan@ibm.net)

ANDREA NYE is Professor of Philosophy and Religious Studies at the University of Wisconsin–Whitewater. She is the author of a number of books, including most recently *Philosophia: The Thought of Rosa Luxemburg, Simone Weil, and Hannah Arendt* (Routledge, 1994), and *Philosophy & Feminism: At the Border* (Twayne, 1995). (e-mail: nyea@uwwvax.uww.edu)

SUSAN MOLLER OKIN is Martha Sutton Weeks Professor of Ethics in Society at Stanford University. She is author of *Women in Western Political Thought* (Virago, 1979), *Justice, Gender, and the Family* (Basic Books, 1989), and many articles on feminist theory and political theory generally. She is currently working on conflicts between claims made on behalf of cultures and women's equality, at three levels of world politics.

OFELIA SCHUTTE is Professor of Women's Studies and Philosophy at the University of South Florida, Gainesville, where she teaches continental philosophy, feminism, and Latin American social thought. She is the author of *Beyond Nihilism: Nietzsche without Masks* (University of Chicago, 1986) and *Cultural Identity and Social Liberation in Latin American Thought* (State University of New York, 1993). Her recent feminist publications include articles in *Hypatia* (Indiana University, 1997) and in *A Companion to Feminist Philosophy* (Blackwell, 1998). (e-mail: oschutte@phil.ufl.edu)

SHARI STONE-MEDIATORE recently received her Ph.D. in Philosophy from SUNY Stony Brook. Her dissertation draws on Hannah Arendt and contemporary feminist theory to investigate the relations between experience, narrative, and political thinking. She is presently Assistant Professor of Philosophy at Ohio Wesleyan University.

MELISSA WRIGHT is Assistant Professor in Geography and Women's Studies at the University of Georgia. She has previously been a researcher at the Universidad Autónoma de Ciudad Juárez, and has published articles on the articulation of the production of things with the production of people in the *maquiladora* industry. Her current work combines a Marxist with a feminist poststructuralist critique of valorization to examine the formation of valuable and worthless subjects in multinational industrial settings.

Index